The Ottoman Gulf

The Ottoman Gulf

The Creation of Kuwait, Saudi Arabia, and Qatar

FREDERICK F. ANSCOMBE

COLUMBIA UNIVERSITY PRESS

NEW YORK

Columbia University Press
Publishers Since 1893

New York   Chichester, West Sussex
Copyright © 1997 Columbia University Press
All rights reserved
Library of Congress Cataloging-in-Publication Data
Anscombe, Frederick Fallowfield.
The Ottoman Gulf : the creation of Kuwait, Saudi Arabia, and
Qatar, 1870–1914 / Frederick F. Anscombe.
p.   cm.
Includes bibliographical references (p.   ) and index.
ISBN 0–231–10838–9 (cl). — ISBN 0–231–10839–7 (pa)
1. Saudi Arabia—History. 2. Kuwait—History. 3. Qatar—History.
4. Turkey—History—1878–1909. 5. Turkey—History—1909–1918.
I. Title.
DS243.A57   1997
953.8—dc21   97–12680
CIP

Casebound editions of Columbia University Press books
are printed on permanent and durable acid-free paper.

Printed in the United States of America

c 10 9 8 7 6 5 4 3 2 1
p 10 9 8 7 6 5 4 3 2 1

To my family, with thanks

contents

	Preface	*ix*
	Preliminaries: Notes on Transliteration and on Currency	*xiii*
	Introduction	1
CHAPTER 1	The Setting	9
CHAPTER 2	Resurrection of the Ottoman Role in the Gulf	16
CHAPTER 3	Midhat Pasha's Inspection of Hasa and His Plan for Its Development	34
CHAPTER 4	The Chance for Adjustment and Stability, 1872–1893	54
CHAPTER 5	The Case of Kuwait	91
CHAPTER 6	Kuwait, 1899–1913	113
CHAPTER 7	Arabia 1896–1914	143
CONCLUSION		167
	Appendix 1. Ottoman Officials and Heads of Arab Shaikhly Families	175
	Appendix 2. Register of Officials, Notables, and Tribes	179
	Notes	183
	Glossary	243
	Bibliographic Note	245
	Bibliography	251
	Index	261

MAPS: The Arabian Peninsula and Neighboring Regions, facing p. 8; Tribes in Arabia, facing p. 34; Kuwait and Southern Iraq, facing p. 112

Preface

It took a book reviewer and an army to arouse my interest and cause me to produce this study of the Gulf during the late Ottoman period. Carl Brown's review of Jacob Goldberg's *The Foreign Policy of Saudi Arabia* drew my attention to the relative lack of information about Arabia before 1914, the period that saw the emergence of Kuwait, Saudi Arabia, and Qatar as stable political entities.[1] Using British sources but focusing on Ibn Saud, Goldberg produced a perceptive, groundbreaking analysis of an Arabian leader's ability to build a durable dynastic state through pragmatic diplomacy in relations with "outside" powers, particularly Britain. Goldberg challenged the implicit assumption upon which the most widely held view of Arabian history is based: that Britain stepped in to fashion stability out of the interminable anarchy of Arabia and to oversee the overnight establishment of the peninsula's current political order. Through some mystical process the Arabian states stepped out of Britain's palm, much as Pallas Athena sprang fully formed from Zeus's head. As in the case of the Greek myth, it makes a nice story but hardly holds up under close inspection. Brown applauded Goldberg for initiating the inspection but noted that his book gave little information about the activities of the state which covered most of the Arabian peninsula—the Ottoman empire. Brown later suggested to me that I find out what "the view from Istanbul" was. His continued interest, guidance, and support were indispensable to completion of this project. He has earned my warmest thanks.

I was frequently surprised by the discoveries I made in the course of researching this study, and the picture that slowly took shape both fascinated me as a story and improved my understanding of the pre-1914 era.

PREFACE

I hope that other historians of the period will find this book equally informative. In August 1990, near the end of my first research trip to Istanbul, the Iraqi army invaded Kuwait, which made clear to me that the issues which I was examining were not just of academic interest. Baghdad's justification for the conquest was that it merely restored the union between Iraq and Kuwait that had existed in the Ottoman period. This book shows that the Iraqi claim to historical rights over Kuwait is very weak: on the fundamental issue of political status, Kuwait was indeed Ottoman but was neither integrated into, nor dependent upon, Ottoman Iraq. Kuwait did have social and economic links to southern Iraq—but they were just part of a wider network of relations that also tied Kuwait to much of the Arabian peninsula, the rest of the Gulf, and India. Although many have disputed the Iraqi historical claim, none could do so convincingly before now because they had only the British perspective of Kuwait's status before World War I.

This study has benefited from the assistance of a number of people who were very generous in giving me their time and advice. They are responsible for much of what is right in this book but for none of what is wrong. I want to thank in particular those who have read and commented upon drafts of this study. In addition to Brown, they include Şükrü Hanioğlu, Heath Lowry, Norman Itzkowitz, Molly Greene, William Ochsenwald, Gregory Gause, Bill Blair, and Michael Hickok. The Fulbright commission provided the grant that made my first stay in Istanbul possible, and the commission in Turkey was very attentive to my interests. The American University in Bulgaria made funds available for subsequent research in Turkey. I am also most grateful to the staff of the Başbakanlık Archives in Istanbul, who kindly helped me to locate the Ottoman documents on which this book is based, and to the staffs of the Public Record Office and India Office Library and Records, whose assistance allowed me to make the most of a short stay in London. Evgeni Radushev and the staff of the Sts. Cyril and Methodius National Library in Sofia made me welcome; I appreciate their kind care and attention. There have been many other people who have given me the benefit of their wit and wisdom. They are too numerous to name, but they all have my thanks.

In addition to those mentioned above, I would like to express my special appreciation to the people of Columbia University Press, in particular Kate Wittenberg and Joan McQuary. Their care and efficiency have made the publication process enjoyable.

Finally, I want to thank several friends and my family, without whose moral and logistical support this work might never have seen the light of

PREFACE

day. Yetta and Theodore Ziolkowski went out of their way to make life in Princeton easier and more pleasant. The members of my family proved themselves, as ever, invaluable. The dedication of this book is but a shadowy suggestion of all I owe to them.

Blagoevgrad, Bulgaria

Preliminaries

Transliteration

Transliteration of foreign words in a study such as this is not simple. Arabic place and personal names have been given according to the Library of Congress transliteration system, with several exceptions. Diacriticals have been omitted, except when confusion might ensue, e.g., to distinguish Qâsim (the shaikh of Qatar) from Qasîm (a region of Najd). Hamza is not marked, but`ayn is rendered as`. Widely recognized place-names and words retain standard English spelling: Kuwait rather than Kuwayt, Bahrain instead of Bahrayn, shaikh rather than shaykh, etc. In general, Ottoman words and the names of Ottoman officials have been transliterated using the alphabet and spelling of modern Turkish.

Personal Names

The fullest form in which Arabic personal names are given follows this pattern: Qâsim ibn (b.) Muhammad al-Thani (Qâsim, son of Muhammad, of the House of Thani). Shaikhly families as a unit are referred to as Al Thani, Al Sabah, Al Sa`ud, etc.

Currency Equivalencies

In an effort to ease comprehension of sums given, statements of money are generally reckoned in Ottoman lira (T£). The value of the Ottoman lira varied in the nineteenth and twentieth centuries; during the period covered in this study it was roughly equivalent to 0.9 British pounds sterling (£). In Ottoman documents sums are frequently, but not always, given in kuruş, of which there were 100 in one lira.¹

Financial reckoning in Gulf affairs is complicated by the use there of a wide variety of monies at that time, including Maria Theresa dollars/ kuşlu riyal, Bombay rupees, and Persian krans. There were several other kinds of Arabian riyals that varied in value. The values of these coins in comparison to Ottoman or British monies also varied over time. In the rare instances when documents record figures denominated in these currencies, rough equivalencies in lira and pounds sterling are determined according to the following scale:² 2.5 krans = 1 rupee; 5 krans = 2 rupees = 1 dollar; 22.5 krans = 9 rupees = T£1;³ 25 krans = 10 rupees = £1 sterling.

The Ottoman Gulf

Introduction

It is commonly but inaccurately thought that to Britain goes the credit or blame for the modern political organization of the Persian Gulf's Arab states. That view underestimates the role of Arab leaders, but more importantly completely ignores the role played by the most important regional state in the pre-World War I period, the Ottoman empire. The growth of the perception is quite understandable, since historical studies of the region have been based almost solely on British records or the often fanciful tales of colorful explorers and post-1918 government officials. To be sure, Britain did have a great influence in south Arabia and Bahrain, where from the early nineteenth century it helped to develop dynastic regimes still ruling today. From Iraq to Qatar, however, the key power was the Ottomans. Iranians and the West know the area as the Persian Gulf, whereas Arabs recognize it as the Arab Gulf. While the Ottomans termed it the Basra Gulf, they thought of it as "our" Gulf—not entirely without reason. They became for a time the recognized authority in that area after a campaign to occupy eastern Arabia in 1871. Britain was concerned with maritime affairs, and if the Ottomans had governed the mainland effectively, Britain would not have become entangled in the territories that were to become the states of Kuwait, Qatar, and Saudi Arabia. The Ottoman administration proved weak, however, and the British were drawn, often unwillingly and even unwittingly, into mainland politics.

Why did the Ottomans fail to control this part of their empire? They had sound security reasons for seeking to stabilize their vulnerable southern border, and eastern Arabia was rich enough to make its administration worthwhile. Contemporary sources did not dispute the govern-

INTRODUCTION

ment's latent superiority of power over local Arabian tribal leaders. Midhat Pasha swept aside the Sa`udi resistance in 1871, and thirty years later Britain recognized that Shaikh Mubarak al-Sabah had no hope of repelling an invasion of Kuwait from nearby Basra. Yet histories of the region give the impression that the Ottomans studiously ignored eastern Arabia after 1871, that in fact they were little more than stage scenery in the political drama from that date until the outbreak of World War I. Examination of Ottoman activity in the Gulf will remedy the shortcomings of present accounts of why key developments did (or, perhaps more importantly, did not) happen.

Several broad themes make this topic of interest for students of the Middle East, the Ottoman empire, Europe, and international relations. The first theme concerns the diplomatic game of the "Eastern Question," i.e., what was to become of the Ottoman empire? Today it is often assumed that eastern Arabia before the discovery of oil was irrelevant to Europe. It was among the regions of the empire affected latest and least by rivalries among the Great Powers. Yet the international tensions engendered by the Eastern Question constantly influenced the course of events in the Gulf, and in distant capitals the region's affairs reverberated much more widely than might be expected of an underdeveloped area, with results that continue to affect global politics today.

Although the international politics of the Persian Gulf in that period did not have lasting resonance in the minds of Europeans to rival events of the Greek war of independence in the 1820s or the Bulgarian atrocities a half century later, it did command great attention in top government circles. Rivalry in the Gulf was one of the persistent problems that soured Anglo-Ottoman relations before World War I. The Ottoman decision to bring eastern Arabia within the empire's boundaries originated in concern about British influence in a vulnerable border region. Consideration of British activities and intentions affected formulation of, and changes in, Ottoman strategic and administrative policies throughout the four decades of their rule south of Basra. Indeed, it contributed heavily to the state's poor performance in the Gulf. Overblown suspicion often diverted scarce resources to meet unlikely outside threats instead of to fix problems caused by maladministration. In addition to fostering local discontent that could be exploited by foreign powers, moreover, the policy options chosen did not check the spread of British influence because they underemphasized "facts on the ground," while relying too heavily on paper promises and principles. One weakness of this approach lay in Istanbul's reluctance to press Britain formally to acknowledge the rights that the Ottomans thought that they had established. Belated realization of the strategy failure led to the explicit demarcation of spheres of interest in an Anglo-Ottoman accord in 1913. Such an agreement had always been a logical solution to the problems raised by mutual misunderstandings; its conclusion only after forty years of haphazard Ottoman administration secured most of the benefits to Britain.

The course of Ottoman rule on the Gulf coast caused as much discussion, thought, and suspicion in London and British India as it did in Istanbul. Among Britain's greatest overseas concerns between the Napoleonic wars and World War I was the security of India. One of the most direct routes from Britain to India ran along the Tigris and Euphrates rivers and through the Persian Gulf; not by coincidence was Iraq the site of the first and longest-running campaign of World War I in the Middle East. Freedom of movement on that route naturally assumed great importance for Britain, and to meet this goal it negotiated agreements with the Arab shaikhs who controlled coasts close to shipping channels in the southern Gulf. These treaties also addressed other issues of concern, notably slave-trading and gunrunning. Extension of Ottoman power down the coast as far as Qatar disturbed Britain, because it seemed to threaten its web of agreements. As apparent Ottoman indifference to issues of maritime peace and trade increasingly irritated them, the British grew ever more willing to widen the scope of their policies. This combined with a perceived threat of rising German, French, and Russian influence in the region to draw Britain into a quasi-protectorate agreement with the shaikh of Kuwait, a territory previously recognized as Ottoman for over twenty-five years. The effects of this were still felt in 1990–91, when Iraq tried to realize a claim to Kuwait that was based on the shaikhdom's tie to Ottoman Basra before World War I, a tie which, in Iraqi eyes, Britain had broken illegally.

This period was the defining era in the formation of four modern Gulf states: Saudi Arabia, Kuwait, Qatar, and Bahrain. The latter three in 1870 were areas with fluctuating frontiers under tribal dynasties of uncertain durability. The Ottoman conquest of the mainland started a process of territorial definition, in the course of which Arab shaikhly families used great power sponsorship to defend themselves against rivals. Some shaikhs became wonderfully adept at playing the outside powers against each other and using the resulting confusion to win domestic security and independence. Gradually Britain became the preferred protector of these nascent statelets, as it grew apparent that it was more steadfast in support than the Ottoman state while demanding less in return. The Sa`udi state reached a nadir early in this period, and its leaders did not play the great power patron game as adeptly as its smaller neighbors. The mistakes of Ottoman policy in Arabia, however, allowed `Abd al-`Aziz b.

INTRODUCTION

`Abd al-Rahman al-Sa`ud (Ibn Sa`ud) to regroup his bedouin supporters after 1901 and to found the state that dominates the peninsula today.

Given the difficulties that the Ottomans encountered in ruling heavily tribal, nomadic areas such as Najd and Hasa, did they still have the ability to rule an empire in the Middle East? As Istanbul lost its Balkan provinces, the idea of a state limited to its Muslim Asian lands began to be discussed. For that scheme to succeed, the Ottomans would need a proven ability to govern tribal regions such as Najd. A very large part of the late Ottoman Middle East had similarly factionalized, unsettled elements among the population, especially in border areas. Kurdish and Arab tribal groups lived along virtually the entire eastern frontier of the empire, from Anatolia to Qatar, and from Yemen through the Syrian desert in the west. The problems that the Ottomans faced in administering these areas fostered a considerable provincial reform program industry in the late nineteenth century[1] and has led to the production in recent years of good scholarship about these sensitive provinces.[2] In a broad sense, the Ottomans in Arabia faced a problem common to much of the empire in its final century: how best to rule internally divided, even antagonistic, populations? The bedouin tribes in Arabia had more physical room for maneuver than had similar groups farther north or the Christians of the Balkans, but the direct European interference so beneficial to dissidents elsewhere was much more limited. Only Britain maintained serious interest in the Gulf coast, and no European state attempted involvement in the Arabian interior. No European government had permanent representatives stationed in Ottoman eastern Arabia. Yet the Ottomans threw away these advantages. They were absolutely convinced that Britain exercised a pervasive, perfidious influence in Arabia. Distracted by fear of an enemy that often was not there, the Ottoman government lost the chance to concentrate on the greater problems of pacifying and administering a tribal area. Britain in fact based its influence among the Gulf population upon a loose skein of alliances with key coastal shaikhs, backed by a small naval presence; this suggests that, with moderate, mobile Ottoman garrisons to protect a few important towns and roads and a naval squadron on permanent patrol offshore, Istanbul could have controlled the area with the help of local notables. This did not happen. The Ottomans' exit from eastern Arabia was one of the most ignominious endings to their rule in any of the Arab provinces, coming with barely a struggle at the hands of a desert chieftain. Their inability to govern in the Gulf gives a picture of overwhelmed administrative and military capabilities that did not bode well for their capacity to continue to govern the Middle East.

INTRODUCTION

The vicissitudes of government in eastern Arabia, in turn, give additional insight into the potentials and problems of modernization, both material and administrative, in the Ottoman empire as a whole during its last half century of existence. Of interest to students of Ottoman history, be they of the empire's early or late periods, are questions of how provinces were governed: who held positions of authority, how much discretionary power did they enjoy, and to what extent were rules of provincial administration shaped to meet local conditions. The Ottoman *Sancak* of Necd was established shortly after enaction of laws in 1864 and 1871 that reordered and streamlined provincial administration across the empire.[3] It is tempting to see uniformity in administration across the empire in the decades after 1871: a common four- (later five-) tiered provincial hierarchy was established, staffed by a professional bureaucracy centered in Istanbul. This study reminds us that a considerable capacity for adaptation of practices to local conditions continued to exist under the reformed regime. Istanbul preferred to appoint officials with knowledge of, and experience in, Arabia or similar neighboring lands; ties to locale were often desired, not abhorred. Exemptions from rules and regulations were granted to officials and people alike, if conditions so warranted. Integration of eastern Arabia into the empire in its waning years was to some degree reminiscent of the flexibility shown by Istanbul when absorbing new territories in its days of youthful vigor.[4]

Yet ultimately Istanbul could not steel itself to allow enough flexibility. Closely related to these issues of provincial administration is the question of how decisions were made.[5] One desired result of not only the provincial reform laws but also the wider modernization of the Ottoman empire was increased centralization. Istanbul wanted to direct affairs throughout the empire. This desire developed quite naturally for a variety of reasons, including the need to prevent local incidents involving European nationals or protected people that could prompt diplomatic confrontations with a Great Power. Despite the flexibility shown in administering eastern Arabia and Iraq, officials in those territories still had to await Istanbul's orders in most important matters. They seemed closely integrated into the centralized Ottoman system—yet that centralization in some ways was more formal than practical. Istanbul may have made decisions, but those decisions were essentially shaped by information coming from provincial officials. Local civil and military authorities could push Istanbul to back moves that they desired by providing slanted, or outright false, information. Even if an official could not persuade Istanbul to adopt his preferred course of action, he could often at least sow enough doubt in central authorities' minds to prevent implementation of policies that he did not want. The empire did not have the ships, roads, railroads, and telegraph lines needed to gather sufficient information for decision-making in Istanbul and to ensure that policies were implemented properly. Ottoman confusion over how to treat Mubarak al-Sabah of Kuwait after 1896 is an excellent example of these problems. In general, the Ottoman empire lacked the modern infrastructure vital to true, effective centralization, in which real decision-making passed from the provinces to Istanbul.

The Ottomans' communications limitations, made so evident in this study, highlight the problem of the physical modernization of the empire. The Tanzimat reform era is reckoned to have ended in 1876, shortly after the government ran out of money. Sultan Abdülhamid II came to power in the same year, ushering in a more "reactionary" phase in Ottoman politics. He did not stop all reform processes, however, but rather pushed ahead aggressively in areas he thought important, such as modernizing the army and building railroads. By examining in detail the reform and modernization process in one area of the empire, this study deepens our appreciation of the strong and weak points of the Ottoman approach. The daunting problems caused by lack of money and other resources, including at times military manpower, are clear. This book also emphasizes the importance of foreign powers to the process, both as instigators of modernization and as hindrances to change. While many Ottoman plans for the Gulf region—from improving maritime security and shipping aids to construction of the Baghdad Railway—were prompted directly or indirectly by British threats or complaints, British objections to anything that might threaten their position in the Gulf in turn complicated their implementation. A government attempting modernization under such circumstances must feel much as would a troupe of actors trying to improvise a five-act play before a crowd of violent, heckling devotees of Shakespeare; the audience in both instances would judge the performance haphazard and not entirely serious.

The Ottomans were not guilty of the latter charge, but for various reasons their rule did come to appear too haphazard. The final Ottoman collapse in the peninsula could have been avoided. Midhat Pasha, the man most responsible for the 1871 expedition, devised a plan of administration that, while imperfect, could have been the basis of good government. He left his supervisory position before his ideas could be fully implemented. Distracted by problems elsewhere and lulled by the general absence of major disturbances or challenges, the Ottoman government did not give the weak local administration the concentrated attention it deserved over the next two decades, preferring instead to follow sporadic, ambitious dreams of territorial expansion. The knotty problems pressing

INTRODUCTION

upon the empire in this period made it hard to devote enduring attention and resources to Arabia until a serious threat emerged, such as the revolt in Qatar in 1893, the growing Anglo-Kuwaiti connection, and the revival of Sa`udi power. The weaknesses of the Ottoman condition by that time often prevented effective counteraction. Irregular communications, neglected local administration, money shortages, inadequate military forces, mixed quality, and rapid turnover of officials, and a lack of firm decision-making were shortcomings (often created by the chaos attendant on reform efforts pressed by European powers) common to much of the empire and among those responsible for decay in Arabia.

The Ottoman perspective of events in this period is the primary focus of this study, but where possible British and Arab views are also examined. Secondary works on the Persian Gulf are relatively limited, but several excellent accounts cover most of this period, generally using British sources. Records from the Başbakanlık Archives in Istanbul are the main source of information on Ottoman views. Collections consulted include the Yıldız Palace papers, Grand Vezirial correspondence, minutes of meetings of the Council of Ministers, papers of the Council of State and imperial decrees (*Irade*). Correspondence on financial matters found in the Sts. Cyril and Methodius National Library in Sofia, Bulgaria was also consulted. British government papers in the Public Record Office and India Office Archives supplement these Ottoman sources.

The study consists of seven main chapters. Readers are strongly encouraged to consult the endnotes while reading the text, since the notes often contain further comments and information in addition to source references. Chapter 1 gives a brief overview of eastern Arabian geography, society and history. Chapter 2 examines the reasons behind the decision to absorb Arabia into the empire and the course of the Ottoman expansion. It makes clear the importance of concern over British intentions as a catalyst to Ottoman policy formulation. A discussion of Midhat Pasha's ideas for the development and security of the newly conquered territory forms chapter 3. Midhat introduced plans that gave the Ottomans reason to hope for long-term success in eastern Arabia. Chapter 4 covers roughly two decades after Midhat's resignation from the governorate of Baghdad. This was the period in which the Ottomans should have been able to refine their administration and put their local authority on a sound basis. This did not happen, according to the British, due to lack of interest and malign neglect. The Ottoman government in fact did show frequent interest in Arabia, but its schemes to make its authority more effective were ill-founded and underfunded. As a result, fundamental problems left unaddressed encouraged outbreaks

INTRODUCTION

of lawlessness and rebellion, such as happened in Qatar in 1893. In chapters 5 and 6, a close examination of the Kuwaiti bid for independence illustrates the state of decay into which Ottoman government had fallen. Although Shaikh Mubarak had committed serious crimes and was vulnerable to Ottoman pressure, he completely confounded all Ottoman moves against him by a masterful blend of sweet talk, false rumors, bribery of officials, and recruitment of allies. His escape into virtual independence under British protection dealt a very serious blow to an already weak Ottoman regional administration. Chapter 7 chronicles Istanbul's last attempts to restore its authority in Arabia in the face of the dire problems that it had helped to create. It made a belated alliance with a local leader, Amir `Abd al-`Aziz al-Rashid, and even sent an occupation force to central Najd to support its ally against Ibn Sa`ud. After that force wasted away and the amir died, the Ottoman presence in Arabia slowly withered to the point where Istanbul was content to conclude an agreement with Britain in 1913, in which it was stripped of all but Hasa. When Ibn Sa`ud conquered that territory one month later, the Ottoman phase of Gulf history effectively came to an end.

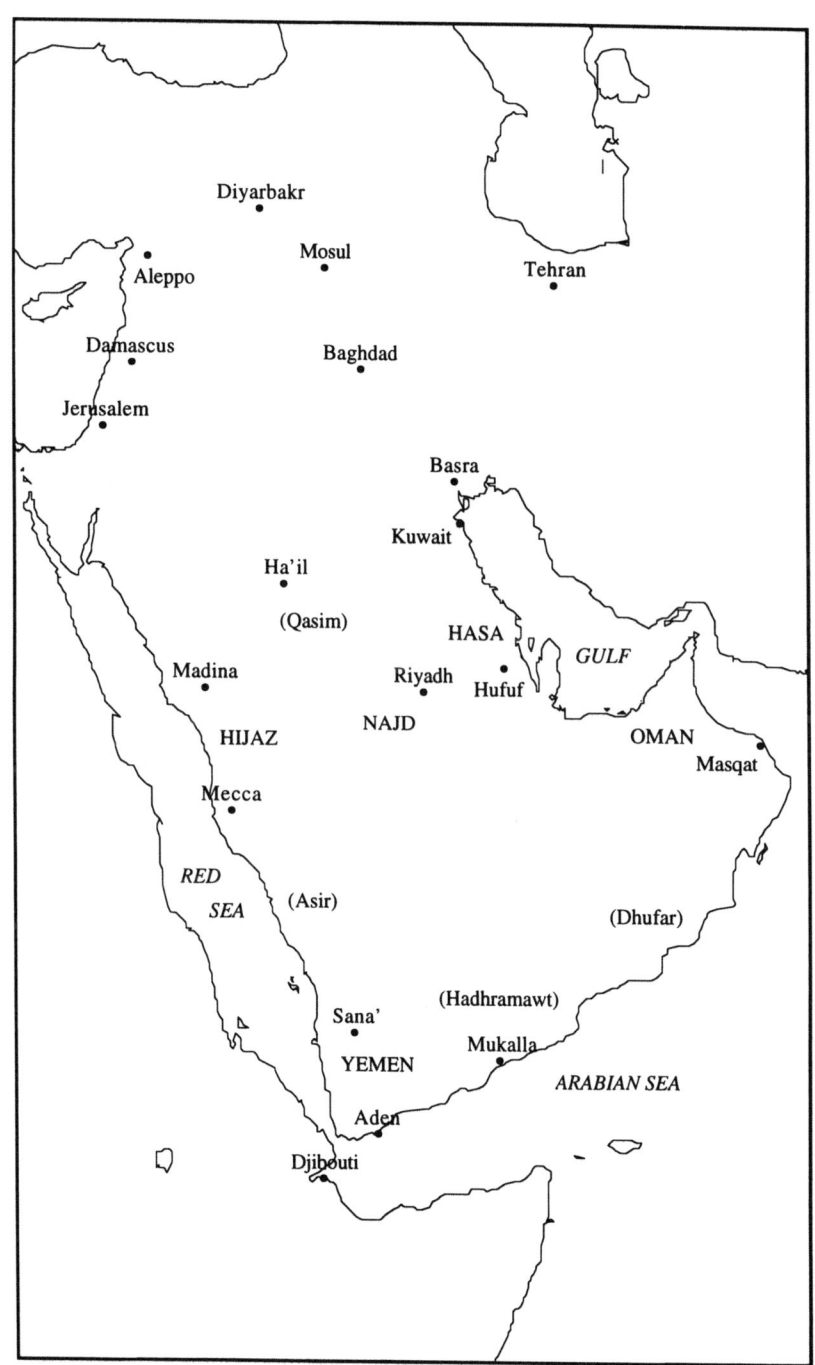

THE ARABIAN PENINSULA AND NEIGHBORING REGIONS

Chapter 1

The Setting

Arabian Geography

Eastern Arabia has an austere appearance and climate. The Gulf coast extends almost 750 miles (c. 1,200 kilometers) from Kuwait to Ra's Musandam at the peninsula's closest point to Iran. Between Basra and Masqat it has only one good harbor, namely Kuwait, and is hemmed in by shallows, reefs, and islands in many areas. Stretches of mangrove swamp lie scattered from the head of the Gulf at Kuwait, along the Hasa[1] coast to the Qatar peninsula. A century ago sizable communities, supported by trade and cultivation of dates and other crops, clustered around the most dependable sources of good water, notably in the oasis areas of Hufuf and Qatif in Hasa. Other settlements, such as Kuwait and Doha, the main town in Qatar, relied on fishing, pearling, and trade for survival. Outside of these settlements, the coastal plain was a sparsely settled, often hilly land. Much of this plain was dry, but by Arabian standards a large number of springs and waterholes existed (roughly 4,000 by Ottoman reckoning), and in hollows water could be found by digging about a meter below the surface.[2] A few established tracks and trade routes connected settlements and the coast to the interior. To the west of Hasa the country slopes up to the central Najd plateau (elevation over 1,000 meters, over 1,500 m. in western areas such as Jabal Shammar), where communities and date-farming again relied primarily on permanent sources of ground water.[3]

Society

The Arabian peninsula north of present-day Yemen and Oman fell into three distinct zones: the thinly populated expanse of the Najd plateau, the arid Hijaz falling away to the Red Sea in the west, and better-watered Hasa sloping down to the Gulf in the east. Cultural differences echoed the geographic separations.[4] Hasa, Qatar, and Kuwait would not rest easy under the rule of Wahhabis from Riyadh, despite sharing some social patterns with Najd.

Arabian society throughout the peninsula in the nineteenth century retained a strong tie to its tribal origins. This was particularly true of Najd, where even those who had settled in towns or villages maintained strong tribal identities.[5] Strengthening this sense of a tribal society was the great superiority of numbers of bedouin tribesmen over the settled population in Najd. Settlements depended directly on the nomads for much that made life tolerable—not just animals and their products but also all trade and other contact with other lands. Personal security considerations also were important to maintenance of some bond of identity between bedouin and settled. It was sensible for the relatively few townsmen to keep the protection of a kinship group among the more numerous nomads who observed the rules of the "blood feud." The society of Najd was comparatively closed and conservative. Religious conservatism may have resulted partly from the austerity of physical conditions in Najd, and perhaps partly as a reaction against the religious practices of "decadent" neighboring populations: Ibadis in Oman, Shi`a in Yemen and Hasa, and even the Ottomans in the Hijaz, Syria, and Iraq.[6]

Various alterations of the Najdi pattern marked society in Hasa, Kuwait, and Qatar. Closer contact with the world beyond the peninsula and the greater degree of sedentarization gave eastern Arabian society a less closed, more cosmopolitan flavor. While tribal identity certainly continued to exist, it was to some degree less exclusive, at least in the towns. Distinct—and sometimes antagonistic—subdivisions of the `Utub tribe (which itself claimed connection to the great `Anaza group of northeastern Arabia and Syria)[7] had achieved paramountcy in Kuwait, Bahrain, and Qatar after the mid-eighteenth century. The main towns of Hasa (Hufuf, Qatif, and Mubarraz) did not have long-lived leading political families, since they were ruled directly by Sa`udi-Wahhabi governors for much of that time. All of those areas also contained members of many other tribes, settled and nomadic. They had in addition significant populations that would have no place in a social order oriented solely around the local Sunni tribes. The towns of Hufuf and Kuwait, and perhaps others, included Jews.[8] Communities of Indian traders lived in port towns, especially Qatif and Doha, as well as in Bahrain. Iranian traders lived in Qatif. The slave trade with East Africa introduced a black and mulatto population. Many settlements included Shi`a as well; in some areas, such as Qatif, they probably formed a solid majority.[9] Diversity existed within the Sunni ranks as well, with adherents of all four schools of Islamic jurisprudence (*madhhabs*) present. Najd, by contrast, was very heavily Hanbali, generally considered the most conservative *madhhab*.

Much of this diversity resulted from extensive contact with other areas, especially through long-distance trade. The mainland ports were in contact with Iraq, the Persian coast, Bahrain, Oman, India and East Africa. Trade flowed not only through the Gulf, but reached in the other direction into Najd. Traders were the richest, most influential members of society, especially in ports such as Kuwait and Doha that had no cultivable hinterland. They exported pearls, dates, date syrup, clothing (*abba* cloaks), camels, horses, donkeys, and hides, importing in turn food, spices, coffee, textiles, and metals.[10] Shopkeepers and artisans, including *abba*-makers and workers in copper and iron, formed the other important sectors of town society. Most of those in the surrounding country and villages were peasants, who were relatively better off than those of Najd but were vulnerable to bedouin raids.[11]

People living on or near the coast supplemented the means of support listed above with occasional acts of piracy. Marine brigandage extended to the Gulf waters the bedouin practice of raiding the property of those outside the protection of the tribal or regional shaikhs. Indian and British traders fell into that category, thus inevitably drawing the British Indian government into Gulf coast politics as the volume and value of its subjects' shipping to Basra and Iran increased.

Hasa avoided British interest for a relatively long period because for several reasons its inhabitants contributed relatively little to the turmoil in Gulf waters. The shaikhdoms of Oman, Qatar, and Bahrain had better ports and lay within easier striking distance of international shipping routes than did Hasa. The greater wealth and importance of the Hasa interior, including the oases of Hufuf and the road to Riyadh, did not force the people to look to the sea for survival. The towns of Hufuf, Mubarraz, and Qatif had the resources to support relatively large populations (15,000–30,000)[12] who in turn had a great demand for the livestock products of the bedouins.

Whereas the settled people in Hasa came from various tribes, the nomads of eastern Arabia and Najd traveled in more distinct, self-contained groups. Each tribe had a recognized *dira*, or area over which traditionally it sought pasturage. Contact between tribes occurred most regularly when *dira* boundaries overlapped and when bedouins encamped around towns to sell animal products and buy goods and agricultural produce. To supplement income from pastoralism, some nomadic and semi-nomadic Arabs tended date groves and raided caravans. Intertribal raiding (*ghazw*) also was a means to get the most important bedouin asset, camels. Among this sector of eastern Arabian society, the more important tribes with whom the Ottomans had to contend were the Muntafiq and the Dhafir (around Basra, lower Iraq), the Mutayr and the Bani Khalid (around Kuwait), the `Ajman and the Bani Hajir (between Kuwait and Qatar), and the Al Murra (south of Hufuf). In Najd to the west were the Shammar, `Utayba, Dawasir, and Qahtan.[13]

Little feeling of kinship or solidarity linked these various groups. Tribes feuded with each other, in addition to preying occasionally on settled areas. Even the internal cohesion of tribes varied: `Ajmani clans, for instance, intermingled freely, while the Bani Hajir had sharp internal divisions. Intertribal enmities and alliances sometimes held fast, sometimes shifted rapidly. Religion also could not always strengthen ties: some tribes (e.g., `Ajman, Al Murra) were Hanbali or Wahhabi, while others, such as the Maliki Bani Khalid, were not.[14]

History

Its diversity of population and severity of climate made the Arabian peninsula historically very difficult to rule effectively as a single unit. Oman and Yemen remained practically independent of external control for much of their history. Rough terrain and brutal climate often kept Najd free of outside influences. Although more accessible by sea than Najd, the Gulf coast similarly resisted domination by distant rulers: the Qaramita movement in the tenth century was the clearest example of this.[15]

Since the mid-sixteenth century, Istanbul had maintained a claim to the peninsula, but its ability to enforce it waxed and waned repeatedly. Following the conquest of Baghdad by Süleyman the Magnificent in 1534, the empire slowly expanded southward to include Hasa. Hasa submitted voluntarily to the Ottomans in 1550, preferring their rule to that of the Portuguese. The Ottomans at that time apparently were more interested in denying Portugal dominance in the area than in tapping Hasa's potential wealth, as the leisurely pace of extension of their control to valuable interior date-producing regions indicates. Their rule never wholly destroyed the power and freedom of action of local leaders, and the empire's internal problems in the seventeenth century further loosened Istanbul's hold. The subsidence of the Portuguese threat in the Gulf also removed a powerful reason for a vigorous Ottoman presence. The Bani Khalid tribe finally ended this first phase of Ottoman rule in 1670.[16] The continued decline of the empire's governance and internal cohesion, and the threat to Iraq posed by the Safavi empire, precluded any serious attempt to resurrect Istanbul's control over Arabia until the early nineteenth century. Indeed, even when the Ottomans first forcibly renewed their claim to suzerainty in 1811, it was not the sultan but the semi-independent Mehmet Ali of Egypt who prosecuted the campaigns to retake the peninsula that lasted until 1838.

These invasions from Egypt targeted the only powerful pretenders to hegemony in the interior to emerge during the long absence of Ottoman authority from most of Arabia: the Al Sa`ud. This family harnessed the fundamentalist fervor fomented by the religious teacher Muhammad b. `Abd al-Wahhab to build an empire. Ibn `Abd al-Wahhab preached a return to the fundamental tenets of Islam, which he felt had been obscured by popular practices in Arabia, including saint-worship. In 1744 he cemented an alliance with Muhammad b. Sa`ud, shaikh of a tribe that had settled the village of Dar`iyya. Sa`udi raiders plundered and often killed those who did not follow the strict Wahhabi program. Attracting a powerful following by a mixture of a strong message, the chance for booty, and the desire to escape the movement's destructive raids, the Sa`udi-Wahhabi movement conquered much of Arabia, taking the two main centers of opposition, Hasa and the Hijaz, in 1795 and 1802–4. They incurred the enmity of the Ottoman sultan by their violent takeover in the Hijaz and by brutal raids into Iraq and Syria, and the first Sa`udi kingdom was overthrown in 1818 by Egyptian-Ottoman troops. A second kingdom was established, centered in Riyadh, in 1824. The new kingdom's first two decades were chaotic, featuring internal conflict as well as clashes with Egypt. The redoubtable Amir Faisal al-Sa`ud (r. 1834–38, 1843–1865) learned from his and his predecessors' mistakes and muted his antagonism to the Ottomans, although on several occasions he confronted the British, the new power in the Gulf region. He maintained reasonably cordial relations with the Ottoman government after the withdrawal from Najd of a second Egyptian expedition in 1838, and Istanbul gave him the title of governor of the subprovince of Najd. They similarly recognized his son, `Abdallah, after Faisal's death in 1865. This was little more than a statement of principle, staking a claim to suzerainty over Muslim territory. Although `Abdallah apparently favored the Ottomans, it would be misleading to suggest that Istanbul had any direct authority in Najd.[17]

On the Gulf Coast various foreign powers joined the Sa`udis in contention for influence in the Ottomans' absence. The Portuguese, who had exerted great influence in the Gulf in the sixteenth century, were expelled by 1650, but the British and Dutch maintained a European presence in the area into the 1700s. The Dutch aspired to political power but were finally driven out by 1763; the British sustained a steady commercial presence based on East India Company agents in Bushire and Basra.[18]

Trade at the beginning of the nineteenth century, however, was still relatively small. With conclusion of the Anglo-Ottoman commercial convention of 1838 and technological improvements in transportation (notably the development of steam power), the level of trade through Basra gradually rose later in the century.[19]

Britain's attempts to protect that trade by prevention of violent actions by the sea-faring Arabs of the southern Gulf provided the basis for its strong position in Arabia at the end of the nineteenth century. Backed by naval power, Britain in 1820 persuaded the shaikhs of Bahrain and the Omani coast from Abu Dhabi to Ra's al-Khayma to agree to a General Treaty of Peace, which called for the suppression of piracy and slave-trading. The Trucial Omani shaikhs also signed a Treaty of Maritime Peace in Perpetuity in 1853, renouncing aggression among the signatories in Gulf waters. Agreements in 1838 and 1847 also strengthened the prohibition of slave-trading. Bahrain agreed to similar undertakings in 1861. In case of disputes between signatories of this array of treaties, Britain acted as referee and guarantor of rights.

These arrangements strengthened simultaneously Britain's influence in the Gulf and the security of local leaders. A nomadic or settled community usually recognized the leadership of a shaikh drawn from a noted family, but such a man was more a first among equals than a real ruler. He had to lead by persuasion, since dissatisfied members of the community could throw their support to a rival member of the shaikhly family. In a society as mobile as that of Arabia, they also could simply withdraw from the area, harming the shaikh's prestige and the local economy. Few shaikhs thus enjoyed real security of tenure and influence.[20] Recognition by a strong naval power such as Britain first gave the Trucial Omani shaikhs a source of effective support in the face of internal and external threats. The Al Khalifa shaikh also won recognition as the 'independent ruler of Bahrain' in the convention of 1861,[21] an asset that was to prove its considerable worth in later years. From the signing of the first treaty, Britain acted as a stabilizer, quelling internal arguments in shaikhly families and deflecting demands on them from Wahhabi and Iranian leaders.

When Britain did not interfere in Arab politics, the handful of essentially independent shaikhs in eastern Arabia maintained an often tense intertribal balance of power, in which neighbor jostled neighbor in search of greater security and freedom. These leaders included the Al Khalifa of Bahrain and their often hostile tributaries and kinsmen, the Al Thani of Qatar; the Al Sabah in Kuwait; and the Bani Khalid shaikhs in Hasa. The balance of tensions was disturbed periodically by threats from the Safavis, who claimed Bahrain, and from the Sa`udi amirs of Riyadh. The Sa`udis controlled Hasa in 1795–1818, 1830–38, and 1843–1871. From that base they extended their power to Qatar, Bahrain, Trucial Oman, and the sultanate of Oman (Masqat). Although these areas at times paid tribute to the Wahhabi amirs, the shaikhs under treaty relations with Britain in later years could use its support to retain more independence than could those outside the trucial system.[22] In the Arabian style of network politics, alliance with the British Indian government "tribe" was quickly recognized as a notable asset in the ongoing struggle for advantage in Arabia, and many contestants in the second half of the nineteenth century courted British power.[23]

Chapter 2

The Resurrection of the Ottoman Role in the Gulf

In the mid-sixteenth century, at a time when the Ottoman empire was at its peak of power, it held the western Persian Gulf coast from Basra to Qatar; more than two hundred years after they had withdrawn in the mid-seventeenth century, and when they were thought to be in rapid decline, the Ottomans once again tried to absorb Arabia. Such a surprising effort has puzzled many from that day to this. Prior to the oil age, eastern Arabia was never considered the potential jewel in any potentate's crown. Its economic assets lay scattered across great distances of barren land, and its population was too mobile, independent, and splintered to be ruled easily. Why, then, divert valuable resources to its conquest?

The answer is simple: fear. That most basic of human instincts, self-preservation, could propel even "the sick man of Europe" from his bed to a burst of unusual activity. The years before 1870 brought startling changes, notably a revolution in communications, that seemed to bring the world within easy striking distance of the Ottoman empire. Rapid transit of messages, men, and materiel increased European pressure on once remote provinces, from Iraq to the Hijaz. Istanbul decided to use those same improved means of transit to seize and hold the Arabian peninsula, in order to create a defensive bulwark against foreign encroachment. In the east this task was given to Midhat Pasha, who showed the drive and the intelligence necessary for the job. He deserved great credit for starting to return this long-forgotten area to the status of a fully functioning, productive part of the empire.

The Return of Ottoman Interest in Arabia

That the Ottoman empire chose to reassert its old claim to sovereignty and government over this fractious area caused surprise and speculation among contemporary observers and modern historians. The Ottoman state in 1870, seen from Western Europe, seemed in many respects truly to be a "sick man." The major *Tanzimat* ("organization") reforms after the Crimean War[1] had raised hopes of the creation of a strong, "European" state to replace the sclerotic, Muslim, autocratic administration then directed by Istanbul; but sweeping change did not happen overnight. Policies decreed by Western-looking reformers in the Sublime Porte[2] lost much of their effect by filtration through often ignorant or corrupt lower officials. Modernization, especially in the military, absorbed huge sums of money, often borrowed on ruinous terms in London or Paris. Unrest in Ottoman Europe also laid heavy claims on government attention and resources. Under these conditions, observers of Midhat Pasha's expedition down the Hasa coast in 1871 could only speculate regarding the reasons for the campaign and even whether Istanbul approved the Baghdad governor's scheme to reclaim old imperial domains.

Yet the vitality of the empire at the time should not be underestimated. Fuad and Ali Pashas kept the reform process alive in the late 1860s.[3] They instituted new systems of decision-making and provincial government that had lasting impact. They pushed toward the goals of the 1856 *Hatt-i Hümayun* in social and land reforms. Military modernization also progressed. After Fuad Pasha's death in 1869, Grand Vezir Ali Pasha continued to keep Sultan Abdülaziz's spendthrift instincts in check. Of great importance also was a relative lull in internal and external conflicts after solution of the Cretan rebellion in 1868. In this era the Ottoman state could bear a relatively modest project such as the reconquest of Hasa.

Dissension among Wahhabi leaders provided the catalyst for the campaign. Two of Faisal's sons had competed for succession to the amirate of Riyadh since his death in 1865, courting the tribes of Najd and Hasa for support. `Abdallah b. Faisal had won the amirate in 1866, but rivalry with his brother Sa`ud broke into open warfare four years later. Sa`ud bested `Abdallah and his dwindling allies. Most of the bedouin of Hasa joined Sa`ud, as did many in Najd; of the powerful Arabian leaders only shaikhs of the Qahtan and the Mutayr, and the Sharif of Mecca supported—materially or only verbally—`Abdallah.[4] The deposed amir fled to Jabal Shammar in northern Najd, home of the Wahhabis' sometime rivals, the Rashidis, but the Rashidi amir also submitted to Sa`ud. In desperation, `Abdallah appealed for aid through the shaikh of Kuwait to a yet more distant power, his nominal suzerain, the Ottoman sultan. This gave Midhat Pasha, the *vali* (governor) of Baghdad province immediately to the north of Najd, the opportunity to intervene.[5]

`Abdallah's petition gave the excuse for intervention; it did not cause the response. Viewed from Britain (and India), the Hasa campaign demonstrated a desire in Istanbul to establish a "'Holy Ottoman Empire'" that, like its Roman counterpart, would combine "an ideal universal Church, the fiction of [a previous] empire, and a feudal monarchy."[6] Such empires could claim nominal sovereignty over countries that acted freely, without reference to their supposed suzerain. This view reserved to Britain the freedom to treat with local rulers without regard to Ottoman claims in Arabia, while it also kept at a minimum the possible points of contention between the two great powers. Britain had only a handful of interests that it felt strongly committed to defend, centered primarily on Trucial Oman and Bahrain, whence pirates, slavers, and gun smugglers could operate most easily; it abhorred involvement in politics on land.[7] It was not necessary, and thus not desirable, to oppose Midhat's expedition, although Britain judged Istanbul's interest to be essentially expansionary.

Modern historians have generally accepted this view, that the Ottomans simply snatched a golden opportunity to expand their authority into Arabia.[8] To that the scholar J. B. Kelly has added some broader historical perspective. He notes Istanbul's efforts to consolidate and expand its Arab provinces in 1870, suggesting that the *Tanzimat* or a "premonitory feeling" that it could not preserve its European possessions spurred a turn to Asia. Ali and Fuad Pashas had relied on French support to push their reform program; France's defeat by Prussia increased the influence in Europe of anti-Ottoman, pro-Slavic Russia. Prompt Russian repudiation of the Treaty of Paris clauses forbidding their armament on the Black Sea dimmed the prospects for Istanbul's continued control of the Balkans, while the opening of the Suez Canal in 1869 facilitated the projection of Ottoman power in the Arab territories.[9]

Kelly's analysis correctly identifies some of the influences on Istanbul but misses other major factors behind Midhat Pasha's expedition. The opening of the Suez Canal, for example, did facilitate communication and the projection of power beyond the Mediterranean coast, and the Russian threat did disturb the sultan's government. Yet the Ottomans certainly had not given up hope of retaining their position in the Balkans. A desire to strengthen their European frontier and to improve their role and reputation in great power politics inspired the *Tanzimat* until its end in 1876, and Sultan Abdülhamid II thereafter also devoted much of his energies to European problems. Asia as the bastion of a new empire did not gain serious consideration among the ruling elite until the turn of the century. The Ottomans did not seek to shift the weight of the empire from Europe to Asia but rather sought to prevent the occurrence in Asia of the piecemeal encroachment by Western powers that was happening in Europe.

RESURRECTION OF OTTOMAN ROLE IN THE GULF

Ottoman Asia had felt the gradual increase of foreign, especially British, pressure on its frontiers for decades before 1870. In the Red Sea area, Egypt since the reign of Mehmet Ali (1805–1848) had followed a practically independent course. Undoubtedly due to events there and in Algeria, which France occupied in 1830, the Ottomans retook control of Tripolitania in 1835—stepping in, as they were to do in Hasa, when a protracted power struggle broke out among members of the ruling dynasty, the Qaramanlis.[10] French and British influence in Egypt rose as the Khedives turned to Europe for money and expertise necessary to their own modernization schemes. "Turkish" rule waxed and waned in the Sudan, but Egypt was the real governing power. Since 1839 Britain had controlled Aden, which lay close to the narrow southern entrance to the Red Sea. With Aden as a base, the British seemed ready to expand their rule up the eastern shore of the Red Sea by adopting clients among the fractious Yemeni tribes. The opening of the Suez Canal, built with European money, eased access to Asia for Britain and France as much as for Istanbul. This increased the risk of a final loss of Ottoman influence in the Red Sea, including governance of the vital Holy Places in the Hijaz. Such a threat helped to prompt in 1870 an Ottoman expedition to resecure western Arabia, including Yemen.

Control of eastern Arabia became desirable to support the campaigns in Yemen and Asir, and other strategic reasons increased its value. Order in Najd would subdue a hinterland that provided a refuge to tribes beyond the sway of the Sharif of Mecca and would secure direct land links between Iraq and the Hijaz. A base in Hasa would permit quicker reaction to any threat from the Wahhabis of Riyadh, who in the past had raided Iraq, Syria, and the Hijaz. Security for the shipping lanes between Basra and Jidda also gained importance as Iraq became a major supplier of grain to the Hijaz after 1864;[11] domination of the Gulf coast would remove some potential threats to these supply routes, be the danger from pirates or the forces of a foreign power based on the peninsula. Although Britain had no permanent representatives stationed in eastern Arabia, the scope of British interests seemed to threaten Ottoman supremacy not only in the southern Gulf but in Iraq as well. The Lynch Company enjoyed a veritable monopoly on Tigris and Euphrates steamer traffic after 1841, despite repeated attempts to establish an Ottoman service.[12] Several British concerns prepared plans for rail lines between the Mediterranean and the Gulf in 1856 and 1867–1872.[13] The plans remained unfulfilled, but Istanbul remembered them well, suspecting well into the next century that Britain wanted to establish a land link from Egypt to India. The laying of a telegraph cable in the 1860s from India to Faw, at the southern tip of Iraq, confirmed official British interest in strengthening ties to the Gulf. By 1870, it seemed possible to Istanbul that Britain could develop a dominant hold on communications—and thus on overall affairs—through the heart of Ottoman Asia, from the Straits of Hurmuz to the Syrian coast, unless Istanbul took preventive steps.

To meet these challenges on the state's southern borders, in short, the Ottomans made vigorous efforts to extend their active control over lands and peoples, in order to make Asia a complete unit of the empire by improving its defense and administration. The Asian territories resembled a fork, one tine of which passed through Syria to the Hijaz, while the other followed the Tigris and Euphrates to Basra. Communication between the two was indirect (through Diyarbakr) or difficult (through the Syrian desert).[14] The failure to extend state boundaries from ill-defined points in the barren interior to natural limits on the coast invited future sovereignty disputes with local and foreign powers. If foreigners established bases in the south, they could easily agitate the unchecked tribes of the interior; the bedouins could advance between the tines into the heart of Ottoman Asia to create havoc among the settlers and nomads of Syria and Iraq. By directing the Arabian tribes, weakening Ottoman control and increasing their commercial and political presence along the two tines, foreigners could come to dominate much of Ottoman Asia. Securing the Arabian peninsula under Istanbul's control could close the gap between the tines and stop the scenario. This was to be attempted by moving troops down the coasts to occupy the important settlements and by posting a squadron of ships to patrol the rest of the shoreline. At the same time steps were taken to reassert control over tribes of the interior, especially in the Syrian desert.[15] The full success of the plan, however, required the spread of Ottoman authority to the southeastern Arabian coast as well; the government never seriously attempted that, despite frequent discussions of plans to build influence in Oman and the Hadhramawt. Unable to control the coast from Aden to Abu Dhabi, the Ottomans could not hope to succeed in eradicating British influence in Arabia.

Events Contributing to the Decision to Occupy Hasa

Whereas the immediate spur to the campaign came with the plea from `Abdallah al-Sa`ud, troubles in Bahrain had already caused the Ottoman government to consider strong action. Shaikh Muhammad al-Khalifa, the ruler of Bahrain, had called for Ottoman aid in disputes with the Wahhabi amir in 1849 and 1853; in 1859 he requested official protection from the *vali* of Baghdad (and coincidentally made similar overtures to the shah of Iran).[16] These appeals had had little practical effect, beyond building a stronger feeling of community of interests between the two parties. Further troubles, which led to British deposition of Shaikh Muhammad in 1868, naturally attracted attention in Baghdad. Britain's bold actions as kingmaker over the next year[17] led the Ottoman ambassador in London in January 1870 to protest this interference in a "permanent possession" of his state.[18]

At the same time Midhat Pasha took the first concrete steps to counteract the spread of British influence in the Persian Gulf. In 1869 he had bought three river steamers for the government's shipping company, the Oman-Ottoman administration, to compete with the British Lynch Company on the Euphrates. By February 1870 he was attempting to organize a naval force in Basra as part of a remedy for the Bahrain problem.[19] His preparations did not meet with much success. His force presumably was to be a major part of a naval squadron designed to monitor the entire Arabian coast; Istanbul had earlier ordered five ships to perform such duty but had had to reassign them to the Aegean. Seven months later the fleet and shipyard at Basra were still in a backward, disordered state.[20]

Midhat achieved more lasting success with the submission of Kuwait to Ottoman authority. Before Midhat arrived in Baghdad the Ottomans had wanted to establish a presence there by sending a customs official and secretary in order to recoup customs losses caused by livestock exporters bypassing Ottoman authorities in Basra. The Ottomans had shelved the idea, however, when the shaikh of Kuwait assured them of popular opposition to the measure.[21] Midhat revived, altered, and pushed vigorously the idea of establishing Kuwait as Ottoman territory. According to information supplied by him to the Grand Vezir, Kuwait in its early period had been a dependency of Basra and thus was and remained an Ottoman land—most of its natives' boats, in fact, had flown the Ottoman flag. Over time, however, as it had been neglected, it had acted with growing independence, which had led Europeans to recognize it as a separate republic.[22] This posed a clear danger to the Ottoman flank. "In view of the situation now in Bahrain, with Britain achieving domination, and foreigners' plots to send ships to seize the Hasa and Qatif coast, and because after that obviously they will move on to Kuwait" (which was practically on Basra's doorstep), Istanbul had to bring Kuwait under proper administration.[23]

To effect the extension of sovereignty over Kuwait, Midhat applied financial pressure on its leaders. Kuwaiti shaikhs for years had received income from land around Basra–dates worth T£500–600 per annum. Midhat cut off that revenue. According to him, the Kuwaiti shaikhs came to petition him on this matter and on that of establishing Ottoman rule in their territory. They claimed to be proud of being subjects of the Sublime State but feared the imposition of duties such as customs and taxes. Midhat replied that the state had no need of them, merely wishing to extend its patronage and protection (*sihabet ve himaye*) over Kuwait. To establish that officially, Midhat named the leading shaikh, `Abdallah al-Sabah, *kaymakam* of Kuwait, under which title he would continue to rule, and requested letters of appointment from the sultan for the Shafi`i judges of the town and patents for five *hutbî* mosques. He also proposed that up to 100 gendarmes (*zaptiye*) be stationed in Kuwait as a symbol of authority. The gendarmes were never assigned to Kuwait; instead, the Grand Vezir suggested that the *kaymakam* be given an Ottoman flag to fly from his residence in order to affirm Kuwait's ties to the empire, in addition to issuing the letters and patents. The sultan then ordered that these recommendations be enacted.[24] The Ottomans thus established a formal claim to Kuwait, although it made little substantive change in the port's day-to-day affairs.

Acquisition of this buffer territory did little to quiet fears about British activities. At the end of September 1870, Midhat sent the small steamer *Asur* on a port-hopping voyage to India, ostensibly to carry trade goods but really to give a special inspector on board the opportunity to gather information on conditions and public opinion in Hasa and Bahrain. The agent returned with a report that practically compelled Baghdad and Istanbul to action.[25]

It painted a scene of chaos, in which malign foreign forces pressed hard upon those of good. Qatif and Dammam were under Bahraini blockade, and the running conflicts between the islanders and the mainland and between `Abdallah and Sa`ud had thrown the people from Kuwait to Qatar into turmoil. Such anarchy in itself was lamentable, but this was especially insidious: the agent's Arab informants—Bahraini and Hasawi alike—blamed Britain for the troubles. Britain backed the Bahrainis, its navy had itself attacked Qatif five times, and one of its naval officers directed the current blockade. With equal surprising unanimity, the informants declared their inclination toward the Muslim Ottomans and professed their wish to be delivered from British thrall. Be that desire real (as it was for the Hasawis) or merely diplomatic (as it perhaps was for the Bahrainis, who would naturally treat a regional power with caution, especially one in whose territory they regularly traded), the chorus of appeals could not but impress the Ottomans.

The impulse to intervene aroused by this news was only strengthened by the agent's information on the `Abdallah-Sa`ud struggle. His report tied Sa`ud firmly to Bahrain, and thus to Britain. `Abdallah on the other hand was not only battling this coalition but also planning to subdue wayward parts of his father's domains, notably in Masqat, Oman, and Bahrain. Not coincidentally, these were all areas under British influence. The *Asur* agent's report made clear that commonality of interests could make `Abdallah a very useful Ottoman protégé.

Even lacking other grounds for intervention, this would have assured Midhat's warm welcome to `Abdallah's plea for help against his brother Sa`ud. The governor, in fact, seemed prepared to invite such a request, should the fleeing amir be slow to make it. Disturbed not only by rumors of secret British provision of money, weapons, and strategic advice to the rebels,[26] but also by reports that Sa`ud had begun to gain control of Jabal Shammar and to suborn tribes based in Iraq, Midhat sent an official to locate and encourage `Abdallah. Coming upon the amir in the desert and finding him in straitened circumstances, the official discovered that `Abdallah nevertheless intended to gather support from various tribes, notably the `Anaza,[27] in order to attack his brother. The amir apparently had already by that time sent a man to Baghdad to ask for soldiers and ships.[28] The official's report on `Abdallah's determination to continue the fight despite his weakness must have fed Midhat's desire to act promptly and forcefully. Made aware of these developments, the Sublime Porte was stirred to request more information.[29]

Midhat submitted to Istanbul an impassioned, three-page petition, in which he argued the case for intervention in Hasa and the means necessary for success.[30] His analysis centered on the opportunities for foreign gains being created by the current situation. The most fertile area of Najd (i.e., Hasa), he wrote, was in danger of being turned into desert as a result of the Sa`ud-`Abdallah rivalry. That struggle might seem to be nothing more than a feud between two bands of nomadic tribesmen, but it invited the interference of the British and Iranians, as had already happened under similar circumstances in Bahrain; indeed, he insisted, Sa`ud relied on the promises of foreigners in undertaking his rebellion, and his campaign in Hasa received material support from Britain.

Midhat placed the blame for Arabia's vulnerability to outside powers squarely upon Istanbul's previous lack of attention to the area. Echoing the *Asur* agent, he averred that the peninsula's inhabitants, as Muslims, all naturally desired a tie to the Sublime State. At no time, however, had the sultan's government offered them meaningful, material support, and the Ottomans had been left behind, even forgotten by the Arabs, as the British presence on the seas increased. The Arabs had been forced to look to foreigners for protection. Midhat had sought to reassert an official presence in the Gulf by strengthening the naval shipyard in Basra but had not had much support from Istanbul. All that he had been able to do was to outfit three cargo vessels that could show the Ottoman flag in the Gulf, of which the *Asur* was one. These alone could not hold back the British.

Midhat sent the Grand Vezir a copy of the report by the inspector aboard that ship as evidence of the severity of the British threat. He scoffed at the idea that the Bahrainis had carried out the blockade of Qatif by themselves: they could not (indeed would not know how to) do it alone.[31] He felt no doubt that real responsibility lay with the captain of the British warship that, he charged, anchored permanently in Manama. Britain sought to strangle the region's trade by sea (unless carried under its own flag), while Sa'ud throttled it by land.

Inaction under such conditions would be disastrous, according to Midhat. The Ottoman state had bestowed on 'Abdallah the title and rank of *kaymakam*; his overthrow by a renegade, backed by foreigners, would critically harm Istanbul's standing among the Arabs and would cause great confusion in the area. Midhat then detailed the forces that he would need in order to ensure 'Abdallah's victory over his brother.[32]

After discussion of Midhat's several reports, the Council of Ministers decided to recommend the expedition to the sultan.[33] Troops from Baghdad, Kirkuk, and Aleppo would act in support of 'Abdallah, who would use this visible backing to gather Arab fighters for his drive to regain the governorate of Najd. To encourage the Arabs further, the Ottoman force would include tribesmen from southern Iraq, including Mansur Bey of the Muntafiq, whose ties to eastern Arabia had enabled him previously to act as a conduit for petitions from Qatifi and Bahraini notables to Baghdad. The ministers clearly hoped that the inclusion of such tribal notables would soothe disquiet among the inhabitants of Najd, some of whom doubtless would be sorry to see 'Abdallah restored to office.

Although they agreed on the necessity of backing 'Abdallah, the Council of Ministers and Midhat differed subtly on the reasons for action. Midhat saw the greatest danger in the growth of British influence in Arabia; the threat to the soft Ottoman underbelly came from abroad. He therefore promoted an aggressive policy, wanting to unfurl the Ottoman flag over the Gulf region through military deployment. A forceful presence offered the best chance for realization of Istanbul's claims to territories dominated by Britain, such as Bahrain. That Midhat kept open the option of using force greater than that involved in simply returning 'Abdallah to Riyadh is illustrated by his ambiguous replies to Britain's voiced concerns over the independence of Bahrain, Masqat, and the free tribes of southern Arabia. Istanbul assured Britain unconditionally that it only wished for a return of peace and order to Najd and had no designs on the other territories. In confirming those assurances to British Consul Herbert in Baghdad, Midhat also restricted his designs to Najd, saying that Bahrain was "not within Turkish contemplation," although his implied definition of Najd seemed rather broad.[34] Judging by this, his concern for the dilapidated Basra naval yard, and his later proposals for the administration of Hasa, Midhat clearly desired a continuing, dynamic Ottoman military and civil presence in the Gulf, from Basra to Qatar, from which future expansion could occur. Full incorporation into the Ottoman empire would secure Arabia from foreign encroachment.

The Council recognized the potential for trouble with Britain detailed by Midhat, but the ministers viewed the disturbances in Najd primarily as a domestic problem. This division foreshadowed the uncertainty of Ottoman administration in Hasa: were reforms to meet a foreign threat needed more than those to improve local conditions in Arabia? The ministers in 1871 clearly felt that, even if Sa`ud had attacked his brother for personal reasons and following bedouin desert tradition of tribal conflict, his most recent actions bore the potential for later, more serious threats to Ottoman security. Having defeated his brother, Sa`ud now showed signs of wishing to conquer the length and breadth of Najd and to dominate Iraq, thus raising a simple feud to a broad revolt against the Ottoman state. The government must have been conscious of the examples of previous, religion-based Wahhabi-Ottoman conflicts, although the Council's missive to the sultan is remarkably free of religious overtones.[35] Rebellion in an area contiguous to the provinces of the Hijaz and Iraq could only bring severe damage to the region. If the British then stepped in to establish a protectorate and block Ottoman efforts to put down such revolts, moreover, other tribes (*aqvam*) would seek their protection.

To stop the spread of this internal decay, therefore, the *vali* of Baghdad was instructed to institute a reformed administration in Najd, with `Abdallah at its head. This would strengthen `Abdallah's loyalty and show the Arabs the power of the Ottoman state. It would also solve the British problem, because under international law Britain could not interfere in measures designed to suppress rebellion in territory under Ottoman sovereignty, let alone extend a protectorate over it. In short, the Council inferred that settlement of the `Abdallah-Sa`ud rivalry would resolve the area's problems. On 3 Muharrem 1288 (25 March 1871), the sultan duly accepted the ministers' recommendation of authorization for Midhat's proposed military campaign.

The British Position in the Gulf, c. 1870

The strength of Ottoman suspicions regarding the extent of Britain's influence among the Gulf Arabs requires further examination of the truth of the information available to Midhat Pasha. As mentioned above, in the first half of the century Britain had established quite limited aims. A message from the Indian government Secretaries of State and Foreign Affairs to the Iranian minister in London baldly confirmed the scope of those goals in 1869: "the sole objects of the British Government in holding the [Bahraini] shaikhs to [their] engagements were the prevention of piracy and of the slave trade and the maintenance of the police of the Gulf—duties of which Great Britain would gladly, if it were possible, divest herself in favor of Persia."[36] Although the message overstated Britain's willingness to abandon its carefully constructed regional position, it did accurately convey the government's general desire to avoid overtaxing India's limited resources in the Gulf. Active policy could not extend beyond matters of trade, licit and illicit.

Pursuit of even these limited aims often required the threat or use of all available force, and British-Arab relations consequently suffered frequent tensions. In 1863–65, when the Indian naval squadron had little presence around Bahrain, Muhammad al-Khalifa harassed and extorted money from Hindu traders in his domains; restitution only came after the British Persian Gulf Resident, Colonel Pelly, seized a Bahraini ship.[37] Muhammad and the shaikh of Abu Dhabi similarly ignored the protests of the Resident after their October 1867 sack of Qatar. Nine months passed before the British could gather a naval force sufficient to the task of imposing a fine on the leader of Abu Dhabi, and a further two months before the deposition of Muhammad could be attempted.[38] The Resident and the Indian government reacted more quickly to Muhammad's invasion of Bahrain the following year; the escalating cycle of attack-counterattack between the island and the mainland threatened to destroy the maritime peace so carefully crafted for a half century.

This delicate circumstance helped to determine Britain's course of action at that time, during which the *Asur* made its tour of investigation. The government of India sought above all to calm the situation. It instructed Pelly to use force to oust Muhammad and to install `Isa as the new shaikh—but not if the population appeared to disapprove. Other steps, regarding punishment of mainland supporters of the rebels and compensation for looted property, remained for future deliberation. Pelly in fact exceeded his instructions by making recognition of `Isa conditional upon his seizure of the chief rebels' property in Bahrain to compensate those whom they had plundered. India, however, authorized no action against the inhabitants of Hasa beyond asking Amir `Abdallah to prevent such raids in future.[39]

In view of India's restraint, how can the tale of British command of the Bahraini blockade of Hasa be explained? Using Arab ships to attack other Arabs would have made a mockery of the very trucial system that Britain's intervention in Bahrain had sought to uphold, especially in this case.[40] It would have meant career suicide if the story leaked, and the involvement of the navy would have made that hard to prevent. It is therefore doubtful that the ship's captain was involved to the extent described to the Ottoman agent. Yet it is certainly possible that Pelly himself simply ignored orders—he was willful, vindictive, secretive, taking unauthorized action on numerous occasions in addition to the case of recognizing `Isa.[41] Although his active direction of the operation is open to doubt, it is likely that at least he dropped a hint in private to `Isa that a blockade might be a good idea.

To claim that full responsibility lay with Britain, however, served Bahrain's purposes well. It allowed `Isa and his adherents to maintain to the agent aboard the *Asur* that, as Muslims, they naturally favored the Ottoman state, but that an outside power compelled them to attack their coreligionists. The assertion of British backing also would give pause to Arabs who would oppose `Isa's plans as well as any who might be tempted to seek British support for themselves. This ploy worked well: Ottoman wrath focussed less on Bahrain than on Britain, while the people of Hasa did not appeal to the one power that openly espoused a policy of opposition to tribal warfare at sea. This was especially important in view of Bahrain's promised reliance on British naval protection. Britain's concerns about its responsibility to protect Bahrain in case of Ottoman invasion in 1871 show the importance attached to that agreement, and the British could not afford to ignore any serious breach of this undertaking by Shaikh `Isa.

Britain's antipathy to naval actions by others in the Gulf, in fact, presented to it the only serious point of anxiety regarding Midhat Pasha's Hasa expedition. The governments in London and Bombay feared that Ottoman maritime operations, which might range from simple troop transport to invasion of Bahrain and Trucial Oman, would encourage all Gulf powers, from the shah of Iran to local shaikhs, to use their own ships at will.[42] Ottoman assurances that their naval operations would not go beyond the transport of troops and supplies to Hasa soothed much of the British anxiety about an eruption of warfare on the waves or an attack on Bahrain, Masqat, or Trucial Oman.[43] Willingness to accept Istanbul's statements increased in proportion to officials' distance from the Gulf, but London finally instructed a more suspicious India to avoid any action against Midhat. Bombay was to observe the expedition; London was to conduct any necessary diplomacy. In the event, Midhat's campaign passed with little British interference beyond warnings against attacks on Bahrain and Oman.

Great Britain's attitude shows that Midhat judged its intentions too harshly. Even the Indian government, despite preferring to block Midhat's troop transports, seemed to accept (grudgingly) that Najd was Ottoman territory—at least that Britain had no legal grounds for contesting it.[44] The thought that London and Istanbul " 'understood ... that the position which the British government has long held in the Gulf is not in any way to be affected by [the] expedition against Nejd' " reassured the government of India.[45] Because Britain had no interest in extending its influence to Hasa, sought rather only to preserve its ties with Bahrain and Oman, its officials failed to understand that others could see its actions as anything but conservative and in the common interest. Consequently, British observers—even the Resident in Baghdad, who noted an Ottoman jealousy of British influence in the Gulf—could not conceive of Midhat's expedition as essentially a defensive move against them instead of a simple case of aggression aimed at all of central and southern Arabia.[46] In fact, the Indian government thought that Midhat was relying upon the benefits of *Pax Britannica* to protect his ships from Arab attack.[47]

That idea exemplified the causes of Ottoman-British tensions in the Gulf during this and later periods. Both sides perceived weaknesses in their regional positions, targeted essentially conservative goals, but due to misperception of the other's attitudes and intentions each empire felt impelled to act more forcefully and offensively than circumstances might have warranted. Midhat felt alarm about his southern frontier because of exaggerated reports of British might and intentions. At that time, however, Britain had no conception of itself as an offensive, hegemonic power. It followed a general policy of seeking the benefits of colonial control without the expense of administering colonies. In southwest Asia this meant safeguarding shipping, to which end it concluded agreements with local leaders in which it assumed few commitments. Even these few responsibilities often tested the limited resources assigned to uphold them. The basis of Britain's influence in the Gulf, the web of agreements with the shaikhs, as elsewhere in Asia rested on the suggestion of power—the resolute behavior of scattered officials, who enjoyed a typically British confidence in their ability to "put things in order"—supported by the occasional judicious use of force. Strong action by another power, even in an area of such small interest to Britain as Najd, threatened that aura of might and eventually fed an urge to rework and strengthen the entire precarious treaty structure so carefully built.[48]

Intergovernmental negotiations could have addressed the separate British and Ottoman concerns in the Gulf. Britain was still one of the European powers friendly to the government in Istanbul; because London had no wish to assume territorial responsibilities (and certainly shuddered at the thought of its European rivals—notably Russia—taking control of the Balkans and Middle East), it preferred to maintain the unity of the Ottoman empire. Britain therefore had little anxiety about Ottoman sovereignty in Najd per se. The British would have been likely to recognize Istanbul's claim to the peninsula, provided that the independence of those areas to which the sultan's authority had never, or rarely, extended (Aden, Oman, Bahrain) were assured. Such an arrangement might have fallen short of the desired control of all Arabia, but it would have given explicit recognition in international law to Istanbul's sovereignty over Najd, which was the goal that the Council of Ministers sought to achieve unilaterally through Midhat's campaign. Britain would gain satisfaction from the security afforded its arrangements for policing the high seas, a function that, the British might argue, should win Ottoman approval as a service in the public interest.

The two sides did negotiate such an agreement, but only on the eve of the First World War. For four decades the Ottomans hoped to improve their position in the Gulf, and the British refused to discuss their affairs openly with the sultan's government, to a significant extent because they also were ignorant of their opponent's concerns. The remarks of the British ambassador in Istanbul upon Midhat's second Grand Vezirate (1876) indicate the difficulties that Britain faced in determining his attitude toward London. The ambassador wrote of his hopes for reform from this energetic modernizer, claiming that Midhat had listened favorably to his advice in the past, but that his attitudes to Britain now were unknown.[49] Although concern for reform and constitutional government gave some common purpose to Britain and Midhat in Istanbul, the latter's prickly independence and devotion to Ottoman interests precluded the appearance of becoming a puppet to European reformers.[50] In light of Midhat's often difficult relations with Britain while in Baghdad and Istanbul, it is ironic that British pressure led to his return from exile in 1881 after he had fallen from Sultan Abdülhamid II's favor and helped to persuade the sultan to commute the death sentence passed on him following his return.[51]

The Ottoman Campaign in Hasa and Qatar

On 26 May 1871 an Ottoman force of 3,000 men, supported by 1,500 Arabs, landed in Hasa at Ra's Tanura.[52] Qatif and Dammam fell in early June after minimal resistance. One month later the troops captured

Hufuf, where they established a base in which to recover their strength. At that point the campaign bogged down, for several reasons. The area most vulnerable to British interference had been captured, but the gains had not yet been consolidated.[53] Reports given the British also stated that the army had little food, 400 men had died of starvation, and more than one third of those remaining were sick. Many of the Arab auxiliaries returned home, including the shaikhs who were to persuade the local leaders to welcome the Ottoman forces.[54]

Events in the Najdi interior later in the summer heightened the sense of paralysis. Midhat received a report, confirmed by the British consul in Baghdad, that Sa`ud had defeated `Abdallah in battle.[55] Midhat's information listed Sa`ud in the wounded and `Abdallah (wrongly) among the dead. Sa`ud's victory allowed him to make peace with `Abdallah's supporters, and he entered Riyadh as the new amir. Although the new Wahhabi leader might be expected to remain in the capital, licking his wounds for a time, the defeat of their client demanded an Ottoman strategic reappraisal and made a drive to Riyadh more necessary.

Several problems forestalled an immediate campaign, however. Current climate conditions raised the first obstacle. The late summer heat and several years of drought made a march into the interior unwise; knowledgeable locals informed the Ottomans that an expedition from Hufuf would need seven days to reach Riyadh along a route with only one waterhole.[56] Even if the weather cooled and some rain fell, the troops in Hasa could not safely proceed without reinforcements, because of losses from disease[57] and war, and the need to ensure peace in the newly conquered territory. Istanbul had ordered the V Army Corps in Syria to second several battalions to reinforce the Najd command, but those units were not ready. Midhat could not spare more men from the VI Corps in Baghdad, because Iraq's tribal disturbances had flared up again.[58] The only material attempt to redress the situation in Najd was the dispatch of troops to the Hijaz for an attack on Riyadh from the west, in response to an appeal for help from `Abdallah to the amir of Mecca and the *vali* of the Hijaz.[59]

The lack of stability in Hasa also concerned the Porte; Midhat and the general commanding the expedition, Nafiz Pasha, had yet to institute a regular provincial government and administration. The *vali*'s lassitude in this matter may well have arisen from uncertainty in his own mind about Najd's future. He was developing a mistrust of `Abdallah, who was proving fickle and strangely lethargic in meeting the challenge from his brother, but no possible Ottoman substitute governor had real knowledge of the area. Midhat himself knew little about Najd, including Hasa, and so could not be sure whom among the local leaders he might trust to be his deputy. With the uncertainty over who controlled Riyadh, he also had to postpone final decisions on provincial districting and chains of command. The continued administrative vacuum unsettled the Porte, however, and Istanbul wanted the situation stabilized preparatory to any advance on Riyadh.[60]

Again the likelihood of strong action receded as the situation in Najd reverted to stalemate. ʿAbdallah's uncle and the people of Riyadh drove Saʿud from the town, whence he retired to his tribal supporters in the area of Qatar, the ʿAjman and Al Murra. The expedition from the Hijaz was postponed until settlement of affairs in Yemen could free troops to augment the small body sent by Istanbul; a large force would then resolve problems not only in Riyadh but also among the troublesome tribes of western Arabia. Istanbul felt that the situation in the interior was sufficiently stable to allow delay. Saʿud was destroying his popularity unaided in Riyadh, and shaikhs of the important areas of Qasîm and Jabal Shammar had declared their loyalty to the Ottoman cause.[61] To the east ʿAbdallah proved reports of his death to be premature, surfacing at the Ottoman camp in Hufuf at the urging of his brother Muhammad.[62] Nafiz Pasha was content to entrust Riyadh to the care of the amir's uncle, giving him the title of *müdir* (town administrator) and sending him money and supplies preparatory to the return of ʿAbdallah.[63] The amir, however, remained in Hufuf, either because of his own lack of initiative or because of increasing Ottoman doubts about the wisdom of allowing him to escape their observation. ʿAbdallah justified any mistrust by carrying on an intermittent negotiational correspondence with his brother Saʿud.[64]

For his part, Saʿud largely stayed clear of the Ottoman army in the autumn of 1871 but did wreak havoc on Qatar. His actions there and in southern Hasa had already given the Ottomans an opportunity to spread their influence south. A British ship calling at Doha in mid-July had found the imperial flag, raised by Shaikh Qâsim b. Muhammad al-Thani following a visit from an Ottoman official, flying over the port, while his father's flag flew over the fort.[65]

Intertribal rivalries provided the opportunity for Ottoman interference in Qatari affairs, much as the ʿAbdallah-Saʿud struggle did in Najd. The shaikhly family of Qatar, the Al Thani, headed by the elderly Muhammad b. Thani, clung to a less certain leadership position in the peninsula than did the Al Sabah in Kuwait and the Al Khalifa in Bahrain.[66] They felt external pressure as well, pushed on one side by their sometime overlord and rival, the shaikh of Bahrain, who still controlled the small port of Zubara on the northwest coast of the Qatar peninsula, and who still expected yearly tribute payments from Doha. On their other side, Sa'ud and his allies plundered the Al Thani domains and even cut off Doha's water supplies. The natural source of help for the Qataris in that situation was the Ottomans, who were seeking to capture Sa'ud and were known to disapprove of an independent, British-protected Bahrain. Ottoman aid seems to have been particularly desired by Shaikh Muhammad's son, Qâsim,[67] who very likely wanted to secure a powerful ally who could aid his succession to the shaikhdom and protect him while he developed his own influence.

Qâsim therefore requested aid from Nafiz Pasha. The general had been previously instructed to bring Qatar into the Ottoman orbit, because it was a tribute-paying dependency of Najd.[68] He immediately sent four flags to Qâsim to signify clearly the inclusion of the Al Thani territories in the Ottoman empire. The young shaikh raised one over his house in Doha, sent another to his father in the nearby town of Wakra, the third went to the shaikh of al-Khawr to the north and the last to 'Udayd, a small port at the southeastern base of the peninsula that the shaikh of Abu Dhabi also claimed.[69] The flags thus marked the important and most distant points of Al Thani territory, adding the weight of the sultan's state to their inviolability.

Qâsim al-Thani and his father used the Ottoman presence when it suited them, notably as a shield for defense and an excuse for noncooperation with British demands. The two Al Thani shaikhs accordingly tailored their accounts of Great Power involvement in Qatar to suit the differing interests of their Ottoman and British audiences. Midhat stated that both Qâsim and Muhammad had sent Nafiz Pasha requests for military aid against their enemies.[70] They had claimed that Sa'ud's followers harried Qatar only because of the inhabitants' allegiance and submission to the sultan. Regarding Bahrain, they had charged that it was a base for smuggling supplies to Sa'ud for his struggle, and that blood ties to the Bahrainis sapped the Qataris' ability to oppose their island rivals. To play further on Midhat's fears, the Al Thani shaikhs had said that British warships pressed them for payment of tribute (zekât) worth 9,000 riyals (c. £400) to Bahrain (neglecting to mention that they had agreed to this payment in 1868).[71] This pressure they had stoutly resisted, saying "we are under this [Ottoman] flag; while it is here we recognize no other." Midhat repaid their devotion by dispatching a full battalion of troops to subdue the Wahhabi outlaws—and presumably to forestall British coercion.[72]

Such was the situation as seen by Midhat; the Al Thanis gave a more independent tone to the scene for other observers. Following the visit of the British warship to Doha in July 1871, Pelly sent his assistant to investigate the reported Ottoman presence in the port. Muhammad al-Thani told his visitor that the shaikh of Kuwait had called to persuade the Qataris to acknowledge the sultan's suzerainty. Muhammad claimed to have refused to do so, but his son, he admitted, had accepted the Ottoman flag. The British also received later an account of the landing of the troops, which were sent by Midhat upon Qatari request, that emphasized the opposition of the rulers and people of Doha to any Ottoman military establishment in the town. Again the cited presence of the Kuwaiti shaikh, acting for Midhat and Nafiz Pasha, reduced the appearance of direct cooperation with the Ottomans.[73]

To determine which picture is more accurate—the Qataris as a proudly independent group, cajoled into reluctant service of Ottoman interests by a respected tribal leader, or as devoted subjects of the sultan—is difficult; probably neither version was completely true. The secondhand reports of Qatari resistance came to the British after the events described,[74] which would allow some post facto exaggeration without fear of contradiction. Midhat Pasha, a self-confident, assertive man, also tended to gloss over uncertainties in his reports. It is nevertheless certain that Qâsim, and probably also Muhammad, saw the advantages of accepting Ottoman suzerainty in principle in order to strengthen Qatar against enemies or rivals in Bahrain, Abu Dhabi, and Najd. Qâsim indeed won Ottoman recognition as the heir apparent to the shaikhdom. As had the Kuwaiti shaikhs, the Al Thani would even accept the formal appointment of a few officials by Istanbul, such as a judge,[75] but any prolonged troop presence would make them fear for their independence of action. The Qataris would not have expected such vigorous Ottoman action, however, before Midhat's inspection tour to Hasa in November 1871; by autumn Nafiz Pasha's troops were showing few signs of activity.

Chapter 3

Midhat Pasha's Inspection of Hasa and Plan for Its Development

Lacking the knowledge necessary to formulate plans of military advance, government, and economic development in the region, Midhat felt compelled to inspect Hasa personally in November 1871. His reports to Istanbul following the tour show that he now thought possible a quick pacification of Najd, to be followed by extensive improvement of infrastructure (emphasizing projects with military applications) and regularization of political and economic affairs—in short, a full fusion of Najd into the Ottoman empire.[1] Many of his plans mirrored his attempts at reform in Iraq and, before that, while *vali* of the Danube province. Wherever he served, Midhat showed himself to be a man of energy and vision. Hasa in 1871 taxed those qualities to the utmost, however, for famine and political unrest had severely debased the people's quality of life.

Midhat's tour lasted some six weeks, and based on his observations over that time he was able to give the Grand Vezir estimates of the economic potential of each town or district, and of what Hasa needed to ensure its security. Although Midhat maintained an optimistic tone, this information indicated the formidable obstacles facing his plans, including the expense to be borne by a financially strapped empire. Each important town required money for upkeep and improvements. Along the Hasa coast Ra's Tanura had the best harbor and served as entrepôt for the military's reinforcements and supplies. It had no fresh water supply, but water could be brought from a spring two to three hours away or could be distilled from seawater.[2] The ports of Qatif and its dependencies, such as Dammam, all had such treacherous shallows as to make them of limited use. Qatif's climate was worse than Basra's, and troops stationed

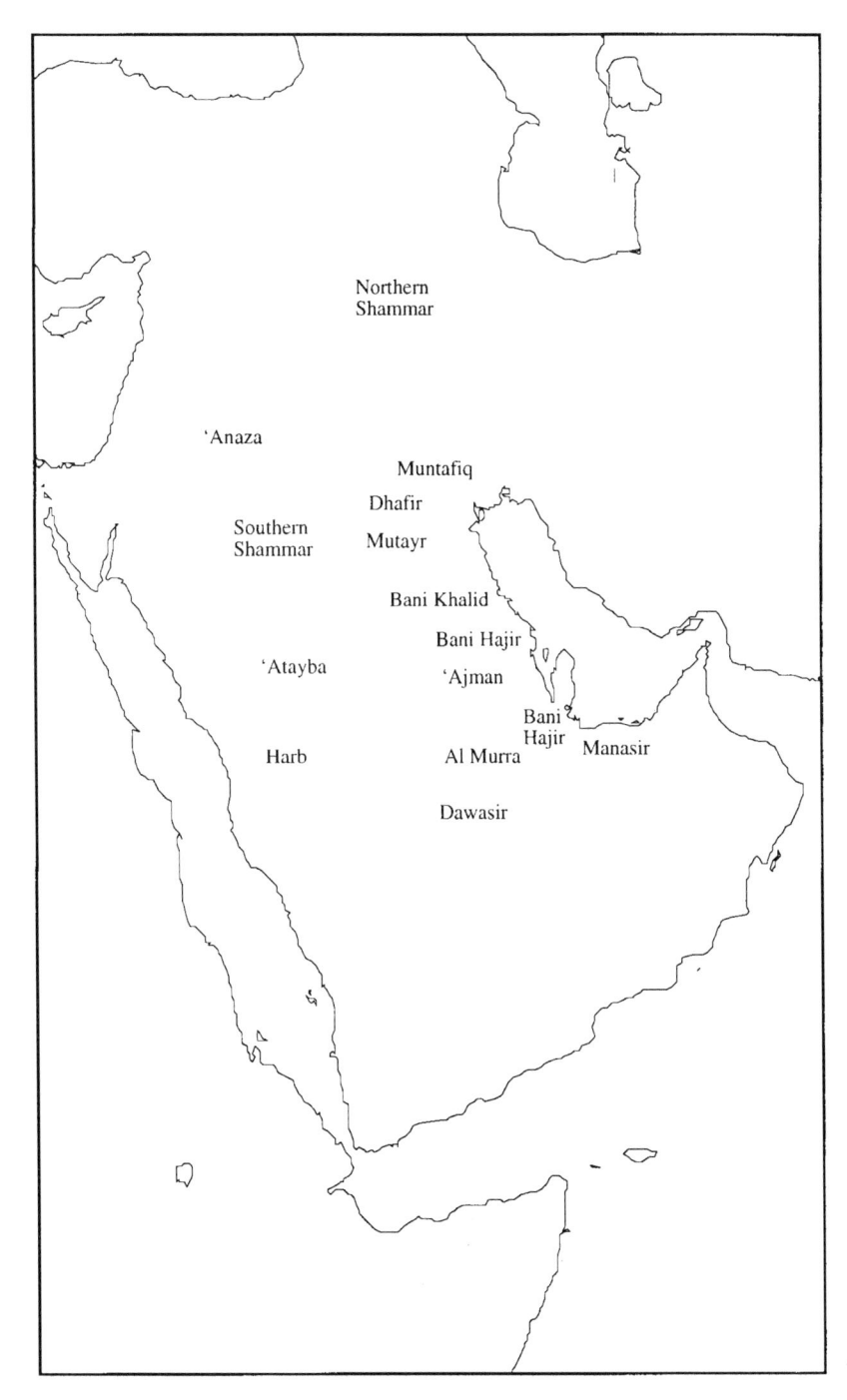

TRIBES IN ARABIA

there had suffered from fever. Midhat wanted to station a battalion of troops in a new barracks to be built at a cooler altitude outside the town. He also wanted to staff small forts at Dammam and on Tarut island (between Ra's Tanura and Qatif). There were in addition three forts in and around Qatif and Tarut that had no military value, but in Midhat's view they had to be maintained; their destruction could encourage disorder among the populace, although there was at the time little likelihood of unrest.[3] The people of the area, many of them Shi`is, had suffered heavily under the Wahhabis, and the easier rule brought by the Ottomans had generated great goodwill.

Despite a sharp degeneration caused by Wahhabi misrule, Qatif and its dependencies held impressive economic potential in Midhat's eyes. Numerous springs supported date trees similar to Hufuf's, in addition to other crops. Bedouin raids had combined with the Al Sa`ud family's oppression to lay much of this territory to waste, but with the return of peace the people had already started to repair the damage.

More problems, but also great potential rewards, lay in the Dhahran district between Qatif and `Uqayr. Due to its hilly terrain, the area had a better climate than Qatif. Numerous water sources until recently had supported a productive agricultural sector, centered again on date farming, but Bani Hajir tribesmen had devastated the region during the Wahhabi administration.[4] Midhat felt confident that the Dhahran area could recover, provided that the Ottomans took one of two steps: settle the Bani Hajir on the land, or drive them away and establish another, sedentary group in their place. The ease of execution of either plan, and the number of troops and fortifications necessary for enforcement, however, were questions left unaddressed by Midhat. The task would turn out to be very difficult, in fact, and the goal of pacification never was fully met. The Bani Hajir were to feature frequently in British reports of piracies and raids in the 1870s, although before 1878 much of the raiding originated in the vicinity of Qatar.[5]

Between Dhahran and Qatar lay less hospitable country under the sway of the restive `Ajman and Al Murra tribes. The only important point lay at `Uqayr, which served as the main port for Hufuf, twelve hours distant. As at Qatif, only shallow draft vessels could enter `Uqayr.[6] Because of their valuable position in Hasa's economy, `Uqayr and the road to Hufuf had suffered terribly from bedouin marauders. The road posed natural difficulties as well, running through forbidding, hilly, rocky desert until within two hours of Hufuf. Midhat declared that perfect peace had returned, however, maintained by troops—including Arab dromedary cavalry auxiliaries—stationed in guardhouses along this important communication route.[7]

Hufuf's importance as the proposed center of Ottoman administration and economic life in Hasa prompted Midhat to devote special attention to its security arrangements. The region's defenses would rest on three main forts around Hufuf that were sufficiently close together to ensure the garrisons' mutual assistance in case of unrest. Much of the oasis area's garrison, in fact, would be at the two posts outside the main town, because Hufuf's rich water sources gave it a humid climate and a susceptibility to fever in autumn. Midhat foresaw a permanent troop presence of not less than four or five battalions. Some of the present fortifications met Midhat's standards, but he wanted to add a large new barracks and a hospital to form a complete base for the region's security operations, which would grow in scope as the area of cultivation spread to remote springs.

Economic Potential and Paths to Development

One of the crucial issues that Midhat had to address in making plans for Hasa was its ability to produce revenue for the state. Baghdad and Istanbul had found the money for the 1871 military campaign, but they could not continue the exercise indefinitely if Hasa turned out to be economically worthless. Midhat was able to reassure Istanbul on this point, describing the oases' surprisingly rich potential. To turn it into reality, moreover, Midhat had developed a plan for making life predictable and rewarding, especially for farmers. The keys were taxation and land tenure. With their reform, Hasa could pay for itself and even reverse the flow of money from the capital.

Hufuf's riches made the proposed extensive and expensive security measures worthwhile. Midhat estimated that the combined population of Hufuf, Mubarraz, and about thirty surrounding villages reached between 15,000 and 29,000 households. He praised the climate, land, and water supply. The date groves roughly equaled in size those of Baghdad and Hilla in Iraq, while exceeding them in productiveness (*mamuriyet*), although no official had yet undertaken an exact inventory.[8] Midhat reported that this area produced so much that it had to import nothing beyond cotton, calico, and thread. Their products had brought the oases around Hufuf T£400,000–500,000 yearly in the past, but as elsewhere Wahhabi misrule had weakened the economy. The amirs of Riyadh had taxed the people into poverty, taken their possessions and done nothing to stop bedouin depredations. Midhat felt sure that production would regain its earlier richness, however, once Ottoman rule had restored peace and justice to the land. The addition of Hasa to Baghdad *Vilayet* would increase the wealth of the province and, by extension, of the empire as a whole.

In light of Midhat's own description of the difficult conditions obtaining in Hasa at the dawn of this new Ottoman era, which contemporary accounts generally confirm, it is tempting to dismiss his projections as those of an optimistic dreamer. Midhat may have been an optimist, yet his visions were not beyond reason. Among Hasa's assets his reports identified important sources of taxable income in agriculture, pearls, trade, animal husbandry, and fishing, centered on Hufuf, Qatif-Dammam, and `Uqayr. If the annual productive value of the oases around Hufuf were to reach T£500,000, with half as much again from the Qatif region, then Hasa would indeed be a valuable acquisition. The British Resident in the Gulf, Colonel Pelly, in the account of his journey to Riyadh in 1865, reported that the oases near Hufuf sent revenues of about T£60,000 to Amir Faisal, with all of Hasa returning a little less than T£90,000.[9] This supports Midhat's projections of the region's potential, as both Pelly and Midhat claimed that these revenues indeed came from standard canonic tax and customs rates of 10% (*öşür*). Midhat also reported, however, that Faisal's sons `Abdallah and Sa`ud had effectively sacked Hasa by gouging the people with taxes of 33%, 50%, even 67%, imposing arbitrary fines, and allowing bedouins to raid unchecked. Midhat gave no hard estimate of the resulting decline in the region's wealth, but it must have been substantial.[10]

This omission is surprising, because Midhat clearly acknowledged the severity of the matter in his report on the provisional financial and administrative organization of the new *sancak*. The tenth and final section of the document stated that the problem most pressing and deserving of official attention in making Hasa flourish was the expansion of the cultivated area by bringing empty or abandoned land into production and by developing water resources. Midhat confidently claimed that, if the people were to settle down, in a short time they would begin production on the fertile but currently empty land. The populace would live in complete contentment, and income accruing to the state would multiply five- or tenfold.[11] In this instance also, because the report gives few details on the extent of farm desertion, it is difficult to determine the proportions of the predicted tenfold increase that would come from reclaiming abandoned farms, from "making the desert bloom," and from intensification of agriculture on land already under cultivation.[12]

Because of the important role given to broadening the scope of agriculture in securing development and prosperity in Hasa, half of the *sancak*'s administrative regulations addressed issues of land tenure. Security of tenure—the confidence of a farmer that he would have a continuous, undisturbed right of cultivation on a piece of land—had disappeared in the general confusion caused by political turmoil and bedouin raids.

Uncertain of their ability to harvest a crop, or at least to profit from it, peasants had limited their planting.[13] According to the only specific assessment of this process that Midhat made, some 300 date palm groves around Hufuf, Mubarraz, and Qatif had reverted to the state after their cultivators had abandoned them.[14] The most important step to a speedy economic revival was the assignment of guaranteed rights of cultivation wherever security of tenure had weakened. The state technically owned most of the land, and the Hasa government could dispose of the right to restore abandoned fields. Farmers assigned such plots, or those among disputants found to have the strongest claims to currently cultivated land, would receive a kind of title deed (*tapu senedi* for agricultural land), which would be registered with an official brought from Baghdad to establish the land title office.[15]

The administrative regulations identified several means of assigning usufruct rights. A land-seeker could acquire the use of government (*mîrî*) land at a fair price through open auction, by payment of a similar sum without an auction,[16] or without any charge on condition that the recipient bring the land under cultivation.[17] Midhat expected the latter process to prevail in reviving agriculture around Dhahran (an indication that the town and its surrounding villages had suffered especially in the past, since free titles were given for land that required the digging of wells and the expenditure of much labor) and in the settlement of bedouin tribes.[18] Whatever the means of gaining the usufruct rights, every new landholder would receive a *tapu senedi*. In theory the state would also issue title deeds to every current landlord whose claim to his property was long-standing and undisputed, but after stating that, Midhat immediately allowed exceptions to the rule. He acknowledged that there might be people who did not know of the *tapu* system or did not understand it, so they would not be forced to accept *sened*s.

This provision is quite interesting, since such an exception to the registration rule threatened to negate much of the benefit that it aimed to achieve. The *tapu* system was designed to improve agricultural output by making the cultivator sure of his long-term rights to the land. Without the state forcing all farmers to register their holdings (let alone conducting a cadastral survey), recurring arguments over boundaries and ownership would remain a probability.

Yet the flexibility of this approach was not necessarily shortsighted. Midhat's earlier experiences as governor of Baghdad must have affected his approach to questions of land tenure. When instituting a title deed system in Iraq, he had shown a willingness to experiment, altering regulations from district to district,[19] and the lessons learned in the process influenced his program in Hasa. Land registration in other provinces, including the *vilayet* of Baghdad, had met with resistance, since farmers often viewed it as a step toward improved tax collection and military conscription. Midhat foresaw that the Hasawis might react similarly. By making registration optional for the most established landholders, Midhat probably sought to minimize conflict with leading community members during the volatile period of transition to Ottoman rule. Reluctance to force too many innovations upon a generally conservative population also surely influenced Midhat in this and other areas of administration. To judge from his repeated remarks that the people felt great gratitude to their new rulers for the removal of Wahhabi tyranny and extortion, Midhat expected popular good will to play an important role in sustaining Ottoman government and wanted to keep it as long as possible. Restraint in innovation would limit condemnation in the court of public opinion but, if executed as planned, the registry scheme might have caused more problems among the agricultural sector: the exemption of the most influential would exacerbate the mistrust of those forced to accept *tapu* deeds. Midhat's scheme to foster agricultural development without arousing local resentment and even opposition in some sector of society faced a real possibility of falling short of both goals to some degree unless emended as problem areas became clearer.

The potential problems in land tenure measures raise doubts about Midhat's prediction of a rapid, massive increase in Hasa's agricultural production. The settlement of *tapu* titles and the distribution of vacant land would require time, since the Ottomans had little knowledge of the area and its previous land use patterns. Even if land questions were settled quickly, the most valuable crop, dates, would need investment of time and energy to return to the level of production achieved ten to fifteen years before.[20] Trees left untended since Faisal's death in 1865, or since a cholera outbreak almost a decade before that, could have suffered from disease and insect infestation. Many groves probably had lost their regular water supply as neglected irrigation networks crumbled. The destruction of canals and drainage systems would have deprived some fields of water while swamping others, easing desertification in one case, soil salination in the other. If many groves needed replacement, it would take years to realize Hasa's full potential; palms could begin to produce dates in two to five years, but ten to eighteen years were needed to reach full maturity.[21] A more rapid rise could be achieved more easily in seasonal crops such as wheat, rice, and vegetables, but to expect a quick five- or tenfold increase in agricultural production from a declining tree crop grown on degenerating land seems optimistic.

While Midhat may have misjudged the time and effort that would be necessary to restore prosperity to Hasa, in truth he did not mistake the region's long-term potential. Engineers of the Arab-American Oil Company (ARAMCO) after World War II estimated the crop area of Hufuf oasis at 25,000 acres (c. 10,000 hectares), supporting over two million date palms, and saw "immense" potential for an increase in agricultural area.[22] Midhat's predictions echoed that of Palgrave, who noted the profusion of cereals and legumes around Hasa but thought that "under a better administration [they] might be multiplied tenfold."[23] The food and animal products of Hasa were generally of very high quality; Hasawi dates of the *khalas* variety had few, if any, equals in the world, and the Ottomans could have developed a lucrative export trade. Artisans of the area also crafted clothing and metalwork of distinction and repute.[24] Hasa clearly had the potential at least to pay for its own defense and administration, if the Ottoman government were actively to promote development by providing security and services to the inhabitants.

In the provision of agricultural extension services, Midhat did not intend to inflict radical change on existing systems, as he partially did in instituting the *tapu* deed program, but rather sought to ensure that they functioned fairly and efficiently. An office was established to provide oversight of state *mîrî* land and another to manage lands that became the Sultan's private estates. Among other duties, these offices would have oversight of the springs and canals.[25] As elsewhere in the Middle East, irrigation water was considered a "communal good" and thus subject to impartial management, either by local leaders or by public officials. The Ottoman administration in Hasa therefore was instructed to manage the water and eliminate wastage. Another area of government action was the distribution of seeds to some peasants, namely those given the opportunity to work abandoned *mîrî* lands. This was not a state subsidy to poor farmers, however; it resembled a common form of sharecropping, in which the land owner (the state) provided land and seeds, and the peasant kept some of the crop in return for his labor.[26] This scheme did not introduce a new pattern of landlord-labor relations, but by specifying the shares of the crop belonging to the owner and the worker it reduced the crushing rents that landholders often charged their tenants.[27]

In an area akin to rent regulation, taxation, Midhat did emphasize the break with the immediate past precedent. Midhat's ideas are by no means unique in modern history: slash imposts, and the resulting growth in the tax base will more than offset any initial drop in revenue. He repeatedly charged `Abdallah and Sa`ud with causing much of Hasa's economic deterioration by bad tax policy. Levies of up to two thirds of crops, arbitrary fines on rich men of 1,000–2,000 riyals (T£220–440) and confiscation of goods had discouraged the people, while customs duties cut off imports and exports.[28] Hasa's new regulations abolished those taxes and reintroduced those commended canonically: the tithe on agricultural produce (*öşür*) and one fortieth of livestock (*zekât* or *bedel-i zekât*). The provincial treasury in Baghdad was also to receive the revenues from state lands and other properties, as well as a few "trifling" taxes.[29] Although Midhat did not identify these minor taxes (perhaps consisting of bureaucratic fees for permits and transactions, including registration of land in *tapu* registers), he clearly intended to exempt Hasa from the extraordinary taxes that had become institutionalized in other parts of the empire.[30]

Whereas Midhat's tax reforms departed from local (and to some extent Ottoman) practice, they roughly paralleled his actions after he had assumed the governorate of Baghdad in 1869. He had banned several special duties, notably those on produce carried to the capital, water wheels for irrigation, river craft, and fuel brought to Baghdad by boat. *Öşür* had become the main source of revenue.[31] He had not eliminated all government imposts, however. The Hasa regulations make no mention of labor impressment or military conscription, practices that he continued or introduced in Iraq. Two factors account for his even greater restraint in Hasa. For reasons discussed below, Midhat had to minimize friction between the Ottomans and the Hasawis; conscription would have soured relations with the Arabs, as it did in Baghdad,[32] although a native corps would have been extremely useful in the maintenance of security. The *vali* also had no development plans to match such grandiose schemes in Iraq as construction of a canal between the Tigris and Euphrates, for which he levied a special tax and impressed laborers.[33] He expected to be able to finance his building projects in Hasa from the region's revenues. This caution in planning may well reflect the precarious situation in Hasa, where even projects for the public good might excite trouble from some section of the population. By contrast in Iraq, although the canal project failed, Midhat's attempts to reform and develop the province made a lastingly good impression on its inhabitants.[34] As noted above, Midhat hoped that his regularization of taxes would have the same effect in Hasa, removing a cause of the area's decay and arousing the people's lasting gratitude.

About how lasting their goodwill might prove, however, Midhat apparently had greater doubts than he indicated to the Grand Vezir. The populace certainly welcomed the reduction of taxes, but they could well wish for veritable abolition of payments. In his 'memoirs' (compiled by his son) Midhat alluded to several factors that forced him to be cautious. Sa`ud and his supporters remained at large, threatening attack. The condition of the region and the temperament of the people also made taxes very unwelcome. Midhat's bugbear, the British, influenced the issue: the example of de facto British protectorates from Aden to Trucial Oman, where, he claimed, no taxes were levied,[35] always beckoned to the neighboring Ottoman subjects. He thus had to avoid imposts beyond *öşür* and *zekât*.[36] The absence of such cautionings from his missives to the Sublime Porte can be attributed to his desire to minimize any challenges to Ottoman rule in Hasa and Najd when addressing Istanbul—he bore primary responsibility for its planning and institution, after all.[37]

The Tribes and the Sa`udis

Among the trickiest but most important matters that the Ottomans faced in making Hasa a profitable part of the empire was that of keeping the nomadic tribes in check. The 1871 expedition had driven a wedge between them and the subversive British, but the bedouins still posed dangers. When Midhat wrote that bringing vacant land into production was most deserving of official attention, he also stated that the prosperity of the people and the economy depended on their protection from "the evil of bedouin Arabs and tribes." He did not give a clear solution to the problem of how to achieve that security, however, beyond hoping that the nomads could be held in check until they recognized the benefits of settling down to a life of farming.

Tribal unruliness demanded the attention of the governors of most of Ottoman Asia to differing degrees. Yemen, Hijaz, and Iraq frequently had bedouin troubles, and eastern Anatolia and Syria also suffered periodic unrest. The standard Ottoman treatment of the tribal problem involved a varying mix of carrot and stick. The government often sought to co-opt the shaikhs, usually by the payment of subsidies and the conferral of official titles and functions. The government also often tried to build up communities around which nomads might settle as they saw the benefits of agricultural life and the encroachment of such settlements on the lands supporting their original pastoral livelihood.[38] When these tactics did not prevent serious breaches of the peace, and sufficient troops and money were available, the Ottomans launched campaigns of military retribution.

It is interesting to note that the basic Ottoman approach to controlling the tribes did not differ much in principle from that used by the British along the wild northern frontiers of India. The British tried to secure a valuable core settled area against raids launched from mountainous hinterlands, using subsidies and other economic inducements to prevent attacks by tribesmen, and deploying strong military force to punish raiders when the subsidies failed to prevent violence. The British, like the Ottomans, never managed to eliminate attacks by tribal raiders on their borders, however; the British suffered severely from violence on the northwest frontier in the late 1890s, when the Ottomans in Hasa also saw increased bedouin raiding.[39]

During his tenure as *vali* of Baghdad, Midhat showed a willingness to use the "stick" against unruly tribesmen, while he preferred a more subtle form of the "carrot" than simple bribery through subsidies. Previous governors had played tribe against tribe, spreading lucrative tax farms among their supporters. They had tried repeatedly to subvert the power of any group, including allies, that showed strength or independence, most notably the Muntafiq and Khaza'il. Midhat faced a large-scale tribal uprising shortly after his appointment that resulted primarily from his predecessors' machinations and fiscal demands. He met this revolt energetically with all of the military resources at his command. As he proposed doing in Hasa, he then left permanent reminders of Ottoman authority in the countryside by constructing an impressive array of forts to guard communication routes.[40] In a more pacific development he improved relations with the Muntafiq by recognizing Shaikh Nasir as head of their confederation and making him *mutasarrıf* of a new Muntafiq *sancak*.[41] Shaikh Nasir remained an important Ottoman officeholder, and stabilizing influence, for over a decade. In dealing with the Muntafiq and other tribal groups, however, Midhat used the distribution of land titles as his primary means of establishing control. He felt that this process would persuade the seminomads of Iraq to settle and eventually would tie all of the tribes to specific lands.[42] If Midhat had been able to serve a longer term as *vali*, correcting over time the deficiencies of the *tapu* system, perhaps his strategy would have had the desired effect. His successors, however, arbitrarily revoked and awarded titles to prevent various tribes from becoming too secure and strong, thus destroying any hope of effectiveness for Midhat's policies.

When confronted with the restless nomads of Arabia, Midhat adopted measures akin to those he introduced into Iraq. These aimed to turn bedouins into farmers, as he explained most specifically in the case of the Bani Hajir around Dhahran. To any nomad reluctant to accept a *tapu* title, he seemed to believe that demonstrated Ottoman military might would prove persuasive. A battle with the most resistant group, Sa`ud's followers, Midhat felt to be of particularly salubrious effect. In the fight near Hufuf 1,600 Ottoman riflemen defeated 7,000–8,000 "vermin" (*haşeran*) of the `Ajman and Al Murra tribes, inflicting lopsidedly heavy losses. This reportedly caused as much satisfaction in the people of Hasa as it did in Midhat.[43]

Among Sa`ud's Arab alliance the campaign did have some effect, but of no great endurance. On 21 January 1872 the commanding officer of the expeditionary force in Hasa reported to Midhat that an `Ajmani shaikh came to him under safe-conduct. The officer persuaded the shaikh to turn his followers from Sa`ud and submit to the sultan. The shaikh's people were then to settle in towns and villages between Kuwait and Hufuf and take up farming. As the general phrased it, they thereby would attain comfort and peace. The shaikh agreed to this but would not settle his followers immediately, because it was winter (generally a slack time for agriculture) and because his people were in disorder following Sa`ud's difficulties. He promised to return to settle later in 1872 and also persuaded an Al Murra shaikh to visit the Ottoman officer. The general reported that this shaikh, a trusted ally of Sa`ud, likewise agreed to abandon the Wahhabi leader after being received in Hufuf as an honored guest. He also left the Ottoman camp to gather his men. The officer hoped that this marked a general breakup of Sa`ud's supporters, which could lead Sa`ud himself to submit. The general surmised, however, that the `Ajmani shaikh had come originally in order to assess the truth of rumors that the Ottoman force was shrinking. His suspicions of the bedouins' motives gave the general little confidence in the durability of their submission and other promises. In his view such marauders would take the first opportunity to return to their old state of rebellion. As a precaution, therefore, he requested reinforcements, just to be sure that pacification continued.[44]

As he did in Iraq, however, Midhat preferred not to rely excessively upon military solutions to tribal matters. He saw little reason for greatly increased troop levels in Hasa or for alarm about Arab intentions. He agreed that the shaikhs were a devious bunch, whose word inspired no confidence, but he thought that their military setbacks had robbed them of the power to disturb the peace. They would naturally have to follow the path of submission. He recognized that the general needed troops to keep the tribes cowed and to dissuade `Abdallah and Sa`ud from patching up their quarrel and turning on the Ottomans, but he was confident that the commander already had a sufficiency after the dispatch of three fresh battalions as part of a troop rotation. The Hasa command then still had almost 5,000 men of various types.[45]

Midhat expected that future commanders would not need quite so many men as his administrative measures took effect. Temporarily heavy spending on military and civilian officials could not be avoided in the early stages of any new territory's absorption into the empire, and Hasa would certainly prove no exception, due to its unsettled nature and the general Ottoman ignorance about what could be expected there.[46] Even when peace returned to the land, however, a significant garrison would remain in Hasa, according to Midhat's plans. Permanent troop and police strength would reach as much as 3,000 men: four or five battalions around

Hufuf, plus those to be stationed in the many forts and guardhouses along communication routes and the proposed new military base outside Qatif. These would have the task of controlling some greater number of tribesmen.[47] Normally a garrison of such size might have difficulty in controlling so many nomads (although the soldiers benefited from superior weapons and training), because the soldiers would have to spread out to protect many points vulnerable to attack by mobile marauders. Midhat's plan of basing most of the troops as strategic reserves near Hufuf and Qatif might foil even a massed attack on a road or post, however, if they themselves had the mobility to react quickly. It could be expected, moreover, that the mutual antagonisms of the different tribes would usually prevent such concerted action; relatively small local garrisons could probably handle most small-scale attacks even in remote areas.

Future governors would have an additional, powerful tool for controlling the bedouins of Hasa and especially Najd. Only a few places in Arabia grew enough food to export the dates and rice valued by the pastoralists (or could serve as entrepôts for imports), and they were concentrated in Hasa. As Midhat pointed out to the Porte, although places in the interior such as Riyadh, `Anayza, Burayda, Jabal Shammar, and Yamama all had some date groves, because of the difficulty in raising groundwater they could support no more than one quarter or one fifth of their populations. Therefore their inhabitants and all of the bedouins naturally depended on Hufuf, Qatif, and Qatar. If the Ottomans controlled those areas and built forts at key trade points, they would inevitably dominate Najd.[48] It was a valid point. It was the flow of money, food, and goods from Hasa that in the past supported the Sa`udis and their followers in the interior, especially in times of drought. Of the Amir Faisal's revenue reported by Pelly in 1865, Hufuf, Qatif, and `Uqayr produced 58% of the total with only 23% of the population.[49] While not an infallible weapon against individual tribes, economic sanctions could be an especially potent antidote to widespread unrest in the hinterland or troublesome alliance leaders such as the Sa`udis.

This very dependence of the desert interior on the Hasa settlements, expected to grow with implementation of Midhat's development measures and to be used to advantage under the security arrangements, may have lulled the Ottomans into offering too feeble a carrot to match the stick. In neighboring tribal areas of the Hijaz and Iraq they offered meaningful, immediate rewards for cooperation and just as importantly managed to gain the support of leading local shaikhs. They gave money and grain subsidies to the bedouins along pilgrimage and trade routes and did not collect taxes from helpful tribes in the Hijaz. The assistance of the amir of Mecca, who acted as intermediary between the *vali* and the tribes, facilitated Ottoman administration there.[50] In Iraq Midhat did not give lucrative tax farms to shaikhs, as had his predecessors, but instituted instead the land title grant scheme to raise Arab living standards. Those already engaged in farming would benefit immediately by this measure, while pastoral nomads would enter the agricultural system more gradually. Midhat also had the valuable support of a powerful leader in southern Iraq, Shaikh Nasir of the Muntafiq, who in return received the open support of the state. The amir of Riyadh could best have played the part of Ottoman viceroy in Arabia, but the Midhat-`Abdallah alliance broke down. Several later attempts to find a substitute for a Sa`udi ally failed, and in the absence of an example of cooperation set by a powerful, widely respected Arab leader, persuasion of the numerous local shaikhs to settle in Hasa remained difficult. Natural conditions in Hasa also contributed to the difficulty of settlement. The big leap from nomadism to labor-intensive irrigation agriculture could not be broken up by easing into less labor-intensive rainfed farming, as happened in greater Syria, for example.[51] The time needed for the advantages of the *tapu* system to attract bedouins to farming would also be greater in Arabia, where a larger percentage of tribesmen still followed a fully nomadic lifestyle than in the Fertile Crescent.

Subsidies in cash or kind could have been used to achieve peace in the period before prosperity made the benefits of landholding clear to all, but Midhat viewed that policy with caution. He gave presents of fine clothes and swords to important Arab shaikhs, a long-standing, widespread Ottoman practice of moderate efficacy.[52] Midhat was occasionally willing to pay important local notables as a temporary measure to avoid an imminent policy setback or in cases where the state received revenue in return, but generally not as a routine method to ensure quiet. He budgeted a large sum (T£8,000–9,000) for official salaries in the first year of administration, citing the need to resolve the initial chaos in the establishment of Ottoman rule, but this did not include widespread payment of subsidies.[53] He had decrees (*buyruldus*) sent to shaikhs of 24 tribes and towns, including Riyadh, Jabal Shammar (Ha'il), `Anayza, and Burayda, formally investing them with administrative powers until the final appointment of a *kaymakam* for a projected *kaza* of Najd (Riyadh), but he made no mention of salaries or other payments.[54] In fact, a similar *buyruldu* went to Shaikh Qâsim al-Thani, naming him *kaymakam* of Qatar, and Midhat stated specifically that Qâsim received no salary because Qatar produced no revenue.[55]

In one instance Midhat was nevertheless clearly ready to assign regular payments to an Arab leader: `Abdallah al-Sa`ud. The amir, his brother Muhammad, and their followers received food rations from the

Ottomans, and Midhat allocated a generous monthly salary of 1,200 riyals (c. T£265) to ʾAbdallah. His was an exceptional case, in part because he was the Ottoman official to whose aid the expedition came; any strengthening of public identification of the amir of Riyadh with the Ottoman state reduced the chance of protest over the invasion from either the populace or Britain. It also strengthened Istanbul's claim to areas that had formerly paid tribute to the Saʾudis, including Bahrain and Oman. ʾAbdallah's good will was also important, however, because he was the only person (except his brother Saʾud) who could act as an intermediary with local tribes, just as the amir of Mecca did in the Hijaz. By the same measure he could be a dangerous opponent. Midhat felt forced to pay in order to avoid giving ʾAbdallah an excuse to break relations with the Ottomans. Any split would embarrass them and have a bad effect on general Arab opinion. Nevertheless, despite Midhat's efforts, ʾAbdallah broke with him shortly thereafter, thereby forfeiting all rights to the *kaymakamlık* in the *vali*'s view.[56]

This rupture of relations, coming before the end of Midhat's Hasa tour, has caused in the past some uncertainty over the original Ottoman plan: did they wish to restore ʾAbdallah as ruler with a specific link to the sultan's government, or did they never intend to allow a member of the Wahhabi al-Saʾud family to reign over Najd and Hasa? The British gave little credence to assurances from Baghdad and Istanbul that the expedition sought to support ʾAbdallah as an Ottoman functionary, not to assume direct administration, although Midhat's original instructions accorded in effect with those assurances.[57] Midhat's reports after his inspection tour trace his growing uncertainty over how to treat his erstwhile ally.[58] He recognized the value of the amir to restoration of stable administration in an Ottoman district of Najd, but as the campaign progressed ʾAbdallah's actions gradually disillusioned him.

According to Midhat, ʾAbdallah proved to be an unreliable ally as soon as Ottoman troops landed in Hasa. While they took Qatif and Hufuf, the amir remained in Riyadh, fearing Saʾud and his brother's bedouin supporters. Repeated letters from Midhat and Nafiz Pasha failed to free him from his funk; they finally had to consider sending soldiers to fetch him. That such a timid, wavering man should serve as *kaymakam* seemed impossible to Midhat, but he did not feel free to depose him. Ottoman troops had come to confirm ʾAbdallah in his office, and abandoning that promised goal would stir trouble among the Arab tribesmen, who attached great importance to such matters. Events soon drove ʾAbdallah to embrace the Ottomans again, however, thus postponing resolution of a looming problem. Saʾud defeated his brother in battle, and ʾAbdallah could find no safer refuge than the military camp at Hufuf.

He stayed there only as long as he felt threatened by his rival brother. After the battle in which the Ottomans defeated Sa`ud's `Ajman and Al Murra supporters, `Abdallah waited long enough to thank the troops individually for their bravery and determination and to send a letter of gratitude to Baghdad. Purportedly at the urging of the Wahhabi *ulema* of Riyadh, `Abdallah and his brother Muhammad (whom, Midhat noted, Ottoman troops had freed from Sa`ud's prison in Dammam) then fled from Hufuf to Najd just prior to Midhat's arrival in the town. From Riyadh he wrote to Midhat to explain his escape. He averred that Ottoman actions were affecting his standing in the region. Three months previously the government had said that it could not sanction his family's continuance in the *kaymakamlık* because of its depredations. In response to his own plea for help, however, Ottoman troops had come and punished Sa`ud. Then after confirming him as *kaymakam*, these soldiers were to withdraw.[59] Thus the Ottomans had first attacked his aura of legitimacy, an injury that their subsequent action did not wholly heal, and now they threatened to withdraw their material support. `Abdallah had been forced to go to Riyadh in order to rebuild his power base.

The amir concluded his letter by declaring himself forever to be an obedient servant of the Ottoman state, an avowal that Midhat immediately put to the test. He flatly denied that the government had ever intended to remove completely the late Amir Faisal's family, including `Abdallah, from the *kaymakamlık*. The people of Hasa had suffered so miserably under that family's oppressions that they had announced their readiness to emigrate, should the Al Sa`ud or their appointees regain power. These complaints of abuse having been verified, Midhat proposed to confirm `Abdallah as *kaymakam* only of Riyadh and its dependencies in Najd, upon the condition that `Abdallah return to Hufuf within fifteen days.[60] Midhat did not really expect `Abdallah to return to the Ottoman fold under such circumstances, but he felt that he must publicly give the amir a chance to retain his office. A failure to appear would then register among the populace as a renunciation of rights to the *kaymakamlık*. `Abdallah did not appear. This enabled Midhat to declare that no man who shirked his responsibilities, in spite of being treated with all honor and respect, could possibly serve the Ottoman state. He announced `Abdallah's deposition and sent the letters of temporary appointment as administrators to local leaders in Najd.[61]

British accounts of Hasa affairs generally corroborate the main points of Midhat's account of his dealings with `Abdallah, although they differ in details. `Abdallah did show extreme reluctance to cooperate with the Ottomans, except when Sa`ud seemed strongest. This was in spite of the fact that the Hasa campaign was waged specifically in his name, as Nafiz

Pasha proclaimed in Qatif a month or so before the alleged declaration of the Al Sa`ud's unworthiness to serve as *kaymakam*s. The British reports conflict with one another on whether `Abdallah escaped from Hufuf before or after the Ottoman victory over Sa`ud's men and on the timing of his deposition from office. One source says that Midhat revoked the *kaymakamlık* before reaching Hufuf, prompting `Abdallah to flee; another records that he did it after leaving Hufuf.[62] This latter contradiction is easily explained in light of information contained in Midhat's report. During a meeting with Nafiz Pasha before the *vali*'s arrival, `Abdallah was informed that his mistreatment of the Hasa inhabitants made it necessary for him to be content with official power only in Najd. The half-revocation of office was made complete only after `Abdallah failed to return to Hufuf while Midhat was there.[63] Although the British believed that the Ottomans intended `Abdallah's downfall from the beginning of the campaign planning, this result did not match initial intentions. Midhat by stages abandoned the idea of employing the amir as his lieutenant in Arabia as it became clear that `Abdallah sought to use the Ottomans only to maintain his own freedom of action. The pains taken to minimize damage to public opinion show that Midhat was aware of the potential disadvantages in his course of action, but a break with `Abdallah had become the lesser of two evils.

Governmental Structure

Having decided against continuation of the extant regime, even in modified form, Midhat had to devise a new type of government. As he did with land registration, he opted to extend for the time being the system that he helped to spread in other Ottoman territories. He created four districts (*kaza*s) centered on Hufuf, Qatif, Mubarraz, and Qatar.[64] These four *kaza*s and Najd constituted the new subprovince (*sancak*) of Necd, of which Hufuf would be the administrative seat. That town would house the governor (*mutasarrıf*), his adjutant (*mutasarrıf muavini*), a treasurer (*beytülmal müdiri*), a shari`a-court judge (*naib*), a court of appeal (*temyiz-i hukuk*) and an administrative council (*meclis-i idare*). Various secretaries and other staff rounded out the civil administration. At the district level, each *kaymakam* also had a treasurer, an accounts officer (*sanduk emini*), a *naib*, a *meclis-i idare*, an Arabic and, if necessary, a Turkish secretary (*tahrirat kâtibi*), and a claims tribunal (*meclis-i daavi*).[65] Midhat had developed this administrative system while governor of the Danube *Vilayet* in 1864–67 and introduced it into Baghdad during his tenure as *vali* of that province.[66]

Whereas in Baghdad Midhat brought many Iraqis into the administration, he did not immediately recruit Hasawis into the new *sancak*'s administration. His decree that each *kaza* should have a secretary schooled in Arabic suggests that officials' first language would be Ottoman; the provision for Turkish secretaries where needed indicated possible future inclusion of local leaders in government, however. The upper echelons of the regime initially consisted almost entirely of officials from Iraq. The military commander, Nafiz Pasha, became the *mutasarrıf*, one of his leading officers *mutasarrıf muavini*. Nafiz Pasha's treasury accountant was previously the accountant (*muhasebeci*) of Şehr-i Zor (Kirkuk). The *kaymakam*s of Qatif and Mubarraz were respectively a former *kaymakam* of Samarra and a Qatif treasury official (almost certainly originally from the Baghdad government).[67]

Under existing circumstances Midhat had little option in this area. To establish regular administration quickly, experienced, well-paid men were a necessity; those who had already learned their duties in Iraq were the obvious choice. Towns such as Hufuf and Qatif—recently freed of the control of outsiders and with populations of very mixed tribal and religious backgrounds—had no natural single supreme leader to match those of more homogeneous communities such as Kuwait, Doha, and Riyadh.[68] Where a respected shaikh already ruled and was ready to recognize Ottoman supremacy, Midhat was willing to confer official standing, as his appointment of Qâsim al-Thani to the *kaymakamlık* of Qatar shows. In other regions Midhat might well expect that impartial outsiders, aided by advice from local notables on the administrative councils, could best control tensions between groups and individuals. As the confusion and novelty surrounding introduction of the new regime died down, of course, changes could be made and more local men included in government.

Midhat's economic and administrative arrangements promised to give a sound structure to Ottoman government in Hasa, yet all plans remained unrealizable in one area: Najd. The interior plateau of Arabia remained outside the direct control of officials in Hufuf and Baghdad, in spite of its dependence on Hasa. Although the Ottoman army had not moved from Hufuf in months, except to meet a direct challenge from Sa'ud, Midhat entertained hopes for a renewed campaign early in 1872. He proposed an ambitious advance to Riyadh that could last for months. Should the Ottomans capture the town, some threat of isolation naturally would face a garrison and governor in such a poor, isolated, hostile region. Midhat considered the risk too small to negate the advantages of driving out the Wahhabi amirs and securing the peninsula's core; he believed that communications could be maintained over routes from Iraq via Jabal Shammar and from Mecca, should the vulnerable road from

Hufuf be cut.⁶⁹ He never did extend to Najd his Hasa arrangements, however, as he resigned the Baghdad *valilik* before any expedition could be mounted. The question of a permanent replacement for `Abdallah thus became moot.

Other Improvements

In those areas that he did control Midhat supplemented his political and economic regulations with social and infrastructural development akin to projects he advanced as *vali* in Iraq, Bulgaria, and Syria. He worked hard to modernize the means of life, not only through measures such as land tenure reform, but also in transportation and education. While in Iraq, he had built a tramway in the capital, bought steamers for the Tigris and Euphrates, planned a Baghdad-Karbala rail link and extended the telegraph network. He had also founded a hospital, an orphanage and industrial school, and an official newspaper in Baghdad.⁷⁰

Baghdad province's newest *sancak* would get much less ambitious government expenditure. Midhat did not intend to link Hasa to the telegraph terminal at Faw, nor lay railroad track or even improve roads (beyond bettering security). The only large outlay of funds for communications that he proposed was the purchase of a steamer to ferry troops and supplies between Basra and Qatif.⁷¹ Events would later show that he should have paid more attention to the problem of communications. He did turn his eye toward social improvements, but he chose not to use tax revenue to pay for them, at least initially, perhaps out of reluctance to introduce too many innovations too quickly for adjustment by the Hasawis. The clear bounds placed on taxation, which similarly arose from that concern about innovation, naturally also limited the range of projects that the local administration could afford to undertake. Midhat thus allowed most social services to remain tied to the traditional institution of the *vakıf* (pious endowment), in which land or other capital was set aside for a specified charitable purpose.

Unless strictly regulated, the *vakıf* system tempted corruption, since it could be misused to safeguard family wealth against government interference and other threats, and in Hasa it had fallen into confusion. No *vakıf* registry existed, and no deeds or other documents formally recognized the endowments' existence and purpose; supervision was impossible. A large number of date groves in theory supported the mosques and schools in the *kaza*s of Hufuf, Qatif, and Mubarraz, but under previous administration much of their income stuck to the hands of their managers and others. The mosques and schools had thus fallen into decay. Because these groves had popular recognition as charitable properties, the government could not simply assume control of them, but Midhat proposed a strict regulation of their administration and purpose. In making this change in local practice, Midhat brought to Hasa the push for a new system of state oversight of *vakıf* that was happening throughout the empire.[72] He wanted to introduce proper registration and bookkeeping of endowments in the newly taken territory. The income of all trusts was to be divided among three categories of recipients. First of all, regular monthly payments would support mosques and their staffs. Local councils received the second share to spend on primary (*sebyan mektebleri*) and religious (*medaris*) schools in each town quarter. The third allotment was to go as alms to widows, orphans, invalids, and other poor, and where possible to create an industrial school for orphans and other children in each town.[73] Subsequently Midhat was to revise his proposal, suggesting that the state should open a secondary school (*medrese-yi rüşdiye*) as well as an industrial school. The state would support these from its local revenues to supplement *vakıf* income and would bring instructors from Iraq.[74]

Midhat's reports on circumstances and measures to be taken in Hasa show that he devoted great time, thought, and energy to planning the future of the new *sancak*. As soon as the Ottomans were convinced that the debatable premise of British determination to absorb much of Asia was true, then Midhat's program became the most logical to follow. He wanted to replicate steps taken in Iraq, another heavily tribal land whose wealth was geographically concentrated. Reforms there—in taxation, land tenure and security arrangements—had settled the country and increased revenues, and Midhat felt confident that they could do the same in Arabia. If Ottoman interests were purely economic, of course, the investment of resources could probably have brought greater returns elsewhere, but Hasa was occupied in order to be a border march, not a breadbasket. The expected excess of revenues over the costs of defense and administration was merely an added bonus to the security benefits of Hasa's occupation.

The scale of Midhat's ambitious schemes for the twin development of the region's security and economy made them vulnerable to criticism. They demanded significant expenditures, especially in military affairs, and if the land's riches did not turn from potential into reality quickly, the government might be tempted to reduce its presence rather than to spill red ink indefinitely. If that happened, the Ottomans could have trouble keeping the bedouins in check. Midhat was probably too blithe in his assessment of the tribal threat and in his assumption that administration would quickly become smooth, efficient, and in harmony with the populace, in spite of the possible lingering effects of the region's recent, troubled history and the general Ottoman unfamiliarity with local conditions. If for no other reason than its harsh climate and distance from seats of power, moreover, officials appointed to Hasa would tend to view it as a punishment post, unworthy of assiduous attention to good government. Baghdad would need to monitor Hasawi affairs as closely as limited means of communication would allow.

These were potential problems, however, not irremediable flaws; to dismiss Midhat's experiment in integration of a new territory into the Ottoman empire as doomed to failure would be wrong. If implemented as planned, the new economic, administrative, and social regimes would have been marked improvements on the decaying institutions of the Wahhabi era. The confusion and adjustment problems attendant on any radical system change would have diminished under the attention of a good governor. Although he was not universally liked, Midhat Pasha was widely acknowledged to have the necessary qualities: energy, intelligence, incorruptibility, and a willingness to try innovative solutions to problems. Much depended on the regional administration's ability to adapt to changing needs. Unfortunately for the Ottomans, Midhat did not stay in Baghdad long enough to refine his ideas on Hasa's administration. His successors did not build on his initiatives, and the upheavals that were soon to strike the empire distracted Istanbul's attention for the remainder of the decade. The bad effects of official neglect were to appear within several years of Midhat's departure from Baghdad in 1872.

Chapter 4

The Chance for Adjustment and Stability, 1872–1893

Hasa After Midhat

Midhat left to his successor in Baghdad a newly subdued unit of the province that had not yet had the chance to become a fully incorporated, smoothly administered part of the empire. He had begun work on this problem but departed before his plans could acquire much permanency in the new territory. Even in Iraq, where he governed much longer, the importance of strong, progressive provincial leadership became clear as his reforms in Iraq withered under his more ordinary successors.

In Arabia, the relative lack of immediate, serious challenges to their authority over the next two decades gave the Ottomans the opportunity to integrate the new *sancak* into the sultan's state and to devise an effective government, yet the administrators of Hasa received minimal guidance in instituting a new style of regime. Too often Istanbul delegated the tasks of defense and administration to Arab governors, hoping that their knowledge of the locale and Arab ways would allow them to keep the peace and keep out the British without having to use significant resources. Local officials, in turn, did not give Istanbul the information needed to address questions before they turned into problems. Sporadic outbreaks of major and minor unrest drew fairly rapid responses—often the reinforcement of undermanned garrisons—that quelled the trouble, but sometimes only until crises elsewhere again took attention and resources from Arabia. When high authorities were able to think of the region, instead of pursuing Midhat's dream of making the area a productive unit of the empire, too often they concentrated more on countering suspected schemes to boost British and other foreign influences than on refining the half-formed administration at the *sancak*'s core. Grand plans were followed that never achieved their aims and absorbed scarce money needed to fund economic development and improve communications. As a result of the empire's extreme financial troubles in the period, anything that was to be attempted in Hasa was to be done cheaply. Money was not to be invested there, it was to be extracted. In such a harried atmosphere, political efficiency received as little attention as the economy. Consequently, little trace of Midhat's plans survived, and when challenges to the Ottomans' position rose thickly in the 1890s, they found that it rested on a fatally flawed foundation.

An important influence on the stability of the Ottoman position was the degree to which the state could persuade the local population that their interests coincided. This was both a precondition and an expected by-product of Midhat's plans. As happened frequently elsewhere in the empire, especially outside the core provinces, the Ottomans in eastern Arabia dealt primarily with leading individuals or groups rather than with all classes of the local society. In Qatar and Kuwait, the Ottomans had contact almost exclusively with members of the Al Thani and Al Sabah families. In the towns of Hasa, where the Sa`udis left no similarly dominant families, the Ottomans built close ties to traders and other notables, including land owners and local shaikhs. The state provided security for commerce and agriculture, and in principle taxation was limited. In return for these benefits, the local notables worked with the government to collect taxes and funds for special needs, in some cases having taken official positions. Predictably, the support of notables eventually weakened when the Ottomans failed to ensure security yet demanded too much revenue from the people.

For many people in Hasa, contact with the state was probably limited to payment of taxes and, if involved in a legal matter, appearance in court; in both cases, they might well be dealing with another Hasawi rather than an outsider. On some levels, however, the general population, both Sunni and Shi`a, could be seen as at least passive supporters of the Ottoman regime as long as the administration performed its duties properly, since the restraint of bedouin raiders and the removal of Wahhabi control over social and religious affairs was welcome to most people.

Of all of Midhat's hopes of bringing change to different areas, it was probably in social conditions that alterations were quickest, longest-lasting, and most widely accepted. The more relaxed, cosmopolitan nature of society near the coast in comparison to the heavily Wahhabi interior was responsible for much of this ease of change. Education saw an expansion of opportunities. The Ottoman central and provincial authorities wished to encourage the spread of education among the Hasawis, although the limited tax revenues from the area made the cooperation of the local population very important. The state had to ask the people to undertake the task of building schools in 1887, for example, because it could not afford to do the job without levying taxes that would exceed the limited tax regime proclaimed by Midhat in 1871.[1] With public or private funding, educational facilities during the Ottoman period included numerous elementary schools, especially in Hufuf, as well as an elementary and a secondary school run directly by the state, in addition to the religious schools.[2] A survey of certain economic and social statistics for Qatar lists similar facilities in that *kaza*, counting thirty-four mosques and fifteen elementary schools (*mekatib-i ibtidaiye*) serving a total population of 20,000 in 1891.[3] A roughly contemporary report for Doha alone listed ten elementary schools for basic instruction in reading, writing, and the Quran, and a six-grade government *rüşdiye* school with a more advanced program.[4] Educational opportunities may still have been limited by the 1890s, but they had improved noticeably since the Ottoman conquest.[5]

Some of the restrictions on popular practices imposed by the Wahhabis disappeared with the change of regime. The Ottomans gave permission for the establishment of cemeteries, which the Wahhabis had banned out of their disapproval of undue veneration of the dead. Other traditional sites of customary importance were repaired, as was the old Istanbul-style mosque of Hufuf that was a relic of the first Ottoman era in Hasa. Tobacco and snuff reappeared.[6] If a report received by the British is to be believed, the desire for change (or just entertainment) led Nafiz Pasha's army to bring to Qatif 70 Baghdad prostitutes and 80 wine sellers.[7]

Designs for sustained economic improvement made less impression, and Midhat's financial legacy in the whole of Baghdad *Vilayet* was the subject of considerable contemporary and later debate. The province's economic output did grow during his tenure as *vali*. This resulted not only from land tenure reform but also from regularization of taxation, improvements in communications, peacemaking, anticorruption measures and increases in military efficiency. Midhat's Iraq also benefited ironically from the growth of British shipping, which fed a booming demand for dates in India, Europe, and America.[8] Reform plans also naturally tend to raise expenditures, however, and Midhat's increased outlays gave his enemies a pretense for attack. Opponents in Baghdad and Istanbul pressured him to resign with charges of bankrupting the province.

Against these accusations Midhat mounted a vigorous and plausible defense, supported with income and expenditure registers. The damage was done, however. Midhat asserted that his achievements in Iraq were threatened by the enmity and greed of ignorant officials in Istanbul who had not set foot outside the Sublime Porte, and of disgruntled Baghdad subordinates who had been punished for misconduct. Rather than continuing to serve while subject to such harassment, he resigned.[9]

Midhat had had support while the reformist Grand Vezir Ali Pasha still lived; after Ali's death in 1871 his successor, Mahmud Nedim Pasha, out of a long-standing dislike for Midhat would have been ready to believe any bad report about his enemy, including those of informants who had never been to Baghdad. The assertion—readily accepted by the British[10]—that the Hasa expedition had caused Midhat to strip Iraq of its resources indeed seems exaggerated. Midhat had not spent even half of the funds initially allocated by Istanbul for the campaign by the end of 1871.[11] Midhat's projected building program in Hasa might have worried Istanbul, but given the ignorance of the region prevailing in government circles, Mahmud Nedim had little evidence with which to challenge Midhat's predictions of future costs and profitability. In fact, a British report on Baghdad *Vilayet* as a whole confirms the general truth of Midhat's assertions and economic assessments. This source listed provincial revenues (excluding customs) of T£648,435 and expenditures of T£285,880 in 1874. Stagnation set in thereafter, however, and thirty years later income had fallen sharply while outlays increased.[12]

Economic development in Hasa followed a path generally similar to that in Iraq, except that Midhat's reorganization had even less chance to take root before his resignation than it did to the north. Economic conditions throughout the empire also soon entered a bad period (as they did in much of Europe as well), further hurting development in Arabia. In Hasa, as elsewhere during the last quarter of the nineteenth century, the *mutasarrıf*s and *kaymakam*s were pressed to spare no effort (but all major expense) to extract revenue for the central government. The spendthrift instincts of Sultan Abdülaziz, unchecked since the death of Ali Pasha in 1871, pushed the weak Treasury beyond its limits. Debt payments fell into arrears after October 1875, and six years later the empire entered a form of bankruptcy with creation of the "Council of the Public Debt."[13] The government thus had little money to invest in the provinces yet needed large returns of revenue.

Such pressure for revenue production led to the corruption or abandonment of much of Midhat's plans. By 1874 the general shift to 'local' administrative and security personnel, who were neither well paid nor well trained, disrupted some governmental functions. For this reason or on grounds of cost, registration of land titles did not progress far before lapsing altogether for a number of years. Some state land was distributed, only later to fall outside all government supervision. Other lands were never freed but were added instead to the sultan's privy purse. When troops were withdrawn from Hasa's garrisons to save money or to serve elsewhere, communication and trade routes became vulnerable to marauders. With neither capable security forces nor easy access to markets, the zone of cultivation and settlement did not expand as much as had been hoped.

Shaping an efficient, tolerable tax regime proved no easier. Tax registers appear not to have been updated regularly for a time. Tax farming (*iltizam*) seems to have been a recurring practice after Midhat left Baghdad. Selling the right to collect agricultural, excise and customs duties is tempting to a state poor in income and trained personnel because it produces immediate revenue with little bureaucratic bother. It also almost invariably leads to corruption, overtaxation of the populace and reduced long-term income for the state, as seems likely to have happened finally in Hasa.[14] The potential for abuse existed even when rights to taxes were not, strictly speaking, sold, since collection responsibility was often delegated to an intermediary, such as a village headman (*muhtar* or *müdir*).[15] Officials after Midhat also ignored his abolition of levies beyond the *öşür* and *zekât*, introducing notably internal tolls or excise taxes. These could be quite heavy, and it sometimes happened that goods from Iraq could be taxed twice, once in Basra and once in Hasa. Midhat had abolished such duties in Iraq and was infuriated by their imposition in Hasa; he correctly assigned much of the blame for the unrest there two years after his resignation to these levies, which contravened his earlier public promises of no noncanonical taxes.[16] By 1889–1890, over one third of Hasa's government income came from such "assorted taxes and revenues."[17]

Even in the levying of the canonical taxes, there was room for manipulation, if not outright extortion. The tithe on dates was the main revenue source in Hasa. Assessment and collection of the tax were not straightforward, however. The *sancak*'s administrative council set the prices for dates. Consultation (i.e., negotiation) with local notables could affect the prices set. The *mutasarrıf* then sent out men to assess tithes on date crops. Officials inevitably faced the temptation to fix high prices to increase the value of the tithe. The assessors, who might or might not be trained officials, could in turn be tempted to overestimate yields.[18] Hasawis found the taxation system tolerable under a good *mutasarrıf*; a bad one had great opportunities to make life hard for the locals.

The Hasa garrison could add pressure on the populace's finances, largely because of the uneven nature of revenue flow. Because dates were the main source of state income, very little money entered the Treasury except in the fall. Troops thus were paid late, if at all.[19] Some resorted to armed extortion in order to keep themselves in funds. Some garrison commanders were among the corrupt, and there was little that civil authorities could do to check them. They could send reports to Istanbul, but poor communications meant that any disciplinary action would be delayed. The Ottomans never really solved the challenge of the narrow timeframe of revenue intake, which, combined with the later decline of *öşür* receipts, made corruption so tempting. The state wanted to tax the pearl trade, which was lucrative and peaked in the summer, thus easing both problems, but the Ottomans discovered that this was hard to do.

Careless administration of assets that were under state control compounded Hasa's financial problems. When government registers were not updated to record improvement or deterioration of properties, popular distress could rise. Agricultural decay could occur because tenant farmers did not have the interest in improvements that Midhat had wanted to establish through the *tapu* system. According to the British Residency Agent in Bahrain in 1882, trouble arose around Qatif because of abusive practices. The *kaymakam* ordered village headmen to care for government groves; the headmen ordered peasants to perform the task without pay. Sloppy care and production decline resulted. The Treasury assessed taxes energetically, however, and misery on state lands grew as assessments became unpayable.[20] Two statements of Hasa's finances illustrate the discrepancy between registers and reality: the first (unsigned, undated, but probably written by the *mutasarrıf* in 1886–87) claimed the existence of three million date groves around Hufuf and Qatif, which produced almost T£40,000. Yet several years later the Basra Gazette stated that the *öşür* produced less than T£17,000 for all of Hasa, or about T£0.005 per grove of some of the world's finest date trees—a paltry sum even in a period of depressed date prices.[21]

Scant official accounts of fiscal returns from Hasa reveal a general, gradual decline in wealth after 1871, as happened also in Iraq, although revenues could fluctuate markedly. Midhat reported a first year's revenue of T£35,000 and expected at least T£50,000 in the next, largely from *öşür* and *zekât*. Baghdad *Vilayet*'s official Gazette of 1883/4 assessed Hasa's revenue at T£30,277 in 1879/80 and T£28,526 in 1880/81 and 1881/82.[22] The 1886–87 report that valued Hasa's annual revenue at T£40,000 repeated the claim of levying only the canonic *öşür* and *zekât* on produce and animals. Other revenue sources must have been developed energetically, however; for example, customs clearly generated an important share of income.[23] Two years later the Basra provincial Gazette stated that Hasa produced T£26,353, of which only T£16,948 came from *öşür* and none from *zekât*.

Just as the sums shifted from year to year, the reasons for the variations differed. In 1889–1890, for example, a slump in the date market and the outbreak of bedouin disturbances must have caused much of the

CHANCE FOR ADJUSTMENT AND STABILITY

marked drop in revenue.[24] In the period 1878–1882, by contrast, extremely sloppy bookkeeping threw the Hasa accounts into chaos. Records of individuals' payments and of tax arrears were not kept, and a change of accounting practices led to the keeping of two or three sets of books which did not agree with each other.[25] Another problem that may have caused revenue to slump in the late 1880s was the issue of money itself. Istanbul tried very hard to keep coinage Ottoman. It banned acceptance of foreign money as legal tender in most of the empire, although it did grant exemptions to border regions, such as Libya, Yemen, the Hijaz, and Baghdad. Basra was belatedly exempted in 1887, but as late as 1899 several Iranian traders were arrested in Hasa for importing foreign coins.[26] Ottoman coinage was not plentiful in Basra province, however, and its value was high in relation to the riyal, the native coinage, and to rupees and krans, even after they became supposedly acceptable.[27] The value of tax revenue in Ottoman lira must have declined as a result. Whatever the individual causes, Hasa seems never to have produced as much for the Ottomans as Pelly estimated it produced for Amir Faisal in 1865. As income declined, so did expenditure on administration. Midhat proposed to spend T£20,000 in the first year; the government budget for Necd *Sancak* in 1889/90 was T£15,792. Necd produced the least, received the least and was the least profitable of Basra *Vilayet*'s four *sancak*s in that year.[28]

The government inattention that facilitated this decline arose from a complacent confidence that the demonstrated Ottoman ability to conquer Hasa would solve all problems of administration. Several months after taking office in Baghdad, Midhat's replacement as *vali* turned his attention to other projects closer to his capital, including preparation of a Tripoli (Syria)-Baghdad railway line, further development of Ottoman Tigris-Euphrates shipping, and efforts to settle Iraqi tribesmen on *tapu* land. The reports of the new commanding officer in Hasa (Nafiz Pasha was replaced shortly after Midhat resigned) continued the assurances of his predecessor and Midhat that peace was firmly established, thus encouraging his superiors to attend to other problems.[29]

According to the commander, the significant body of troops in the garrison was in good condition. Some soldiers suffered from malaria, but measures were being taken to control the spread and intensity of disease. Local food supplies were adequate, and it was hoped that future harvests would increase with the introduction of new strains of wheat. The Ottoman forces also had enough money to buy what they needed from the Hasawis—as Midhat had noted earlier, local products and materials were quite inexpensive. Complete, lasting peace ruled the land in mid-1872, and the Ottoman position seemed secure.[30] This claim reflected

CHANCE FOR ADJUSTMENT AND STABILITY

continued confidence that even the very independent Al Murra and `Ajman tribes could soon be induced or forced to settle on the land. The Ottomans began to realize within a few months that the task would prove harder than expected, however, when their arrest of a leading `Ajmani shaikh caused unrest in that tribe.[31]

The rise in Ottoman-`Ajmani tension marked a partial reversal of fortune for the would-be Wahhabi amir, Sa`ud. Midhat's desired campaign to capture Riyadh had been shelved as Ottoman concern about Arabia diminished. The government had apparently accepted his statement that some control of the Najd plateau could come from possession of the Hasa coast, a statement that the current situation made credible. Amir `Abdallah seemed powerless, ruling a Riyadh racked by famine. Sa`ud had a recognized potential for causing unrest, and the Ottomans tried to induce him to come to Baghdad, where his potential could be prevented from developing into something more real. He resisted the idea, sending instead his brother, `Abd al-Rahman, who was detained as a surety for his brother's good behavior.[32] Sa`ud in any case had been reduced to metaphorical and literal wandering in the wastes before the resurgence of `Ajmani support allowed him to drive his brother out of the Najdi capital in 1873. The Ottomans still felt able to ignore the change in circumstances. They paid no more heed to the defeated amir's plea for help than they did to Sa`ud's attempts to win appointment as *mutasarrıf* of Najd and Hasa. `Abdallah had proven himself too irresolute an ally, and, although Britain refused Sa`ud's request to intercede on his behalf in his quest for acceptance, the Ottomans were too sure that Sa`ud was London's tool to allow him any power or recognition. The Ottomans were content to continue to ensure his passivity by keeping `Abd al-Rahman hostage in Baghdad.[33]

Adoption of unpopular measures such as the arrest of potential malcontents and the extraction of new taxes became the most striking aspect of Ottoman administration in its early years, marking an emphatic darkening of Midhat's exciting, optimistic vision. Another kinsman of Sa`ud, Fahd b. Sunaytan, was sent a prisoner to Baghdad in 1873, as were some who objected to a new *mutasarrıf* in 1874.[34] British reports noted popular discontent with the oppressive rule of Ottoman officials and soldiers. Despite local informants' tendency to exaggerate Ottoman or British misdeeds to stir their audience's support, these stories gain some confirmation from ensuing events.

In 1874 open revolt broke out, encouraged by several misguided Ottoman measures designed to "localize" the administration. The first move was a virtual abandonment of another pillar of Midhat's plans. The government withdrew from the garrison the regular troops (*nizamiye*) who had maintained relative stability in Hasa for three years, replacing them with a detachment of gendarmes and mounted Arab scouts.[35] The bad climate and bad water had taken their toll on the *nizamiye* troops, and the material cost of keeping them in Hasa was seen as a useless drain on the Treasury.[36] Their replacements were more poorly armed and disciplined than the regulars. Such a significant downgrading of the garrison did much to limit the governor's authority to Hufuf, Qatif, and their environs and weakened his ability to overawe the stronger nomadic tribes.

To balance the effects of this change, the government simultaneously made another policy shift: instead of sending a military officer from outside the region to act as *mutasarrıf*, they appointed a local tribal shaikh with the expectation that his reputation, followers, and knowledge of the area could compensate for the lost troop strength. The idea of reappointing `Abdallah found some support in Istanbul, notably at the Ministry of War. Given the status of the Al Sa`ud among Arabia's tribes, the choice of one of their number was logical. Others in Istanbul, however, were not yet ready to overlook `Abdallah's flight from the Ottoman camp in 1871. The government nevertheless did not rule out appointment of `Abdallah at a later date, should no other appointee prove capable.[37]

Instead of `Abdallah, the Ottomans chose Bazi` b. `Ara`ir, son and grandson of shaikhs of the Bani Khalid, although he had been living in southern Iraq prior to his appointment.[38] The Bani Khalid were the once-dominant tribe in Hasa, but the Al Sa`ud had lastingly damaged their power and prestige when they took control of eastern Arabia. By the 1870s the Bani Khalid could not be sure of dominating such strong tribes as the Bani Hajir, Al Murra, and Mutayr, nor did they have the necessary stature always to control the mixed populace of the towns.[39] The protests, and subsequent arrests, of local leaders at Bazi`'s accession show a notable Hasawi initial reluctance to accept his authority. Resistance predictably grew among those who did not acknowledge the worth of the holder of power.

The violence and arrogance shown by Bazi` and his men broadened and deepened popular dissatisfaction. Bazi` enrolled in the gendarmerie members of the Bani Khalid and other "wild" tribes, who abused their new power. The arrests and confiscation of property of notables in Hufuf caused tension between the local populace and the gendarmerie, which led some people to abandon their lands. Revenue dropped. It fell further when Bazi` and other members of the Bani Khalid seized state-owned date groves as their own property. The local administration collected by force extraordinary taxes and excessive customs and excise (*rüsum-i ihtisabiye*) levies, which choked off trade and caused more people to flee their lands. When officials in Hufuf precipitated a confrontation with a shaikh of the `Ajman, moreover, dissatisfaction was no longer confined to the settled people of Hasa.[40]

A third Ottoman action set a flame to this tinder: the release of Fahd and `Abd al-Rahman al-Sa`ud from detention in Baghdad.[41] `Abd al-Rahman moved to Bahrain, whence he sent agents to stir revolt among the mainland tribes. Late in 1874 he landed at `Uqayr to lead a band of `Ajman, Al Murra and other tribesmen against the *mutasarrıf*; the latter found himself besieged in the Hufuf citadel after the rebels overran the other forts. The Bani Khalid chief survived, however, because Shaikh Nasir al-Sa`dun, head of the Muntafiq, *mutasarrıf* of Basra, and Bazi`'s brother-in-law, came speedily to his relief with a large force.

Britain thought that `Abd al-Rahman wanted to win appointment as *mutasarrıf* himself by creating unrest that only he could quieten.[42] This is possible, yet such a direct challenge to Ottoman authority suggests an attempt to expel the government, not to join it in any fashion. A subsequent Ottoman explanation, that he was merely engaged in the troublemaking for which the Sa`udis were so well known, was even more erroneous.[43] Non-Wahhabi townspeople were also discontent with the current administration. To ascribe blame for the 1874 unrest simply to ingrained Sa`udi boorishness betrays a remarkable ignorance about changes of opinion among a once grateful populace.

This episode, and Bazi`'s governorship in general, was a severe check to the Ottoman position in Hasa. Some townspeople joined the uprising, as punishment for which Nasir allowed his men, notably Muntafiq tribesmen, to sack for three days the quarters of Hufuf outside the citadel. They took not only money and goods but women as well.[44] This dealt a blow to the goodwill and the revenue production for which Midhat had had such high hopes. The government, moreover, could ill afford to ease some of the resentment by lightening the tax burden. It had to keep levying excise taxes to help meet the costs of local reform.[45] For example, Istanbul faced demands for compensation from Basra and Baghdad traders who had been in Hufuf during the uprising and had lost to the rebels money and goods worth T£1,500.[46] It also had to find the funds for replacing some of the gendarmerie with a battalion of regular infantry and one hundred cavalry.

This alteration of the garrison was but one part of a reorganization prompted by the Ottoman realization that the Necd *Sancak* needed closer supervision. In 1875 it became part of the new *vilayet* of Basra, whose governor, Nasir Pasha al-Sa`dun, had greater familiarity with Arabia than had any Baghdad *vali*.[47] The Ottomans replaced the ailing and unpopular *Mutasarrıf* Bazi` with one of Nasir Pasha's sons, Mazyad.

Bazi' and the Bani Khalid could not keep Hasa quiet; the government hoped that Mazyad could do so with the more powerful Muntafiq of southern Iraq.[48] Mazyad resigned the post a year later, however, pleading an inability to become accustomed to either the climate or the water of Hasa.[49] This was to be the last serious attempt to install a local shaikh into that office; the only other logical such candidates for the position, members of the Al Sa'ud, inspired even less confidence in the sultan's government after 1875 than they had before.[50]

Events of the following two decades did little to restore a Sa'udi reputation for stability. Sa'ud won Riyadh and the amirate, only to die of smallpox in January 1875. The inhabitants of the town chose as his successor his brother 'Abd al-Rahman, who presumably viewed the amirate as a helpful step toward either becoming *mutasarrıf* or driving the Ottomans from Hasa. August saw his defeat and deposition by his brother 'Abdallah, however. That maladroit but tenacious individual retained the title of amir for twelve years, but continuous feuds with his brothers and nephews greatly limited his power. Except in 1878, when the late Sa'ud's sons stirred unrest in Hasa,[51] the Ottoman authorities could perceive little overt Wahhabi threat in this period.

Although Sa'udi and other Arabian shaikhs were generally too untrustworthy or too weak to serve as *mutasarrıfs*, the Ottomans did frequently appoint to that post Arabs or officials with long service in Arab provinces. As practical as this policy might seem, it was not always applied in other sensitive Arab areas, such as Jerusalem, where knowledge of a Western European language was deemed more important than knowledge of Arabic.[52] Since *mutasarrıfs* did not have to contend with European consuls in eastern Arabia, the Ottomans benefited from being free to seek governors with practical knowledge and skills useful for service there. Among these were Said Bey, an Arabic-speaking army officer who served in Basra prior to his appointment; Sayyid Akif Pasha; Ibrahim Pasha, formerly governor of Hudayda (Yemen); Musa Kazım Efendi, former *Mutasarrıf* of 'Asir (Yemen); Sayyid Talib Pasha of Basra; and Said Pasha, a native of Baghdad, who served thirteen years in Hasa. The simple fact of knowledge of Arabic or service in Arab territories did not ensure effectiveness, of course, no doubt in part because the Hasawi dialect was very difficult for outsiders to understand.[53] Yet their terms in office seem to have been longer and somewhat calmer than those of *mutasarrıfs* who were probably non-Arab.[54] Istanbul also showed a distinct inclination to appoint military officers as *mutasarrıfs*.[55] Both of these patterns indicate the great importance and delicacy that Istanbul attributed to the position, born of the political-strategic reasons that caused the Ottomans to move into Hasa and Qatar in 1871. The state wanted representatives who knew local customs, were not cut off from the populace, and had the experience to counter domestic and foreign security threats.

As it did in its Gulf economic policy, in geopolitics the Ottoman government adopted a strategy that aimed to maintain, and even expand, the rewards of rule without major expenditure of resources, in this case their formal claim to sovereignty over the Arabian peninsula. The military force stationed in Hasa was only intermittently sufficient to ensure a measure of security for caravans and large towns. Small, ragtag garrisons[56] could not inspire the popular confidence in enduring peace that Midhat had hoped to establish, however, and the troops were never able to eliminate low-level banditry. Major disturbances also erupted in the countryside on several occasions.[57] In short, the military force in Hasa was insufficient to safeguard the territory's well-being by itself: Ottoman tribal policies had to provide the needed help.

The government followed two sometimes complementary strategies to impose limits on bedouin actions, each of which eventually showed shortcomings after initial success. Both resembled policies tried elsewhere, but conditions peculiar to Arabia subverted them. The first, and most continuous, policy strand was financial. Midhat had not wanted to bribe the tribes, but the government adopted the practice after the unrest of 1874. From 1875 to 1903 the state—or, when the state did not have the funds, the local settled people—paid subsidies to the bedouins, the amount depending on the tribe's size and the strategic importance of its *dira*.[58] Using revenue from livestock taxes (*deve rüsumu*) collected from the tribes and excise taxes, the Ottomans paid T£330/year to six shaikhs of the `Ajman and three of the Al Murra; shaikhs of the Bani Hajir, Bani Khalid, and Manasir also received stipends.[59] In the cases of Qatar and Kuwait, the government also paid stipends to the *kaymakam*-shaikhs.[60] In return for the money or food provided, the bedouins were to refrain from attacking roads, towns, and other places under direct Ottoman control, while the *kaymakam*s were to protect Ottoman sovereignty rights in their territories. The subsidies also could have a broader pacifying effect, because they could dampen other conflicts such as intertribal raiding that could damage the entire territory's security and thus provoke official reaction. A further safeguard was provided by a second monetary tie, the payment of tribute by tribes to the state, generally in the form of *zekât* or *deve rüsumu*.[61] A shaikh who tendered tribute could expect in return access to town markets, Ottoman aid against foreign powers, and even official support in intertribal disputes.[62] These mutual financial bonds, maintained in conjunction with army or gendarmerie forces, did much to reduce the use of force among Hasa's inhabitants.

CHANCE FOR ADJUSTMENT AND STABILITY

Over time, however, defects in the system became clear. Mutual payoffs could be at best a minimizing, status quo policy. It only reduced violence to a tolerable level, it did not eliminate it. Subsidies did not reduce much the need for capable garrisons. Perennial insecurity of roads and property hampered economic growth and burdened the Treasury.[63] The subsidies did nothing to further progress toward the cherished dream of settling the nomadic tribesmen and turning them from economic threats into producers. In other areas of the empire where the Ottomans had some success in this kind of effort (Palestine, Syria, Transjordan, even Libya), nomads settled because the state could bring significant force to bear on an area quickly, or it promoted new communities to which nomads (and others) would gradually be drawn and encouraged to settle, or because possibilities for escape into a great hinterland were limited for geographic, economic, or other reasons.[64] With an often minimal garrison and a vast, uncontrolled hinterland to the west and south, the Ottomans in Hasa faced serious obstacles to overcoming bedouin resistance to settlement.

Another serious problem inherent in this system was that it was a balancing act, which outside forces could disrupt with some ease. Because Ottoman authority did not encompass all of the Arabian peninsula, powerful tribes intent on attacking the government and people in Ottoman territory could find refuges from retribution. This in itself damaged Ottoman power and prestige, and resentment could build in tribute-paying tribes that suffered from such attacks yet saw no Ottoman response to their plight. The sons of Sa`ud thus could arouse a rebellion around Qatif in 1878, and when it failed they and their supporters could escape Ottoman pursuit in Bahrain and the Najd interior. Their supporters, the `Ajman, similarly could stay beyond Ottoman reach in Najd until they were satisfied that they would not be severely punished for their attack on Hufuf in 1880. Through most of the next decade the frustration of the Qatari *Kaymakam* Qâsim al-Thani grew as he battled the shaikh of Abu Dhabi for control of `Udayd. Despite reportedly paying the Ottomans at least T£400 annually,[65] he received no meaningful aid from them. Such payments brought support against the encroachments of foreign powers but not those of foreign-protected tribes. Bitterly disappointed by this and other disputes with Ottoman officials, Qâsim encouraged the unrest that broke out in Qatar in 1887 and in Hasa in 1890.[66] Since the Ottomans never completed their conquest of Arabia, the payoff policy could not always work effectively.

Magnifying the effects of the system's flaws was a technological revolution. The government for too long thought that it could counter any internal unrest by the quick dispatch of some soldiers to the troubled area, as in 1874 and 1878, but this became much more difficult in the 1890s. The tribesmen were closing a previously wide weaponry gap in this period. As Europe's armies improved their equipment, superseded (but still high quality) rifles flowed into the world arms market, some passing through Djibouti to western Arabia and through Masqat to the Gulf; Muhammad al-Rashid's possession of field artillery shows that heavier weapons were also available.[67] The arms trade overwhelmed all efforts at containment. Although Britain tried increasingly to limit arms smuggling,[68] the involvement of traders from India and Gulf ports under British influence convinced the Ottomans that the steady stream of weapons entering Arabia was one of their rival's means of weakening their rule in Hasa. Muhammara, Kuwait, Qatar, and especially Bahrain were suspected of involvement in the trade.[69] Bedouins grew bolder as they bought weapons almost as good as those of the soldiers in Arabia or Iraq.[70] The Ottomans tried to regain superiority by deploying more, better-equipped soldiers and developing new tactics—most importantly increased use of camel and mule corps—but the expense of these changes delayed progress.[71] The narrowing of the firepower gap not only disturbed the first method of bedouin control, it also made the government more reluctant to rely on their other tribal policy.

The second plan with which the government experimented was also a policy that had brought results in other provinces: winning authority through co-option of a supremely influential shaikh. As noted earlier, this strategy helped the state to govern the Hijaz, with the help of the sharif of Mecca, and southern Iraq, where Muntafiq Shaikh Nasir al-Sa`dun became first *mutasarrıf* in Suq al-Shuyukh and then *vali* of Basra. Although the Ottomans could never find a suitable lieutenant among the most powerful family, the Sa`udi amirs in Riyadh, twice in the nineteenth century they did attempt to buttress their authority in eastern Arabia with that of a tribal leader. The first experiment was twofold. The appointment of Bazi` b. `Ara`ir as *mutasarrıf* sought not only to use his authority as a leader of the Bani Khalid but also to bring the power and influence of the Muntafiq (Shaikh Nasir was Bazi`'s brother-in-law) to bear more fully on Hasawi affairs. Bazi` proved to lack standing among his neighbors, however, and Nasir's reputation was not enough to compensate for Bazi`'s (and his successor Mazyad's) shortcomings.

The second attempt to rule through a tribal leader came a decade after Bazi`'s removal from office and was more successful; yet the nature of Arabian politics again eventually limited its effectiveness. The intrafamily feuds among the Sa`udis after the death of Amir Faisal created a power vacuum in central Arabia that permitted the rise of new leaders, the most important of whom was Muhammad al-Rashid, ruler of Ha'il and shaikh of the Shammar. By 1884 he was the most powerful man in Najd, and from 1887 to 1902 Rashidis ruled Riyadh. The Shammar *dira* extended well into Iraq, and contacts with the government there and in the Hijaz impressed upon Ibn Rashid the power of the Ottoman state.[72] The interest was mutual. Sultan Abdülhamid II noted the emergence of the new supreme leader in Arabia. He sent a commission to Jabal Shammar in 1886 whose ostensible mission, according to British accounts, was to gain permission for establishment of an Ottoman mosque and school in Ha'il.[73] The commission's real objective, however, was to assess the condition of the lands and people ruled by Ibn Rashid, his attachment to the sultan, his relations with neighboring tribes, and his influence among them.[74] Ibn Rashid refused the mosque and school but sent the commission away with presents (and presumably information). Ottoman-Rashidi relations remained relatively good for some time, strengthened by the exchange of numerous gifts, honors, and declarations of good intent.[75]

The Ottoman government was at times pleased to see Ibn Rashid become its enforcer in Arabia. The Shammar leader defeated rivals in neighboring regions and tribes, acting always in the name of an Ottoman state that could not, by its own admission, come to the assistance of distant supplicants.[76] When the Ottoman-Rashidi alliance reached a brief peak after the capture of Riyadh in 1887 and the killing of three of Sa`ud's sons in 1888, the government was tempted to use Ibn Rashid to make progress toward the final conquest of all of Arabia. The scheme targeted Oman.[77] Sultan Turki b. Sa`id of Masqat died in 1888, and the succession of his son Faisal soon brought turmoil to an internally divided land. He distanced himself from his father's British allies, but the conservative Omani faction[78] also withheld their support from him. Faisal found himself isolated, facing a challenge from his uncle and two sons of the late Imam `Azzan b. Qays. The highly colored Ottoman information on the situation came from the conservative faction and emphasized British villainy. Britain supposedly tried to use the Omani disorder to establish a protectorate on the grounds of defending Indian traders on the coast.[79] The Omani Arabs refused the British overtures, declaring that they would turn to their coreligionists of the Ottoman caliphate if they needed help. Encouraged by this story, the sultan's government considered allowing Ibn Rashid to intervene on the conservative side. Britain could not hold Istanbul responsible for the shaikh's actions, because he held no official Ottoman title or position, and in any case Britain had no internationally recognized right to interfere in Omani affairs. An Ibn Rashid-Faisal clash would be a dispute between two independent leaders.[80]

The proposed intervention never occurred, perhaps in part because government doubts about the suitability of using Ibn Rashid within

Ottoman territory grew.[81] The author of the proposal to unleash Ibn Rashid on Oman suspected that the shaikh might try to realize dreams of conquest in times of Ottoman weakness, although he would not at present dare a direct challenge to the state.[82] By 1890 reports of Ibn Rashid's supremacy in Najd, the large number of weapons and men at his disposal, his propensity to stir conflict in Arabia, and his alliances with some of the most unruly tribes in Iraq deepened the Porte's mistrust, although further investigations refuted some of the rumors.[83]

Recognizing that Ibn Rashid was formidable, the government had to develop ideas for subduing him if indeed he turned against Istanbul. Some of the suggested measures could have had results: subject tribes' access to town markets could be cut, and rival tribal leaders could be urged to topple the shaikh. Other steps held less promise, such as declaring him to have acted against the sultan's wishes by capturing Riyadh, killing Muslims, and murdering the *kaymakam* of Najd, `Abdallah al-Sa`ud, two years before. An accusation of British influence was also hinted.[84] The proposals betray a certain naïveté about the ease with which a prestigious, powerful shaikh might be replaced but do show that the state was prepared to turn on its supposed lieutenant.[85]

The policy of alliance with strong shaikhs to manage tribal affairs thus had only limited effectiveness, not merely on the grounds of suspicion. One limitation for rule in Ottoman Hasa was simply geography: the seats of power of leaders willing to act for the state lay far from Hufuf. Ha'il is roughly 500 miles (c. 800 km) from the Hasa capital, and overland travel by indirect tracks would take weeks to accomplish. Ibn Rashid's control over areas south of Riyadh (c. 350 miles/560 km from Ha'il) was often shaky, which raised serious questions about his ability to police more distant territories. Attacks on caravans made by bedouins based in areas nominally under Ibn Rashid's control contributed to the growth of Ottoman distrust of him.[86] His greatest use for the Ottomans lay in the check he provided to Sa`udi power[87] and in the limited reduction of tribes' ability to flee government retribution that his control of Najd provided. Ibn Rashid also lacked the religious authority that made the amir of Mecca an effective Ottoman ally, an authority whose only other possessor in Arabia was the Wahhabi leader, the Sa`udi amir of Riyadh.[88] Because it depended upon the personal fortune of a distant individual, the alliance with Ibn Rashid could not serve as a long-term instrument of control among the Arab tribes.

Britain in the Gulf: A Stealthy Counterattack

Whereas Britain's Gulf policy in 1871 featured cautious restraint in tracking Midhat's expedition, its attitude over the next quarter century gradually hardened into a predisposition to challenge Ottoman authority throughout Arabia. A long-standing piracy problem spurred the move to a more aggressive stance, while changes in European great power politics prompted more forceful delineation of the British sphere of influence. As at the start of Ottoman rule in Hasa, misunderstandings about intentions and regional politics helped to shape the Anglo-Ottoman relations of this period.

The course of these relations in the Gulf was also influenced by increasing tensions between the two empires as European powers. British support for Istanbul in the face of Slav nationalism and Great Power intervention in the Balkans came much less willingly than before. Britain promised to help the Ottomans retain and reform their Asiatic possessions after the 1878 Berlin Conference, and its support during the peace negotiations there facilitated the sultan's recovery of Bulgarian and Macedonian territories that he had lost in the Balkan wars of 1876–78. As the price for its assistance, however, Britain demanded, and received, control of Cyprus. In combination with the 1875 purchase of the Egyptian khedive's shares of the Suez Canal, this gave Britain an alarmingly great stature in the eastern Mediterranean in Istanbul's view.[89] The public outcry in Britain over reported atrocities in Bulgaria in 1877–78, and Ottoman resentment following the British takeover of Egypt in 1882, caused both sides to reconsider the value of their former de facto alliance. The marked contrast between British constitutional liberalism and Abdülhamid II's autocracy further alienated the two powers after the sultan dissolved the recently elected Ottoman parliament in 1878.

Within the local context of the Gulf, Anglo-Ottoman tensions crystallized around the problem of piracy along the Hasa and Qatar coasts. The first of the periodic outbreaks of attacks on shipping occurred off the coasts of Qatif and Qatar in 1878. A weak Ottoman presence and the turmoil caused by the uprising led by Sa`ud's sons encouraged the lawlessness in the former *kaza*; that of the latter was tied to the continuing Bahraini-Qatari rivalry, which centered on the town of Zubara opposite Bahrain.[90] Although the British government could claim only a small interest in the recovery of stolen property,[91] as the guarantor of maritime peace it felt compelled to resolve all cases of piracy. To that end British warships seized stolen ships and suspected pirate vessels at sea, while representatives in Iraq demanded punitive action by the Ottomans in Hasa.

The measures taken along the Arabian coast by the Ottoman local authorities failed to impress the government of India, however, causing it to debate greater freedom of action for British warships in Ottoman waters and indeed the limits of land to be acknowledged as Ottoman. In response to British complaints, the authorities in Basra *Vilayet* approved various policing actions, including several raids on suspected pirate nests at Jubayl and near Dhahran, and the assignment of two steamers to patrol the coast. These and other measures failed to capture the ringleaders or recover stolen goods.[92] Receiving friendly assurances of action in Istanbul and Basra, yet detecting little practical result in Hasa, some British officials advocated permitting the navy to attack pirates in Ottoman waters and to pursue them on land. This proposal raised the question of what waters should be recognized as Ottoman. Opinion among government officers in the Gulf, Baghdad, India, and London varied from recognition of Istanbul's rule as far as `Udayd[93] to acknowledgment of control only as far as Qatif *Kaza* or `Uqayr. In 1881 the British opted for tacit acceptance of the Ottoman claim to rule Qatar, but in the absence of Ottoman ships to police the coast British naval commanders were to deal with pirates without reference to the three-mile (4.8 km) territorial water limit (although prisoners captured within three miles of the coast were to be turned over to the authorities in Hasa).[94] This was an important step toward Britain's eventual, northward-creeping denial of Ottoman claims to sovereignty over points on the coast.

It was not only British actions in this and later situations—secretive, inconsistent, and of dubious legality—that guaranteed the creation of diplomatic problems much greater than the scattered acts of piracy warranted; similar mistakes by the Ottomans only made the British more determined to act without reference to Istanbul's claims (which naturally increased Ottoman antagonism, and so on). The Indian government's representatives in the Gulf initially advocated an assertive maritime policing policy, such as was adopted in 1881, because they felt that the Ottoman authorities were ignoring their complaints. If the piracy incidents are viewed through Ottoman eyes, however, the justification for the British officials' tone of righteous indignation over this inaction loses clarity for several reasons. First, officials in Hasa and Basra undoubtedly resented the forceful interference of a power with little legitimate claim to involvement. Britain pressed damages for, and sought resolution of cases involving, not only British Indian merchants but also local Muslims, most notably Bahrainis; its right to interfere in the Doha-Zubara rivalry was especially debatable. Second, the reports of incidents and evaluated damages given to the British did not tally with those gathered by the Ottomans. In cases involving non-Hasawi merchants such as the Bahrainis, the government presumably preferred to believe local statements that minimized the incidents to claims advanced with British help.[95] Third, Britain appeared to apply a double standard in judging complaints. It demanded redress for crimes committed by Ottoman subjects but turned a deaf ear to claims against Trucial shaikhs. When in 1879 the British urged the Hasa government to extradite a captured raider to Bahrain, the *mutasarrıf* raised a counterclaim for the extradition from Bahrain of an accountant accused of having embezzled government funds in Qatif. The British refused to treat the cases as equal, nor is there any indication that they later addressed the Ottoman complaint.[96]

This incident followed another example of variable standards that was more offensive to Ottoman sensibilities, the sack of 'Udayd. Although their position in the Gulf rested upon agreements with autonomous shaikhs to ban maritime warfare, the British permitted the shaikh of Abu Dhabi to attack by sea former tributaries who had left his territory for 'Udayd over a dispute with him. Britain acknowledged that the shaikh of 'Udayd had raised the Ottoman flag, claimed Ottoman protection and paid tribute through Doha to Hufuf as a mark of that protected status. Yet British officials considered that this did not "justify the Turks in asserting their jurisdiction over the place."[97] Since the Ottomans based much of their tribal (and geopolitical) strategy upon the sovereignty implied by payment of tribute and flying of flags, they could not accept this argument.[98] The distrust of British intentions felt by many Ottoman officials may well have caused some provincial authorities to stall efforts to address Britain's concerns.[99]

There were other constraints, however, that were as much to blame as local officials' sheer bloody-mindedness for the disparity between Istanbul's promises and the results obtained in the Gulf. As will be seen in this chapter's next section, high-ranking members of the Ottoman government in Istanbul and Basra did recognize the need for better policing of the Arabian coast, but fiscal constraints prevented quick, effective action. Lacking adequate naval resources, governors had to rely primarily on the gendarmerie and the army, although their effectiveness and visibility in fighting piracy were more limited than light coastal patrol boats would have been.[100] In the period immediately following the Qatif rebellion of 1878, the military and civilian authorities in Hasa may have felt reluctant to exacerbate tensions with the locals by taking harsh action in a matter that had little direct tie to internal Hasawi affairs. Perhaps the most consistent cause of the disparity between words in Istanbul or Iraq and actions in Hasa, however, was the difficulty of communication. Orders to the *mutasarrıf* could be over a month in transit, leaving ample time for the pirates to disperse and dispose of their loot.[101] In short, the Hasa administration's isolation, understaffing, and internal preoccupations did more to undermine security than did the mere indifference or antagonism charged by Britain.

CHANCE FOR ADJUSTMENT AND STABILITY

Despite misinterpretation of the piracy problem, Britain did have reason for concern about the broader political competition with the Ottomans in the Gulf. Some in government saw an Ottoman intention to use the suppression of piracy as an excuse to extend sovereignty over Bahrain and Trucial Oman.[102] This opinion also overstated the danger posed to the British regional position, but the worsening of bilateral relations in Europe and the growing British assertiveness in the Gulf encouraged the Ottoman desire to pick at their rivals' foundation of influence. In 1879 double quarantine charges were levied in Basra on ships arriving from any harbor between Bahrain and the boundaries of Aden, on grounds that they had avoided the sanitary regulations in those "Ottoman" ports.[103] Indian traders in Hasa after 1880 suffered from illegal export duties and other harassments, which contributed to a marked decline in the value of their trade.[104] After 1886 the recrudescence of Ottoman schemes to detach the Trucial shaikhs from their ties to Britain also caused alarm and convinced the British of the need to gain a sturdier, formal basis for their position in Arabia.

The weakness of Britain's legal grounds for forceful action in Arabian affairs greatly concerned the British and Indian governments. Protests to the Sublime Porte had to be tempered when treating matters not covered by the Anglo-Arab agreements, the stipulations of which rarely could involve Istanbul. Britain usually preferred not to discuss, or even acknowledge the existence of, its treaties with the shaikhs,[105] not only because publication could reveal the legal limitations of the accords but also because overt guardianship of foreign lands could provoke counterclaims from European rivals.[106] Yet continued reliance on de facto supremacy in the Gulf lost attraction as perceived challenges from Iran and European rivals as well as the Ottoman empire threatened to require increased military and administrative expenditures.[107] It remained for the personal initiative of the Gulf Resident finally to solve the dilemma and determine the future course of Anglo-Arab relations.

Rumors of a planned invasion of Bahrain by Shaikh `Isa al-Khalifa's old adversary Nasir b. Mubarak in 1880 spurred the Resident, Colonel Ross, to action. Fearing that the aborted attack signaled Istanbul's intention to weaken `Isa's position by force, an Ottoman attempt to establish a coal depot in Bahrain having failed, Ross felt that his ally needed a new weapon to fend off foreign designs.[108] The Resident proposed that the shaikh and his successors should not enter negotiations or treaties with other states, nor permit establishment of foreign diplomatic posts or coal depots in Bahrain, unless with the British government's consent. The bond did not affect "customary friendly correspondence" with neighboring local rulers on routine matters.[109] Shaikh `Isa agreed to the conditions, at least partly because he wanted reassurance of security in the face of Nasir b. Mubarak's challenge. He recognized more fully than did the British that, while it preserved his relative freedom of action domestically, the agreement made British responsibility for Bahrain's security nearly total. Neither Ross nor the viceroy of India saw that it increased the government's responsibilities, nor did they realize that peer rivalry would make other Trucial shaikhs eager for similar accords.[110] His superiors thus forgave the Resident his unauthorized action and ratified the agreement in 1881.

With this accord as precedent, similar pacts were reached with other rulers between 1887 and 1892. Ross repeated his Bahrain action in Masqat in 1887, signing an exclusive agreement without authorization. In this case the Indian government did not immediately ratify the accord, although its principles were included in an 1892 Anglo-Masqat commercial treaty.[111] Ottoman and Persian overtures to the shaikhs of Trucial Oman led Britain to sign Bahrain-type agreements with these rulers in 1887, and the activities of French agents in the same area five years later made Britain broaden the ban on all foreign contacts there and in Bahrain.[112]

By 1892 Britain thus had markedly strengthened the defenses of its position in the Gulf. Two decades earlier its prestige had lain in its rather informal role as regional arbiter and policeman; like the British bobby, its representatives' authority was largely symbolic, not based on ostentatious displays of armed might. Initially unsure of how to react to the intrusion of outsiders into its bailiwick, Britain finally opted for much tighter control over its Arab clients' foreign interests. Military and civilian observation of affairs on the Arab side of the Gulf became more frequent or permanent. Most importantly for Istanbul, a willingness to question Ottoman rights on the mainland grew to the point where Britain began to regard the Ottomans not as the governors of Hasa but rather as its occupiers.

Ottoman Reform Proposals

This chapter's previous sections have suggested several major areas of weakness in the Hasa administration that, if left unremedied, could hasten the end of Ottoman control. Piracy and the opportunity it gave for foreign intervention remained a nagging problem after 1878. The preference for cheap government, spending no more than necessary to ensure collection of a moderate level of revenue and thereby promoting a shortsighted squeezing of the populace, eroded local attachment to the empire. The elastic leash with which the administration hoped to check the bedouins' worst impulses could snap under the stress of changing conditions. The Ottoman administration had to prove that it could change as well, if it hoped to retain a solid grip on Arabia.

Accounts of British observers leave the impression that the Ottomans never attempted to address problems in Hasa, but this was certainly not the case. The 1880s were a decade in which the government reconsidered its program in many areas, in large measure due to its recent territorial losses in the Balkans, Anatolia, and Egypt and to its need for more revenue from its remaining provinces. Painfully aware of its ignorance about its remotest possessions, Istanbul sought data from any and all sources. Sultan Abdülhamid and the Porte gathered information on territories especially remote, thinly populated, and vulnerable to foreign interference, including Yemen, Libya, Dair al-Zor, Iraq, and eastern Arabia.[113] Given the impulse behind this search for information, however, it is not surprising that some reports stressed the evils wrought by foreigners. This was especially the case in the Gulf. As in other regions, however, the biggest obstacle facing efforts at reform was money.

Whereas Britain thought that the sultan's government simply ignored its complaints about piracy, a plan of action presented to the sultan on 15 January 1880 shows both that the protests were heeded and that considerable problems stood in the way of their resolution.[114] An attack on a boat from Karachi stirred action in Istanbul, because it occurred embarrassingly close to Basra and because the vessel carried a British flag.[115] The alarm of the Sublime Porte arose not only from the material damage inherent in such lawlessness but also from the opportunities that the repetition of piracy was creating for foreign intervention that infringed upon Ottoman rights. The Basra naval commander had been sent firm instructions to capture the bandits, but his resources were not equal to the task. He had only two steam corvettes, one of which badly needed to return to Istanbul for repairs that the local naval yard was too ill-equipped to make. The government dispatched a small steamer to replace it, but this was only a temporary substitute. Istanbul also designated for Basra service two other corvettes currently completing overhaul in the Istanbul dry dock in order to give the squadron more substance. Even should the refitting finish quickly, several problems would yet inhibit effective police action. The corvettes drew too much water to seek or pursue small Arab boats along the coast.[116] They consumed coal too rapidly to permit long patrols.[117] If the warships needed repairs, they had to go to, and replacements had to steam from, Istanbul, which made maintenance of full squadron strength extremely difficult. Until these problems were solved, pirates would continue to act with impunity in the Gulf.

To escape these limitations the Naval Council proposed construction of four small gunboats. They were to draw no more than six feet of water, which would allow them better (but not total) access to the inlets and other hiding places of the pirates.[118] Their range would exceed that of the corvettes because of lower coal consumption.[119] The Basra naval yard would also receive the equipment necessary to maintain the new boats, eliminating the need to send them to Istanbul or Bombay in case of breakdown. The estimated cost of the four vessels, T£31,600, turned out to be the most formidable obstacle to the dawn of a new age of Ottoman Gulf security. The imperial Treasury was empty. The Council had to try to find the money by squeezing other items in the service's budget, notably by deferment of salaries and other payments.

It was not enough to permit quick execution of the project. Two years later the boats still had not been built or bought. The plan had been complicated by the discovery of the great extent of work required to outfit the Basra naval yard. The naval yard staff was proving ineffective, making improvements slow.[120] Unrest in Basra province may also have occasioned delay, as the depredations of several mutinous tribes along the Tigris and Euphrates drew the attention and resources of civil and military authorities. One result of this was that the government amalgamated Basra *Vilayet* into the province of Baghdad, hoping to improve the efficiency of administration and security in Iraq, but the move made the affairs of Hasa and the Gulf less pressing by making the area more remote from the seat of power.[121] A reported cessation of piracy in 1880 also probably eased the pressure for immediate action.[122] For any or all of these reasons, a resurgence of attacks in 1883 found the navy still ill-prepared.

Fresh incidents of piracy did not revive the debate over how to improve command of Arabian coasts, however, because it had not ceased. To examine the problem further, the Navy Department had set up a commission to examine this question that submitted its conclusions in January 1882.[123] The report's recommendations recorded a shift in thought that was to harm Ottoman planning in future, namely a strengthening inclination to view piracy solely as a cover for European schemes of expansion rather than as a legitimate problem in itself. In a way, the analysis resembled that of Midhat a dozen years before but lacked his concern for consolidation of what had been already gained.

The problem that was preoccupying the Porte again at this time was the expanding European presence around the Red Sea. Italy encouraged its people to emigrate to Assab (Eritrea), the British fomented tensions between the amirs of Shihr and Mukalla (Hadhramawt), while the French claimed Obokh (off Djibouti) and had reportedly landed troops in Yemen.[124] To affirm the Ottoman claim to the Arabian peninsula and its surrounding seas—areas whose delicacy and importance it expected to see grow continuously—the commission enlarged the original proposed Basra flotilla into a three-part naval force. The first squadron would patrol the Gulf, the second the coasts of Dhufar, Hadhramawt, Somalia, and Zanzibar, and the third would cover the Red Sea. The force would include sixteen steamers, including five then being built, and be based in Basra, Jidda, Hudayda, and Dhufar. Coal depots and other necessary infrastructure would be installed there and at the Basra naval yard, which would be the common organizational and support base, commanded by an officer schooled in naval science and practice.

Again, Istanbul's plans did not create results to match intentions; nor did disappointment cause a radical rethinking of the problem or the scale of possible solutions. Coming a month after establishment of the Council of the Ottoman Debt, the Naval Council's ambitious plan had little hope of being fully funded at once. Several inexpensive steps were carried out,[125] but the overall Ottoman position changed little over the next two years. A report by the Basra naval commander, Rıza Ali, brought the Arabian issue to the fore again in 1884–85 with detailed descriptions of decay in the state's authority there, its roots and remedies.[126] He at least acknowledged British concerns, correctly identifying the importance of trade. Yet Rıza continued the tendency to view it mainly as the cover under which Britain had recently widened its sphere of influence among nominal Ottoman subjects. Protection of Indian merchants provided the pretext for Britain's conspicuous naval presence and, upon disagreements between the traders and the locals, intercession to force payment of damages. The insidious spread of foreign influence through visiting officials and missionaries promoted popular allegiance to Britain and the conclusion of secret pacts with shaikhs. Rıza's mistaken regard of the concern for trade as primarily a blind for purely political ambition resembled Britain's suspicion that Midhat in 1871 was simply making a senseless land grab in Hasa, despite acknowledgment of the common Ottoman suspicion of British Gulf activities. Thus in neither case did the states address each other's publicized, legitimate concerns.

In appraisal of political ties to the other important western Gulf group, the Arabs, Rıza showed a similar mix of realism and misjudgment. He seemed absolutely convinced that the shaikhs, as a group, were quite undependable. They oppressed their people and made secret agreements with the British, which suggested a severe lack of principles.[127] The shaikhs between Kuwait and Aden had to be bypassed in order to appeal directly to the people. Such consideration of the problem of building a sense of unity between the state and its subjects was too often lacking in Ottoman reports from the Gulf after Midhat. Rıza repeated the claim—made so often in the past and in the future, and with reason when loyalty placed no onus on the subject—that the Arabs inclined by nature to the sultan. The ultimate aim of his report was to suggest means of fixing that affection to the caliphate[128] and making the shaikhs irrelevant.

The methods proposed were not all as reasonable as this goal, however. On the principle that people who did not share the burdens of state (i.e., taxes) had no more than a pretense of loyalty, Rıza wanted officials appointed to key settlements from Kuwait to Masqat. Not only would they gather regular revenue for the Treasury, they would also assert Ottoman regional supremacy by police action, especially by patrol of pearling areas. Each post would have a small ship at its service to reinforce the officials' authority, at least until easy relations with the locals were established. This step would strengthen the control arising from the proposed appointment of talented local leaders at more spots from 'Uqayr to Aden, who would rule under the protection of the Ottoman flag and with the support of regularly patrolling warships.[129] The obvious weakness of this scheme was that it was designed to address Britain's ambitions more than the interests of the local people. Alliance with Britain had advantages: shaikhs retained considerable freedom of action in internal affairs, gained greater security of tenure, paid no taxes, and might even be given subsidies.[130] The people might gain as well from the British police of the sea, where most coastal Arabs earned their living. The religious bond to Sultan Abdülhamid counterbalanced some of these advantages but by itself could not conquer all dissatisfaction, as sporadic unrest in Hasa indicated. Neither Rıza nor the government in Istanbul questioned the assumption that the Arabs all desired Ottoman rule, probably because of a mixture of ignorance about the area and the political inadvisability of criticizing the Islamism of Abdülhamid II.

Even if the plan had been fully implemented, such an oversight raises serious doubts about its chances for achieving lasting security in the Gulf. The question must remain moot, however, because like its predecessors the program was too ambitious. The plan to bring the Omani and Dhufari coasts under Ottoman rule required construction of six ships, supply depots at Kuwait, Ra's Tanura, Masqat, and two towns in Dhufar, as well as a complete new naval yard at Basra.[131] The mass of expensive, expansionist ideas was unfortunate, because it distracted attention from a few more practicable, sensible suggestions on how to improve mastery of waters already accepted as Ottoman. These ideas were also intended primarily to counter a perceived British threat, in this case to control of the navigable waterways of Iraq. Improvement of security and shipping along the vital Tigris-Euphrates communications route, however, was very valuable regardless of its motivation. Rıza's recommendations included addition of four gunboats to the two already assigned to the Tigris and the Shatt al-Arab and revival of the Oman-Ottoman administration, the state shipping line that served the Tigris from Basra to Baghdad and was hoped to be an important source of revenue.[132] Because it was vital to the plans for the defense of Arabia and indeed all of Ottoman Asia, Rıza also included some ideas on means to secure the head of the Gulf between Basra and Kuwait, most notably by assertion of Ottoman control over the shipping channel from Faw to Basra.[133]

Abdülhamid's government had to proceed cautiously with this long list of measures, slowly picking a few each from the Arabia and Iraq programs. Decisions depended on an independent inspector's confirmation of Rıza's report,[134] a better listing of priorities among the measures and an estimate of the most urgent steps' cost. These came in over the following year, and on 10 January 1885 the Council of Ministers finally recommended making three T£10,000 annual additions to the naval budget to buy ships, develop the Basra naval yard and revive the Oman-Ottoman administration. Navigational markers and lighthouses were to be placed at suitable points around the entire Arabian peninsula (except the territory of Aden).[135]

Even with this restricted agenda, Istanbul was hard pressed to achieve a lasting impact in any area, due to a mixture of poverty and bad luck. Ottoman shipping service on the Tigris and Euphrates remained weak for twenty years, despite several abortive attempts at revival.[136] Two naval ships arrived for duties in the Gulf in 1887; more were promised, but the Basra squadron remained under strength and poorly equipped.[137] The naval yard improved slowly but did not gain first-class status, despite continuing to receive much more money from Istanbul than most naval facilities did.[138] The government also did not place lights or other navigational markers outside recognized Ottoman waters, in the Shatt al-Arab, or anywhere else where Britain felt an interest in supervising commerce. It did start to build a fort at Faw to secure the mouth of the Shatt in 1885, however, and erected three guardhouses at other points on the river in 1890–94.[139] Regarding the steps suggested to improve control of the Arabian coast, the main change (an increase in land personnel only) was at Doha, where the government hoped to tap into the port's pearling wealth and to prevent a possible British takeover.[140] Kuwait remained undisturbed,[141] and the navy was slow to assume an aggressive police of the pearl fisheries.[142] Many factors undoubtedly combined to prevent fulfillment of various goals—feared or actual British complaints, the loss or diversion of ships—but cost must have been the biggest obstacle. Even if T£30,000 were spared for the building program in a time of indebtedness, the sum would not be enough for completion. A relatively straightforward project, repair of the decrepit Basra naval office and its dock, was expected to cost T£700; the cost of constructing the other buildings, workshops, and dry dock, and equipping them with heavy machinery would have swallowed much of the budget, leaving little to pay for ten or twelve ships.[143] The difficulty of finding the necessary sums must have slowed work and reduced the impact of the program.

Among the most striking aspects of this and the other reform plans was how little direct attention the piracy problem received. It was, after all, at the root of Britain's increasing willingness to chip away at the basis of the Ottoman presence in the Gulf. Convinced that the real problem was the British navy, not the depredations of a handful of tribesmen in boats, the Ottoman government failed to develop an efficient policing plan for this specific problem, despite the expenditure of so much effort and money. When it sent ships, they were suited more for showing the flag in the most important ports than for shallow-water patrols. Ships continued to be based at Basra, not at any of the Arabian harbors. Most importantly, there was almost no consideration of methods to address the problem from land—identification of the culprits, their home bases, their modes of operation, the ways in which they could be controlled. Despite noting turbulence caused at that time by unruly tribes, Rıza's only suggestion for concrete internal change was the creation of a Najd *vilayet*, which despite its altered name would still be run from Basra. His immediate aim was to boost security within Hasa, but the change might also affect maritime unrest. Rıza hoped to restore a proper attitude of respect for the sultan and the state among the people by raising their home from the lowly status of a remote appendage of Baghdad. This suggestion probably influenced the decision to reverse the 1880 incorporation of Basra into Baghdad province.[144] The change, and the resulting shortening of the lines of communication, indeed may have contributed to a decrease in the unrest reported by Britain in the next few years except in Qatar.

Yet the case for deeper internal reform remained largely unargued for several more years until the presentation of proposals by a *mutasarrıf* in Hufuf, probably Mehmet Salih Pasha.[145] Most of his five-page document reflects the empire-wide fiscal problems by suggesting ways to increase local revenues. These included ideas about settling deserted districts such as Dhahran and widening cultivation around Hufuf that resembled Midhat's measures. It also resurrected the notion of finally bringing the Najd interior under direct supervision, although it inflated the estimate

CHANCE FOR ADJUSTMENT AND STABILITY

of the region's revenue.¹⁴⁶ Other suggestions originated from more recent incidents: an anti-Qâsim Qatari shaikh's request for an Ottoman customs house in Doha aroused the intention to post more (tax-collecting) administrators there, while an 1887 crisis between Qâsim and his Anglo-Bahraini nemeses reawakened the desire to place an official in Manama.¹⁴⁷ These statements of potential goals did not form a comprehensive plan to rival Midhat's, however, because the author gave few details of possible methods of improving Arabia's finances. He noted that the Hufuf area had groundwater sufficient to triple agricultural production but did not explain the reasons that had prevented its full utilization, be they security, taxes, or ownership disputes. Although British reports discussed the pressing need for updated tax (and population) surveys, no *mutasarrıf* carried out such a step until after the turn of the century.¹⁴⁸

This oversight is quite surprising, because some Ottoman reformers elsewhere were aware of this far from unique problem and tried to make it an issue of attention. Reformers in Hasa generally seemed to ignore the problem, because they did not see clearly its connection to countering the British threat. Mehmet Salih's silence on the issue nevertheless is surprising, given his administrative responsibility for the area.

Mehmet Salih's most specific suggestions, however, did address two particular, important problems: commerce and communications. Trade interested the author primarily because of its tax potential. He valued Hasa's annual exports at T£250,000, much of which could be subject to varying duties.¹⁴⁹ To facilitate this trade he proposed that the shipping channel connecting `Uqayr to the sea be deepened, or that a new one be cut through the spit of land opposite the harbor.¹⁵⁰ To encourage commerce further, the *mutasarrıf* also wanted to establish a regularly scheduled shipping service, in which every week one or two small vessels would carry mail, passengers, and goods from `Uqayr to Basra with stops at Linja and Bushire on the Iranian coast, Bahrain, Qatif, and Kuwait. Not only would this encourage trade, it would tighten the ties of key peripheral areas to the government centers, Hufuf and Basra. The governor felt frustrated by the length of time necessary to send messages by camel rider to Basra and to areas nominally under his supervision. Piracy notwithstanding, sea mail also was more secure than camel post. An added benefit would result from an Ottoman demonstration to the Arabs of an ability to organize and execute such a visible project, which might persuade them to obey the state's wishes or (it is inferred in the case of Bahrain) to acknowledge Ottoman sovereignty.

The problem that the shipping and other proposals were designed to solve, the difficulty of communication with the rest of the empire, was indeed a major hindrance to government responsiveness to local needs and conditions. Because action on important issues often had to await instructions from remote superiors, seeming government inaction aroused resentment; the Arabs noted that the *mutasarrıf* gathered taxes promptly but was slow to act on local petitions. Mehmet Salih wanted a telegraph line extended from Faw to Hufuf to reduce further Hasa's isolation from the rest of the empire. The area's importance and the delicacy of its current situation justified the expense. If Istanbul were to pay for a submarine cable from Faw to Qatif or `Uqayr, Hasa could afford to install a land line to Hufuf. This improvement and the shipping project would undoubtedly help to smooth administration and improve government-populace relations, thus making future reforms easier to carry out.

Mehmet Salih had one other suggested means for improving the Ottoman position in Arabia that did not require significant investment in hardware. Rıza Ali's proposal to move the *vilayet* capital from Baghdad to Basra had been intended to ease the resentment of Hasa's inhabitants by speeding the government's reaction time. It did not fully resolve the problem, and so Mehmet Salih took the next logical step, suggesting that the Necd *Sancak* be made independent, i.e., answerable directly to Istanbul, not to a provincial capital in Iraq.[151] Such a change might seem questionable at first—why should a region of modest population and wealth be made independent of the empire's *vilayet* structure?—but on further consideration the question of why the area did *not* become independent seems more appropriate. Istanbul created a number of independent *sancak*s during Sultan Abdülhamid II's reign, most if not all for one or more of the following reasons (in declining order of importance): the immediate threat of foreign influence and interference (e.g., Mount Lebanon, Jerusalem, Binghazi, Biga); other security issues, including bedouin depredations (e.g., Zor in the Syrian desert, Binghazi, Istanbul's defense perimeter at Çatalca); and remoteness from any suitable *vilayet* capital (e.g., Binghazi, Zor).[152] The Necd *Sancak* met all of these criteria, yet Istanbul never detached it from Basra. There are several probable reasons for this. The region was too remote: it would take Istanbul weeks to communicate with Hasa and could gain very little idea of conditions there, given the lack of telegraph and reliable shipping services. It would gain little by cutting Basra out of the communications and command chain; despite their distance from Hasa, officials in that Gulf port would have a better sense of regional conditions than would those in Istanbul, and all communications would have to go through Basra anyway.[153] A second reason for keeping Hasa tied to Basra was the Ottoman analysis of the threat to be met. It held that British designs encompassed not only Arabia but also Iraq. In order to frustrate Britain's intrigues, which drew no line between Basra and Arabia, the Ottoman authorities in Basra needed a similarly seamless arena in which to implement defense strategies. Istanbul thus several years later granted the local military command an unusual temporary exemption from the need to await orders from Iraq and the War Ministry before taking action against foreign and bedouin threats, because of the slowness of communication, but Hufuf still needed to give post facto justification of military operations.[154] Necd *Sancak* otherwise remained administratively subordinate to Basra.

Much of the rest of Mehmet Salih's program of action similarly was at best only partially realized, although, as happened with Rıza Ali's proposals in maritime affairs, it became a basis of Ottoman policy in the Necd *Sancak* in following years. Part of the blame for this must go to Istanbul, because the marked recrudescence of its concern about British designs on Arabia after 1887 caused the government to concentrate ever more on expensive geopolitical schemes at the cost of delaying attention to deep administrative reform. Istanbul did enact several measures clearly related to trying to gain the favor of locals and improving their condition. The Porte tried to appeal to sensibilities of locals, including Arabs outside Ottoman control (i.e., in Bahrain and Trucial Oman), by giving precedence to Shari`a instead of secular state law (*kanun*). As in the Hijaz on the other side of the peninsula, religious judges (*kadi, naib*) were to head the courts of first instance and appeal.[155] State secular (*nizami*) courts were phased out. In an attempt to improve the locals' commercial ties in 1887–88 the successor to Mehmet Salih as *mutasarrıf*, Rifaat Bey, made sporadic, unsuccessful attempts to develop a port for the import/export trade, although the chosen site was not `Uqayr but rather Darin near Qatif.[156] His successor, Akif Pasha, also attempted to improve Hasa's shipping connections, adding Doha to the list of scheduled ports of call, but it did not come to fruition.[157] In all other attempted reforms, improvements in administration, trade and quality of life seemed to be of only secondary importance.

Akif Pasha particularly influenced Istanbul's inclination to preoccupation with regional geopolitics after 1889. The Council of Ministers adopted his recommended policy initiatives, which retained some ideas of Mehmet Salih and Rifaat Pashas but were much more concerned with countering British influence.[158] Akif renewed the urgent call for a telegraph line to link Hufuf to Basra and even persuaded local notables to promise to contribute T£1,000 to the cost. His support for improvement of shipping in the Gulf was partially a quid pro quo for this contribution, but the scope of his plans show that he wanted political more than commercial gains from expansion of the Ottoman fleet. Ships calling regularly at ports around the Arabian peninsula, Iran, Baluchistan, and India, supported by stationing local agents and coal depots, would allow the Ottomans to gain a presence in places where they had little or none. In Trucial Oman and Bahrain, that presence might later lead to incorporation of the land into the Necd *Sancak*. Along all the Gulf coast the demonstration of Ottoman strength to rival Britain's was expected to tighten the allegiance of the Arabs to the sultan. Maritime security was also to be increased to deal with pirates who refused to behave properly. On land as well a substantial increase in the undermanned garrison (including camel- and donkey-mounted troops) was to control bedouin unrest.[159]

Troops, camels, fortifications, ships, supplies, telegraph—all required money; how did Akif propose to pay for them? Much of the cost would have to be met by Istanbul, but Akif (and the Council of Ministers) thought the threat from the British severe enough to justify the burden on a straitened treasury. The burden, in fact, was too great. Istanbul did not have the money to lay telegraph lines, build enough ships, or buy camels. Trying to close the shortfall, Akif did search for quick ways to raise funds locally, primarily by extending tax regimes to areas that had not produced real revenue before. He wanted to establish customs houses at Darin and Doha to gain immediate benefits from any increase in trade.[160] In Qatar, in fact, Akif suggested eventually introducing a broad range of taxes as part of a plan to bring the *kaza* more fully under regular Ottoman administration. Before 1889 the only "Ottomans" in Doha were *Kaymakam* Qâsim al-Thani, a judge (*naib*), and a garrison of gendarmes. Under Akif the Ottoman contingent grew to include a deputy *kaymakam*, a secretary (*tahrirat kâtibi*) and assistant secretary, and a proper administrative council was to be formed. Since almost all residents of Qatar except Qâsim were poor, the members of the council from the local population were to be paid a monthly salary in order to make sure that the council took its duties seriously. A harbor master for Doha, who would collect fees from native boats and monitor foreign ships and passengers, was named but did not assume his post. Akif furthermore told Qâsim that the state in future intended to erect buildings in the town and levy taxes on pearl dealers and other merchants. Finally, to complete Qatar's defense against British intrigue, Akif also assigned administrators (*müdirs*) and gendarmes to the disputed towns of Zubara and ʿUdayd, but they, like the harbor master, did not assume their posts after Akif fell sick and left Hasa.[161]

Illness, which felled Akif and other key people, complicated reform in the Gulf, as it could elsewhere; it did not, however, cause damage to rival the several problems that consistently delayed Istanbul's attempts to secure control of Arabia. Money caused chronic headaches in Arabia, as it did throughout the empire. Having lost wars, territory, and solvency, Istanbul demanded revenue from Baghdad and Basra. They in turn tried to squeeze more from their *sancak*s as Iraq's own productivity declined. This meant that Hasa could not use much of its modest surplus to improve security and the economy. Projects that could have reduced Arabia's isolation, such as telegraph lines and port improvements, thus proceeded slowly, if at all.

As a result, communications failed to meet the needs of reform. Provincial officials could not, or would not, cooperate to form plans. Without thorough consultation with others, individuals were left to address their own concerns. Naval officers thought the key was more ships and bases; soldiers saw more men and materiel as the answer; civil authorities felt that more administrative assets were critical to improvement. Members of the different services battled each other for influence in Istanbul and control in the Gulf. Despite Istanbul's close interest in Gulf affairs, it lacked the means both to gather information that could guide it to a sound choice of reform measures and to monitor officials in order to ensure their cooperation and good behavior.[162] The government therefore opted for programs that made most sense in the imperial capital: as elsewhere in the embattled empire, problems were the fault of foreigners, in this case Britain; Britain was a naval power; the Ottomans thus needed to build a fleet to match the Royal Navy. Events were soon to prove, however, that this was a mistake, as Hasa was caught unprepared when insecurity and chaos erupted in the 1890s.

The Ottoman Crisis of Control: The 1893 Qatar Revolt

The reformers of the 1880s wanted to correct problems in security and administration that were reducing the state's control or collection of revenue, problems that an enemy might be able to exploit in the future to drive the Ottomans out of Hasa; after 1890 the challenge to the government's authority was direct and immediate. It moreover came, unexpectedly, from within Ottoman territory. The Hufuf administration managed to survive this bout with tribal marauders, discontented townspeople, and rebellious shaikhs, but its prestige suffered lasting damage. Twenty years of relative stability ended, and a slow but marked decline began.

Unrest in the Najdi interior caused by bedouin raiders blossomed into a crime spree in 1889–1890 within Hasa's core, as Al Murra, Bani Hajir, and Manasir bedouins attacked caravans traveling between 'Uqayr and Hufuf.[163] A brief respite from the raids followed the reappointment of Said Pasha as *mutasarrıf* in 1891. Having a nice judgment of the possibilities of government in a tribal area, Said had earned a good reputation in almost eight years of previous service in the post and was able to effect a reconciliation with the bedouins, in part by resuming payment of subsidies, which might have lapsed due to insufficient funds.[164] The truce collapsed in May 1892, however, when about 300 members of the three tribes sacked another caravan. For much of the next four years roads remained insecure, subject to sporadic attacks, and travel was safe only in large, well-armed caravans guided by tribal *rafiqs*.[165]

This new insecurity of trade and travel brought to a climax the frustration of many Hasawis. Incensed by the robberies and murders, including that of a noted merchant in the May 1892 raid, traders petitioned the Grand Vezir for action, pinning blame for the bad situation squarely on the local administration. Government officials had but one interest: squeezing money from the people. They demanded more than the legal taxes, either to enrich themselves or to win promotion by remitting more money to the state. In return for taxes they were obligated to ensure public safety, yet they did not even pretend to take action against the marauders, few in number though they were. The townspeople could not protect themselves, moreover, because they were strictly forbidden the use of weapons. This situation shamed the sultan and the state. If the robber bands remained unpunished and the Hasa settlements effectively besieged, the merchants threatened to resort to the traditional Arabian method of protest, emigration.[166]

Although their complaints might be attributed to the panic of people overwrought by a recent attack on fellow traders, there is evidence to support their charges. The Ottoman military presence in Hasa had again fallen to a level too weak to restore order in 1892, and a serious tribal revolt around `Ammara, north of Basra, prevented the province's military and civil authorities from responding quickly to the Arabian crisis.[167] The Hasa government took little effective action against the bandits before receiving reinforcements totalling 800 regular army troops.[168] Restiveness among the population had been growing for some time over this and other problems. By February 1890 Istanbul had heard enough of Hasawi dissatisfaction with the local administration and justice system to order an investigation. The people's charges were heard in the Qatif *Kaza* claims tribunal and the Hufuf court of appeal but apparently were not permanently resolved, perhaps because the Ottoman legal system itself was a target of complaint.[169] If the Hasawi merchants' petition was accurate, the local officials managed to win relief of the pressure from their superiors by lying about their progress. Those superiors tended to equate reform with increasing the Ottoman civil and military presence throughout the *sancak*, as called for in the reform plans of the 1880s, however unwelcome it might be to such influential people as Shaikh

Qâsim in Qatar. The government seemed not to appreciate fully that loss of support from the settled people due to mismanagement invited problems with the British and the bedouins.

These changed circumstances of Arabia in the 1890s invited a direct challenge to the state by a leader seeking to widen his sway; Shaikh Qâsim gave in to the temptation. The Qatari ruler had become disenchanted with his Ottoman overlords in the 1880s. They had given him limited or no support in confrontations with Britain in 1882–83 and 1887 and with Abu Dhabi throughout the decade.[170] He fell into disfavor in 1885–86, when Istanbul received a stream of complaints from Qataris about Qâsim's abuses and oppression, which officials in Doha and Hufuf generally confirmed.[171] The Ottomans also accused him (wrongly) of signing an agreement with the British Consul in Bushire that led to his active role in stirring violence in Hasa.[172] They did not try to remove him, however, at least in part because such an action would dissuade every shaikh from `Udayd to Masqat from submitting to Ottoman authority.[173] Qâsim in turn suspected them of supporting two Qatari rivals in 1885–87, which probably caused him to reconsider their old usefulness as guarantors of his shaikhdom. Istanbul continued to pay him an annual stipend[174], but the plans for stronger civil and military contingents in Doha threatened to reduce his political and financial independence. To protest this he submitted his resignation from the *kaymakamlık*, but it was refused. Nevertheless, on several occasions he withdrew from Doha, leaving it and nearby areas open to bedouin attack.[175] At one such time, February 1893, recalcitrance became defiance when Hafız Mehmet Pasha, the *vali* of Basra, came to Doha with a garrison reinforcement to examine conditions in Qatar, restore peace, take measures to combat the spread of supposed British influence, seek payment of back taxes, and investigate the shaikh's involvement in Hasa's recent unrest.[176].

Fearing that the pasha had determined to take him dead or alive, Qâsim refused to meet him, with a plea of illness as his reason for remaining in the interior. Protected by a large band of Manasir and Bani Hajir bedouins, and using his brother as an emissary to stall any Ottoman action, for a month the shaikh continued to ignore Hafız's messages. Conscious of Qâsim's strength, the *vali* abandoned command for entreaty: all would be forgiven if the shaikh dispersed the bedouins and submitted to the state (although it seems unlikely that the Ottomans would permanently renounce all claim to the customs and other taxes that they charged Qâsim with having withheld for some years).[177] The shaikh countered with an offer to pay Hafız T£10,000 and to address the outstanding Ottoman complaints, if the pasha withdrew with his troops.[178]

Hafız Mehmet was soon forced to take the offensive. Qâsim's bedouins cut his land links to Hasa, seizing messengers and documents. Hafız thus lost contact with the body of Arab tribesmen under the command of Mubarak al-Sabah, brother of the shaikh of Kuwait, that was coming to his assistance. The proximity of this force made credible the rumors in Doha that Qâsim planned a preemptive, surprise attack on the Ottomans. To quell the rising tension, the *vali* arrested some leading Qataris who were suspected of involvement in the imminent attack and sent a column of troops into the desert. This party was to gather information in the interior, raze one of Qâsim's strongholds at Waqba, and seize the weapons stored within it.[179]

The column halted at the dilapidated fort of Shakba, a half-hour journey from Waqba; when the march resumed, 3,000–4,000 bedouins, armed with modern rifles, attacked the cavalry vanguard.[180] The troops retired to Shakba, where they held out until evening. Fearing that they could not hold the crumbling fort through the night, they attempted a withdrawal to Doha; weakened by thirst, hunger (Ramadan had begun), and the day's heat, the soldiers could not withstand the bedouins. A relief force from Doha rescued some of the troops, but not before 117 soldiers were killed, some in the battle, some by having their throats slit by their captors after surrendering. Many more were wounded, and the tribesmen captured 152 rifles and the column's 3-pound cannon.

Leaving the vulnerable Doha fort to a garrison of 100 men, the *vali* and the remaining soldiers embarked on two corvettes, which later withdrew from the harbor to lessen the threat of Qatari attack. The garrison and the departing troops came under fire from the town, suffering further casualties, which caused the corvettes to shell the town while the evacuation was in progress. The garrison was besieged, its water supply cut, until the *vali* released the Qataris he had arrested earlier. The Ottoman mounted troops were then permitted to leave for Hufuf.

As if to confirm Ottoman suspicions of British involvement in the affair, several weeks later the Resident arrived from Bushire in a warship. Qâsim had written to him shortly before the battle, imploring his protection, but the Resident did not act until the Foreign Office learned of the conflict and instructed him to mediate between the combatants. Britain hoped to prevent the dispatch of a large Ottoman force to an area of disputed authority.[181] The *vali* refused to allow him to land in Doha, and the only result of his mission was a meeting with Qâsim's brother, Shaikh Ahmad. Ahmad agreed on Qâsim's behalf to accept any decision by the Resident concerning the affair and asked for a British-protected refuge on the Qatar coast. He also wanted to renew the 1868 Anglo-Qatari agreement or enter a pact similar to those binding the Trucial

Omani shaikhs. Action on these requests would undoubtedly cause a crisis with Istanbul, and thus Britain ignored them. Qâsim nevertheless later put the episode to good use by asserting to the Ottoman officers sent to inquire into the affair that the Resident had offered him protection, which he had refused out of his loyalty to the sultan.[182]

Qâsim's claim helped to protect him from any retribution by his nominal suzerain. The tale of a British offer of protection carried the implicit warning that the shaikh could still turn to a powerful defender—who, once established in Qatar, would be difficult to dislodge—should the Ottomans attempt to punish him for his rebellion. Even if Britain did not interfere, the expense and the large number of troops that would be required to hunt down the culprit bedouins discouraged the state from seeking reprisal.[183] The Ottomans therefore opted for reconciliation, to realize which they appointed a committee of Arab notables, headed by the *naqib* of Basra.[184]

The delegation succeeded in restoring relations between the two sides in June 1893. The Ottomans were to restore calm in the area, allowing the residents of Doha to return safely to the homes they had fled following the fighting, and were to give Qâsim a full pardon. The shaikh was to pay taxes regularly and to bring about the return of the weapons captured by the bedouins.[185] Qâsim immediately evaded the latter condition by claiming that most of the weapons had been seized by Bahraini Na`im tribesmen, who returned home with them, thereby diverting the Ottomans' aggressive intentions from himself to his more innocent neighbor.[186]

The only other important question of the settlement, Qâsim's future role in government, also came to no clear resolution. Qâsim again asked to be relieved of his duties as *kaymakam* on account of his advanced age;[187] again, the resignation was refused. The point was largely moot, however, since after 1893 Qâsim generally delegated the duties of office to his brother, Ahmad, in order to avoid personal contact and cooperation with Ottoman officials. Istanbul did consider transferring the *kaymakamlık* to Ahmad in 1893–94, and again in 1905, but did not follow through.[188] They and everyone else in the region recognized that Qâsim was the most influential man in Qatar, regardless of title and seclusion, and to prevent a further loss of control in the peninsula they had to forgive his sins and permit him unusual independence of action, hoping that the weak check of holding an official position would keep that independence within some limit.[189]

In effect unchastised and unrepentant, Qâsim remained a prestigious figure on the stage of Gulf politics until his death in 1913, not least because he was the living symbol of the most humiliating defeat for the

Ottomans in Arabia since their return in 1871. Previous setbacks, such as the 1874 uprising in Hasa, involved posts overrun by surprise attacks, and relief columns quickly restored the state's supremacy. In Qatar it was the relief column itself that was defeated, despite being heavily armed and prepared for action. The Ottomans then made little attempt to punish the accused tribes, and they allowed the rebellion's leader to escape severe sanctions.

The Ottomans' flaccid response to Qâsim's challenge caused real, long-term damage to their position in Arabia. Qatar became a burden, draining scarce resources, as maintenance of any control there required larger permanent civil and military posts. The garrisons in Hasa also had to be expanded, because a greater display of power was needed to restrain the growing, violent impudence of some tribes.[190] The increasing insecurity made implementation of numerous old and new proposed reforms even more urgent, yet the immediate expense of military and civil reinforcements further weakened a Treasury already too lean to finance many projects. Above all, the hope of impressing upon the Arabs the might and efficiency of the empire died.

This should not have happened as the result of one blow. The Ottomans had had twenty years of relative peace in Arabia—a great opportunity for them to foster solid, mutual ties with the populace, based upon sound methods of keeping the peace and encouraging growth. The desire to protect the well-being of the Gulf's Muslims by ensuring the tranquillity necessary for them to prosper underlay Ottoman policy in the region, but Istanbul assumed that the bonds of religious loyalty tying the Arabians to the sultan could bear almost any burden. When suddenly challenged not by the British, against whom its energies had been concentrated, but rather by its own subjects, it found itself without strong, committed allies and turned indecisive.

As the appearance of beleaguered government gained strength after 1893, local leaders became more willing to act against Ottoman wishes. These included not only Qâsim but the Rashidi amirs of Ha'il and Ibn Sa`ud. The most striking example, however, would prove to be Mubarak al-Sabah. In command of the Arab force that neared Doha in support of *Vali* Hafız Mehmet, Mubarak saw at close range the efficacy of Qâsim's methods of handling his Ottoman overlords. He absorbed the lessons of 1893 and three years later gambled that similar strategies would win him an independent domain in Kuwait. This they did.

Chapter 5

The Case of Kuwait

The previous chapter's description of the problems besetting the Ottoman administration in Arabia concluded with an example of the consequences to be expected from weakened control, the 1893 Qatari unrest. That event foreshadowed the troubles surrounding Shaikh Mubarak al-Sabah's bid for independence in Kuwait. This case deserves investigation in some detail, not only because this period determined the very existence of modern Kuwait, but also because it illustrates so clearly the shortcomings of Ottoman administration in a vital area.

The state could ill afford to let the port fall completely out of its control: Basra and the Shatt were within easy striking distance of it, and as a thriving harbor, it influenced the interior. As Midhat had observed, control of the coast could mean control of Najd, and Ibn Sa'ud was able to start to establish the state of Saudi Arabia largely because of help received from Kuwait. Yet from 1896 to 1914, the Ottomans never found an effective strategy to restore influence over the little town that lay so close to the capital of Basra province.

This record of ineptitude was the result of conditions, already noted in Arabia, that also afflicted Iraq. Too little money, too little manpower, too little equipment hamstrung policy makers. More debilitating were corruption and the related increase in popular dissatisfaction with unfair, arbitrary rule. Most important, however, was the problem of communication. Corruption flourished because officials had little supervision or fear of retribution. Policy had to be shaped in Istanbul without the benefit of prompt, accurate information about events in distant areas. As a result, initiatives did not target the most important possible goals, partly due to overblown concern about Britain, or were outmoded by changed conditions before they could be implemented.

The case of Kuwait also makes clear the crucial role of dynamic local leaders in using Ottoman weaknesses to achieve their own ends. Mubarak created independent Kuwait. He had simple wants—the accumulation of wealth and influence, and the independence in which to enjoy them—and he was not overly particular about how to win them. There was nothing inevitable about his shift into the British camp. Kuwait had lived comfortably under Ottoman suzerainity. If the Ottomans had acted quickly and practically, Mubarak and Kuwait would have remained "theirs." Instead, they gave Mubarak the opportunity to play diplomatic games. He assessed and targeted the fears and desires of the Great Power rivals, and his gambits won him assets from both. Much to the detriment of Ottoman control in Arabia and Iraq, he became the exemplar to be emulated by notables who wished to gain their own independent domains.

Kuwait to 1896 and the Accession of Mubarak to the Shaikhdom

In the quarter century after Midhat Pasha resurrected Ottoman sovereignty over the port and its hinterland, few people other than its inhabitants gave Kuwait much thought. Under the well-established political leadership of the Al Sabah, the community avoided serious disturbances. This allowed the merchants of Kuwait to thrive. The town was practically autonomous in many respects, but it was tied into a thriving regional economy that stretched from the northern Gulf to India and East Africa. Throughout the Ottoman period the port grew in importance as a commercial center, being a natural entrepôt for Najd and southern Iraq, but it still was small in comparison to Basra.[1] Istanbul felt that its rights over the territory were already established and saw no pressing need to break Midhat's promise not to collect taxes or station officials there.[2]

Kuwait was accorded the status of a *kaza* attached to Basra, and the Shaikhs ʿAbdallah (1871–1892) and Muhammad (1892–96) were given the title of *kaymakam*; the Basra provincial gazette in 1890–91 listed no other officers for it while naming twenty-two for Qurna, the other *kaza* attached to Basra.[3] After their defeat by Qatari bedouins brought home the threat of weapon smuggling, the Ottomans toyed with the idea of stationing a corvette to police the trade in Kuwait.[4] There was also some thought given to assuming direct control of the *kaza* at that time, as there was every few years after Rıza Ali's reform proposal in 1884.[5] The only result of these and earlier plans was the award to Muhammad of a generous stipend in 1893 on condition that he preserve Ottoman rights in the area.⁶ Except in providing arms, Kuwait played a purely peripheral part in the intertribal disputes recurring in Najd and southern Iraq, only acting to defend itself against threats from Ibn Rashid and factions of the Muntafiq, Dhafir, and Bani Hajir.⁷ The Sa`udi pretender `Abd al-Rahman b. Faisal and his son `Abd al-`Aziz (Ibn Sa`ud) took advantage of Kuwait's peacefulness, enjoying refuge there as Ottoman pensioners after 1893.

The port's low profile in Gulf affairs saved it from Britain's scrutiny. Throughout the British government's internal debate about the extent of the sultan's sovereignty over the Arabian coast that began with the outburst of piracy in 1878, Kuwait's status never entered dispute. The southern limit of territory acknowledged by Britain as Ottoman gradually shrank from `Udayd to Doha to `Uqayr, but as late as 1893 the Ottoman foreign minister was informed that sovereignty was admitted from Basra to Qatif.⁸ The Sabah family also owned date-palm estates along the Shatt al-Arab near Faw, strengthening the perception of a Kuwaiti tie to the Ottoman empire. Britain in 1895–96 seriously considered holding Istanbul responsible for an attack on the Indian ship *Haripasa* by men of those estates.⁹

Kuwaiti participation in Ottoman military and political schemes deepened the British impression of the sultan's sway over the area. *Valis* had called upon the military assistance of the *kaymakam*-shaikhs in 1871, 1892, and 1894 for operations in Hasa, Qatar, and southern Iraq.¹⁰ Mubarak figured prominently in these operations, leading Kuwaiti land forces in 1871 and 1892, and probably also aided the government during the 1878 troubles in Qatif and southern Iraq, for he was given the rank of *istabl-i amire payesi* (equerry to the sultan) in August 1879.¹¹ In 1893–94 Istanbul considered, and may have granted, honors to reward Mubarak for services rendered in the Qatar campaign, although the value of his assistance was much in dispute.¹² By 1883 the Ottomans had already used his diplomatic services often enough to cause considerable disquiet among the British when he visited Bahrain.¹³ Britain therefore took little immediate interest in Mubarak's murder of his brothers Shaikh Muhammad and Jarrah, regarding it as an Ottoman domestic matter.

Mubarak and his men killed his brothers in the early hours of 8 May 1896 for reasons that are still disputed. The explanation of a recent analyst, for example, that Mubarak resented being rusticated to the desert by Muhammad to take charge of tribal affairs seems unsatisfactory,¹⁴ since Mubarak had acted as bedouin leader under his brother `Abdallah at least as early as 1871.¹⁵ Yet this theory is better than the explanation that gradually won favor among some British and Arab historians. It states that Kuwait had suffered under the weak rule of the indolent

Muhammad and Jarrah, who had shown little determination to defend the land from bedouin attack. They were about to give the government into the hands of a brother-in-law (or maternal uncle; in either case a man without a clear right to rule), Yusuf al-Ibrahim, who was thought to be intent on a policy of Ottomanization. Mubarak—a man as brave, principled, and open-handed as his brothers were weak and grasping[16]—could not allow the continued deterioration of Kuwait's affairs and was forced into drastic action.[17]

This common interpretation is unfortunate, because it suggests that ideology made an irreparable Kuwaiti-Ottoman rupture inevitable. Money more than politics caused the quarrel that resulted in the murder of Muhammad and Jarrah.[18] An early explanation of Mubarak's motives by the British Consul in Basra was that he had killed his brothers to usurp the position and seize the property of Muhammad, who was reportedly quite wealthy.[19] The early twentieth-century historian al-Rashid cites the Kuwaiti *naqib al-ashraf*, who was closely involved as a mediator in the family argument: Mubarak (and his two younger brothers) felt that they had not received their rightful share of the family's wealth, and that Muhammad, Jarrah, and Yusuf al-Ibrahim were too unfairly tight-fisted when Mubarak needed money.[20] Rashid's contemporary al-Qana'i generally confirms this.[21] Even Khaz'al lists Muhammad and Jarrah's tight control of Mubarak's finances as one of the main reasons for the feud.[22]

Mubarak Confounds the Ottomans, 1896–1897

J. G. Lorimer wrote that "the attitude of the Turks toward Shaikh Mubarak was for a considerable time one of neutrality."[23] The statement is misleading, since it implies a lack of interest in Istanbul. Kuwait was a serious preoccupation for the state (and vice versa) from the moment of the murder. It saw the need for a response, but its seeming neutrality arose only from its inability to judge between several loud, determined parties.

Mubarak's actions immediately after his coup make clear that his first thoughts, too, included his relationship with the Ottomans, and that he hoped to preserve the amicable, loose tie formally linking Kuwait to Istanbul. Having gained power by violence, he had to impress upon the government that he now represented continuity, even tranquillity. He wanted above all to win confirmation as the new *kaymakam*, which would simultaneously seem to give an official, routine blessing to the change of ruler and secure to him payment of Muhammad's annual stipend. If he could not attain appointment to the post, at least he had to create enough confusion in government ranks to short-circuit any attempt at armed retribution, to which he was very vulnerable. Spending much to win more, Mubarak immediately started to use his brothers' wealth to recruit supporters among the powerful in the government.[24]

In this effort Mubarak took advantage of the weaknesses in the local Ottoman administration. Bribery and graft had become a serious problem; much of the bureaucracy was very poorly paid, while the dispersal of power among several local authorities allowed top officials to pocket money while blaming others for the province's deterioration.[25] Mubarak thus was able to gain the interest of several key men. The most important of these were Receb Pasha, Marshal of the VI (Baghdad) Army Corps; Ebülhuda, Sultan Abdülhamid's close adviser; and Mehmet Cemalüddin Efendi, the *Şeyhülislâm*.[26] Over the course of the campaign to secure Ottoman recognition, Mubarak continued to purchase the aid of high and lesser officials in Basra, Baghdad, and Istanbul. Their assistance was often decisive in undermining any coherent Ottoman reaction to the developing Kuwait problem.

Mubarak's attempt to win acceptance and appointment as *kaymakam* did not immediately succeed, however, because one key official refused the proffered bribe. Within two days of the slaying of Muhammad and Jarrah, the *vali* of Basra, Hamdi Pasha, was urging Istanbul to order a military occupation of Kuwait,[27] and even a reported offer of T£10,000 from Mubarak could not sway his antagonism.[28] This represented only a partial setback for Mubarak, however, since his other efforts ensured that Ottoman attention shifted from him to a series of long-distance, multi-party arguments among Basra, Baghdad, and Istanbul.

As a governor of his disposition might, the mercurial Hamdi burst into his superiors' consciousness like a sudden thunderstorm on a sultry day, painting a picture of crisis where there had been but relative calm before. He bombarded the Porte with reasons to act against Mubarak. It was wrong that Kuwait, the best Gulf port, should be independently ruled by its shaikhs when more distant areas (Qatif, Hufuf) had proper officials. Britain would renew its twenty-year-long campaign to make of Kuwait a Bahrainlike dependency. The Kuwaiti people had long wanted to be freed from despotic Sabah rule, and the violence among them could infect others. Dissension (*fitne*) would spread. To prevent this, now was the time to strike; 300 men would be more than enough to restore order. Kuwait could then be reconstituted as a regular *sancak*.[29]

Hamdi cited every circumstance that had guaranteed government reaction in the past, yet in this case his cables caused more irritation than alarm in Istanbul. Messenger obscured message. The Minister of the Interior passed the *vali's* telegrams to the Grand Vezir under cover of a sour commentary on Hamdi's abilities. The suggestion that Kuwait should be invaded and ruled directly contradicted the long-established policy of leaving the *kaza* in the local shaikhs' hands. In Arabia, on the other hand, war with Britain had almost started over the control of Zubara in 1895 due to Hamdi's bungling. Then he failed to prevent the *mutasarrıf* of Necd from deserting his post and coming to Istanbul without authorization; he did not even appoint an interim deputy to govern that important territory. During these past and present crises, Hamdi failed to give Istanbul important information or sent conflicting messages. This administration, the interior minister concluded, was beyond salvation.[30]

Istanbul eventually replaced Hamdi, but not until more than five months passed; in the meantime it had no authoritative source for the intelligence it needed to begin consideration of possible responses to Mubarak's coup. The Porte began to receive new information six weeks after the event, but again the reports conflicted. According to one story that reached Istanbul, the British Resident in Bushire had instigated the assassinations as part of a plan to achieve hegemony over the Gulf. Muhammad and Jarrah were killed because they refused to join an "Arab confederation" with Qâsim al-Thani, `Isa al-Khalifa, and Ibn Rashid.[31] The Ottomans did not act on this challenging report, however; according to the British embassy councilor Stavrides, they were unwilling "to cause a new complication to arise."[32] After hearing this rumor, in fact, a simultaneous message from the VI (Baghdad) Corps Marshal had blunted whatever impulse Istanbul felt to interfere in Kuwait.

Mubarak picked a very capable supporter in Receb Pasha. The arguments advanced to forestall action against Mubarak were practically as compelling as those used to promote it and went far beyond the one attributed to him by a Kuwaiti chronicler, that this disaster was but one of the normal, unending occurrences among the bedouin that would cost far too much to police.[33] Receb pointed out to the Minister of War that, with the death of Muhammad, Jarrah, and their sons,[34] Mubarak was now clearly the fittest candidate to head the Al Sabah. Under the circumstances, the Kuwaitis absolutely rejected any thought of retribution, even by any heirs. Given the lack of Ottoman experience in governing Kuwait, leaving it without a shaikh would make it vulnerable to local and foreign intriguers. More important than any search for the killer was the restoration of peace and order; the best way to do this was to follow precedent and appoint Mubarak *kaymakam*.[35]

Receb's arguments carried weight. Without a suitable alternate candidate for the shaikhdom, removal of Mubarak would necessitate creation of an entirely new administration in unfamiliar territory. It would break precedent and surely ruffle Kuwaiti opinion. Istanbul had found the present *vali* of Basra wanting in the discharge of his normal duties; could it trust him to undertake a difficult new task with a reasonable hope of success? Such considerations must have given added potency to Mubarak's advocates in Istanbul, for orders were sent to Hamdi to cease all plans against Mubarak, preparatory to appointing him *kaymakam* in late June.[36] The central government continued to hesitate before taking a final step, however.

Almost two months had passed before even this hint of action arose, yet with the passage of time the view of the affair from Istanbul grew ever cloudier. Two diametrically opposed opinions had been advanced by top-rank provincial officials, and each argument sounded plausible. No independent official of high rank who could investigate authoritatively was available on the scene. The voices of other interested parties also multiplied and clamored to be heard. They too were in disagreement. Mubarak requested appointment as *kaymakam* and tribal chief of Kuwait and avowed his devotion to Istanbul. Telegrams bearing the names of notables and others in Kuwait supported Mubarak, warning that they might have to flee their homes if he were not named to protect them from neighboring tribes. Hamdi promptly disputed these supporting telegrams' veracity and authenticity. The slain shaikhs' sons (who had lately surfaced in Basra) also demanded the righting of the wrongs done by their fathers' killer, Mubarak.[37]

Deliberation among Ottoman officials remained stuck at this fruitless level for a further eight months. The details of the arguments varied slightly. Generally Mubarak and his supporters swore their past and future fidelity to, and willingness to serve, the sultan and emphasized the pacifying effect that his official appointment would have. The anti-Mubarak faction pressed the Porte to take military action, stressing the unsettling effect that leaving such a severe injustice unpunished would have on the region. When a deadlock between the two sides became clear, each charged the other with working for the British. In July 1896 Hamdi forwarded reports from anti-Mubarak informants on the suspiciously friendly reception accorded a British warship in Kuwait.[38] Mubarak's followers later charged that Yusuf al-Ibrahim, the protector of the murdered shaikhs' sons and supposed ally of the Ottomans, was a foreign subject spending vast sums in a campaign to spread anarchy.[39] The (incorrect) information of both sides did not tip the balance of argument in favor of either; it merely added to the pressure on Istanbul for a decision it felt incapable to make.

At last a resolution seemed to take shape after two necessary steps were taken: the appointment of a new *vali*, Arif Pasha, to Basra[40] in September 1896 and the submission of this new arrival's reports on the Kuwait affair over the following six months.[41] Although more equivocal than Hamdi's, Arif's findings came to support the anti-Mubarak side in the dispute. In January 1897 he had stated that, although the shaikh's guilt in the killing of his brothers could not be officially proved, there was not much doubt of it. Nevertheless Arif had apparently seconded Receb Pasha's idea that resolving the affair quickly by naming Mubarak *kaymakam* was better than getting justice by time-consuming military operations. While he recognized that it was preferable to avoid radical change in the *kaza*'s administration, by March he came to the conclusion that neither the local inhabitants nor the Ottomans would benefit from the usurper's continued presence in Kuwait.[42] Regarding the case of the murdered men's sons, at present not only was Mubarak denying them their inheritance, he was also effectively holding their mothers and wives hostage in Kuwait. Nothing short of a military occupation could force Mubarak out and restore justice; this would be expensive, but the introduction of customs, taxes on pearls, and quarantine and port fees could defray the costs.

Having finally received firm information from a source that he trusted, the Minister of the Interior submitted an urgent appeal for action. He grasped the key point of the affair—one that had been missed four years earlier in Qatar—that permitting such an egregious crime and insult to the state to go unpunished, especially in a place only one day's march from the provincial capital, would tempt every ambitious man in the already unruly region to defy the government. It was vitally important to preserve government rule by seizing Mubarak and, if necessary, his confederates, removing them to Basra and naming one of Muhammad's sons *kaymakam*. This would keep the post, as before, in Sabah hands, while choosing an amenable candidate would allow the Ottomans to exercise better control of Kuwait in future. The plan worked its way through the Council of State and Council of Ministers toward approval in late May 1897.[43]

The passage of a full year between the birth of the crisis and the first serious attempt to solve it raises questions about Istanbul's alarmingly sluggish reaction, given that all officials recognized the importance and delicacy of the situation. The Porte had other pressing concerns closer to Istanbul: the worsening of Greek nationalist violence in Crete, which broke into open revolt in January 1897, and the resulting heightened tensions with Athens, which led to a month-long war following the Greek invasion of Janina (Epirus) on 10 April.[44] Competing nationalist groups based in Bulgaria, Greece, and Serbia intensified campaigns of violence in Macedonia, further distracting attention and resources from Asia. More intriguing is the issue of Hamdi's continuation in office for almost half a year after the Interior Minister led such a strong attack on his credibility. It is very likely that he had 'friends in high places', possibly in the Palace. In the early stages of the Kuwait problem Abdülhamid's interest was aroused but not inflamed,[45] and the influence upon him of Ebülhuda and other friends of Mubarak probably weakened any impulse at Yıldız for action as urged by Hamdi. The sultan presumably knew of the *vali*'s personal probity through his extensive intelligence system, however, and this would have been much in Hamdi's favor. That Hamdi had potent allies during this bureaucratic fighting is indicated not only by his six-month continuation in Basra but also by his subsequent reappointment to the post in 1899.

Mubarak Invites Britain to Enter the Scene

The damage done to the empire's prestige and position in the Gulf by its overlong process of picking a program of action might have proven only temporary, if the other actors in the drama had been content to sit passively awaiting developments. They were not, however. Mubarak did not rely solely on the chance of being named *kaymakam*; as he exhausted the most immediate means of effecting a reconciliation with his nephews and Yusuf, he gradually expanded the scope of his campaign. This opened the road to a plea for British protection as his despair of other solutions grew.

Mubarak and his supporters hoped to convince the Ottomans that he did not represent discontinuity and disruption (vide Receb's claim that the assassinations were part of normal bedouin practice), and the most persuasive piece of evidence for that would be an open reconciliation with his nephews and Yusuf. He tried hard to achieve one by blandishments and influential intermediaries. For a short time after his coup he might have thought a containment of the quarrel easily achievable: the sons of the murdered men remained in Kuwait, where the shaikh could exert some control over them. Although they may have stayed only to discover the depth of popular support for a counterattack against Mubarak, their continued presence in Kuwait presented an image of normalcy to the outside world. When they and some supporters finally fled to Basra and the protection of Hamdi, that illusion was broken.[46] Mubarak then concentrated his efforts on Yusuf, their elder adviser, protector, and financial backer.[47]

One of the few strokes of good luck that Yusuf enjoyed in this affair was his absence from Kuwait at the time of Mubarak's coup. Mubarak almost certainly would have killed him, his brothers' closest associate. Yusuf had earlier retired to Qasr Sabiya on the headland opposite the main port, however, where he was in a good position to ward off all but a determined attack from Kuwait. Mubarak quickly sent a messenger to Yusuf to promise him security of life and property if he were to return to Kuwait, but Yusuf gave the assurances little credit. He remained in Qasr Sabiya until a Kuwaiti source warned him of a rumored impending attack. He thereupon left by boat for Basra and his home at Dawra, which lay on the Shatt al-Arab below Abadan.[48]

Far from discouraged, Mubarak continued to press Yusuf by other means. Even as he attempted to persuade the government that Yusuf had killed the two shaikhs,[49] Mubarak sent his rival sweetly worded letters that urged a reconciliation for the good of Kuwait. When that did not work, he sent a delegation of notables led by his brother Hamud. Again Yusuf rejected the assurances. Mubarak then sent an envoy to Bombay to ask another member of the Al Ibrahim to restrain his near relation. The man denied that he had any power to curb Yusuf's freedom of action. Finally Mubarak turned to Yusuf's powerful neighbor, Shaikh Miz`al of Muhammara (Khorramshahr), who acted for a time as intermediary until being assassinated in a separate dispute in 1897.[50]

From May 1896 to February 1897 Mubarak's hopes of winning his rivals' acceptance of his fait accompli seemed to get no closer to realization, but he could take some satisfaction in other developments. His orchestrated campaign of petitions and testimonials, seconded by the support of suborned officials, had created confusion in Istanbul, where the lack of hard facts made decision on a firm plan of action impossible. Mubarak had hastened the fall from grace of Hamdi, his most determined foe in the government. He reportedly bribed Hamdi's successor, Arif, which seemed to bring reconciliation with his Ottoman suzerain almost within his grasp. It was even rumored that Arif had given his own recognition of Mubarak as *kaymakam* early in the new year.[51]

With little warning, however, the situation soured. The confusion sown by Mubarak now worked against him, and Istanbul continued to hesitate on the appointment of a *kaymakam*. Any doubt about the value of Arif's aid that this failure caused must have been magnified by the arrival of the quarantine inspector in February. Within several months of the purported handsome bribe to the *vali*, Mubarak found himself saddled with the first non-Kuwaiti Ottoman official ever to be stationed in the port. That a chill fell on his relations with Arif seems clear from the *vali*'s rather negative report on the Kuwait problem in March 1897. Mubarak could be excused for feeling that the Ottomans were "grasping and unreliable."[52] He now began to consider seriously an application to the British for support. The British Consul in Basra reported that Mubarak wanted an interview with the Resident in Bushire, in which he would ask for establishment of a British protectorate over Kuwait.[53]

Rather to the relief of Britain's officials, the interview was delayed until September. Circumstances prevented either Mubarak or his representatives from going to Bushire, while the British saw no need to travel to Kuwait in search of unnecessary entanglements. Changes of Gulf personnel also temporarily blunted any drive for aggressive diplomacy, as the Basra Consul (serving since 1895) and the Bushire Resident (since 1894) were replaced by inexperienced men in March and June 1897, respectively. Policy makers in India and Britain also needed the time to gather information about Kuwait and to argue amongst themselves about its status.

Discussions about Kuwait's dependency on Istanbul tied into those about the *Haripasa* piracy case of September 1895, responsibility for which was attributed to men from Muhammara and from the Sabah date groves in Faw.[54] The Bushire Resident and the Baghdad Consul had urged that the Ottomans be held responsible for the Kuwaiti action, but no official demand for justice or compensation was ever lodged, in part because of the Istanbul embassy's description of Kuwait as practically independent.[55] This objection was later weakened as details of Mubarak's recent relations with the Ottomans became known. His energetic campaign to win the *kaymakamlık*, and his rumored acceptance of the post from Arif, seemed clearly to establish Ottoman influence, if not protection, over Kuwait. Mubarak also flew the Ottoman flag, and a visit from a British man-of-war in July 1896 had caused him considerable alarm and embarrassment.[56]

Yet even with private acknowledgment of heavy Ottoman influence in Kuwait, London did not want to raise another messy issue at a time of tense relations with the Porte. The chill between the two powers that developed following the British occupation of Cyprus and Egypt deepened sharply in the 1890s. Negotiations over Egypt finally broke down in 1894. From 1895 to February 1897, Britain was the only European power to put serious pressure on Istanbul to improve treatment of Armenians, many of whom died in pogroms in 1894–96. The prime minister/foreign minister, the marquis of Salisbury, even briefly considered seizing Jedda to force acceptance of reform. Britain was also one of the Hellenophile states among the powers that imposed an end to the war with Greece, by which resolution the Ottomans had to give up control of Crete and all of the territory won from the badly beaten Greeks.[57] The government of Salisbury had abandoned the old policy of preserving the Ottoman empire, but raising the issue of sovereignty over an obscure corner of the

THE CASE OF KUWAIT

Persian Gulf promised more pain than it was worth. The British contented themselves with unofficially raising with the Ottoman foreign minister the idea of a mixed Ottoman-Iranian commission to investigate piracy in the Shatt. Since Istanbul and Teheran were not on good terms, the minister instead suggested that Britain give a simple warning to Kuwait. This was the course finally adopted in mid-1897.[58]

Although Britain's stance on Kuwait accorded well with its longstanding Gulf policy—no involvement unless British subjects or the Trucial chiefs suffered damages[59]—it did mark an intangible shift. Whereas Ottoman sovereignty between Basra and Qatif had been explicitly recognized as recently as 1893, the unofficial talk with the Ottoman foreign minister that led to Britain's warning to Mubarak about piracy set a precedent. The meeting gave mutual recognition that both states had interests in the area.[60] On a psychological level, moreover, the airing of arguments on giving protection to Kuwait brought the idea into focus in official minds and gave it a certain legitimacy. It began to win a few supporters, notably in the Indian government.[61] Britain refused Mubarak's application for protected status in September (just as it had not responded to a request for support from one of Muhammad's sons in July),[62] but the very act of soliciting protection suggested that Mubarak was an independent ruler.[63] The discussions of 1896–97 thus greatly weakened several potential obstacles to Britain's volte-face of 1899, when it was to conclude an exclusive agreement with Mubarak.

A Frustrated Istanbul Acts, but Mubarak Gains

Frustrated by the lack of information, an impatient Ottoman government leaned toward a military solution in 1897–98. By this time, however, the confusion of words began to be augmented by one of events. Istanbul was kept off balance by developments, notably the implosion of the Basra regime, that similarly could not be assessed accurately without better reporting. Under such conditions Mubarak and his men found opportunities to improve his chances.

That he survived to make an appeal to the British, Mubarak had to thank his ally, Receb Pasha, and his enemy, Yusuf al-Ibrahim. When ordered to prepare for the expedition to Kuwait, the Baghdad army commander responded very slowly. While a ship, some marines, and a commanding officer were gathered in Basra, no army soldiers were assigned by Baghdad, nor did Receb communicate with the *vali*. Arif complained about this twice to Istanbul over the next six weeks, but to no avail.[64] Without troops or real military authority, the *vali* had no means at hand to react effectively to a crisis created by a supposed Ottoman ally on 30 June 1897.

THE CASE OF KUWAIT

Yusuf al-Ibrahim made a serious mistake by attempting an attack on Kuwait. Having waited thirteen months in vain for effective Ottoman action against Mubarak, and unaware of or unimpressed by the current planned punitive expedition, the shaikh of Dawra recruited and armed a large body of men, many from Iran. These he put in ships, by which a swift descent could be made on an unsuspecting Kuwait. The plan might have succeeded—Mubarak knew nothing of the attack—had the raiders not looted a stray Kuwaiti boat, only to release it after the captain promised not to warn his home port of its impending danger. The boat promptly sped to Kuwait, and Yusuf had to withdraw without firing a shot when he found his enemies on alert.[65]

The abortive raid accomplished nothing save the disruption of the Ottoman attack on Kuwait. It dismayed the government for at least four reasons. Many of the marauders were from Iran, a country that Istanbul viewed with great suspicion. It also suggested that Yusuf had acted like an independent potentate, smuggling arms and setting up strongholds on the Shatt. Such activity might confirm Mubarak's charge that he was stirring trouble in the service of Britain. Such an extralegal resort to force could also tempt neighboring tribes into unruliness (a point that Receb Pasha soon pressed by warning of imminent trouble among the Muntafiq).[66] That would expand the present opportunity to meddle that Yusuf had given to the British. Although Britain had had absolutely no involvement in the scheme, the presence of an Indian navy ship in the vicinity and a rumor about its contacts with those involved made the Ottomans suspect strongly that its officers directed the plot.[67] A report on the British ship's visit to Kuwait, submitted by the captain of an Ottoman gunboat on quarantine patrol, deepened suspicions. He stated that a British officer offered Mubarak assistance, including delivering Yusuf to him, but that the Kuwaiti shaikh refused, claiming to follow the orders only of his protector, the Ottoman state.[68]

The bundle of newly acute threats to stability that Yusuf's scheme presented to the Ottomans reopened the case of Kuwait just a few weeks after it seemed on the way to resolution. The army officer and naval ship assigned to the Kuwait expedition went to the Faw area instead, where they tracked down and seized several of the raiders' boats.[69] Yusuf had to flee to Bahrain, where he vainly sought British assistance.[70] As his opponents sank into disgrace, so Mubarak rose in Ottoman opinion. Alarmed just as others were by the threats of British interference and spreading anarchy, Arif abruptly shifted to Receb's position. He advised Istanbul to resolve the *kaymakamlık* dispute immediately by giving the office to Mubarak, on condition that the murdered shaikhs' sons' rights of inheritance be satisfied.[71]

Sultan Abdülhamid asked the Council of Ministers to reopen discussion of the problem, which also was to be investigated by a military commission. The council reviewed old and new arguments before returning to the basic dilemma. Two possible paths of action lay open: send in troops to restore peace and order, or use a soft approach, trying to gain goodwill. The first course was more appropriate, but the various dangers brought to light by the recent raid made it risky. There was no guarantee of success, and no one could foresee the ramifications of violent action. The second choice was now becoming more attractive, especially since Mubarak had recently sent the Porte and the Palace telegrams confirming his devotion and service to the sultanate. He asked to be named *kaymakam* in order to restore peace and the glory of the state to the area. The Council therefore decided that the immediate gains to be won by a quick, bloodless resolution of the *kaymakam* problem now outweighed the disadvantages and so recommended giving the title to Mubarak.

Several conditions were added to the recommendation, however, that were sure to displease Mubarak. The Council, and the military commission of enquiry, were much troubled by the continuing weakness of the government in Basra, of which the total absence of direct Ottoman influence in Kuwait was the prime example. To increase both Mubarak's dependence on the Porte and the state's means of controlling affairs in the *kaza*, the ministers advised giving the shaikh a regular salary and appointing a qualified member of the Basra *ulema* as canonical court judge (*hâkimüşşer`*). A body of gendarmes would accompany this official to help him maintain order. It was hoped that a gradual reformation of Kuwait's administration could thus be introduced. The complaints of those outside the *kaza*, including the slain shaikhs' sons, also would be examined and resolved justly.[72]

Timely implementation of these recommendations—which might have forestalled Mubarak's application to the British a month later—proved impossible when the Basra government gave definitive proof that it was incapable of swift, coherent action. In August and September 1897, before the local administration completely collapsed, it gave Mubarak glimpses only of the stick, none of the carrot. He was warned (without effect) to release the families of his nephews,[73] and the provincial administrative council tried to transfer to the dead shaikhs' sons the title to a small part of the Sabah date groves.[74] The latter action had been discussed but not ordered by the Porte, which led Mubarak's coalition in Iraq immediately to charge that it resulted from British-financed bribery by Yusuf in Istanbul and Basra. This in turn helped to launch a welter of accusations (concerning shady land transfers and the navy's continuing inefficacy in policing the Gulf) that led to the general breakdown of

Basra's government into squabbling factions. The *vali, defterdar,* Basra naval and military commanders, provincial administrative council, junior officials, and local Arab notables (including Talib, son of the Basra *Naqib al-Ashraf* and one of Mubarak's allies, Mubarak himself, and Yusuf al-Ibrahim) suddenly in mid-September hurled at each other various colorful charges: bribery, larceny, graft, incompetence, drunkenness, dereliction of duty, mistreatment of officials, false reporting to Istanbul, and attempted murder.[75]

Obviously nothing could be done about Kuwait until the mess in Basra was cleared up and a more capable *vali* appointed;[76] on this occasion Istanbul managed to take quick action. The *vali* of Diyarbakr was selected to inspect and settle the situation.[77] When new circumstances almost immediately forced the government to try to get as speedy a resolution as possible, however, it gave the task to a nearer official—Receb Pasha.[78] The development that put a premium on swift action was a report that Yusuf had struck an alliance with Qâsim al-Thani, the Ottomans' old Qatari nemesis, to attack Kuwait. Such an extension of the conflict to the most recalcitrant of Arabs was to be feared more than the ill effects of appointing a fratricide to the *kaymakamlık* of Kuwait. Selection of the markedly pro-Mubarak Receb thus became acceptable, even desirable, since he was most likely to mend relations with the Kuwaiti leader.[79] Receb in fact excused himself from the task on account of pressing matters at his Baghdad headquarters, but his place was taken by his like-minded chief of staff, Muhsin Pasha. Muhsin was to become one of Mubarak's staunchest allies. He speedily restored some order to Basra and was soon able to inform Mubarak of his appointment as *kaymakam*.[80]

This apparent victory for Mubarak did not resolve the crisis, it merely moved it to a new phase, as once again confusion in the government disrupted execution of a clear policy. For one and a half years the Ottoman government had allowed the problem to grow, as administrative turmoil blocked action but amplified alarming noises. Now that it had chosen and executed one of the two basic policy options (i.e., the soft approach, accepting Mubarak as *kaymakam*), it promptly ensured the shaikh's further alienation by continuing its confusing activity. For Mubarak it was undoubtedly unsettling to see the Ottomans gathering a large force, whose goal was rumored to be Kuwait, at the same time that they were recognizing him.[81] He had little chance of defeating such a force, especially if it attacked in conjunction with Qâsim al-Thani's band from the south.

Ironically this army was originally gathered to prevent by force the shaikh of Qatar from attacking Kuwait, and Mubarak himself inadvertently helped to pressure the government into assuming a threatening military posture. When he learned of Yusuf's agitations in Doha, he sent a message and a "handsome gift" to the *mutasarrıf* in Hasa, Said Pasha, asking him to warn Basra about the violent disruption of the peace made imminent by Qâsim's unjust assault on a faithful servant of the Porte.[82] Said did send alarming reports about Yusuf and Qâsim's preparations for war, which included arming and mounting members of several powerful, barely controllable tribes. He also alerted Basra that Qâsim was trying to draw the Al Rashid into the conflict, thus threatening to spread unrest far to the west and north. His messages warned that he could not stop the raiders, although other tribes might be able to help.[83] The idea of giving the `Ajman, Al Murra, and Manasir free rein to make war, even on Qâsim's followers, could hardly be well received in Istanbul.

Increasing the pressure on the Porte did not ease that on Mubarak, however, but rather almost forced realization of the oft-discussed plan to occupy Kuwait. Istanbul became so worried about eruption of a major "Arab incident" that it undertook to meet Qâsim's ends, if he would forswear violent means and return to Qatar. Qâsim had telegraphed that, while he did not intend to act against the sultan's wishes, as one of Abdülhamid's officials he had to address the complaints of Mubarak's nephews. They had requested, and waited in vain for, help from the authorities in Basra before turning in desperation to the *kaymakam* of Qatar. Since Qâsim claimed to be acting in his official role, it was easy for the state to adopt as its duty an investigation of Mubarak's actions in the murder of his brothers and the dispute over their estates. Reassured slightly by his tone, the Ottomans now hoped it would suffice to order Qâsim, on pain of severe reprisal, not to attack Mubarak. Instead of adhering to the original plan of sending troops directly to Qatar to avert the threatened clash, Istanbul now wanted the force to march into Kuwait and thus allow a full investigation of all complaints.[84] Yet again, an end to the twenty-month-old problem seemed at hand.

It never materialized. As happened so frequently to Istanbul's plans in distant Arabia, creating a consensus for a forceful policy proved difficult, and changing circumstances overtook slow-moving preparations. Time was needed to gather and ready the expeditionary force. Because the Porte could not trust any official in Basra—many of whom, including *Vali* Arif, were being replaced because of the recent scandals—it wanted to send a high-ranking man from Istanbul to investigate the various complaints. A tour of such a troubled, distant province would take at least three or four months. This was not supposed to delay action concerning Mubarak and Qâsim, but it could nevertheless create a certain amount of nervous turmoil and hesitation among the local authorities.[85] Of greater consequence were changed perceptions of those not immediately party to the troubles. Naming Mubarak *kaymakam* amounted to forgiving him for the murder of his predecessor; the theft of his nephews' inheritance was now the only real charge outstanding against him.[86] Having failed for one and a half years to bring Mubarak to book for several serious crimes, could the government now attack him over one accusation just after it accepted him into its own ranks? Such action would only confirm the local image of the Ottomans as an erratic, arbitrary power.

This in turn could give greater scope to another growing problem perceived in Istanbul, the awakening of European interest in the Kuwait affair. When recommending the action against Kuwait, the ministerial committee noted certain foreigners' preparations to take advantage of the unrest, as well as the increasing talk about the affair among ambassadors in Istanbul.[87] Anxiety about Great Power interference found a focus in February 1898, when the Ottoman Consul in Bombay reported a British build-up of troops and ships off Oman. Although the event purportedly sparking the muster was unrest in Iran, which had led to the killing of a British telegraph official in Jask, the possibility of the flotilla's turning to aid a strike on Hasa's coast by Qâsim and Yusuf could not be ignored.[88] Tying up troops in Kuwait at a time of renewed threat to the south lost attraction. Heightening Istanbul's concern was a detailed analysis of Anglo-Ottoman relations and in particular Britain's aspirations in the Persian Gulf, which the vice-consul in London submitted to the sultan in March 1898. Among the document's points was a judgment that rivalry with Russia made Britain determined to win an unchallengeable position in the Gulf, or even to take over the entire southern tier of the Ottoman empire—creating a land link from Egypt to India—should Russia move into Anatolia.[89] The vice-consul suggested steps to strengthen the Gulf Arabs' ties to the state. One important recommendation was to treat the people, who were largely of bedouin background, according to a swift, straightforward code of simple justice. The present corrupt, arbitrary administration alienated the Arabs and gave foreigners an excuse to meddle.[90] From its beginning the Kuwait problem had been handled so badly that belated military action might only make the situation worse.

For five months, therefore, the troops remained encamped in Basra, ready to act should Qâsim start to march but otherwise ignored, until they had to disperse. The force included much of the VI Army's reserves, whose recall Receb requested in May to handle a serious outbreak of violence in Mosul province; the troops also had to be moved before the Basra summer could wreak havoc on them.[91] In fits and starts the soldiers moved north.[92] The task of resolving the Kuwait problem now devolved upon the *naqib al-`ashraf* of Basra, Rajab Efendi, who was somehow to persuade Mubarak to come to the provincial capital in order to investigate all complaints.[93] He also was asked to go to Qatar to investigate a recent confrontation between the people and the garrison of Doha.[94] His appointment emphasized Istanbul's frustration over the inefficacy of civil and military officials in Basra province.

Rajab Efendi was becoming one of Abdülhamid II's most trusted agents of influence in the area. The sultan recognized that religion was one of the strongest factors binding Arabia to Istanbul, and he tried through his Islamic policy to strengthen the tie. He thus turned for help in Basra to Rajab, who as leader of the town's community of descendants of the Prophet Muhammad enjoyed great local prestige. Other authorities having produced little visible result in the affair, Abdülhamid now sought, in using a religious dignitary, to win Mubarak's submission to him, the caliph, by emphasizing their bond of faith. This decision carried certain risks, however: as a leading member of the local community, Rajab had long-established ties to many Arab notables, including the shaikh of Kuwait, and the exclusivity of his identification with Istanbul's interests in this case was open to question. The course of events suggests that, while Receb and Muhsin Pashas insulated Mubarak from a military strike, Rajab Efendi joined the ranks of religious leaders who softened other Ottoman pressure tactics.

Rajab's friendly attitude toward Mubarak was of importance because Istanbul's policy on Kuwait was entering a new phase, in which it tried to reduce tensions by letting Arab leaders play a leading part as intermediaries or surrogates for the Ottomans. After the murder of Muhammad and Jarrah, the Ottomans had had numerous opportunities to initiate a forceful policy but had frittered them away. The longer the dispute continued, the wider its repercussions spread as both sides looked for help in breaking the stalemate. After mid-1898 the Ottomans found that they had maneuvered themselves into a position where they could do little but react to developments initiated by others. Discredited and hamstrung by weak, squabbling officials, the government had to rely more on third parties to coax or threaten Mubarak into submission;[95] except in rare circumstances, it confined itself to a modest campaign of (often legalistic) harassment. The use of intermediaries was a tactic of the hard-pressed (cf. Mubarak's search for someone to stop Yusuf's calls for justice in 1896), and the appointment of the *naqib* surely expressed Istanbul's view of the futility of working through its own subordinate organs in Basra.[96] So did the sultan's unusual decision to form an independent commission to settle the inheritance argument. In order to ensure that its decision would be accepted, its members were to be reliable people with no con-

THE CASE OF KUWAIT

nection to the matter and acceptable to both sides.[97] Since both parties had had such bad experiences with government officials, this condition limited the pool largely to local notables. Thus one of the first members selected was Ahmad Pasha, brother of the *naqib*.[98] Intermediaries and arbiters, even if independent, usually can apply only moderate pressure to recalcitrants, however, and in this case they had almost no ability to force Mubarak into compliance. Less than six months after the commission was proposed, the shaikh of Kuwait finally won Britain's protection.

Mubarak and Britain

Commitment of Britain's firm support to Mubarak did not come about because of any new wooing stratagem of the shaikh; indeed, he did not ask again for its protection. Although his position was by no means certain, his enduring success in defying the Ottomans was heartening. They had not sequestered the income of the disputed Sabah properties in Iraq, and his highly placed friends made it unlikely that any surprise attack would catch him unprepared. He maintained good relations with Arab leaders, such as Shaikh Khaz`al of Muhammara, and tribes, notably the `Ajman. These ties lessened the threat of attack from nongovernmental foes; his boast that his followers outnumbered Qâsim's raiders by more than five to one,[99] while perhaps exaggerated, was not totally misleading. He felt sufficiently secure in mid-1898 to have the `Ajman take the offensive against Qâsim's allies, the Bani Hajir and Manasir, thus breaking his own promises of good behavior, including those of a truce recently brokered by the *naqib*.[100] The immediate consequences seemed to justify his confidence: the raid brought him only a rebuke from the *vali*, a demand for the return of booty and another round of the *naqib*'s diplomacy. When the British Resident arrived from Bushire to conclude an agreement with Mubarak in January 1899, therefore, he found that Mubarak considered his position more secure than it had been when he first asked for Britain's protection.[101]

Thus the causes of the abrupt British decision to reach an accord with the shaikh of Kuwait lay not in changed conditions in that territory but rather in altered perspectives of British and Indian policy makers. One important change was the culmination of a long process. During the 1890s the Age of Imperialism finally reached maturity; the Great Powers of Europe had grabbed much of the underdeveloped world and were beginning to fight over the remaining available pieces. The Fashoda crisis of 1898 marked the climax of Anglo-French rivalry in Africa and threatened to spark a war. The race for Siberia, China, and Southeast Asia caused several diplomatic conflicts and one major military clash, the

Russo-Japanese War of 1904. The Persian Gulf also became one of the arenas of contest. France opened a consulate in Masqat in 1894, and later a coal depot, which led to a brief crisis with Britain in 1899. Germany's appointment of a consul in Bushire stirred unease in some in Britain.[102] Russian influence grew ever stronger in northern Iran; war with Britain would result from a concerted effort to extend it to the Gulf, a gateway to India.[103]

One influential man who had long argued forcefully for a major expansion of the British presence in the Gulf to counteract the Russian threat was Lord Curzon, and his appointment as Viceroy of India in November 1898 gave him the opportunity to push his program. As subtle as an elephant, he brushed aside all arguments against turning the Gulf into a British lake. When he was named to the post, he drew up a strongly worded memorandum arguing for assumption of a protectorate over Kuwait.[104]

Curzon's views on the shaikhdom had been reinforced by those of another recently appointed official, the Bushire Resident, Major M. J. Meade. Meade came to the post with no prior experience in Gulf affairs. The little background information that he possessed had come from Curzon's grand testimonial to the virtues of expanding Britain's imperial reach, *Persia and the Persian Question*, published in 1892.[105] Meade therefore enthusiastically supported the idea of a protectorate over Kuwait from the moment he learned of Mubarak's wishes. He had no illusion that Mubarak had any natural inclination toward the British,[106] but that only made Meade more eager to establish their influence there before another power could. He and several other like-minded officials adduced a number of reasons (of dubious validity) for protection: control of a major center of piracy and slavetrading, security of a terminus for a long-discussed railway from Port Said, and prevention of an Ottoman takeover that would seriously threaten British trade.[107] These arguments met with some skepticism in high circles, but not when reiterated privately to Lord Curzon.[108] When the subject of protection arose again in late 1898, therefore, Resident Meade and Viceroy Curzon were in accord and well supplied with arguments for extending a British shield over the shaikhdom.

The event that caused reconsideration of British policy, and which fed on the changes of circumstance listed above, was a Russian plan to build a railway from Tripoli (Syria) to Kuwait. If realized, the scheme threatened to penetrate the carefully constructed buffer around India. Should the railway later be connected through Iran to Russia, a path to the subcontinent much easier and faster than through Afghanistan would open to Britain's rival. Although their fears about the rail plan were exaggerated (Count Kapnist, the concessionaire, lacked influence, money, and government support; nor was a Gulf railhead the same thing as a conquering army in India), British officials suddenly listened much more closely to Curzon's counsels.[109] A December 1898 rumor that Russia's finance minister was supporting the plan finally tipped the scale in Curzon's favor. Meade was to conclude a nonalienation bond under which Mubarak would agree not to cede without British consent any territory, in any manner, to a foreign government or subject. This was not the equivalent of a protectorate, although in Curzon's opinion the difference was small. The distinction was further reduced by Meade's inclusion, against government wishes, of a clause barring reception of "the Agent or Representative of any Power or Government" in Mubarak's territory without prior British agreement.[110] In practice the primary difference between a bond and a protectorate was that the former could be better kept secret; an open move on Kuwait would cause trouble with Istanbul and might lead Russia to demand a Gulf port as compensation.[111]

On 18 January 1899 Meade was given the task of concluding an agreement as quickly and quietly as possible; to ensure success he was permitted to offer Mubarak a stipend or a lump sum. Such "negotiating papers" only gave added warmth to Mubarak's welcome to the belated British response to his earlier overtures. A Great Power ally could counter the most serious continuing threat to his position in Kuwait, an assault by Ottoman regular troops. Most importantly, however, it could exert pressure in Istanbul and Basra to prevent a move against Mubarak's most vulnerable point, his estates in Iraq. The question of British "protection and assistance" on the latter point, in fact, was the only real issue of negotiation. Mubarak refused to sign the nonconcession bond when Meade stated that he had no authority to give assurances beyond a separate letter promising Britain's "good offices." He even tried to pressure the Resident with tales of recent overtures from the French. The shaikh relented only when Meade threatened to leave Kuwait to ask for instructions. Mubarak's two remaining brothers, however, continued to refuse to sign any agreement that did not promise aid for the Iraqi estates.[112]

Mubarak proved to be more acute than his brothers. While the promise of the British government's "good offices" was not as explicit as might be desired, the letter and bond implied Britain's willingness to champion the shaikh's rights in Iraq. The agreement included a clause extending it "to any portion of [Mubarak's] territory ... which may now be in the possession of the subjects of any other Government." Meade intended by this to prevent transfer of houses in Kuwait owned by Ottoman subjects to Russian or other nationals, although such transactions seemed already to be barred by other clauses. Mubarak might be excused for thinking, as did at first the Indian government, that it referred to the Faw properties currently under Ottoman pressure.[113] Since the object of the clause and the rest of the bond was to maximize territory under Kuwaiti, and thereby British, control, Mubarak could feel confident that Britain would inevitably enter the dispute over the Iraqi lands. In any case, he could ill afford to wait for a more explicit guarantee: if Britain needed one and a half years to respond to the request for protection, how much more time would it require to consider this new issue? As events unfolded, Mubarak's judgment was shown to be sound: Calcutta soon told Meade that "a hope may be held out to Sheikh Mubarak that British Government will do what they can to protect him and his brothers in the matter of their estates near Fao."[114]

After two and a half years of having to resort to various stratagems to counter Ottoman attempts to establish some control over him, Shaikh Mubarak had finally won a guarantee of security from a mighty, outside power. Largely freed from anxiety about his own long-term survival and more sanguine about his ability to resist seizure of his lands, he enjoyed greater freedom of action than when he stood alone. British supervision was not tight and rarely interfered with his schemes of aggrandizement. Where previously he had irritated the Ottomans by his stalling strategy of ignoring orders and blandishments, he now felt free to take steps certain to arouse their wrath. His audacity increased with the success of many of these moves, while Britain protected him from the repercussions of his failures. The Ottomans would find the task of reestablishing control over him after January 1899 much harder than before.

KUWAIT AND SOUTHER IRAQ

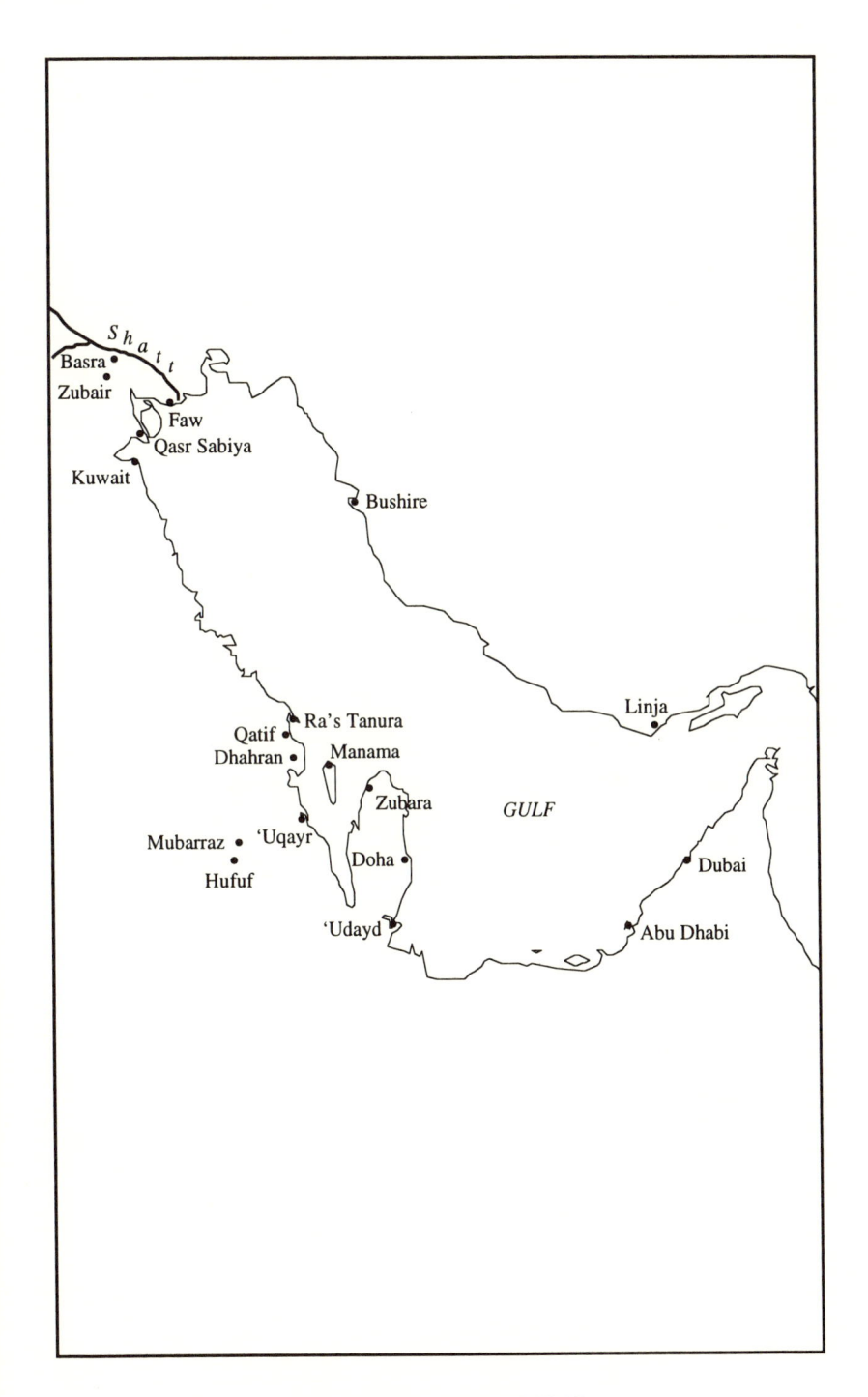

Chapter 6

Kuwait, 1899–1913

Adjustment and Transition: 1899–1901

In the decade following the establishment of the Anglo-Kuwaiti tie, the leading actors explored the new openings or limits to their actions. The process favored those who could act quickly; the Ottomans continued to be hampered by poor communications and indecisiveness. Past failure came back to haunt them: Hamdi returned as *vali*, but the trauma of his earlier experience made him very cautious. As Hamdi was withdrawn again, Mubarak was able to buy the support of Hamdi's successor, Muhsin, as he had with Receb Pasha. Istanbul itself should not be blamed too harshly for its failure to reabsorb Kuwait, because it lacked vital information: the existence and nature of the 1899 Anglo-Kuwaiti concession bond remained secret until 1912. In 1901 the Ottomans agreed with Britain to honor the status quo without knowing what the status quo was. Mubarak, on the other hand, adapted to the new situation with alacrity. In one sense he was still quite weak: the resources at his immediate disposal remained unstable. For defense he relied upon neighboring bedouin tribes, whose loyalty in turn depended on the liberal gifts given from the Iraqi estates' revenues. Those properties could still easily be seized by a determined Ottoman administration. Yet Mubarak began to display to the fullest degree his marvelous ability to get others to do for him what he could not do himself. He pursued aggressively his dearest aims: the increase of his own wealth, the strengthening of his authority over Kuwait, and the weakening of rivals on his borders. This repeatedly put him in a vulnerable position, but by a smooth mixture of sweet talk and threats he gave pause to his opponents or prodded Britain to use its promised "good offices." Britain occasionally balked at the demands of its new ally—and felt considerable irritation at Mubarak's repeated waywardness—but was nevertheless drawn step by step toward identification of its own interests with those of Mubarak. The notable increase of interest in Mubarak exhibited by Britain in the Gulf, Istanbul, and London hinted to the Ottomans that their nightmare, foreign intervention in an integral part of the empire, was being realized. Their uncertainty of the nature or extent of the Anglo-Kuwaiti tie, however, made adaptation of policies even harder than before.

Continuation of the governmental feebleness surprised the new allies. Both Britain and Mubarak had reason to expect more determined opposition; they knew that the Ottomans were fully aware of Meade's visit, which was soon followed by the alarming news of the reappointment of the shaikh's old nemesis Hamdi as *vali*.[1] This was one of several moves that seemed likely to erase any advantage to Mubarak in the involvement of the *naqib*.[2] The government also considered a pardon for Yusuf al-Ibrahim and eased pressure on the murdered shaikhs' sons, allowing them to return to Basra. They had been widely scattered—Yusuf in Bombay, the others in Zubayr or Ha'il—and living in much-fallen state. They had had to remain in exile after Mubarak laid charges against them for the 1897 attack on Kuwait. Their enforced absence blocked progress on the accusations against Mubarak. Istanbul also gave serious consideration to Yusuf's request to move the court cases to a neighboring province, on the grounds that his enemy's influence in Basra was too pervasive.[3]

The reassembly of much of the original anti-Mubarak team in Basra raised strong public expectations of an imminent attack on Kuwait. The rumors were also fed by Mubarak's audacity in establishing new customs regulations in Kuwait. It was a step of great importance to the port. Making all goods pass through, and pay duty to, his customs post gave Mubarak a powerful means of controlling the town's heretofore independent traders, as did his perfection of a market taxes regime. As Kuwait's importance as a trading center grew during his reign, these commercial taxes joined the Faw estates, building taxes, and payments from Britain as the leading sources of Mubarak's income.[4] It was a measure of the shaikh's confidence in his local and British supporters that he now dared to make the move: to make customs duties inescapable, he made no distinction between goods from overseas and those from Basra.[5] Only a public proclamation of independence could have been more challenging to the Ottoman authorities.

Contrary to general expectations, Hamdi's reaction was muted. When the director of the Basra customshouse complained to him, he reportedly asked that the matter be allowed to rest until he had settled into his new post and studied all the circumstances.⁶ Hamdi's deliberation may well have been due in part to fear that an open trade dispute would surely cause the involvement of the British.⁷ He was already aware of the heightened British interest in Kuwait, which he understood to arise from a fear that Istanbul might allow a rival Great Power to establish itself there.⁸ Also of importance were the lessons he drew from his previous experience as *vali*. Hasty advocacy of bold action had made him vulnerable to attack by Mubarak's allies in government. Now he had to work closely with a firm friend of the shaikh, General Muhsin Pasha, with whom every governor since Arif had had to cooperate on such security matters as Kuwait. Hamdi could not but work circumspectly.⁹ Caution carried no guarantee of success: he formulated a top secret plan for a fast, September dawn attack on Kuwait by a small body of troops that only survived tenuously until Muhsin's opposition and fears of the British reaction to the use of armed force killed it.¹⁰

It was thus left to Istanbul to push through a visible response to the most recent provocation. An August 1899 report from Qatar that Mubarak was preparing to sell land at Faw to a British subject, possibly the Bushire Resident, hurried a new decision to assert some supervision over the shaikh.¹¹ Within a week the Naval Ministry sent a man to Kuwait to act as harbor master, apparently assuming that Mubarak would accept him as he had quietly received the quarantine officer in 1897. Mubarak immediately sent this appointee back to Basra, however. Taken aback, the ministry could only suggest naming a Kuwaiti to the post in consultation with Mubarak. Hamdi disagreed: it would gain nothing (after all, if the shaikh's title of *kaymakam* did not make the port Ottoman, what use would an ordinary Kuwaiti be as harbor master?) and, if the title were refused, it would strengthen foreigners' impression of the area's independence.¹² Under pressure from the India Office, the British ambassador also protested the affair to the Ottoman foreign minister. Although Istanbul believed that they had clearly refuted any British right to interfere in territory long recognized internationally as Ottoman, the Porte thus found it wise to shelve the scheme.¹³

As the nineteenth century ended and the twentieth began, there was nevertheless a certain degree of optimism in Istanbul, despite the nagging persistence of the Kuwait problem. The Ottomans thought of Mubarak as "extremely ignorant" (as Hamdi described him) and thus vulnerable to the intensified intrigues of sophisticated foreigners.¹⁴ Istanbul still did not have enough reliable intelligence about Kuwait to make informed judgments; that a Muslim shaikh might seek the aid of infidels against the caliph-sultan to whom he repeatedly swore devotion did not get sufficiently serious consideration. The government thought that Mubarak had not yet succumbed to British blandishments (notwithstanding Hamdi's late report that "everyone" knew that the shaikh had made an agreement with Britain after applying in vain for the protection of the Shah of Iran).[15] With so many other options now discredited, the Ottoman government saw its best hope in outbidding the outsiders for the "ignorant" man's allegiance. It decided to try to dazzle Mubarak into submission by offering him a promotion in rank and a nice decoration. The *naqib* was assigned the task of going to Kuwait to impress upon its leader the importance of the religious ties binding him and his people to the caliphate. He was also to warn Mubarak of the damage to the Kuwaitis, the state, and Islam that would result from giving in to foreigners' enticements. If Mubarak were to give a written avowal of allegiance and submission to the sultan, he would be awarded the promotion and honors.[16]

The *naqib*'s mission met with apparent stunning success. Mubarak gave the written declaration and—never loath to exploit an opportunity—asked for the resumption of the stipend of dates given to his brother Muhammad.[17] It was granted. The shaikh received a promotion of two grades (to the rank that he had almost won in 1893), the Order of *Nişan-i Mecidi* and the cash equivalent of 108 metric tons of dates.[18] This was the stipend that Ottoman records showed that his brother had received (but 172 tons less than Mubarak had claimed it was) and was probably given with the same conditions: the shaikh had to maintain good order and protect all Ottoman rights in his territory. The transaction had a calming effect on both parties, making the ensuing months one of the most stable periods of the post-1896 Ottoman-Kuwaiti connection. Steady communication was maintained through intermediaries;[19] the inheritance case was not pressed too hard; Mubarak kept the British at arm's length;[20] and he honored the sultan-caliph by asking his blessing on a new mosque in Kuwait town to be named for Abdülhamid.[21] That Hamdi was recalled and Muhsin became *vali* and military commander of Basra—a move clearly intended to make government more coherent—in early 1900 also relaxed tensions.

The second factor to deflect the urge to reclaim Kuwait immediately was the political maneuvering attendant to the Baghdad Railway. The German-led project was to link Europe and the Gulf by land, Berlin to Basra. As had been clear not only to the British when the Russian Kapnist plan had surfaced, Kuwait was a better natural port than Basra, and the German planners quickly eyed it as the preferred terminus. The prospect of a fast route to the Gulf outside of their control perturbed many in Britain and India, which led the Foreign Office to drop dark hints to Istanbul and Berlin in April 1900 that, because of certain agreements, nothing could be done at Kuwait without British approval.[22] The Ottomans knew well that the current coolness of relations with Britain made London less unwilling to act unilaterally to safeguard its interests. A crisis in Kuwait or even Basra thus seemed possible. On the other hand, Istanbul welcomed the advent of a European champion of Ottoman rights over Kuwait, especially since Germany had closer ties to Britain than had Kapnist's Russia. The Ottomans saw a possibility of delaying British action long enough to bring the railway to a point from which a quick extension to Kuwait might be forced through. They did not anticipate a strong reaction against such a move from Mubarak: a German commission was warmly received in Kuwait in January 1900 and left with the impression that the shaikh favored the railway.[23] Basra thus became the nominal, but not intended, railhead.[24] Istanbul felt hopeful that, if the line eventually did reach Kuwait, it would firmly establish Ottoman rights (as grantor of the railway concession) and influence there. That hope could continue as long as Mubarak seemed at all friendly to his sovereign.

All sides seemed content with the stability of the status quo until the eruption of a crisis in an unexpected arena: central Najd. The protagonists this time were Mubarak and `Abd al-`Aziz al-Rashid (Ibn Rashid), nephew and successor of the redoubtable Muhammad al-Rashid, amir of Ha'il and ruler of Najd.[25] Muhammad had died in 1897, and his talents as chief of vast territories in the Arabian and Syrian deserts were sorely missed. `Abd al-`Aziz al-Rashid was a man of action, not policy; he resorted to force to achieve his goals more readily than had his predecessor. Muhammad had avoided active interference in the Kuwait problem, giving shelter to several of Mubarak's nephews but not joining Qâsim's aborted attack of 1897.[26] `Abd al-`Aziz, however, chose to appoint himself champion of the dispossessed Kuwaitis. He brought Yusuf al-Ibrahim to his side and began to petition the Ottomans for resolution of the inheritance case.[27] Several factors encouraged Ibn Rashid to become actively involved in Kuwaiti affairs. Mubarak was strongly suspected of responsibility for robbing and killing Ha'il traders in a caravan from Kuwait while Muhammad Ibn Rashid was still alive.[28] Mubarak's growing influence among the bedouins was also worrisome to a leader surrounded by jealous rivals. Control of Kuwait would be very useful to Ibn Rashid, because it was the best port through which Ha'il could import arms and other supplies. Most importantly, `Abd al-Rahman al-Sa`ud and his son `Abd al-`Aziz (Ibn Sa`ud) were living in Kuwait under Mubarak's protection. They were trying to stir unrest in central Najd that had been helped already by Ibn Rashid's rash release of Sa`udi prisoners upon his accession in 1897.[29] On Mubarak's part, fear of Rashidi might, anger over his nephews' refuge in Ha'il, and ambition to eclipse Ibn Rashid as Arabia's eminent power underlay his enmity for Ibn Rashid. He worked hard to weaken his rival through raids and Sa`udi subversion, a challenge to which Ibn Rashid responded with alacrity.[30]

As if by agreement, both sides prepared for war (Mubarak and the Sa`udis allying with the renegade Muntafiq shaikh, Sa`dun),[31] leaving the Ottomans and British scrambling to avert any incident that might upset the current hard-won stability. The new Resident, Colonel Kemball, hurried to Kuwait in October 1900 to gather information and to warn Shaikh Mubarak against action. The shaikh was in the interior. Muhsin had already sent Talib Pasha, son of the Basra *naqib*, to remonstrate with Mubarak, but in vain. Turning to Ibn Rashid, he promised to address the amir's complaints. When this failed to calm Ibn Rashid, Istanbul ordered the dispatch of trusted intermediaries to persuade him and Sa`dun to desist. The simultaneous advance of Mubarak's men and Ottoman troops in November finally forced Ibn Rashid to withdraw temporarily.[32]

The status quo appeared restored to some extent. Mubarak retreated to Kuwait, escorted by the *mutasarrıf* of Muntafiq. On the way he detoured to meet Muhsin at the *naqib*'s house near Zubayr. He went with Muhsin to Basra for the first time since 1896, where he apparently had a telegraphic reconciliation with Istanbul.[33] The peace was not likely to last, however: neither side had materially weakened its rival, and the amir of Ha'il still had not received restitution of looted property. Frequent skirmishes induced Mubarak to attempt a grand blow to crush his adversary.

Having gathered an impressive army of Kuwaiti townspeople, Sa`udi loyalists, and bedouins from all the important eastern Arabian tribes, Mubarak advanced into Najd. His aim was to tear away the southern part of the Rashidi dominions, notably `Anayza, Burayda, and Riyadh. He had moderate success until the campaign's only major battle, at Sarif (near Burayda) in March 1901. Of the Kuwaiti force, hundreds fell and the rest scattered; a brother and one or two nephews of Mubarak were killed. The defeat effectively ended Mubarak's dream of becoming the new, undisputed Arabian leader and threatened to cost him control of Kuwait.[34]

Sarif naturally also affected the two concerned powers. Its earlier warnings to Mubarak to desist having fallen on deaf ears, the British government hurried to check an initial report that he had been killed. When a more accurate picture was formed, it stationed three warships in or near Kuwait to dissuade any Ottoman advance, warned the Porte not to disturb the status quo, and told Mubarak not to visit Basra to account for his actions. Mubarak, who had been sufficiently desperate for immediate help to ask the Russians for their public protection, was impressed by Britain's demonstration of potent support.[35] Their continuing military presence around Kuwait did much to comfort him over the ensuing months of tension with the Ottomans.[36]

Reports of Mubarak's defeat and death caught Istanbul similarly by surprise. The Porte knew of the possibility of fighting but was largely ignorant of where and when it might happen. Muhsin had no reliable information to give.[37] The focus of concern, and military preparations, was not disorder in central Arabia but rather the renewed possibility that Qâsim al-Thani would join an attack on Kuwait by Ibn Rashid.[38] Sultan Abdülhamid had been trying by peaceful persuasion to restore calm, using his customary semisecret channels, and had seemed to be succeeding with Ibn Rashid. His orders had no effect on Mubarak, however, whose advance dissolved Rashidi restraint.[39]

Since Istanbul had not anticipated the possibility of Mubarak's defeat, it reacted too slowly to take advantage of his brief vulnerability. The first official to pinpoint possibilities for action after Sarif was not Muhsin but rather a tax inspector visiting Suq al-Shuyukh. Reporting Mubarak and Sa`dun as killed and the victorious Ibn Rashid as arriving at Kuwait, and noting Kuwait's importance as a trading and weapons-smuggling center for Najd, he recommended the immediate establishment of a customs bureau there. The idea excited great interest for a week, until Muhsin's repeated messages persuaded the Porte that Mubarak still lived.[40] The ensuing brief delay for revision of Ottoman plans gave Britain the opportunity to marshal resources for Mubarak's protection.

For a time Mubarak's fate hung in the balance, because for one final time the Ottomans toyed with the idea of a military solution. Receb Pasha no longer commanded the VI Army Corps, and his successor, Ahmet Feyzi Pasha, had none of his predecessor's kind feeling for Mubarak.[41] He met with enthusiasm the opportunity to put the weakened shaikh under a tight rein. With or without Mubarak's consent, a garrison was to be established in Kuwait. In April Feyzi began to gather troops, dispatching men from Baghdad and going to Basra himself.[42] The imminent possibility of armed confrontation between Ottoman and British forces seemed very real—until the usual Ottoman bad luck reasserted itself. An outbreak of plague in Basra made the only logical base for a large expedition unusable. River traffic stopped. Troops approaching Basra were halted, while those already there had to enter quarantine.[43] A small body of troops was given dispensation from the strict seclusion regulations, on condition that they follow fumagatory and other sanitary precautions, but the idea of using a large force had to be suspended.[44]

Until Basra became fully functional again, the Ottomans had to be content once more with cajolery, not diktats. They had no more real success than in previous attempts. Words begat words, not deeds. Escorted by the detachment excused from quarantine, Muhsin sailed into Kuwait on 19 May. He was to persuade Mubarak to accept the stationing of troops and the establishment of an Ottoman customs post and harbor master.[45] Although the discussions were cordial and the offered terms relatively lenient,[46] Muhsin pressed his old friend hard enough to leave Mubarak greatly worried. The shaikh refused all proposals for substantive change, saying that they would weaken him in his struggle with the Rashidi amir, but he also took pains to appear to be well-disposed toward his suzerain. He accompanied Muhsin and his escort to Faw, using Ottoman-flagged Kuwaiti ships, when the *vali* departed on 23 May 1901. There he remained long enough to send another telegram to the sultan professing complete submission and allegiance.[47] The only other result of Muhsin's mission was a vain renewal of Mubarak's request for a British protectorate.[48]

Despite the continuing absence of protectorate status, Britain's alliance with the shaikh of Kuwait was daily becoming clearer for all to see, making it harder for Istanbul to be satisfied just with Mubarak's general declarations of faithfulness. British ships (naval, cargo, and postal steamers) were now always to be found in the harbor. Rumors began to reach Abdülhamid that an agent's office, flying a British flag, was being established as a result of the frequent port calls, and that Britain was installing navigational lights and markers. When queried, Muhsin had to confirm much of this. Worried about his own security of tenure, he could not afford to feign ignorance of Britain's involvement in Kuwait, since a protectorate might be declared at any moment. The way in which he phrased his information, however, made it difficult to hold him responsible for any bad developments. He blamed Feyzi Pasha's ostentatious gathering of forces, coming after the defeat at Sarif, for stampeding Mubarak into an agreement with Britain. The fault lay with Marshal Feyzi and the British; Mubarak at heart was still loyal to the sultan. Ottoman control could be asserted again over Kuwait, Muhsin advised, if Feyzi stayed in Baghdad, the Rashidi amir were restrained, and calm restored. Mubarak could then be lured to Basra and forced to accept an Ottoman garrison. If these steps were ignored, the *vali* could not prevent a deepening of the Kuwaiti-British bond.[49]

Istanbul had to listen to the advice of its man on the spot, but outside pressure spurred the government to act before Muhsin had wanted. Not only did the sultan desire a tangible sign of his authority in Kuwait, Britain's European competitors were growing more anxious to forestall their rival's quiet march to hegemony in the Gulf. Early optimism about a quick agreement on the Baghdad railway question died as Britain balked at plans to finance the project.[50] Just as the sultan hoped to use Germany to reattach Kuwait to his empire, the Germans and others wanted to use the Ottomans to confound the British. The French ambassador told the Ottoman foreign minister of the rumored raising of the British flag and the constant presence of warships in Kuwait; he forcefully urged that Istanbul firmly reestablish its rights and influence there by opening offices, including customs and harbor master posts. France's own interest in the Gulf and that of its ally Russia, as well as its continuing general dislike of Britain, account for Paris's entry into the dispute. Germany strongly seconded the French advice in the hope of gaining easy access to the preferred Gulf railhead.[51] Since this only strengthened the sultan's own sentiments, Istanbul ordered action before the heat (literal and metaphoric) had eased around Kuwait.

The *vali* was directed to induce Mubarak to come to Basra, where he could be compelled to accept a garrison and customs and harbor officers. The message to Mubarak was blunt: the favors bestowed by Abdülhamid required in return real loyalty, not just the renewal of old promises.[52] A fresh troop concentration spawned more rumors of an attack on Kuwait. Since it was preferable to avoid outright conflict to prevent giving Britain an excuse for intervention, some of these soldiers at most might have formed the new garrison; the majority were for use in Iraq.[53] Some officials nevertheless may have hoped that the preparations would scare Mubarak into cooperation, but the main result was to steel British determination to resist all Ottoman advances, by force if necessary.[54]

The September 1901 Status Quo Agreement

Britain's extreme alarm induced the sudden climax to the Kuwait dispute before the *vali* could execute his orders, and the Ottomans—as usual caught underprepared—could only watch as hope of reclaiming the port took its most serious blow. The troop concentration had led the British government to issue orders to the navy to prevent the debarkation of Ottoman soldiers in Kuwait. When the corvette *Zuhaf* made a port call while on routine patrol from Basra to Qatar on 24 August 1901, therefore, as a precaution the captain of a British warship warned him that landing men or supplies would be resisted by force. The Ottoman captain misunderstood the warning, probably as a result of a tense meeting with Mubarak, and hurried back to Faw to report that Britain had established a protectorate over Kuwait.

Reaction in Istanbul and Berlin was swift and strong. Foreign Minister

Tevfik Pasha and the ambassador to London protested most vigorously the contravention of the territorial integrity of the empire and of the sultan's rights within it, which Britain had long formally recognized, most clearly in 1876–78, when Britain promised protection of Istanbul's rights in return for control of Cyprus.[55] The German Foreign Ministry lodged a similar complaint. Both countries felt particularly outraged because the British had always denied any intention of assuming a protectorate over Kuwait, most recently to a German diplomat on 30 July and to Tevfik on 20 August.[56] London hastened to quieten the complaints, since it disliked the idea of a lengthy public discussion of its legally dubious position in the shaikhdom. The British Foreign Office offered no apology for the threat of force in Kuwait but affirmed that no occupation of the town was intended, as long as the status quo was not disturbed. Germany saw the contradiction recognized by many in Britain: if no protectorate existed, how could the sultan legally be barred from action in land recognized, however hazily, as his? The British move itself disturbed the status quo. German objections continued to be an irritant to relations with Britain, but the disagreement soon became an unresolvable routine.[57]

Istanbul was sooner satisfied. Britain's qualified assurances came as a real relief to the government, in part because they seemed to reaffirm Ottoman interest in Kuwait and because the state was momentarily powerless to demand anything better. A serious dispute with Paris had arisen in July, when Istanbul refused payment of T£500,000 allegedly owed to two French contract-holders. The French navy sent warships to Mytilene as a pointed demonstration of the wisdom of not disputing the accounts. Since the Treasury was as bare as usual, the possibility of a protracted confrontation with France was real.[58] As the German government pointed out, the Ottomans could ill afford a simultaneous break with a second Great Power (especially France's main rival). Istanbul's recent rocky relations with London had just entered a phase of particular tension due to events in Yemen, where Ottoman and British soldiers had come to bloody blows at the end of July.[59] The Ottomans thought at first that Britain planned to repeat its pugnacious Yemeni action by occupying Kuwait under cover of the French distraction. When London offered to forswear such a move on condition that the Ottomans send no troops to the town, therefore, Istanbul thought that it had forced London to retreat.[60] In return, the government was willing to agree to maintain the status quo.[61] After all, a promise not to move the military into the town accorded well with the policy since Midhat's day of not governing Kuwait directly.

The agreement of 1901 marked the effective end of the phase of the Kuwait question in which the Ottomans had a real chance to reclaim control of the port, and it could be argued that Istanbul acted in haste only to repent in leisure. In principle, a mutual promise to respect the status quo was a very useful step, since it reduced the uncertainty about intentions that could drive disagreement into warfare. In this case, however, the Ottomans might be excused for feeling rather cheated of that benefit. The basic flaw in the accord was that it did not define the status quo.[62] To Britain the phrase signified acceptance of its place as the preeminent power behind the independent shaikh of Kuwait. London recognized the sultan's suzerainty there but denied his sovereignty (the distinction between the two terms was never clear to the Ottomans);[63] since all Ottoman authority over the town was denied, any act that affected Kuwait could be considered a change of the status quo. To Istanbul the status quo consisted of the conditions listed by Foreign Minister Tevfik Pasha at the time of the accord: Kuwait was a part of the empire, whose integrity Britain had often agreed to respect, and its shaikh was thus unable to conclude agreements with foreign powers.[64]

Such incompatible views were sure to lead to trouble in the future, yet, openly stated though they were, neither side wished or was able to spare the time, effort, and resources necessary to convince the other of its mistakes. Britain wanted no scrutiny of Kuwait that could draw in Russia, Germany, and France. The Ottomans had too many other problems—Macedonia, Yemen, Mytilene, the state's perpetually poor finances—to spend more time on Kuwait. Although Germany urged the Ottomans to bring Britain before the international tribunal at The Hague, Istanbul preferred an instant half-solution and hoped to be able to muddle through any resulting future difficulties.[65]

Reports from Basra undoubtedly encouraged Istanbul to accept the British proposal, and it was to be the course of events there that was to define the meaning of "status quo." Muhsin stated that Mubarak had denied to the *Zuhaf*'s captain that a protectorate had been established, but that he would be forced to accept one if he were put under any pressure. To Istanbul it was a painful indication of the extent to which the shaikh had now come under British influence that he immediately stopped signing letters to the authorities with his usual title of *kaymakam*.[66] The statements of Mubarak and the British persuaded the Porte that matters could only worsen in the near future, making an immediate truce worthwhile, even at the cost of forswearing the use of troops against its recalcitrant subject.

Consciousness of the fragility of the Ottoman hold on Kuwait, and indeed on all of eastern Arabia, led the Sublime Porte to read the new agreement in a more restrictive way than did Sultan Abdülhamid II. The main aspect of Istanbul's agreement to preserve the status quo was its promise not to send troops to Kuwait; the accord said nothing, for example, about the Rashidi amir, Yusuf al-Ibrahim, or the disputed Faw properties. The sultan seemed disposed to support Ibn Rashid, who was threatening Kuwait in September, while the Porte strongly urged the Palace to restrain its protégé. The Council of Ministers, which included Foreign Minister Tevfik Pasha, was more attuned to British sentiments than was the sultan, with whom Tevfik had no influence. The Porte could ill afford to ignore Mubarak's warning about being pressured into accepting Britain's protection. The Porte furthermore could not overlook the ever-feared, real danger that all of Najd might erupt in violence at any time, since it was believed that Mubarak had sent Ibn Sa'ud to rally support among tribes of the interior.[67] Grand Vezir Said Pasha thus felt compelled to warn Abdülhamid that a new crisis with Britain could erupt, unless the Rashidi forces withdrew.[68] Upon its recommendation, therefore, the *vali* of Baghdad was to tell Ibn Rashid to stop his attacks on Kuwait. The VI Corps Marshal and the new *vali* of Basra (Muhsin had finally been replaced) were to treat Mubarak with complete amicability in order to make him feel secure.[69]

Tevfik simultaneously tried to soothe Mubarak's main ally. When the British ambassador complained about the recent military activity, Tevfik assured him that it was intended only to prevent a tribal clash. The minister also proposed that Britain restrain Mubarak as Istanbul pressured Ibn Rashid. Britain promptly agreed, since the idea seemed to recognize its preponderant influence in Kuwait.[70] That the foreign minister should make such a suggestion indicates the Porte's feeling that the danger of a total loss of control in Arabia outweighed the importance of a further concession of protocol. The change was not as momentous as it would have been in the past; Britain had agreed not to strip Kuwait from the empire, and the greater freedom to treat of the shaikhdom's affairs smoothed some of the earlier awkwardness from the rivals' discussions. Talk did not lead to total credulity, however, so Britain sent four warships to prepare Kuwait's defense.[71]

Reacting either to this public reinforcement of Mubarak or to warnings received from the sultan, Ibn Rashid disappeared into the interior; a modest loosening of tension resulted. It did not last long. Laboring under misapprehensions about British determination, Abdülhamid apparently issued several secret orders that, had he consulted more closely with the Porte, he might have known could cause further strong British protests. At the end of October he began to send messages to Mubarak via the *naqib*, calling on the Kuwaiti shaikh to reconcile with the sultan as befitted all Muslims.[72] This was consistent with a recent Council of Ministers recommendation and was not technically a violation of the status quo, since it continued the previous practice of using the *naqib* as an intermediary.[73] Under the new diplomatic rules, however, it quickly became clear that such moves were more risky than before. According to information received by Britain, the sultan had the *naqib* deliver an ultimatum to Mubarak in early December: the Kuwaiti shaikh could live luxuriously in Istanbul as a member of the Council of State, accept an Ottoman protectorate, or be evicted by force. Mubarak asked for, and received, time to consider. He consulted with the captains of the several British warships at Kuwait, dropping broad hints that he would have to accept Ottoman protection if he were not helped. The officers thus willingly followed Mubarak's suggestion that they should threaten to fire on Kuwait if its shaikh heeded the sultan's demands. The *naqib* could do nothing but sail away to report this new instance of British high-handedness.[74]

If true, the incident showed severe misjudgment by Abdülhamid and deft maneuvering by Mubarak. The latter turned the situation to his advantage, concocting a scenario in which he could flatly disobey his suzerain without seeming responsible, while strengthening British protectiveness. The accuracy of this story, however, is questionable. The key details—the Ottoman threats and promises—came only from Mubarak, who proved himself capable of giving them in half a dozen different versions, as one high British official remarked.[75] Mubarak knew about the status quo agreement; what better way to win Britain's protection than to suggest that the Ottomans were about to attack Kuwait? The only certain fact is that the *naqib* and the *vali*'s brother brought Mubarak a message from the sultan, calling for his return to the Ottoman fold.[76] From the reaction in Istanbul to British complaints about the *naqib*—almost ignoring him as either irrelevant or the subject of a false tale, in favor of discussion of Britain's new attack on Ottoman suzerainty—the Porte and the Palace may otherwise both have been telling the truth when professing bewilderment over the story. Whatever the case, Abdülhamid was starting to discover the new limits of what was safe to attempt before British resistance stiffened.

Unbeknownst to both his would-be suzerain and his protectors, Mubarak continued his habit of reaching out to other parties that might be useful to him in his quest for security and practical independence. Two Russians, a naval officer and the head of the Consulate-General in Bushire, visited Mubarak on 10 December 1901. He said that he would welcome more frequent visits to Kuwait by Russian ships and that "he would prefer to turn to the Russians for help rather than to any other nation if Kuwait got in trouble."[77] Contravening the conditions of the 1899 Anglo-Kuwaiti Bond, Mubarak did not inform the British of these talks, let alone receive their blessing. His statements to Russian representatives on this and later occasions make clear that Mubarak was prepared to abandon his British allies, should they not protect him fully against the Ottomans or should they try to place limits on his freedom of action.[78]

Mubarak could have no reason for deep displeasure with the British in 1901–2. The *naqib*'s visit and the ensuing months left no doubt that, when Britain thought that the Ottomans had overstepped the limits of the status quo, it could make life in Istanbul uncomfortable. Tevfik was informed that the affair of the *naqib* violated the status quo and that, if Istanbul kept raising such questions, London might be forced into a settlement less favorable to Ottoman interests. Since the Porte was ignorant of the purpose behind the *naqib*'s visit, Tevfik passed the protest directly to the palace.[79] A similarly strong complaint was lodged several weeks later when it was learned that exports of food from Basra had been banned, a move particularly aimed at arid Kuwait. In this case, Abdülhamid was clearly responsible. Again the Foreign Ministry was caught unprepared to respond vigorously, because the sultan had bypassed the Porte in ordering the ban. London's pressure, made potent by Istanbul's belief that the British were trying to take over Kuwait,[80] contributed to Abdülhamid's rescission of the order, just as it caused him to abandon any thought of bald intimidation.[81]

These instances of pressure applied to Mubarak annoyed top British officials, who had so recently thought the Kuwait question stabilized, and the reasons for Abdülhamid's actions are obscure. A threat to evict the shaikh, if one were made, was almost unenforceable, since Britain had practically promised a protectorate at the first sign of military action. Why, then, ask for trouble? Always very jealous of his sovereign rights, the sultan seemed to see in several semi-innocent events a plan to spread British influence through Arabia. The consul in Basra had sent a letter to Ibn Rashid in late September 1901, suggesting that the shaikh of Muhammara mediate a settlement with Mubarak. Ibn Rashid reportedly sent a rather dramatic account of the offer, and of his refusal, to Abdülhamid.[82] The sultan could easily be excused for seeing in this an attempt to replicate in Najd the insidious creep of London's influence through maintenance of "long-standing ties" with "independent shaikhs" that had already happened in Bahrain, Qatar, Kuwait, and Yemen. Another alarming new sign of British designs on Najd was the appearance of well-armed Egyptian bedouins traveling through the Syrian desert to support Mubarak.[83] These were probably recruited by western Arabian enemies of Ibn Rashid, but their departure from British-held territory made other suspicions inevitable. Hearing these reports, the sultan must have felt that he had to remove the key local malcontent by whatever means possible in order to save Arabia. His view that Britain had been forced to retreat from establishing a protectorate in September 1901 seemed to give him confidence that he was not running an overwhelming risk by doing so. It was the paucity of his own leverage, however, that was made painfully clear by the total failure of his efforts; the uselessness of the grain embargo in particular was soon realized. It was an annoyance that would only push Mubarak further into the arms of an alternate supplier (Britain, whose ships' presence in Kuwait had earlier been ascribed by Mubarak to the need for imported grain) and, as the Germans pointed out, strengthened the appearance of Kuwait's foreign status.[84]

The outcome of these events was a narrowing gap in opinion between the Porte and the Palace over policy, at least regarding the futility of direct attempts to reclaim Kuwait. Both seats of power came to believe that the sultan's schemes had almost resulted in Britain's seizure of Kuwait. The commander of the ship carrying the *naqib* had reported a British ship captain's opinion that the port's independence had been recognized in the status quo agreement, and that the British officer had hauled down the Ottoman flag and raised a "Kuwaiti" one.[85] The ensuing alarm, which spread to other governments, notably Russia's, diverted some attention from the sultan's controversial initiatives. When London reaffirmed its disinterest in a protectorate and explained that the flag had been lowered only to permit temporary shore-to-ship communication, Istanbul even felt that it had managed a victory of sorts. The news that in January 1902 British ships had landed heavy guns near Kuwait was a setback, however, an indication that London's recent diplomatic retreat should not be mistaken for feebleness. Abdülhamid threatened to remove by force the guns, which were to defend against Rashidi attack, and warned that the case would be taken to The Hague if the maneuver were resisted. Britain eventually withdrew them after Ibn Rashid retired into Najd.[86] While the sultan might feel that important points of principle on Kuwait had been reaffirmed, the entire sobering sequence of events made it clear that Britain could not be shaken easily from its position there, at least by direct confrontation. As long as the principle of Kuwait's inclusion in the Ottoman empire was not openly challenged, therefore, the Porte and the Palace henceforth largely accepted Britain's definition of the status quo.

In one sense, this seeming limitation to Ottoman authority became a blessing to Istanbul. Once the heatedly debated option of sending the army into Kuwait had been removed, the government found it much easier to take more measured steps. An initial instance of this new-found alacrity followed Ibn Rashid's appearance near Kuwait, which led to the dispute over the British guns. Istanbul asked Ibn Rashid to withdraw, and to ease the trip back to Ha'il the Treasury offered him a large gift.[87] The government continued to watch Ibn Rashid's movements closely.[88] It also took concrete steps to prevent renewed clashes between the amir and Mubarak, deploying troops south from Basra to act as a buffer force.[89]

Given recent disputes, Britain—especially the Indian authorities—viewed the advance of Ottoman units toward Kuwait with deep suspicion. The affair of the *naqib*, the grain embargo, and Ibn Rashid's uncertain intentions predisposed many to jump to the conclusion that the Ottomans still fully intended to crush Mubarak regardless of promises to respect the status quo. The stationing of troops at Safwan, Umm Qasr, and Bubiyan island thus was assumed to be an obvious pressure tactic to cow Mubarak by gradually tightening a noose around Kuwait. The government reluctantly concluded that it could not rightfully protest the Ottoman actions, because they did not disturb the status quo in Kuwait itself, but it did consider them as breaking the spirit of the agreement. This rather unjustified irritation was to have the later effect of easing British consciences over breaking their own commitment to respect the status quo.

British antagonism may be termed unwarranted because the Ottoman intention behind the troop movements was very much defensive. The deployments were part of a wider plan to meet threats in Arabia, not to mount them. The perceived main threat to be met was from Britain (admittedly a circumstance justifying a degree of concern in London and India), but Istanbul had no intention of attacking London's local allies, as was feared (although in the case of Kuwait the sultan surely wanted to keep open the option of using soldiers to remove any British guns temporarily landed around Kuwait bay). It wanted rather to prevent recruitment of new proxies.

Events of 1901–2 in Arabia strengthened and sharpened suspicions aroused by Britain's increasing reluctance to champion Ottoman territorial integrity. Midhat's old fear that Britain would use unruly tribes to strike the soft southern Ottoman underbelly had been revived with a vengeance for an ill-informed and worried Istanbul. In contrast to Arabia in 1871, Britain did now have major commitments that conflicted directly with Ottoman aims. Each side grew ever more reluctant to admit the validity of the other's interests. A forward policy in Yemen had already caused a clash in 1901, and diplomatic arguments and reports of further troop movements from Aden suggested that the border might not be set by negotiation.[90] Istanbul showed for some time great diplomatic and military determination to prevent admission of British border claims.⁹¹ From the Gulf coast came garbled accounts of a British ship having raised three flagpoles on an island off `Uqayr, and of the unsettling effect on the Arabs of such warships' frequent unchallenged appearance in Ottoman waters. Combined with coincidental bedouin unrest in Hasa (suspected to be the result of machinations by Mubarak and/or `Abd al-`Aziz Ibn Sa`ud, whose January 1902 capture of Riyadh was itself a severe setback to Ottoman fortunes in Arabia), this made Istanbul fear that the British were on the point of, or indeed already were, establishing themselves on new parts of the Gulf coast on the old excuse of the lack of local Ottoman control. The government quickly dispatched fresh soldiers to Hasa and tried to transfer warships to the Gulf, in order to restore order and to be indisputable markers of Istanbul's authority over the area.⁹²

The aims of military advances from Basra to as far south as Bubiyan island fit into this overall pattern. The sparsely settled shore between Basra and Kuwait had no permanent Ottoman representatives. Zubayr had become a focus of all sides' attention by this time, and when Istanbul learned from Basra that it had no officials there, the Council of Ministers hurried to begin formation of a formal *kaza*, complete with security forces.⁹³ The area of Khawr Zubayr (the long inlet of the Gulf west of the Shatt, and on or near which lay Umm Qasr, Zubayr, and Safwan) had become especially favored by gun smugglers in the absence of close official scrutiny. As elsewhere on the coast, they were a dreaded threat to a shaky government and were to be pursued vigorously.⁹⁴ Pirates also lurked nearby, and a complaint by Yusuf al-Ibrahim that Mubarak had had one of his trading vessels seized (thus raising the specter of a renewed attack by the anti-Mubarak alliance) probably gave added impetus to the coastal deployments.⁹⁵ Khawr Zubayr had also suddenly become important for another reason: with Kuwait's inviolability now being protected by British guns, Umm Qasr offered the most promising alternative for the terminus of the Baghdad Railway.⁹⁶ The Ottoman-German convention for the line's construction was ready for signature in January 1902; it planned a route through Zubayr to an unspecified port.⁹⁷ Istanbul saw the wisdom of establishing posts around Umm Qasr before Mubarak and Britain could claim it and its approaches as Kuwaiti territory.⁹⁸ Finally, there was the problem of Ibn Rashid and the other anti-Mubarak agitators, whose activities were one of the original reasons for the international interest in Zubayr. A stronghold of the anti-Mubarak faction, the town was a focal point of frequent raids and counter-raids by both sides. Since these did not threaten Kuwait directly, Britain was not stirred to try to compel their cessation, and the Ottomans were more concerned to prevent a major clash between the rivals. Each Great Power also was reluctant to restrain its client because it held the other party guilty of the original aggression. The Ottomans were finally forced to apply more pressure to restore calm to the Zubayr area, however, when the combatants tried a new scheme.

It was illustrative of the peculiar relationship yet existing between the Ottoman government and Mubarak's Kuwait that, despite all the turbulence, the Ottoman overland mail service between Basra and Hasa had continued routinely to pass through this nominal Ottoman *kaza*. It was a sign of Kuwait's inclusion in the empire that both sides were careful to preserve: Istanbul because it had so few other signs of its authority there, and Mubarak because it was one of those gestures of fidelity to the sultan (such as continuing to fly the Ottoman flag) that cost him little but whose removal could cause trouble. When Rashidi supporters in Zubayr rifled the mail for letters from Kuwait in January 1902, Mubarak knew that he could pressure the government to restrain Ibn Rashid by stopping the Ottoman post. Not only did this challenge Istanbul's claim of sovereignty over Kuwait, it reduced communication with Hasa into dependence on unreliable shipping. The plan succeeded. The government ordered the Zubayris to leave the post alone, and having received assurances from them and conducted negotiations with Mubarak, it got the mail started again in return for a written promise of the Kuwaiti post's protection.[99] This affair was one of those that, had Britain had real knowledge of them, might have reassured somewhat the officials who suspected darker designs behind the Ottoman moves in the desert.[100]

If the extension of authority to Zubayr and other towns had led to clashes with Ibn Rashid, the state's sole notable tribal ally in the Arabian interior, the security initiatives could only have been deemed a disaster. Several coincidental developments prevented that by distracting Ibn Rashid's focus from Mubarak. One was Ibn Sa'ud's capture of Riyadh, which initiated a marked decline of Rashidi fortunes in central Najd. Within several months Ibn Rashid had to shift his attention and resources from Kuwait to the interior.[101] The other change occurred in Basra, where the court case against Mubarak for ownership of the Sabah date groves suddenly came back to life. The shake-up marked by Muhsin's dismissal from military and civil command in Basra must have removed much of the opposition within the provincial regime that had blocked earlier cases and execution of decisions. The government presumably pressed for action, deeming it preferable to have the inter-Sabah rivalries fought out in court rather than with guns. Mubarak was summoned to appear, and, when he refused, his nephews' right to one of the smaller properties was confirmed.

This result was to Ottoman advantage. It was a slap at Mubarak that the British could not legitimately protest as a rupture of the status quo, and it showed both the nephews and Ibn Rashid that satisfaction could be found in a peaceful way. Mubarak indeed grew greatly alarmed and demanded British protection of his interests. All that his ally could do, however, was to have the shaikh appeal the ruling to a higher court, thus threatening further to delay settlement of all claims for years.

This appears to have infuriated the nephews, and the government also did not relish the idea of interminable legal wranglings. When the *vali* reportedly tried to resurrect the idea of an independent arbitration commission, the plaintiffs refused to take part, spurning partial satisfaction in the hope of getting full justice, even vengeance, with the aid of friends. Unfortunately for them, by the time of their refusal Ibn Rashid was already turning his eyes to Riyadh, which by then had been in the hands of Ibn Sa`ud for several months.[102]

Although the legal gambits thus seemed futile, they not only helped to alleviate tension at a delicate moment, they also reminded all parties that a less objectionable, more pacific path to a solution might still be pursued. As a new trial was about to start in April 1902, the sultan suspended proceedings in favor of a new arbitration committee, and Mubarak and his nephews in fact settled their dispute in 1903 through negotiations, involving not only the shaikh and the *vali* but also local notables and the British Consul Wratislaw.

That negotiations on this issue of such interest to the nephews and, especially, Mubarak eventually proved successful suggests that all parties realized that a durable stalemate was settling around Kuwait; the Ottomans in particular could see with relief a check to their decline in that area in 1902. Of course, they still had no means of influencing directly events in Kuwait proper, but no longer could they only react to Mubarak's moves. The occupation of key points in the desert "no-man's-land" prevented later preemptive Anglo-Kuwaiti claims to other possible termini for the Baghdad Railway or to posts valuable to the defense of Basra and Hasa. The new garrisons on Kuwait's doorstep dealt a blow to Mubarak's regional stature as a chief who could tweak the Ottoman lion's tail with impunity, as well as forcing him to act with greater restraint. Partly as a result of this, the Kuwaiti shaikh found it less easy to direct strikes at distant enemies. An immediate indication of Mubarak's alarm engendered by the military moves and the court case was his reported attempt to buy Basra *Vali* Mustafa Nuri's assistance for T£10,000 in February 1902.[103] Although communications between the two after that were not always as productive as in the case of the mails dispute, they were frequent and had a relatively friendly tone, with Mubarak repeating protestations of his undying devotion to the sultan.[104] This, in turn, probably helped to still any impulse in Istanbul to devise a more aggressive policy.

Also continuing to restrain the sultan's aggressive instincts was the reluctance of the Sublime Porte, which had responsibility for the handling of the daily problems of executing foreign and domestic policy, to risk renewed rupture of relations with Britain. When Abdülhamid wanted to advance troops to two towns on Kuwait bay in spring 1902, Sabiya and Kazima, the Council of Ministers argued strongly against any further moves toward Kuwait. While the sultan apparently hoped to limit further the size of the "British" enclave on the coast and to prevent further supply of arms and assistance to Ibn Sa`ud, the ministers were well aware of possible British retaliation. They could also appreciate better than a ruler obsessed with preservation of his own sovereignty the British view that such a move would alter the status quo, since both towns were occupied by men clearly under Mubarak's control. The combined protests of Britain and the Porte finally pressed a grudging disavowal of the plan from the sultan.[105] Once again, Abdülhamid's grasp of what was possible under the status quo agreement had been refined, and another point for Mubarak's defense had been established. The Kuwaiti frontier was beginning to take firm shape along a line roughly akin to the present border, with the notable exception of the contested islands of Bubiyan and Warba.

The Final Phase: Kuwait After 1902

The events of the six months following the status quo agreement settled the final direction of Istanbul's Kuwait policy, which was to be maintained with greater coherence than in the confusion of earlier years. As the 1901 accord made action easier, it also gave the Ottoman government an easily graspable point on which to focus: Britain was dangerously close to realizing its dream of hegemony in Arabia. Mubarak was its tool to that end. Ottoman policy therefore targeted Mubarak as such, as the key point in Britain's plan. The efforts to restrict the area that might be claimed for Kuwait were to prevent extension of Britain's notorious "relations" to neighboring shaikhs. Istanbul also tried hard to keep Mubarak from contact with rebels in Najd and Iraq. Finally, it attempted to persuade Mubarak that he had nothing to fear from it, no reason to accept a British shield. Steps included the accelerated settlement of the inheritance dispute, restraint in pressuring the shaikh and efforts to achieve amicable relations or even a reconciliation.

The initiatives had some success, but the gains were too modest to arrest the decline caused by Mubarak's actions. The status quo agreement limited what was possible by removing the threat of attack on Kuwait. Also of importance, however, was Istanbul's misunderstanding of Gulf politics. It assumed that Britain was pulling weak men from the empire, not that the initiative came from the shaikhs. Concentration on Britain obscured the bad effects of leaving Mubarak unpressured. By letting him enjoy his long-sought prosperity in relative peace, in the hope of enticing him back to his suzerain, the Ottomans made clear to other ambitious men that there was little price to pay for rebellion, as long as it appeared to be done reluctantly. Kuwait thus did not lose importance, even as diplomatic disputes over it lost immediacy.

After the contested frontier stabilized in 1902, Kuwait retreated from its earlier prominence as a center of Anglo-Ottoman rivalry and activity. Action tended to take place at greater remove from the port than previously. The main issues of concern to Britain—the frontier, the disputed Al Sabah lands in Iraq, and the acknowledgement of the British position in Kuwait—were either stable or improving, and any good from pushing them publicly would be outweighed by the sure arousal of jealousy among European rivals. London turned its attention therefore to the knotty negotiations over the Baghdad Railway. In this the Germans, not the Ottomans, were the main opponent. Britain could prevent construction of the line, not due to its position at Kuwait but rather because its permission was needed to raise Ottoman customs levels, from which the funds to provide investors with guaranteed returns were to come. It demanded first a share of the project equal to any other power's and then, when that proved unacceptable, a controlling interest over its southern leg from Baghdad to Basra. Germany's opposition to both proposals deadlocked negotiations.

This shift of attention to Europe did not mean that Kuwait was now ignored; Britain continued a gradual entrenchment of its position there, but London tried to maintain the appearance of respecting the status quo. Several incidents of note occurred after 1902 that yet produced muted reaction from Istanbul or Europe. In 1903 the Viceroy of India finally visited Kuwait during a grand tour of the Gulf. The visit erased any doubts in Curzon's mind about Mubarak's reliability, which some officials still strongly suspected. The occasion aroused Ottoman apprehension, but Mubarak's explanation that he had merely accorded a welcome suitable to an illustrious foreign official who had chosen to visit, as well as the absence of any inflammatory declarations from the controversial Curzon, left Istanbul little ground for serious protest. Such was not the case the next year, when appointment of a British officer as temporary

Agent in Kuwait during the Saʿudi-Rashidi crisis in Najd brought an Ottoman charge of violation of the status quo. The Agent, Captain Knox, was withdrawn in March 1905, much to the chagrin of Mubarak and the Indian government, but rumors about Ottoman activity on Bubiyan and German railroad engineers intending to visit Kuwait brought him back at the end of October. The Agency became a fixture in Kuwait thereafter (again at times to the chagrin of Mubarak, who did not appreciate the semblance of supervision). This time Istanbul reacted more calmly, possibly in part because it felt that the posting was driving Mubarak into a more friendly attitude.

Except in these instances, Britain acted with enough circumspection so that even its own officials felt confusion over policy in Kuwait. Several suggestions and agreements were made, only to be left awaiting execution.[106] Mubarak agreed to a proposal to allow to Britain exclusive rights to establish a post office in Kuwait in 1904; fears of difficulties with Istanbul delayed its opening until 1915. A similar fate befell an idea of 1905-6 to introduce a Kuwaiti flag to replace the Ottoman standard. Plans to increase the Agent's stature by provision of a launch and to secure further possible railway terminus sites by purchase or lease were delayed more than two years, not only by concern about secrecy but also because of disputes between London and India about costs and responsibility. News of the eventual lease agreement of October 1907 was guarded even more closely than that of 1899.[107] Under this seemingly all-inclusive secret agreement, Britain rented or otherwise got rights of priority to most of the possible terminus sites around the bay, in return for £4,000 per year. Among other things, Britain also promised that the town of Kuwait and its boundaries belonged to the shaikh and his heirs, who would remain essentially free to administer it as they saw fit. The bond strengthened the conviction among Mubarak and the British that their fates were entwined, that a veritable protectorate was confirmed, but it hardly helped to make clear to everyone Britain's legal position in Kuwait. Only on limited issues of the "status quo" could it act openly. Public and private policies pursued at variance tend to promote confusion, as the sultan and his ministers might attest.[108]

Whatever the weaknesses of secret policies, in this case circumspection did reduce occasions for direct Anglo-Ottoman confrontation, and the British might be forgiven for thinking that Istanbul had accepted the loss of Kuwait, de facto if not de jure. This was not the case, however, as long as Abdülhamid II still reigned. Just as Britain preferred to act in obscurity, the Ottomans eschewed direct confrontation in favor of indirect pressure on Mubarak. Both Porte and Palace, for instance, issued orders to prevent possible clashes between the Ibn Rashid-Sabah nephews coalition and Mubarak near Kuwait at the end of 1902. Sultan Abdülhamid in particular feared that Britain would use the excuse of aiding Mubarak to establish just such an unofficial protectorate as was then being formed in secret. Britain would then be free to extend its web of treaties into the interior, even to the Rashidi capital. The effects of such a British coup could reach as far as the Hijaz.[109] The united attitude of Istanbul's leaders makes very doubtful Britain's belief that an abortive seaborne attack on Kuwait by Yusuf and several of the nephews several months earlier had at least tacit Ottoman approval. Officials' unresponsiveness to the incident, which did much to strengthen British suspicions, came not from complicity but from the delicacy of trying to punish the protégé of an important client (Ibn Rashid), a general wish to avoid a public reopening of the whole question of Kuwait, and a related suspicion that Britain and Mubarak had concocted much of the story to suit their own purposes.[110] The reaction in both incidents shows clearly that the government now concentrated on Kuwait's potential as a conduit of British perfidy rather than on trying to strike blows to hurt its shaikh.

Even in the several other instances of confrontation where Britain felt obliged to come to Mubarak's aid, the Ottoman initiatives were aimed more at preventing perceived British plots than at punishing the Kuwaiti shaikh. This circumstance generally precluded such strong British protests as those, for instance, in the affair of the *naqib*. In May 1902, for example, Mubarak's agent in Basra was arrested and his papers—including the title deeds to the disputed properties at Faw—seized. The deeds were soon returned upon London's protest, rather to British surprise. The agent had been arrested, in fact, not to attack the Kuwaiti shaikh's source of wealth but to prevent the dissemination (on Mubarak's orders) of a proscribed, London-published newspaper. Similarly in 1908 the authorities tried to bar Mubarak from cultivating reclaimed land on the Shatt that he had appropriated, not to harass him but to prevent his (and by inference British) control of land in the field of fire of the Faw fort.[111] In the years leading up to the Great War the government was ever more concerned about appropriation of state land by private individuals in Iraq, and particularly about the transfer of land to foreign ownership. Mubarak's indeterminate nationality made all of his land dealings worth scrutiny. Istanbul examined several of his acquisitions, but only in those cases with an effect on security did the government try to block the transfer outright. In addition to that of Faw, there was a less well-known case involving the purchase of land from Sa`dun Pasha, sometime outlaw chief of the Muntafiq. Istanbul wanted to limit as much as possible the ties between the two troublesome leaders.[112] Mubarak was already suspected of smuggling British guns to another rebellious chief in `Ammara,[113] and it seemed natural to expect similar support for Sa`dun. The Muntafiq chief in fact was accused of having been seduced by the blandishments of foreigners and of entertaining illusions of (independent) chieftaincy, just like Mubarak.[114]

Istanbul's new policy of trying to restrict as much as possible Mubarak's ability to stir up trouble in unsettled times in supposed furtherance of British interests is to be seen most clearly, however, in the Rashidi-Sa`udi struggle for central Najd. The Ottoman military occupation of Qasîm in 1904-6 came in response to the report of Ibn Sa`ud's having seized the territory and proclaimed himself amir; the *vali* of Basra also stated that the seizure had taken place under the judgment and guidance of Mubarak.[115] Mubarak's strong moral and material support for his friend was no secret to the Ottomans and the British, but neither had great success in limiting his involvement in Najd affairs. He smuggled arms into the interior or equipped directly men who went on to join Ibn Sa`ud in Najd. Noting Kuwait's role as an arms depot, the *vali* later complained that, until the Kuwait problem was solved, no good would come from the reforms planned in Qasîm.[116]

At the same time Mubarak acted as mediator between the Sa`udis and the Ottomans, forwarding messages and taking part in negotiations. These talks led in February 1905 to the relatively amicable agreement on the ground rules of the Ottoman occupation of Qasîm. Mubarak's political experience clearly shaped the Sa`udi strategy during the negotiations. Mubarak and `Abd al-Rahman, father of Ibn Sa`ud, met the *vali* near Basra to affirm the Sa`udi shaikh's submission and devotion to the sultan. At this time, or in subsequent communications, the Mubarak-Sa`udi team told the Ottomans that the British were trying to establish control over the Sa`udis (in truth, Britain did not respond to overtures from Ibn Sa`ud), but that these attempts were resisted on the advice of Mubarak.[117] Such a ploy at that time was practically guaranteed success. In preceding months the government's suspicions had reached a new pitch. Istanbul took jumbled information about separate events (the arrival of Knox as Agent and the loan of money to Mubarak to settle the nephews' inheritance dispute) as evidence of British plans to manage directly the campaign in Najd, although the *vali* discounted such a link.[118] Shortly thereafter several British officials, including Lorimer, came to Kuwait and Iraq to gather information for the *Gazetteer*; both Palace and Porte felt sure that the aims of these visits were political, including a wish to confer with Ibn Sa`ud.[119] The stories spun by Mubarak and `Abd al-Rahman al-Sa`ud immediately after this thus fell on quite credulous ears, further diverting Ottoman animosity and suspicion from the warring Arabs to the British and helping to reconcile Istanbul to the fact of Sa`udi domination of Najd.

That Mubarak eventually managed to win credit for the rapprochement shows just how well he had learned the possibilities of politics in Arabia. The British and the Ottomans knew of—and disapproved of—his involvement in the struggle for Najd; Istanbul became an active participant in the conflict in large part because of Mubarak's activity there. Yet this period saw distinct improvement in the Kuwaiti shaikh's relations with both powers. With each of them he rarely lost an opportunity to address simultaneously their desires and fears: Britain, that he had been ever loyal to it, but that events might force him to break the fragile ties between them, if Britain did not support him wholeheartedly; and the Ottomans, that he was ever loyal to the sultan, but that unfortunate circumstances forced him into reliance on the British. No matter how blatant the lie, both sides preferred to accept his statements as much as possible, in part because they were not sure of the true nature of Mubarak's relations with their rival, and in part simply because they wished so strongly to believe what he was telling them.

If those points are borne in mind, then the last of the strange strands of Ottoman policy on Kuwait becomes more comprehensible. In February 1905 Istanbul was working diligently to limit Mubarak's ability to disrupt his neighbors, the Kuwaiti shaikh had avowed openly his preference for the British over the Ottomans, and the *vali* had to admit that the idea of Mubarak's continuing to function as *kaymakam* had no basis in reality.[120] Yet shortly thereafter the government began to woo Mubarak. Despite the way in which it started, this charm campaign was not merely a hopeless, "it's-not-going-to-work-but-then-nothing-else-will-either" move, which the British view of Kuwaiti affairs might have suggested; the Ottomans seemed to think that there was a chance of drawing Mubarak back from his foreign entanglements. This belief gained strength from reports of tension between the British and their Kuwaiti client.

When the effort began, Istanbul had slight grounds for thinking that Mubarak would abandon the British and adopt a more friendly attitude. Only one month after the meetings with Mubarak and `Abd al-Rahman al-Sa`ud seemed to settle conditions in Najd, Ibn Rashid revived the conflict by raiding some of the Sa`udi supporters. In response Mubarak gave weapons to 500 tribesmen from Qasîm and sent them into the interior. Other bedouins gathered near Kuwait, and war on a wider basis than before appeared probable. The sultan and the Porte ordered the Basra *vali* and the commander of the troops in Qasîm to try to win the hearts and minds of Mubarak and the local people, thus causing them to abandon all thought of leaving their homes.[121] The remonstrances of these officials seemed to gain the immediate goal: there was no Arab mass advance on Qasîm, where the Ottomans were able to set up their new administration.

As that success took shape, another intriguing report came from Basra. The *vali* reported that British officials were planning to build strongholds around Kuwait and up to Umm Qasr, despite the opposition of Mubarak. The British rebuffed Mubarak, saying, "Kuwait is ours; as it is on the coast, we will control it."[122] In one sense this was alarming news: Britain seemed to be reneging on its promise not to establish a protectorate in Kuwait. Yet in light of the current Ottoman effort to woo Mubarak, the report might inspire hope, since it suggested that the Kuwaiti shaikh might be regretting his recent avowed favor for Britain. The report had no relation to fact, which raises the interesting question of why the *vali* should have believed it. Mubarak probably found the rumor useful, indeed may have started it; it would help to repair damage done to the careful balance of outward warmth and distance that he found so comfortable in his relations with his neighbor. He was spreading similar stories later in 1905, telling tales to deserters from the Ottoman army in Qasîm who stopped in Kuwait and then sending them to Basra at his own expense.[123] Mubarak also had the opportunity to drop hints directly to the *vali*, for instance when he submitted a letter to avow the obedience to the Ottomans that he had refused to give in February.[124] Growing resentment of the increasingly heavy-handed Mubarak among Kuwaitis, who might attempt the return to power of the anti-Mubarak party, may have influenced his change of attitude. It could well have resulted also from the realization that the recent posting of an Agent to Kuwait still would not solve all problems with the Ottoman regime; it would be especially understandable if he had heard hints of the Agent's imminent withdrawal.[125] Most upsetting for him, however, probably was news of Britain's high-handed, humiliating treatment of his Bahraini friend and counterpart, Shaikh 'Isa, in March.[126] Mubarak was irretrievably committed to his British connection, but the attendant discomforts must have checked his desire to make final the break with his neighbors.

With both sides finding an advantage in the resurrection of apparent mutual good will, the relationship so recently declared dead by the *vali* regained vitality, as did the lingering suspicions of some British officials. The Basra Consul in January 1906 reported on the clear warming of relations since February 1905. The *vali* appeared friendly and conciliatory to Mubarak, while the latter seemed "to do all he can to meet Mukhlis Pasha's wishes." He subscribed T£625 to the construction of a new barracks in Basra, provided free transport to Iraq for deserters from Qasîm and allowed resumed carriage of the Hasa mail through his territory. Mubarak corresponded frequently with the *vali*, reportedly reassuming the title of *kaymakam* and signing letters as "your dear friend." The government in turn took pains to soothe Mubarak's points of complaint, notably by easing pressure on less sensitive land questions and by releasing the Basra agent arrested three years earlier.[127]

Along with the efforts to restrict his acquisition of Basra real estate, these attempts to maintain some form of continuing, official intercourse with the lord of Kuwait became the government's policy mainstay in the waning days of its rule on the Gulf. In January 1907, the apparent imminent return to Ottoman good graces of Sa`dun Pasha, Mubarak's erstwhile ally at Sarif in 1901 and would-be partner in a recent land sale, for example, raised hopes that that other recalcitrant, Shaikh Mubarak, could likewise be brought back into the Ottoman embrace. The government may have wanted to exploit tensions that had arisen between Mubarak and the British Agent. Abdülhamid ordered the *vali* to make an approach to Mubarak at a gala given by Shaikh Khaz`al of Muhammara, the Kuwaiti shaikh's close friend. The government probably hoped to effect a reconciliation with the mediation of Khaz`al, much as the *naqib* mediated between the *vali* and Sa`dun, and as had Mubarak himself between `Abd al-Rahman al-Sa`ud and Muhlis Pasha.[128] The plan brought no concrete gains, but renewed signs of friendliness from the Sa`udi-Kuwaiti alliance caused the government to try again a little later.[129] Circumstance scuttled that attempt: Mubarak's attempt to buy Sa`dun's land came a month later, precipitating the dispute that was to put a lingering chill back on relations. Britain was able to take advantage of Mubarak's initial anger, in fact, to reach the secret 1907 agreement.[130] Although relations eventually improved again, Istanbul did not retake the initiative. The turmoil of the 1908 Young Turk revolution, the changed priorities of the new regime, the disastrous wars in the Balkans and with Italy, and, not least, the 1909 deposition of the most interested observer of Kuwaiti affairs, Sultan Abdülhamid II, made the fate of the enclave seem less important. The Ottomans treated Mubarak with a good show of courtesy and amicability, but they did not seek any real concessions from him. Istanbul's changing attitude is to be seen in the draft of a message to Mubarak in 1911, addressed to Mubarak al-Sabah, "Ruler of Kuwait and Chief of Its Tribes," instead of to "the *kaymakam* of Kuwait."[131]

For his part, Mubarak was generally willing to maintain an equal appearance of good will and loyalty. In addition to messages expressing devotion to the sultan, his favorite tactic was to donate money to various causes favored by the government. He received an honor reserved for noted contributors to the Hijaz Railway, a project even dearer to Abdülhamid than the Baghdad line. In addition to the funds for the Basra barracks, Mubarak helped to finance construction of a road between Basra and `Ashar on the Shatt in 1909/10.[132] He also gave generously to support the Ottomans in the Italian and Balkan wars that began in

1911/12, for which he received another honor. A committee of dignitaries came to Kuwait to bestow the medal in a ceremony of pomp and circumstance, which included fulsome displays of the love and loyalty felt for the sultan by the recipient and the townspeople.[133]

In one sense, it may be said that the late Ottoman policy on Kuwait had some effect. Occasions for sharp diplomatic clashes with Britain—so frequent between 1899 and 1902—and for Mubarak to meddle aggressively in Arabia and Iraq gradually declined. Judicious application of the Ottoman carrot and stick, however, was not the only restraining influence on Mubarak. The British disapproved of their Kuwaiti client's open involvement in tribal troubles and, as their presence in Kuwait increased, Mubarak found it more difficult to ignore their advice. After the death of Ibn Rashid in 1906, in fact, Mubarak adopted a more even stance in Najd, moderating his support for Ibn Sa`ud and thus becoming less influential there. He did not greatly prefer an unchallengeable Sa`udi amir to a powerful Rashidi leader.[134] In Iraq, restrictions on Mubarak's acquisition of land may have moderated his activity as chief weapons supplier to rebellious tribes, but also of importance was the worsening of his relations with the leading rebel, Sa`dun. This enmity led to a clash between Muntafiq and Kuwaiti forces in 1910; victory by Sa`dun in the battle of Hadiyya also dealt a blow to Mubarak's prestige.

Even with his greater circumspection, however, Mubarak remained an exemplar to other notables who wished to shake off Ottoman control, because no policy succeeded in altering significantly the total absence of governmental influence inside Kuwait that was deplored by *Vali* Muhlis in 1905. Just a month after the ceremonious award of the medal to Mubarak in 1912, for example, a Danish traveler carrying recommendations from the *vali* was met with suspicion, until the British Agent vouched for him, because he was suspected of German sympathies.[135] Mubarak continued to take care not to put himself within reach of the government, for instance by going to Basra.[136] It must therefore be concluded that, despite some success in stabilizing affairs, the policies followed after the 1901 agreement with Britain were as futile as those of 1896–1901 in repairing the most serious damage arising from Mubarak's murder of his brothers. Noting this lack of significant progress and under severe pressure from the Balkan wars, the Young Turk government thus finally entered the negotiations with Britain that were to lead in 1913 to formal renunciation of Ottoman claims to control Kuwait.[137]

These last two chapters' examination of one of the longest-running, thorniest problems complicating Ottoman rule in Arabia presents abundant material from which to draw conclusions about the behavior of the key players in the region. The period 1896–1914 brought fairly rapid change to the Gulf, as commerce and technology advanced. Those who could read and adapt to such shifts flourished at the expense of those who could not.

The story of one of those who did well in the Gulf, Britain, is fairly well known. Although hampered by limited resources around Arabia, the British usually achieved objectives because they used what they had very efficiently. Modern ships reached trouble spots at short notice, showing to advantage in comparison to the slow-moving Ottoman military. These ships also were useful in gathering intelligence, which was passed quickly to India and London. This contributed to Britain's crucial comparative advantage over Istanbul in policy making. Information gathered from a wide variety of sources reached the central government almost immediately, thanks to the telegraph. The informants naturally had personal views on events that could color reports, and their sources of information were not always trustworthy, but they generally did not slant their reports as egregiously as some perhaps corrupt Ottoman officials. Confusion was thus reduced, the formation of policy speeded and the prompt execution of decisions assured. Policies might react to circumstances—Britain had little inherent interest in Kuwait, until the strengthening current of imperialism made them think that no other power should be allowed to possess it—but efficiency in analysis and execution gave Britain the opportunity to initiate action more often than to absorb it.

Britain's crispness in action benefited Mubarak, the man who gained the most in this period. As the possessor of limited power, Mubarak did an amazingly good job of creating a safe niche for himself in the shadow of two Great Powers. He sought wealth and influence, but he realized that it could be won and preserved only under the protection and nominal authority of another power. Without weapons of his own, he had to play upon the weaknesses of potential sponsors, not only Britain and the Ottomans, but also at times the Germans, Russians, French, and even Iranians. His long experience in Gulf politics made him aware of each government's hopes and fears, and he addressed those relentlessly. He approached the Ottomans first, proclaiming his loyalty and devotion while accusing his enemies of being in the pay of Britain. He thereby succeeded in delaying retaliation for having murdered his brothers, but the confusion in the Ottoman government eventually led him to despair of ever winning the right to rule independently as his predecessors had. At times when retribution seemed imminent, he turned in desperation to Britain, using the same strategy. In short, he told each side that he favored them, but that he would go to the highest bidder. Even after the creation of the tie to the British, he pushed them for greater support by threatening to accept proposals from the Ottomans and the Russians. At the same time, he generally maintained fairly cordial relations with the Ottomans, in case British oversight grew too close for comfort or the relationship otherwise soured. His simple strategy of saying anything but only doing what was in his interest indeed worked well. All sides regarded him with some suspicion, but his words made them hesitate and fostered a feeling of tolerance. Mubarak may have been an "ignorant" man in some people's view, but he was no fool. His peers recognized his success, and ambitious notables such as Ibn Sa`ud were tempted to try to emulate him.

That did not bode well for the Ottomans. Their conduct throughout the Kuwait problem displayed all of the shortcomings that were sapping their ability to rule areas like Arabia and Iraq. The problems of communication in comparison to the British have been mentioned. If they bedeviled Basra, which at least had telegraph links to Istanbul, imagine how much worse they were in Hasa, communication with which took not hours but weeks. The sense of remoteness encouraged the spread of corruption and lax administration. In conjunction with confusion in government circles, this engendered a feeling of fundamental disconnection between state and people. For all of Mubarak's lack of religious sensibility, it was natural for Kuwaitis and other Arabs to feel more kinship for the Ottomans than for the British.[138] They drifted away from the state because the seemingly arbitrary rulings on taxes, land registration, gun ownership, and many other locally important matters made life more difficult than it should have been.

If life was tough for those submitting to Ottoman rule, in practice it was often only marginally tougher for those who rebelled. The lack of a coherent policy on dealing with tribes and other semi-independent communities clearly disrupted the effort to regain Kuwait. The state was slow to use the stick, which provided the best hope of checking Mubarak. Without its threat, he and others began to take the carrot almost for granted. The sultan did try partially to correct the imbalance by working more closely with Ibn Rashid, but he was not the power that his predecessor had been. The Ottomans also were to find that he was not always an amiable ally. Without the use of a credible deterrent force, the government felt restricted in shaping policies on Kuwait, lest any move topple the entire precarious order among the tribes of Arabia. Mubarak saw this, and the longer that he avoided military retribution for his acts, the bolder he became. By supplying weapons, intruding into tribal politics, and being an example to his peers, Mubarak sharply accelerated the destabilization of the region. The failure to regain Kuwait dealt a blow to Ottoman rule in Arabia from which it was not able to recover.

Chapter 7

Arabia, 1896–1914

Mubarak al-Sabah's long campaign to create an independent shaikhdom in Kuwait diverted Ottoman attention for too long from the problems of Hasa. The conditions that had stirred unrest beginning around 1890—weak control of better-armed bedouins, the ill fit of the tax system to local conditions—had not been fundamentally altered by ad hoc improvements. The impression of Ottoman indecisiveness spawned by the lack of reaction to the 1893 Qatar unrest (and which the Kuwait problem reinforced) reduced the impact of isolated moves. Yet as long as serious disturbances did not break out, the government did not want to take time or effort from other pressing problems to devise a coherent plan of reform. In Arabia, it preferred to concentrate on Kuwait and the threat of British penetration posed there.

When attention was paid to Arabia, too much continued to center on trying to halt the spread of British influence and too little on addressing the concerns of the populace. The state on occasion showed some initiative in trying to improve government operations, for instance by updating some tax records. These initiatives, however, grew as much out of concerns in Istanbul, including the need to raise revenues, as out of those in Arabia. The efforts to invigorate administration thus could increase local discontent as easily as decrease it. Central and provincial authorities generally allowed local officials to carry on as usual, however, except when problems with Britain and related issues of security demanded action. When it was aroused, as a result, government attention focused disproportionately on Najd and Qatar instead of on the vital Ottoman center, Hasa.

Unfortunately for the Ottomans, the rapport between the state and the local notables in Hasa that had existed since the era of Midhat Pasha continued to suffer from periodic stress. As long as the authorities protected commerce and agriculture from bedouin raids, and taxes were kept at a tolerable level, the key elements of eastern Arabian sedentary society remained reasonably content with, and willing to assist, the Ottoman government. By the last decade of the nineteenth century, dissatisfaction among society's leaders had become quite evident as the state did not fulfill its requisite functions. Shaikhs Mubarak and Qâsim might not have irrevocably sundered relations with the Ottomans, but they certainly showed limited willingness to cooperate with the state. Hasa's traders and other notables remained more closely tied to the Ottomans than the shaikhs of Kuwait and Qatar, but they too protested against government action (collection of customs and excise duties) or inaction (failure to police the roads), which damaged their security of life and livelihood. Farmers suffered from governmental manipulation of date prices and other occasional unwelcome interference, as in 1900, for example, when the garrison commander (acting as overseer of the state land office) apparently assigned water rights without regard to local practice.[1] The dissatisfaction shown in 1890–95 recurred after 1900, and when security practically collapsed in 1913, the Hasawis stood aside while Sa`udi forces pushed the remaining Ottoman garrisons out of the towns. The lack of committed local supporters facilitated the expulsion of the Ottomans from eastern Arabia, be it by force, as in Hasa, or by negotiation, as in Qatar.

The Struggle for Qatar

Throughout the last period of Istanbul's sovereignty over Qatar, the Ottoman position in this dangling *kaza* varied from poor to woeful. Just as with Mubarak in Kuwait, the specter of British subversion complicated the government's problem of prickly relations with its nominal *kaymakam*. Qâsim al-Thani escaped punishment for the 1893 revolt in part by suggesting a British desire to make Qatar a protectorate, and Ottoman policy thereafter was shaped by suspicions of foreign intrigue. London's hardening resistance to admission of Istanbul's sovereignty over the peninsula added body to the thought. Policy therefore followed three channels, all directed to meet this perceived threat.

The most constant element of the anti-British effort in Qatar was the prevention of weapons smuggling from Bahrain. The investigation into the 1893 revolt described the danger of destabilization posed by this illegal trade, and an 1896 memorandum by the *mutasarrıf* of Hasa reinforced the warning. As had the authors of the 1893 report, he wanted to increase the Gulf squadron in order to keep all of the potential entry points under observation. He suggested basing two sailing ships in Qatar to patrol the coast, to be supported by deeper-water steam corvettes.[2] The plan was not realized, probably not only because of expense but also because the author was the same *mutasarrıf* who had been disgraced by leaving his post and traveling to Istanbul without permission.[3] Istanbul nevertheless did keep a ship on station at Qatar with much more regularity than anywhere else in the Gulf and had some success in stopping boats carrying arms.[4] Its presence may also deserve some of the credit for keeping piracy off the Qatar coast at a lower level than off Hasa.[5] Significant supplies of arms still managed to pass through Qatar, however, and it is likely that Shaikh Qâsim did not frown on the trade.[6]

Because of the second element of Ottoman policy, Qâsim within limits was left fairly free to do as he pleased, even if it pleased him to run guns. The government took care not to press the shaikh, fearing that he might at any time reverse his supposed rebuff to British offers of protection. Qâsim lost no opportunity to encourage that view: after the seizure of a shipment of guns, he warned that Qataris would turn to foreigners if the arms were not returned for their own defense.[7] Despite some confusion over which party most desired a British protectorate in Qatar, and over the reasons for their own weakness, the Ottomans had a reasonably accurate idea of basic conditions there. They knew that their influence was restricted to Doha and the waters patrolled by the navy; to speak of their having supreme authority anywhere would be an exaggeration.[8] Nothing could be accomplished by a few officials and a modest garrison without the agreement of Qâsim or his brother, Ahmad. Qâsim was the paramount Qatari shaikh but lived in semiretirement in the interior, leaving Ahmad to represent him in Doha and in most contacts with the Ottomans. Shaikh Ahmad thus in time was able to raise his own influence to rival his brother's. With real authority resting in the Al Thani shaikhs' hands, the Ottomans took care not to irritate either man more than was necessary.

The state thus did not return the seized weapons, but neither did it press the shaikhs hard after incidents of unrest. Qâsim's aborted assault on Kuwait did not draw a harsh response, despite Receb Pasha's suggestion that eight battalions be sent to chastise him; the main result of the Qatari shaikh's mobilization was to cause Istanbul to listen to his complaints. Similarly after residents attacked some of the garrison of Doha, the government tried to soothe relations as quickly as possible by recall of the troops, to be replaced by a fresh battalion under a more capable commander.[9] Many officials appointed by Istanbul gave in to the temptation to be timeservers, content to draw their salaries while involving themselves as little as possible in the actual management of Qatari affairs.[10] Somnolence was easy, since several schemes to reduce Qatar's isolation from Hufuf and Basra by laying telegraph lines or improving the camel post had little effect. It is very doubtful that the officials ever extracted significant tax revenue from customs, pearling, or any other source.[11] As long as they checked the import of weapons, dissuaded the shaikhs from too open involvement in tribal unrest, and kept the Ottoman flag flying in the peninsula, they were in the main left in peace by both Istanbul and the locals.

Although the Ottoman claim to be the sovereign power of the peninsula was thus based more on principle than on an ability to direct events in the remotest villages, the state was not wholly without influence. The garrison in Doha was a check to Qâsim, who exiled himself to the interior to avoid possibly dangerous contact with the Ottomans. He thus was cut off physically from the leading Qatari settlement, and inevitably his influence suffered as Ahmad assumed management of the town. Ahmad in turn could not ignore completely the military force with which he shared Doha.

It is also misleading to dismiss the *kaymakamlık* as just an empty title, borne with indifference by Qâsim. Such official recognition added some prestige to its recipients, as well as helping to insulate them from open governmental antagonism. It worked at times to Qâsim's advantage, as in giving a veneer of legitimacy to his moves against Kuwait, but it did not always get him what he wanted, as in the case of the seized weaponry. He could occasionally gain support for actions that coincided with Ottoman goals as well, notably in problems with Britain. Ottoman pressure could also be cited as an excuse for not taking distasteful action on British complaints. On the other hand, acceptance of the title made acting in direct defiance of Ottoman interests a little trickier. Whatever the effect of disloyalty on public opinion, it certainly made pacific overtures to the British more complicated by raising doubt about his legal independence and reliability.

Presumably because, as a long-established leader, he felt the restrictive aspects of the *kaymakamlık* more than its benefits (especially after disappointments over Ottoman action concerning Kuwait and Zubara), Qâsim tried to resign from the post in 1898. Istanbul seemed prepared to accept his resignation but then reconsidered. It was true that the shaikh now left all the functions of office to Ahmad, but he still wielded great influence in Qatari affairs. Good will might be gained by humoring him in formalizing this arrangement.[12] Yet to release him from his formal tie to the state would be to acknowledge his right to act as he pleased, including the option of drawing closer to the British. Also important to maintain was the principle that Ottoman office and allegiance were not to be assumed and discarded at will; under normal circumstances, it would not be proper to strip a shaikh of his title.[13]

That theory came to the fore in incidents of 1905 which also made clear the potential value of the *kaymakamlık*. Shaikh Ahmad had begun to chafe at his subordinate position as Qâsim's deputy, which probably prompted his overtures seeking some kind of relationship with the British from 1898 to 1903.[14] The approach of ʿAbd al-ʿAziz Ibn Saʿud in the summer of 1905 threatened to precipitate a crisis, since he claimed to be making rounds to settle disputes among tribes of Hasa and Qatar. He also said that he was acting with Ottoman permission. In reality he was coming to aid Qâsim, who had lately been losing a proxy war between his supporters, the ʿAjman, and Ahmad's, the Al Murra. Qâsim sent money and weapons to get Ibn Saʿud's aid against his brother and probably also against the ruler of Abu Dhabi, with whom both allies had quarrels of long standing.[15] Ahmad in turn sided with the Abu Dhabi shaikh and Ibn Rashid, while seeking his own seal of approval from the Ottomans.

Ahmad thus made some interesting proposals to the Doha garrison commander. He tried to do the same thing that Qâsim had done in 1871: gain Ottoman backing that could give decisive protection during a bid to become the next shaikh of Qatar. Ahmad had been treating the Ottoman troops well and now wanted to deepen the bonds between himself and the state. Detailing repeated British attempts to pry settlements away from (Ottoman) Qatar, he asked for the dispatch of fresh troops to block the schemes. Since he recognized that such a deployment might be difficult under present circumstances (all concentration was on the Najdi region of Qasîm at the time), Ahmad offered to pay for their transport or even enough yearly to support one or two battalions. In return he wanted public marks of Ottoman approval, including a rank and people (i.e., to govern). In short, he wanted to become *kaymakam*.

The commander was intrigued by the scheme. It could make control of Qatar immeasurably easier. With Ahmad's help the land could be run by about as many men as were now present in Doha; if the Saʿudi faction came to dominate in Najd and Qatar, no one could foresee the troubles that might ensue. He forwarded the request for troops and a ship to guard against the advent of Ibn Saʿud. The question of the *kaymakamlık* was more doubtful. While wishing to encourage Ahmad, the commander acknowledged that it would be impolitic to take the office from Qâsim without a compelling reason. The best solution would be to give Ahmad a rank and make it clear to everyone that he would succeed his brother.[16]

These events of 1905 give a good picture of the Ottoman predicament in trying to maintain a legitimate claim of sovereignty over Qatar. Although not entirely dependent on the sufferance of the Al Thani shaikhs, any official presence had little chance of real effectiveness without their good will. The shaikhs thus greatly influenced determination of governmental action. This was compounded by the extreme difficulty of consultation with Istanbul: because of the slowness of communications, no decision regarding Ahmad could be taken before he was assassinated five months later.[17] Lacking effective direction from above, local commanders must have felt the strong lure of cooperation with local magnates when it was offered to them. There also was much uncertainty about the true motives of the shaikhs, as happened elsewhere. Although noting Ahmad's interest in gaining Ottoman support in his struggle for power, the Doha commander was inclined to believe that his first impulse was as he said, to block Britain. Given his overtures to the British, however, he surely had no ideological abhorrence of them. Yet in the belief that he was working for that object, the Ottomans considered supporting him in his more personal schemes. Finally, the discussion of the *kaymakamlık* shows how interested the state was in establishing precedents or principles, no matter how weakly they reflected reality. Because of the British and related threats, it was vital to make sure that leading locals held official titles to mark them as Ottomans, even if they carried out no duties. In this effort the state was to expend effort and resources, which might have been better spent on firming the allegiance of the real source of vulnerability, the local populace.

Repeated attempts to expand the area claimable as Ottoman by appointing administrators to disputed settlements was the third, and most prominent, element of Istanbul's Qatar policy. These efforts were notable not only for their endurance but also for their total lack of effect. The state named *müdir*s to Zubara, Wakra, and 'Udayd, intending or trying to install them in 1895 and in much of the period from 1902 to 1912. Since the British disputed Ottoman claims to sovereignty over the peninsula, they objected to the appointments, and no *müdir* remained at his post for long. Istanbul maintained its right of appointment, however, by continuing to name the officials (four to Zubara, six to 'Udayd and two to Wakra), even if they had to stay in Hufuf instead of at their posts.[18] In at least one instance they tried to avoid British objection by assigning to Wakra a local notable, one of Qâsim's sons, first as *müdir*, then, when Britain objected, as a stipendiary "of long standing."[19]

The involvement of the Al Thani in the struggle over the three settlements tempts a conclusion that the government saw it as an opportunity to draw the shaikhs more closely to the state by supporting their interests. It was suggested above that Qâsim found the *kaymakamlık* useful when his and Ottoman goals coincided. Such was the case here. The control of each settlement was at times a subject of dispute. Zubara was the focus of trouble with Bahrain, and `Udayd with Abu Dhabi, while the Al Bu `Aynayn in Wakra were uneasy with the Al Thani.[20] Qâsim wanted to use Istanbul's power to assert his position in the face of his British-backed rivals, and his stories of foreigners' overtures or high-handedness helped to keep Ottoman attention on Qatar's borders.[21] Yet the available evidence suggests that the state took action not to sway Qâsim into being more cooperative in governing Qatar but rather to block British intrusion, to increase control over entry points for smuggled guns and to stop use of these areas as bases for unruly bedouins.[22] The most prolonged period of attempting to establish the Ottoman flag around Qatar, after all, began in 1902, the year of anti-British military reconsolidation elsewhere in Hasa, Yemen, and Kuwait.

The course of events after 1895 raises one outstanding question about Ottoman policy in Qatar: did it have any effect, or was it all wasted effort? It is true that Britain did not reestablish "friendly relations" with any Qatari shaikh by signing agreements. London refused to admit Ottoman sovereignty over the peninsula, but neither did it care to take steps that would inevitably draw protests from Istanbul and its allies until the negotiations leading to the peninsula's independence in 1913. The Ottoman presence in Doha was enough to hinder encroachment before then. It was to Istanbul's detriment that it concentrated discussion upon the problem of raising its flag over scattered, sparsely settled areas (even as distant as Dubai), except when Qâsim threatened trouble over Kuwait. Qatar became utterly marginalized. Men were sent to the peninsula and left to waste away. If the government was determined to keep Qatar Ottoman, the most important step that it could have taken would have been to improve the reliability of shipping between Basra and Doha rather than to worry over uninhabited `Udayd. More regular supply and communication with the garrison and officials would have improved their miserable morale and have been the first step to exerting real control over the Al Thani shaikhs. By ignoring Qatar except in the context of the British problem, the Ottomans guaranteed the upper hand to the shaikhs, and despite all their efforts to keep official ties to them, the Ottomans were unable to influence the selection of leaders or to check inclinations toward Britain.[23] Thus another *kaza* dangled and was lost.

Hasa, 1896–1905

As in Qatar, the Ottoman administration in Hasa limped along without much sustained effort made to reestablish rapport with the settled populace. Two leading concerns of the people had become clear in the turbulent time 1890–95: unfair taxation and the predations of bedouins. The steady trickle of ideas for improvement of control in Arabia that had come from knowledgeable officials in the 1880s practically stopped, however, and without such promptings Istanbul found it hard to devote attention to its distant dependency. Problems were addressed ad hoc. Istanbul generally left the *mutasarrıf* free to administer as he saw fit until a crisis or complaint arose, at which time he was replaced by another, equally poorly guided man. *Mutasarrıf*s instead frequently had to battle rival officials in Hasa for power and money. Several governors lasted a number of years because they had notable success in some areas, but none addressed all of the entrenched problems.

One such *mutasarrıf* was the durable Said Pasha. He was brought to Hufuf to restore order after the hasty departures of two successive *mutasarrıf*s in 1896. As in his three earlier terms, Said succeeded in pacifying Hasa. Lorimer found no significant attack on travelers or towns under him to report.[24] This relative tranquility contrasted sharply with the years before and after Said's rule. Order likely resulted from his practical approach to the two main functions of the state in the eyes of the people: security and taxation.

Papers collected by the Council of State in Istanbul during its investigation of Said's conduct give an example of his flexibility in taxation. After Istanbul ordered a 0.5% increase in the *öşür*, some village *muhtar*s collected it. When the *müdir* of 'Uyun brought that town's share to Hufuf, Said directed him to return it to its former owners.[25] He did this on his own authority, although Istanbul later agreed to postpone collection of this and another tax increase in Hasa because of the people's inability to pay more.[26] Hasawis—if not always Istanbul—must have appreciated Said's practical approach to revenue collection.

In security affairs as well, Said took several practical steps that should have been staples of the Ottoman regime in Hasa. Of great sense was his recruitment of a *hamidiye* force of mounted Arab auxiliaries, including at least some locals,[27] on which he came to depend more heavily than on the regular garrison. The garrison still lacked a mounted section, despite the recommendations of several *mutasarrıf*s since about 1890, including Said.[28] Given the size of Hasa and the mobility of bedouin raiders, foot soldiers faced a difficult task in keeping the peace. Said's success with a force, perhaps recruited on his own authority, presumably did much to persuade the state to create a mounted police force in 1902-3; it seems to have preferred not to recruit Hasawis, however, who would have been best adapted to fighting under local conditions.[29] The government never felt sure whom they could trust in Hasa, which kept them from ever adopting Said's relaxed attitude on allowing weapons into the hands of nomads or settlers.

ARABIA, 1896-1914

Also clearly important to Said's security success was his willingness to use tribal politics to play groups off one another. The example of his response to Shaikh Qâsim's move to attack Kuwait sheds some light on his methods. He met with tribal leaders who might wish to oppose Qâsim's advance and seemed ready to support them in a campaign. In conjunction with the payment of subsidies to friends and the closure of towns to enemies,[30] the threat of instigating counterraids could be an effective check on any bedouin urge to plunder. Said also took care to cultivate contacts among the local populace and notables, which facilitated two-way communication. He was able to disprove rumors of British-directed Egyptians stirring trouble among the `Ajman, Al Murra, and Bani Hajir, for example, by recruiting five Arabs to visit the tribes to gather information covertly.[31] He also reportedly maintained contact with the shaikh of Qatar by employing Qâsim's agent in Hufuf as his personal aide.[32] Said's assorted means of keeping the peace might make Istanbul nervous, but he at least had the experience and willingness to cut corners that allowed him to do what was necessary with the tribes, something that others in the capital and in the provinces often found difficult.

Whereas Said used techniques that disquietened some in government, the other "peace-keeping" *mutasarrıf* followed more orthodox methods. Sayyid Talib Pasha (1902-4),[33] brother of the *naqib* of Basra, benefited from Istanbul's moves to counter British designs in Arabia, about which he helped to stoke concern. Hasa received reinforcements, with which he was able to hit hard several groups of marauders. He may also have used some tactics reminiscent of Said, setting tribe against tribe, since he paid on his own initiative salaries to shaikhs of the Bani Hajir and Manasir for "services to the state."[34] His combination of Istanbul's and local forces restored a modicum of order to Hasa's roads.[35]

It proved temporary, however, because Talib—and even Said—did not correct basic problems hastening the decline of Ottoman influence in the area. Hunting gun smugglers and strengthening the military against Britain and the bedouins could not put administration on a sound footing as long as corruption continued and economic growth was hampered. Too frequently officials let personal financial or career interests interfere with the proper execution of their duties. In the Qâsim-Mubarak affair, for example, Said was guilty of accepting a bribe from the Kuwaiti leader that influenced his reporting to Istanbul. He also was able to do little to control rival officials answerable to other ministries. He was dismissed— and almost put on trial—because of allegations of gunrunning made by the military commandant, who resented Said's reliance on the local militia and coveted the *mutasarrıflık* for himself. Sayyid Talib fell from grace because of abnormally rapacious avarice, the effects of which continued to paralyze the financial and civil administration in Hasa after he left.[36]

Talib exploited, and widened, a gulf between civil and military officials that plagued Hasa's administration for years. Ill-paid, feeling isolated and bored, surrounded by potentially hostile bedouins and townsmen, the gendarmerie was tempted to squeeze money from the people to repay it for the thanklessness of its task. This irritated the civil authorities, who not only found that the increased discontent made their own job harder but resented the competition in corruption.[37] Said fell victim to the rivalry, while Talib was able to hit the richest extortion targets by allying himself with the military. His dismissal restored some restraining balance, but the competition continued, paving the way for riots and a shopkeepers' strike in Hufuf in 1905.[38]

Corruption was but an outgrowth of the fundamental problem in Hasa, heavy and unfair taxation. Reform plans of the 1880s had repeated Midhat's estimation of the area's rich revenue potential, but few steps were taken to realize it. Only the assessment of its wealth was remembered. The temptation to wring more from Hasa became overpowering as Basra's receipts sank further below outlays and as problems in the Balkans heightened Istanbul's need for cash. The spread of unrest and corruption undoubtedly also caused or worsened an apparent sharp decline in Hasa's revenues, which fell well below expenses.[39] In 1900 the tax increases mentioned above, assessed at T£12,000, caused much grumbling before being postponed. A new survey of date trees at Qatif was finally made in 1903 and was to be repeated every five years. The tax base grew but still appears to have been weak.[40] More attention was paid to collecting long-ignored livestock taxes, but with mixed results.[41] The right to collect customs was also farmed out for rapidly rising sums, leading to imposition of trade-stifling, illegal duties and consequent protests from Britain. Other, nontax barriers could be thrown in the way of trade as well: the authorities imposed an embargo on trade with Najd in 1904, for example, in an effort to control Ibn Sa'ud.[42] This, a population survey in 1905–6 preparatory to the levy of a poll tax and, most significantly, dissatisfaction over the administration's setting of date prices and taxes sparked the Hufuf unrest.[43] These acts harmed the interests of all members of Hasa's society, especially the traders, major landholders, and other notables who were the government's main interlocutors among the population. Given their influence in Hasawi society, civil unrest became all too likely when their interests were threatened.[44]

Without the solid support of any broad section of society, by 1905 the Ottomans clearly recognized the danger that Hasa could slip from their grasp. The efforts of 1902 to improve command of the coast and the roads to Hufuf had had some effect, but keeping the peace was still a challenge. The cost of keeping an enlarged garrison also could not be met from the still anemic revenues returned by the local administration. Having received complaints about taxes and the conduct of officials, Istanbul knew that there was much discontent among Hasawis. Yet it could only deal with individuals, not the administration as a whole. The only notable attempt at changing the system was increased experimentation with unification of the civil and military commands; as before, however, there was always someone inside or outside the administration who complained about the governor. With little more than these protests and the general knowledge that talented officers were needed to get the most effect out of insufficient troops, Istanbul often rotated commanders too frequently to restore equilibrium to Hasa's government.[45] No one disputed that the most urgently needed step was the improvement of communications; without the ability to monitor the *mutasarrıf* easily, there was an argument to be made for allowing several groups to vie for power. Money naturally was a major obstacle. The sultan had issued an order for the extension of the telegraph to Hasa in 1899, but the Treasury could not meet the expense.[46]

An equally serious problem was Istanbul's blindness to the real causes of turmoil in Arabia. Excepting complaints from the populace, it was reports about, or protests by, the British that were the most frequent causes of drawing the central government's attention to the area. The Ottomans' thus failed to absorb the lesson of their past three decades of experience: it was difficult to foresee problems when they focused too much on British machinations. Without an accurate picture of the conditions under which Hasawis lived, Istanbul still attributed to outsiders opposition to the state instead of to its natural allies, the Muslim population. Consequently its moves, which at times did show determination and willingness to expend resources, concentrated on issues raised by Britain, notably the defense of Ottoman territorial claims along the coast, instead of the issues of good government. Similarly after 1904 the state was to begin to trace many problems to the supposedly foreign-influenced Ibn Sa'ud, whom it also tried hard to counter.

The Occupation of Qasîm and Ottoman-Sa'udi Relations, 1904–1906

The Ottoman administrative machine may have become more creaky by the middle of the decade, but Istanbul's efforts in Najd showed a surprising willingness and ability to undertake an ambitious program. It launched a military expedition that rivaled that of Midhat in size and exceeded it in ambition: the permanent occupation of towns deep in the Arabian interior. When the troops had to withdraw in 1906, however, they left Najd firmly under the control of Ibn Sa`ud, who could then devote attention to strengthening his influence in Hasa.

The decision to march into the interior resulted from the struggle between Ibn Sa`ud and Ibn Rashid. Conflict between the two had started in earnest in 1902 with Ibn Sa`ud's capture of Riyadh. By late 1903 he had wrested control of large parts of southern and central Najd from the Rashidis. He reached a position from which he could threaten Ha'il when he took the important districts of Washm and Qasîm early the next year. Istanbul's main tribal ally in Arabia, so powerful just two years earlier, faced elimination.

The Ottomans in 1902 did not show much alarm at the incipient Sa`udi revival. Their main concerns centered on Kuwait and on the upsurge in bedouin unrest in Hasa. The latter had some recognized connection to Ibn Sa`ud's activity in the interior, but the government limited itself to having Talib restore order in the strip of land thought to be desired by both Riyadh and Britain. It laid no plans for an advance into Najd, nor did it markedly increase aid to Ibn Rashid.[47]

While not wanting to see the Rashidi amir fall, Istanbul had interests that were served by the struggle in Najd. Ibn Rashid was a useful ally in many respects, but as a powerful, ambitious, and unpredictable bedouin leader he was also at times regarded with fear and suspicion. Istanbul originally became interested in him because of his potential to restrain bedouins who frequently cut the telegraph line between Damascus and Madina. Ibn Rashid also won Abdülhamid's favor, using a constant stream of gifts and protestations of loyalty to convince the sultan of his devotion. His status as an important Muslim leader in the vicinity of Mecca and Madina predisposed Abdülhamid to believe him. Ibn Rashid's actions away from the Hijaz, however, were less open to Ottoman supervision and made the Porte distrust him. He was reported to have a large stockpile of weapons, some of which he had received from that most suspect of the sultan's servants, Qâsim al-Thani. The Rashidi amir was thought to be responsible for raids on `Asiri tribes and for some of the tribal unrest in Hasa in 1900. In 1902, of course, Ibn Rashid was still hovering around Kuwait, where his activities could cause London to declare a protectorate. As long as it did not start a wider tribal war, therefore, the Sa`udi challenge might be useful in limiting Ibn Rashid's ability to cause trouble on the fringes of Ottoman-controlled territory.[48]

They may be excused for not realizing it immediately, but the Ottomans were courting trouble by not helping wholeheartedly Ibn Rashid's campaign against the Sa`udis. Many among the Arabian population had not been enamored of the Sa`udi-Wahhabi movement during its previous incarnations, but there was a significant body of supporters among the conservative population of Najd. There were many people dissatisfied with current conditions in much of the peninsula, where strife on several levels was common. Ibn Rashid's rough methods for maintaining his grasp on the interior caused many to suffer and made trade difficult. The Ottoman struggles with Kuwait and Britain (and by extension most of the Gulf and India) further disrupted trade, which was already undergoing pressure to change as Britain extended its domination over the Gulf economy.[49] The Ottomans showed discouragingly little ability to match British encouragement and direction of economic development in Hasa, Qatar, or even Basra. Ibn Sa`ud was able to tap into both the strain of popular sympathy with Wahhabism and the dissatisfaction with Ibn Rashid and the Ottomans. His stunning exploit in capturing his family's old base, Riyadh, with the help of a mere handful of men instantly won prestige and supporters for himself and the Wahhabi movement. Among them was Qâsim al-Thani, who was swept up in the surge of religious feeling and who also, no doubt, saw a potential welcome ally against the Ottomans. Istanbul's belated perception of the seriousness of this new threat eventually was to stir it to great efforts.

Ibn Sa`ud's attitude also helped to cloud the Ottoman view. He had observed Shaikh Mubarak and learned that the Ottomans, although powerful, could be managed by maintenance of an outwardly friendly attitude. After his capture of Riyadh he dispatched a message to Istanbul, avowing his allegiance.[50] Perhaps because the government thought that Ibn Sa`ud was merely the lieutenant of `Abd al-Rahman al-Sa`ud, who had been a pensioner of the Ottomans for a decade, it was willing to accept the statement for the time.[51]

When, contrary to general expectation, the Sa`udi upstart in 1904 seemed poised to supplant Ibn Rashid as the great tribal leader in Arabia, the Ottomans quickly reversed themselves. The protégé of the British-Mubarak camp could not be permitted complete license in such a sensitive region. The conflict moreover now showed alarming signs of drawing in tribesmen from Iraq as Ibn Rashid searched for help.[52] Already in 1903 the state had started to allow passage of arms through Basra to Ha'il;[53] when that failed to shore up Rashidi fortunes, it proved willing to commit a large body of troops.[54] It was the only means available to prevent the spread of violence to important, settled lands.

Sadly for the Ottomans, the very faults that made Ibn Rashid a more suitable ally than his predecessor—notably his inability to gather allies who could give him the confidence to turn against Istanbul—made him a burden in this venture. Whereas the Amir Muhammad al-Rashid had

had a measure of genuine respect for the Ottomans, his successor, `Abd al-`Aziz Ibn Rashid, treated the troops sent to his assistance with a complete lack of policy, tantamount to abuse. He made little attempt to meet their material needs, made them bear the brunt of the fighting, killed two high-ranking officers who balked at renewed operations, and generally caused confusion in the army by acting as though he were in command.[55] Of the 2,000 soldiers who marched into Najd in May 1904, fewer than 500 survived past September.

Istanbul promptly dispatched a second, larger force. Ibn Rashid enjoyed Sultan Abdülhamid's favor, and criticism of his behavior was consequently muted. Marshal Feyzi Pasha of the VI Corps thus was told to expel the Sa`udis from Qasîm (which would become a buffer province) either by negotiation or by force with the help of Ibn Rashid. Ibn Sa`ud recognized the danger of confronting this expedition; his repeated appeals for British protection unanswered, he renewed his appearance of loyalty to the sultan, sending one of his relatives to Istanbul with a letter for Abdülhamad.[56] This led to the February 1905 negotiations between his father `Abd al-Rahman, Mubarak al-Sabah, and the *vali* of Basra, which resulted in the peaceful occupation of the province.

Qasîm retained an Ottoman presence for more than a year after Feyzi's entry into Burayda and `Anayza, but the orders under which the administration and garrison had to operate reveal some telling weaknesses in Istanbul's conception of Arabia.[57] Construction of workable policies is difficult without a sound sense of local conditions, especially in an ambitious program such as this. The Qasîm venture courted failure because it left the detachment in a very vulnerable position. Istanbul depended too heavily on the validity of local leaders' expressions of loyalty to the sultan. A mere handful of military officers were to head the new *sancak* and *kazas*; the government counted on the existence of a preponderant class of notables, allied to neither Ibn Sa`ud nor Ibn Rashid, to make the administration work. It also hoped to buy the loyalty of surrounding tribes by distribution of honorific titles, salaries, and badges of unity.[58] Istanbul thought that these steps would restore peace quickly, allowing the reduction of the garrison to almost symbolic strength.[59] The great distance from Madina and Basra, moreover, could make supply of even that body of men very hard if they could not rely on the assistance of important bedouin tribes.

The plan limped along for a time in relative peace. The people of Qasîm welcomed the respite from war, and a notable portion of them preferred the Ottomans to Ibn Sa`ud or especially Ibn Rashid.[60] A large faction was aligned with Riyadh, but Ibn Sa`ud thought it wiser at first not to cause directly any problems that might spur a hostile reaction. His father accepted the title of *kaymakam* of Riyadh and a salary, and the Sa`udi notables scrupulously maintained a show of loyalty to the sultan.⁶¹ Acts such as Ibn Sa`ud's "peace-keeping" tour of Hasa and Qatar might arouse strong suspicion, but his demeanor offered the Ottomans no open reason to threaten Riyadh.

All could not be called satisfactory, however, even with the lack of outright opposition. Istanbul sadly underestimated the cost of operating an army in the midst of a vast waste. Ibn Rashid could not, or would not, ensure steady supply of the troops. Many of Marshal Feyzi's original force had died of hunger by the outset of the new regime in Qasîm; more would have starved without provisioning, on credit, from an `Anayza merchant.⁶² Supplies and transport had to be bought and arranged from Basra, Baghdad, and Madina, none of which had the money to outfit enough caravans. Money was transferred from other areas, but the troops never got full rations, let alone pay.⁶³

Expenses soared beyond expectations in large part because the government had not reckoned with the noncooperation of so many of the "brother Muslims" of Najd. Despite his declarations of loyalty, Ibn Sa`ud was happy to let his partisans in Qasîm make life unpleasant for the Ottomans. "Arabs" looted half of the provisions sent from Madina.⁶⁴ Over time incidents of harassment and aggression against the troops grew more frequent; if they retaliated, deputations of shaikhs asked for, and were given, the guilty soldiers for punishment.⁶⁵ In June 1906, after the death of Ibn Rashid, Ibn Sa`ud ordered the tribes that had assisted in any way the supply and communications of the Ottomans to stop.⁶⁶ He consistently blamed all unrest on Rashidi depredations, but this last act made clear even to distant Istanbul that he was being much less than helpful.

Ibn Rashid and his followers were, if anything, a greater problem. Left unaddressed by Istanbul because of Abdülhamid's favor for Ibn Rashid, the difficulties that beset the first expedition only grew worse. For example, one officer reckoned that 41 metric tons of supplies from Madina had been diverted to Ha'il by July 1905; Ibn Rashid also tried to block establishment of a supply route outside of his control.⁶⁷ His refusal to stop interference in Qasimi affairs was very damaging to the Ottoman position. Having long experience of Ibn Rashid's control, the locals had accepted the new administration with the understanding that he would be excluded from the area. He continued to raid tribes and towns opposed to him, however, which quickly stoked popular resentment. Since Ottoman officials were under Istanbul's orders not to oppose Ibn Rashid, they came to be seen in the same light. This, as much as covert Sa`udi agitation, caused the Qasimi-Ottoman tensions that sapped the government's strength.⁶⁸

Ibn Rashid's actions eventually precipitated the collapse of the Ottoman regime in Qasîm. His raids caused Ibn Sa`ud to resume operations after returning from Qatar late in 1905; in an April 1906 battle the Sa`udis killed Ibn Rashid and scattered his forces. Ibn Sa`ud quickly came to an agreement with his opponent's successor, who had to devote his attention to consolidating his hold on Ha'il.[69] The main reason for the Ottoman presence in Najd had abruptly disappeared. Ibn Sa`ud's order to the tribes to stop supplying the soldiers brought a new expedition from Madina, but without any sound purpose for keeping troops tied up in a remote area, Istanbul eventually was willing to withdraw all but a few. The Sa`udis had regained control over their Najd heartland.

A bold beginning thus fizzled, but the anticlimactic end does not erase the interest of the episode. First it must be emphasized that, when Istanbul thought it saw an obvious policy to follow in handling a problem in Arabia, it could act with determination and dispatch sufficient to overpower likely local adversaries. The concerns about Ottoman interests and foreign designs first stirred by Midhat were thirty-five years later still felt strongly by some. At a time when troops were badly needed to quell a revolt in Yemen, as well as to police ever-insecure Iraq, Istanbul was willing to keep several thousand men tied down in Najd. It could even have kept them adequately supplied, given a few changes in policy, notwithstanding the misery they experienced in actuality.[70]

One policy that badly needed reassessment was that resulting from a decision to cast the Ottoman lot with Ibn Rashid's. With "friends" such as this, the "enemy," Ibn Sa`ud, could afford to depart for Hasa and Qatar, leaving his rival to self-destruct. Arguments could be, and had been, made that the state could not rely fully on bedouin shaikhs. In Arabia it therefore more often followed (with middling success) the best alternative to close alliances: be a strong, neutral power that could be the fulcrum of a tribal balance of power. Sultan Abdülhamid forsook that policy by becoming so closely identified with Ibn Rashid, to the point of allowing Istanbul's client to dominate the Ottoman troops in Najd, without a clear appraisal of the shift's advantages and drawbacks. Ibn Rashid was a raider, not an astute or subtle leader. Although a Wahhabi, he had none of the Sa`udis' stature, and much of Arabian society disliked him. This and family rivalries made him insecure and an unreliable ally. While he usually obeyed direct orders from the sultan, he was as determined as Mubarak or Ibn Sa`ud to follow his own immediate interests; unfortunately for him and his allies, however, he lacked his rivals' political acumen. It seems that Abdülhamid came to favor this poor risk so heavily only out of conviction of Ibn Rashid's loyalty, as proven by declarations, annual deliveries of tribute, and enmity for Mubarak al-Sabah.

ARABIA, 1896-1914

Sultan Abdülhamid could not make informed judgments about his ally because of the particular severity in this case of an old headache: communications. The limitations of the usual channels of information from distant provinces to the center were seen in the Kuwait problem. The difficulty of exchanging messages quickly with Qasîm—like Hasa far removed from telegraph terminals—was even greater. What made the problem of transmission of information and orders almost insurmountable was Ibn Rashid's practical monopoly on communications. Messages had to be sent by caravan, under Rashidi control; they could be easily delayed or "lost" and may have been opened regularly. Ibn Rashid could use the delay to present his own version of events first. In effect he had a private line to the sultan. The state supported his personal agents in Iraq, Syria, and Istanbul.[71] They kept Ibn Rashid informed of developments that might affect him, while feeding the sultan information that would further the Rashidi amir's interests. Abdülhamid came to rely on this speedy source of news, ensuring Ibn Rashid's ability to manipulate Ottoman policy. It took a brave man to send reports challenging the Rashidi version of events.

The campaign in Qasîm was the last major project undertaken by the Ottomans in eastern Arabia, and it revealed in acutest form the great weakness of the regime. It was impossible to direct operations from the center, when the center could not see what was happening beyond its immediate horizon. Istanbul could not get the reliable information necessary to alter plans as new conditions emerged. Yet because it insisted on exercising final control, local commanders could not act as they saw fit. The gap between the two left a lot of room in which would-be local rulers could operate. As happened too often, the result was failure to achieve policy ends and personal disaster for many.

The End of the Ottoman Era in Eastern Arabia, 1906-1914

The eclipse of the Rashidis marked the beginning of the final transfer of power in Hasa from the Ottomans to the House of Sa`ud. The death of Ibn Rashid and the withdrawal of the troops from Qasîm gave Ibn Sa`ud the breathing room that he needed to press plans for expansion to the east. Possession of this comparatively rich area would make him a much more formidable leader. At the same time, the authorities in Hasa became more vulnerable than they had ever been, as Istanbul suffered the distractions of the Young Turk revolution, the overthrow of Sultan Abdülhamid II, the conflict with Italy, and the two Balkan wars.

Despite the problems threatening to overwhelm the government, Ibn Sa`ud needed to proceed with circumspection. The Ottomans had to withdraw from Qasîm, but he knew that they could still project daunting power into the area if too boldly challenged. In all of his political activities, therefore, he maintained an appearance of deference and devotion to the sultan, perhaps even more steadily than his mentor, Shaikh Mubarak, had done. At the beginning of his campaigns in Qasîm and Hasa early in 1906, he sent to Abdülhamid a telegram (ostensibly from Qâsim al-Thani) that attributed all disturbances to popular revulsion against Ibn Rashid's tyranny. Ibn Sa`ud was only acting to restore justice and remained an obedient servant of the Commander of the Faithful.[72] He sent several emissaries to Istanbul the following year to reaffirm his devotion, which earned him the title of pasha.[73] The pattern continued even in 1913, when he drove the Ottomans out of Hasa.[74] As had Mubarak, Ibn Sa`ud showed sufficient public restraint to persuade the government that it had more to gain by accepting a fractious "Ottoman" vassal than by punishing him and thereby perhaps driving him into Britain's arms.

Again like Mubarak, Ibn Sa`ud repeatedly sought British recognition in the hope of using them to block what he feared most, another large Ottoman military strike. These overtures generally clustered around moments when his activities, planned or actual, increased the likelihood of reprisal from Basra. Britain had the power to stop ships from ferrying troops to Hasa, leaving Ibn Sa`ud free to act against the isolated garrison. The British rebuffed all of these approaches, because they had no interest in the Arabian interior that equaled the problems involved in starting a new dispute with Istanbul.

Without a British insurance policy, Ibn Sa`ud thought it best to use indirect means to persuade the Ottomans to give up their position in Hasa. His capture of Riyadh and emerging success in Qasîm garnered him growing authority among the bedouin tribes, while some in the towns would have welcomed a shift to Sa`udi rule. Popular unrest had weakened the Ottomans in Qasîm, and conditions favored a repetition on the coast. Ibn Sa`ud could also cite the turmoil as justification for an eventual extension of his rule over Hasa, as he had in the interior. The government might suspect him of stirring the trouble, but he retained a fair degree of deniability by remaining far in the interior. He also probably followed Mubarak's lead in creating further indecision by buying support among local officials.[75]

The success of Ibn Sa`ud's destabilization plan may be seen in a comparison of accounts by two travelers to Hasa: Burchardt in early 1904, Raunkiaer in 1912.[76] Burchardt traveled in a lightly defended caravan from `Uqayr to Hufuf and alone with the post carrier from Hufuf to Doha. Raunkiaer went from Hufuf to `Uqayr, only with an escort of fifty

Ottoman soldiers. He also saw the remains left from several battles and raids pitting troops against bedouins. These raids had become a serious problem again in 1906, when the `Ajman, loyal to the Sa`udis, killed a shaikh of the Al Murra, who at that time were on reasonably good terms with the state. The shaikh had come to Hufuf on a government-issued safe-conduct; when the authorities took no steps to punish the killers, the Al Murra in retaliation started to prey on caravans.[77] The violence spread to other tribes, but the `Ajman took the lead in pressing audacious attacks; armed with modern weapons, the bedouin were frequently successful. Several caravans under strong guard, including regular troops, were plundered.[78] The `Ajman also mauled a force sent to lift their siege of a town. The government managed to restore a degree of security by sending heavy reinforcements and resuming subsidies to the tribes, but tension and violence remained ever close to the surface.[79]

This change is reflected in the travelers' accounts. Burchardt spent an enjoyable fortnight or so as a guest of the local officials. The main problem afflicting these well-educated and well-mannered men was boredom. Their days were filled with drinking coffee, smoking water pipes, and leisurely strolling; there was even a military band that performed every afternoon. When Raunkiaer visited, he found the garrison under veritable siege. Troops had to patrol the marketplace at all times to prevent attacks and thievery. Bedouins made daylight attacks on oasis inhabitants and their property, while no one ventured outside of the town walls after dusk. The fort was full of prisoners, but this seemed to have little effect on security. The situation only increased popular irritation over the Ottoman presence, because arms carried for self-defense were promptly confiscated. Raunkiaer thought that peace might be retrieved if the staff and garrison were doubled and a "forward" policy toward the tribes adopted, but the task was beyond the present authorities.

Such a move grew ever less likely as events elsewhere sapped the attention and resources that Istanbul could afford to devote to Arabia. Ibn Sa`ud was a major concern for a time, because of his potential for disruption, but the state was willing only to let other shaikhs act for them. Subsidies, and possibly guns, were delivered to the Rashidi amir and others in Najd in 1908–9, while the Sharif of Mecca pressed Riyadh from the west in 1910–11.[80] Neither move achieved lasting success. The sharif harassed Ibn Sa`ud but did not cripple him, while internecine warfare brought Rashidi power ever lower and finally caused a break between Ha'il and Istanbul.[81] Neither Ibn Sa`ud nor the other limited matters that continued to draw the Porte's attention after the withdrawal from Qasîm—British activities along the coast, the lack of Ottoman ships, complaints about officials and bedouin violence—could arouse much action following the deposition of Sultan Abdülhamid.[82] Once his dominating influence had been removed, the government at last began negotiating with Britain to establish recognized spheres of influence in Arabia within broader talks about the Baghdad Railway and Iraq.

The negotiations concluded with the initialing of an agreement on 6 May 1913, having been drawn out by Ottoman distraction during wartime and by the Indian government's maximalist demands. The knottiest questions concerned the status and boundaries of Kuwait and Qatar. Istanbul wanted recognition of its rights in those territories, while India thought that any such move could lead to the collapse of Britain's position in the Gulf. Agreement was finally reached when the Foreign Office overrode India's more extreme objections and when the disasters of the Balkan wars persuaded Grand Vezir Mahmut Şevket Pasha that two "unimportant" desert *kazas* should not cause a crisis with Britain.[83] Under the draft agreement, which was to be ratified by the Ottomans but not by Britain before World War I began, Istanbul renounced its claims to Qatar and Bahrain, Kuwait became an "autonomous" *kaza* of the Ottoman empire, and Britain recognized Hasa as Ottoman.[84] Mahmut Şevket in this accord pushed to a logical conclusion the "pragmatic" line of thought on Arabia that had marked the Porte in apposition to the Palace since the turn of the century. Ministers' sense of the need for a breathing space, as well as a clearer definition of immediate, feasible goals, had made them receptive to the 1901 Kuwaiti status quo agreement. The dire distress of the Balkan wars only sharpened that feeling. The Porte knew that Ottoman fortunes in Arabia had been slipping in recent years and that the trend was likely to continue in the foreseeable future. To prevent collapse it was necessary to define the territory most vital to its interests and to win enough time for it to be reorganized when Istanbul's other problems receded. The key was Britain's explicit recognition of Ottoman rights. Since Istanbul viewed London as the source of much of its troubles in Arabia, a check on British freedom of action seemed a very desirable asset. The accord could be a club with which to beat Britain in the ring of Great Power politics, if it tried to interfere in Hasa or to station troops in Kuwait. Withdrawal from Muslim lands was hard to accept, but it was worthwhile if it secured a defensive line south of Iraq that could be tenable until the empire's fortunes rebounded.

The advantages of consolidation were plain to see by May 1913. Moving the Doha troops to Hasa, for instance, would bolster a garrison even more overwhelmed by security problems than had been the case during Raunkiaer's visit the year before. The state had had to withdraw troops to defend Istanbul following the outbreak of war in the Balkans in 1912; four hundred at most remained in 1913.[85] This was only 15-20% of the garrison strength of just a few years earlier.

ARABIA, 1896–1914

This was a situation to delight Ibn Sa'ud. He had been distracted for several years by troubles in Najd, most notably by a strong challenge from six grandsons of Sa'ud b. Faisal, whose struggle with 'Abdallah for the Riyadh amirate had precipitated the 1871 Ottoman invasion of Hasa. Sa'ud's grandsons were defeated in 1912, but one of them took refuge with the 'Ajman (who no longer looked so kindly upon Ibn Sa'ud) in Hasa, whence they raided caravans supplying Najd from Kuwait. This irritant, his newly restored authority in the interior and his long-standing desire to return wealthy Hasa to his family's domain made this province the focus of his attention. Intelligence about the extreme weakness of the Ottomans there convinced him to attempt its reconquest.

It was still a risky venture. Britain continued to refuse to establish meaningful relations with him or to promise him to block any Ottoman attempt to send an expedition by sea. The state's current weakness made an immediate counterattack unlikely, but Ibn Sa'ud had no guarantee that it would not later send a formidable force to quash his challenge. He gambled, however, that Britain would have to become involved if he took control of the Hasa coastline. He was right—up to a point.

The conquest of Hasa was simple; the aftermath gave Ibn Sa'ud some tense moments. In May 1913, just when London and Istanbul were agreeing that Hasa was Ottoman, Sa'udi forces captured Hufuf, Qatif, and 'Uqayr. The garrisons were allowed to depart for Bahrain, as was a relief force sent in vain from Basra. Ibn Sa'ud immediately launched diplomatic campaigns aimed at the two powers. He sent a message to Istanbul, averring that he had no thought of revolting against the sultan, whose obedient servant he remained, but that he had had to respond to the populace's appeals for salvation from corrupt and incompetent administration. He offered to become an Ottoman *vali* and to guarantee security in the province. To the British he sent a message that he had regained his forefathers' dominions and asked for establishment of relations that might block Ottoman retribution. Neither appeal was successful. The Ottomans wanted a return to the status quo, while the British Foreign Office did not want to do anything that might jeopardize the concluded but unsigned 6 May accord.

The course of events changed direction after the May Anglo-Ottoman agreement was formally signed on 29 July 1913, however, and raised some doubt about just how final the accord would prove to be. The Foreign Office bowed to Indian pressure to raise the issue with the Porte. British mediation was offered and declined. It was a very polite, unthreatening exchange, but it can hardly have been wholly welcome to Istanbul. The Porte certainly suspected that Britain had stirred Ibn Sa'ud to action, and British diplomatic démarches in Istanbul and contacts with the amir of Riyadh in the following months only strengthened the idea. Istanbul was determined not to recognize any British right to interfere in territory so recently acknowledged as Ottoman. Perhaps in retaliation for this suspected British trickery, the Ottomans reportedly assured Ibn Sa`ud of carte blanche to conquer Qatar and Trucial Oman during later negotiations over their return to Hasa.[86]

Those Ottoman-Sa`udi negotiations almost came to nothing, in large part because Indian officials gave Amir Ibn Sa`ud a misleading idea of how deep British support would be. Ibn Sa`ud used the usual tactic of playing to Britain's fears to bring it into line behind him. He revealed the conditions demanded by the Ottomans for their return, some of which would effectively close Hasa to unwanted outsiders, and said that he would have to accept them if he did not get London's support. He also raised the threat of taking control of Qatar and Trucial Oman if Britain failed him. It is unlikely that he would have carried out either threat (and the Foreign Office was unmoved by them), but they convinced the Indian officials. Since these were the British government as far as Ibn Sa`ud was concerned, he was emboldened to take a tough stance in the peace talks. It was only as renewed warfare seemed imminent—a prospect that neither side particularly relished—that he and the Ottomans retreated from their extreme positions. In May 1914 they reached an agreement that was to regulate the Ottoman presence in Hasa over the months before Istanbul entered World War I as Germany's ally.

Under this agreement Ibn Sa`ud became the hereditary *vali* of a new province of Najd. The arrangement clearly would allow him great latitude in the territory's internal affairs. In return he agreed to a number of measures that would mark the area as part of the Ottoman empire, including the use of its flag on official buildings, important places, and all shipping; carriage of mail by its postal service; and conformity to its customs regulations. Ibn Sa`ud agreed to leave all foreign affairs in Ottoman hands. Small Ottoman garrisons were to return to the coast, but their size was controlled by Ibn Sa`ud.[87]

The Ottoman-Sa`udi Treaty split the differences between the two sides and clearly would not satisfy either. Neither of them intended to honor it in full indefinitely. It left too much power in the hands of Ibn Sa`ud for Istanbul's comfort, while Ibn Sa`ud was intent on developing a Mubarak-style protective relationship with the British. If he could establish himself as "an independent shaikh" with whom the British had "friendly relations," he could sweep the Ottomans out of Hasa with impunity. For its part, Istanbul was still playing for time. It was developing a new plan for the restoration of its fortunes in the peninsula. A reconciliation with the current Rashidi amir revived the idea of using him as the linchpin of a new Ottoman Arabia. He was given money and guns. Much hope was also put in a grand scheme to create a defensible frontier by building a railway from Madina to Najaf via Ha'il.[88] The Rashidi forces could thereby be supplied quickly and well, allowing them to overrun Najd and, if necessary, Hasa. All of Istanbul's dreams of a return, however, were shattered by the outbreak of world war and the ensuing final eviction of the Ottomans from the Persian Gulf.

In view of the conditions found in Arabia during this last period of Ottoman rule, did Istanbul have a reasonable hope of a return to a leading position there, or did the idea merely show how completely out of touch with the region it had become? Playing the game of "what if..." always risks opening the door to overimagination, but it is interesting to consider what might have happened if Istanbul had chosen the viable option of not becoming Germany's ally in the war. It did not expect to be soon at war with Britain when it reached the 1913 and 1914 agreements. Under foreseeable circumstances it did have some hope of a revival in Hasa (provided that the Foreign Office continued to rein in the Indian government's most expansionary instincts). Tribal politics was always volatile. The rapid rise of Ibn Sa`ud could have ended in an equally precipitous fall, as many expected; it had happened before in that family. The Ottomans' extraordinary weakness of 1913 was not going to last indefinitely, and they still had the inherent strength to crush the Sa`udis. Ibn Sa`ud had powerful Arab enemies who enjoyed Istanbul's support, notably the sharif of Mecca and the Rashidi amir. Their combined forces could have restored the Ottomans to Hasa, especially if Britain were caught in a European war.

Their ability to hold it thereafter would have been an entirely different matter. A simple return to the status quo ante would likely have led eventually to another downfall. In its last years the Hasa administration had no direction. In good times it shuffled along, in bad it was torn to shreds by more focused opponents. To avoid a repeat of 1913, the Ottomans had two options: much closer oversight by Istanbul to give officials more coherent direction, or the creation of a strong governorate with the authority to take action as needed without having to await orders from the center. Neither choice held much attraction for the Ottomans in 1914. Both required heavy investment in infrastructure, most notably a telegraph link and adequate shipping to ensure the speedy passage of information, people, and goods. The importance of this to the first option is obvious, but the need also existed in the second. Aside from the clear value to morale of closer ties to "civilization,"

Istanbul had to have confidence that it could revoke power easily before it could give it to a distant governor. The state might do reasonably well if the governor were Said Pasha, but if Sayyid Talib had unchecked authority, the result would be disaster. Communications were the most important ingredient of any program to combat the corruption and other malpractices that plagued the last years of Ottoman rule in Hasa. The Ottomans planned to install a wireless link between Hufuf and Baghdad a year before Ibn Sa`ud's conquest of Hasa.[89] The state did not have the funds to do it that year, however, and probably would not have had the T£15–20,000 necessary for the project in 1914, even had it not entered the World War. Thus the plan was never realized.

More germane than speculation about whether or not the Ottomans could have made a successful return to Arabia is the question of whether or not they should have wanted to. So much of what they did in Arabia centered on countering the threat of British absorption of most of the empire's Arab provinces. Possession of the peninsula had great symbolic value because of its prominent role in Islamic history, but in the eastern regions its importance lay in keeping the land out of the hands of foreigners, who could use it as a base for expansion into Iraq. The loss of Kuwait and Qatar broke the barrier that Midhat had erected. Through both regions British weapons, money, and influence could now pass practically unhindered into much of Arabia and Iraq. In case of war, moreover, no one could expect Britain to honor its agreement not to send troops to Kuwait and thence into Iraq. If properly administered, Hasa could have had some economic value, and the government was on principle loath to withdraw from any land populated by Muslims. Except for increasing the visibility of the Ottoman flag in the Gulf, however, the strategic value of Hasa by itself was small. It is quite possible that the pessimism about eastern Arabia developing at the Porte would have led to eventual resignation to the permanence of the 1913–14 changes in the region. Istanbul had been willing to settle for only the principle of Kuwait's being Ottoman. It would have been tempting to accept a similar arrangement in Hasa and save the state the great expense of time, effort, and money that would be needed to correct the many problems paralyzing its administration there over the last years.

Conclusion

When an imperial power is expelled from one of its territories by a local tribal leader, it is impossible to term that empire's administration of the area a success. That is especially true when the only consistently felt aim of the government's presence there was to keep it out of the hands of others. The end of the Ottoman era in the Persian Gulf is especially depressing when it is compared to the energetic, forceful, promising way in which its final phase started. Midhat Pasha wrought great changes wherever he went as an administrator, and his plans for the new *sancak* in eastern Arabia marked a promising start. His abrupt departure, however, removed the catalyst behind this creative idea, and his plans never reached full development under his successors. Within less than forty-five years, that supposedly vibrant member had become a veritable carbuncle on the body politic, which the heart could not bear to have removed but could not manage to treat itself. The dismal fate of the Arabian adventure—which until the end the government continued to consider very delicate and important—raises serious doubts about the empire's ability to regenerate itself in this period. The main factors contributing to Ottoman weakness in the Gulf, after all, were by no means unique to that territory.

The search for revenue defined the limits of Istanbul's ability to institute sound administration. Innovation and reform cost money, of which the state had precious little. Perhaps the single most damaging step taken in Hasa by the government was the imposition of extraordinary, noncanonical taxes so shortly after Midhat had promised the people not to impose them. According to the classical Ottoman methods of conquest, this was a cardinal error, and the Ottomans in Hasa were indeed to suf-

CONCLUSION

fer damage from this step. The temptation to use all potential resources to avert impending bankruptcy proved simply too great. The relatively high rate of taxes, the manipulation of date prices, the customs and excise duties, the coinage restrictions, the failure to improve ports, the restrictions on trade with Najd, and the general corruption all caused discontent at various times among the traders, the farmers, and the artisans—the sectors of society vital to Ottoman hopes of binding the territory firmly to the empire. They were also the sectors that had welcomed the expulsion of the Saʿudis. Their disenchantment grew with each decision to withdraw troops to reduce expenses, since this worsened the condition of the economically productive sector of society further by weakening security. Without a powerful garrison, the government had little hope of persuading or coercing the bedouins to give up their wild ways and settle down as farmers.

The nomadic Arab tribes remained the most dangerously unstable element in Arabia, and the Ottomans may be rightly criticized for not showing greater initiative in seeking to control, even sedentarize, them. They essentially restricted themselves to policies that they used elsewhere but, for a variety of reasons, did not apply them energetically. The distribution of *tapu* deeds and the formation of new settlements in tribal *diras*, which had encouraged sedentarization in Iraq and Transjordan, were never seriously attempted in Hasa after Midhat's departure from Baghdad. Even in the payment of subsidies, which was effective in the Hijaz, the Ottomans seemed half-hearted, giving only small amounts or nothing at all to tribal shaikhs. Midhat himself was uncertain when dealing with the tribes. He and Istanbul initially had the idea of co-opting the Saʿudi amir ʿAbdallah, who could have helped to assert control over the desert interior, as the sharif of Mecca did in the west. Midhat's break with ʿAbdallah, however, left him with no solid plan for ensuring security beyond maintenance of a strong garrison and a general hope of persuading the nomads to settle. Consideration of the problem rarely reached even that degree of development after he left Baghdad.

The state did experiment occasionally. It tried using selected shaikhs to extend its control, but these attempts usually did not succeed. Either the leaders (Baziʿ b. ʿAraʿir, ʿAbd al-ʿAziz al-Rashid) proved ineffective, or Istanbul feared that they were too strong (Shaikh Nasir of the Muntafiq, Muhammad al-Rashid). Occasionally a *mutasarrıf* would take the initiative to try to work within the tribal system, using the tribes to maintain the rough balance of tensions that predated the Ottoman return to Hasa. Knowledgeable men, like Said Pasha, were rare, however, and the state often fell back upon the threat of its greater firepower to prevent anarchy. That threat was not kept consistently credible. One way

CONCLUSION

in which the British in India differed in their treatment of the tribal problem was that they took greater care to maintain a real military deterrent. The Ottoman state did not always fulfill its duties toward shaikhs under its protection, such as Qâsim al-Thani, by giving aid when they were threatened or by punishing their peace-breaking enemies. In some cases this was due to a lack of military means, or suspicions of shaikhs' loyalties, but in others where it had sufficient forces on hand (as in Qatar in 1893), the state showed a lack of will. It chose to take the path of least resistance because it was afraid of problems (tribal warfare, British interference) to which firm action might lead. The state conserved its strength in order to address other issues, which might well not be the concerns of the Hasawis. Even though reluctant to expend resources, it should at least have heeded the advice of the vice-consul in London, who advised adoption and strict observance of a simple code of behavior in relations with tribes. Unsure of the rewards for cooperation and of the penalties for antagonism, the bedouins felt little lasting commonality of interests with the state or strong compulsion to heed its commands.

In comparison to other provinces, pacification of Arabia's tribes was an abject failure for the Ottomans. When the bedrock of tribal policy in Arabia—control of the coast and all major towns—was broken by the virtual loss of Kuwait and Qatar, well-armed nomads of the interior felt fairly free to cause repeated outbreaks of unrest. This made control of Hasa, let alone Najd, much harder than before.

With more money available, of course, the Ottomans might have accomplished much more. Hasa would have benefited greatly from the presence of a stable, well-paid garrison. Money shortages also severely limited Istanbul's ability to acquire the physical assets needed to improve administration of Hasa. The central government knew that conditions in Arabia were not matching up to Midhat's projections. As reports and recommendations for action came from the Gulf, Istanbul proved willing to undertake ambitious programs to increase its authority. If some of these improvements—connection to the telegraph, maintenance of dependable civil and military shipping, development of harbors—had been instituted during the first two decades of Ottoman rule, the crises of the last twenty years could have been eased, if not avoided. Even at a late date they would have helped greatly. Yet the money was impossible to find, in Istanbul, in Basra, in Hasa. Capital could come from Europe, but only on ruinous and humiliating terms and with a political price. Practically every region of the empire had needs similar to those of Hasa, and the state simply could not afford to address them all at the same time. Even when fully approved, therefore, important projects took exceptionally long periods to complete.

CONCLUSION

It is a striking feature of the various reform schemes that most of the important plans were concerned in some way with communications, a weakness most debilitating to a centrally run empire. Accurate information is the essential element in sound decision-making. The Ottoman state lacked the means to collect it regularly, and its disadvantage in comparison to Britain and other European powers was marked. Basra was connected to Istanbul by telegraph, which was of enormous benefit to administration. That thin wire could not support the entire weight of the state by itself, however, since no medium could meet all needs. The line was cut frequently by bedouins and others. Telegraphy is also relatively anonymous, and one message sent without seal or signature looks much like another. Local leaders such as Mubarak and Ibn Sa`ud could send telegrams under other people's names to increase Istanbul's impression of their support. The telegraph eased communication between central and provincial authorities throughout the empire, but long, detailed reports were better sent by post. Mail service from Basra to the capital was slow, and from Hasa painfully so.

Of perhaps greater harm was the difficulty of transport for people and supplies. Travel between Istanbul and Iraq or Arabia was a task that few undertook willingly. Most members of the government's upper level had no personal experience of life in these outposts of empire and no intention or way to remedy the lack. Viceroy Curzon toured the Gulf in 1903; no Ottoman minister had the time or desire to undertake a similar tour. The lack of roads, railroads, and river transport not only constricted the flow of information, it also insulated local authorities from supervision. Corruption flourished in part because officials had little fear of close oversight and could survive through patronage. This was not a uniquely Ottoman problem: after all, Colonel Pelly was able to act with impunity as the British Resident in the Persian Gulf because of having a powerful patron, Sir Bartle Frere. Yet the problem was clearer to see in the Ottoman Gulf. Mubarak bought crucial support from such key men in Iraq as Receb Pasha and Muhsin Pasha, while the reputation and efficiency of the administration in Hasa suffered greatly through the extortion of Sayyid Talib and others. Such malfeasance was repeated elsewhere in the empire in varying degree, but because of their actual and mental distance from Istanbul, the central government found it especially difficult to remedy the damage done in Basra and Arabia. The empire was simply internally too ill-connected to be run well from the center.

When officials in the center have no direct experience of a province and only poor means of monitoring its affairs, logically it should devolve power to a local representative. Having had to struggle hard to eliminate

CONCLUSION

overly independent governors early in the nineteenth century, Istanbul was too reluctant to grant wide powers. Istanbul did try to be flexible on many issues, granting exceptions to empire-wide regulations based on local conditions regarding the legal, tax, and monetary systems, for example, as well as military conscription. It did not go far enough, though. To cite but one example, its fear of gun smugglers prevented it from granting the reasonable Hasawi request to be permitted to bear arms for protection. Two of the most effective administrators in the Gulf, Midhat and Said, were men who formally or informally exercised a unified command and showed a flexible attitude toward such issues of local concern. Given Istanbul's difficulty with oversight, it would have helped both center and province to appoint one man with wide discretionary powers of command whom the government could hold responsible for the area's well-being. This was especially true in Arabia but also applied to territories elsewhere in the Middle East.

One of the strongest rationales for not devolving more power to the provinces was Istanbul's need to know about all issues that could involve a European state. Of all the many factors complicating Ottoman efforts at government, and influencing the overall Ottoman position in Arabia and to a noticeable degree in other provinces, perhaps the most important was the specter of foreign intervention. The British determination to exercise absolute control over the Gulf was a twentieth-century phenomenon; for much of the nineteenth, London did not want to do more than was necessary to safeguard respectable trade and ensure maritime peace. Yet Istanbul let the idea that Britain was actively working to absorb Arabia and Iraq govern its actions from the moment Midhat's men marched into Hasa. The 1871 expedition was to safeguard Iraq. Once the territory was secured, administration drifted. In the 1880s attention and money were devoted to grand schemes to attack foreign influence everywhere in Arabia, notably by building naval flotillas and a major base at Basra. Although an increase of the naval presence as far as Qatar would have been useful, its extension around Hadhramawt would hardly have been worth the expense. The money could better have been used elsewhere in the empire, including in Hasa. The fact that officials wanted to extend taxation among nominal Ottoman subjects, which would demonstrate sovereignty to the British but would be extremely unpopular among the new rate-payers, indicates the "foreign" orientation of policy in this period. Ironically, however, British feelings that the Ottomans were being unhelpful or even provocative in matters such as piracy and sovereignty over Bahrain pushed them into the very sort of aggressive policy that Istanbul thought it was combating. Finally, the government's virtual paranoia about perfidious Albion helped to make it

CONCLUSION

freeze at key moments when quick action was needed. Qâsim al-Thani escaped punishment in 1893 in large part because of the fear that it might drive him into Britain's arms. He set a precedent that Mubarak al-Sabah followed. Istanbul's decisions on Kuwait were frequently influenced by perceptions of a British hand hidden behind the shaikh or his adversary, Yusuf al-Ibrahim. From this evolved the campaign in Qasîm and the later watchful but cautious attitude toward Ibn Sa`ud. In each case the Ottomans had relative freedom of action for a time, but the conviction that Britain would interfere if action were taken caused Istanbul to miss its best opportunities.

Arab shaikhs quickly learned how to take advantage of this Ottoman fear to achieve their own goals. They became the real source of change in the Gulf. Leaders wished to retain the freedom of action that had characterized the fluid, pre-1870 pattern of tribal politics, but each also wanted to gain a powerful guarantor of his domain and dynasty. While expanding their influence at the expense of their neighbors, shaikhs told tales to the British and the Ottomans to force attacks on their adversaries, win support for themselves, or at least escape retribution for their own actions. Mubarak al-Sabah had the most success in this. Circumstances belatedly brought him to British attention in 1899, but thereafter he was able to push Britain into giving him vital support, while at the same time blunting the Ottoman threat. Leaders from Ibn Sa`ud to Ibn Rashid saw how he was able to carve out a protected shaikhdom for his family, and they in turn sought a British tie in the hope of replicating his feat.

It was these Arab shaikhs of the Gulf who profited the most from the changes of this period. Kuwait became an internationally recognized, separate entity, one step removed from independence and statehood. Bahrain and Qatar were lastingly parted and also received recognition of rough boundaries. These influenced the final territorial dimensions of the present Sa`udi state, whose predecessors had encompassed so much of the Arabian peninsula. The politics of the Anglo-Ottoman rivalry in this period also had a great effect on basic Sa`udi policies: Ibn Sa`ud discovered the value of patient, pragmatic realpolitik. He restrained the uncompromising religious drive that had spurred the rapid rise and equally swift fall of his forebears. As a result, he, too, was to win the international recognition that had served to safeguard the Al Sabah and Al Thani dynasties in Kuwait and Qatar.

While extension of British protection may have been essential to the eventual international recognition of Gulf dynasties and states, it was found to carry a price that had not been immediately obvious to the shaikhs. Britain let it be known that it was concerned with the foreign relations of the Arab leaders and did not really want to interfere in

CONCLUSION

domestic affairs. As the Ottomans discovered, however, the separation between internal and external affairs blurred with increased European political and economic penetration of borders. In time, the shaikhs of Kuwait, Qatar, and Bahrain came to resent British oversight. Shaikh `Isa of Bahrain had already met with harsh treatment at British hands in 1904–5, and Shaikh `Abdallah of Qatar (1913–1948) was very disappointed by Britain's lack of interest in his concerns from 1916 to 1935.[1] Shaikhs of Kuwait came into conflict with the British not only in World War I but mostly clearly in 1922, when the British gave a large chunk of Kuwaiti territory to Ibn Sa`ud.[2] Only with the discovery of oil in the shaikhdoms in the 1930s did Britain's treatment of their rulers become gradually less high-handed.

The gains for Britain in this era seem clearer at first glance. It consolidated its leading position in a region about to be proved fabulously rich in petroleum. It also made any attack on India from the Gulf very difficult. Britain's creep up the coast made it the natural candidate to take over Iraq after World War I. Yet not all results were so pleasant. Britain's sunny moment in the Gulf was brief, as, locally loathed, it had to withdraw from Iraq and Iran after the next war. Its rivalry with the Ottomans in this region, moreover, was one of the handful of long-running, intractable territorial disputes (including Egypt and Yemen) that were key to driving the formerly friendly powers apart. In this sense, Gulf-bred antagonism was a noteworthy factor in determining both empires' roles in World War I. The British took the lead in fighting the Ottomans in the Middle East, a surprisingly tough task.

On the whole, Britain's experience in the Gulf prior to the war was positive, especially when compared to the mixed fortunes of the Ottomans. In one sense the saga of their sojourn in eastern Arabia was hardly forlorn. Istanbul sought to stop the deepening British penetration into Arab, Muslim territories, and that process was successfully slowed. The extension of Ottoman influence along the coast and into the Najdi interior also reduced for several decades the threat of bedouin unrest sweeping into the rich cultivated areas of Iraq and Syria. Istanbul did not do this very efficiently, however. The Ottomans did not fully exploit the economic potential of Hasa, and in later years Arabia became a serious drain on finances as well as men and matériel. The seemingly intractable problems of administration caused headaches in a distracted capital, while the heightened tensions with London damaged Istanbul's international position. By 1913, the usefulness of the Arabian experiment had become clearly outweighed by its drawbacks.

Appendix 1

Ottoman Officials and Heads of Arab Shaikhly Families

Al Sa`ud Amirs of Riyadh

Faisal b. Turki   1834–1838
Khalid b. Sa`ud   1838–1842
`Abdallah b. Thunayyan   1842–1843
Faisal b. Turki   1843–1865
`Abdallah b. Faisal   1866–1870
Sa`ud b. Faisal   1873–1875
`Abd al-Rahman b. Faisal   1875
`Abdallah b. Faisal   1875–1889
`Abd al-Rahman b. Faisal   1889–1891
`Abd al-`Aziz b. `Abd al-Rahman (Ibn Sa`ud)   1902–1953

Al Rashid Amirs of Ha'il

`Abdallah b. `Ali   1835–1848
Tallal b. `Abdallah   1848–1868
Mut`ib b. `Abdallah   1868–1869
Bandar b. Tallal   1869–1872
Muhammad b. `Abdallah   1872–1897
`Abd al-`Aziz b. Mut`ib (Ibn Rashid)   1897–1906
Mut`ib b. `Abd al-`Aziz   1906–1907
Sultan b. Hamud   1907
Sa`ud b. Hamud   1907–1908
Sa`ud b. `Abd al-`Aziz   1908–1919

APPENDIX 1

Al Sabah Shaikhs of Kuwait

Jabir b. `Abdallah   1812–1859
Sabah b. Jabir   1859–1866
`Abdallah b. Sabah   1866–1892
Muhammad b. Sabah   1892–1896
Mubarak b. Sabah   1896–1915
Jabir b. Mubarak   1915–1917
Salim b. Mubarak   1917–1921

Al Thani Shaikhs of Qatar

Muhammad b. Thani   1860–1876
Qâsim b. Muhammad   1876–1913
`Abdallah b. Qâsim   1913–1948

Al Khalifa Shaikhs of Bahrain

Muhammad b. Khalifa   1843–1868
`Ali b. Khalifa   1868–1869
`Isa b. `Ali   1869–1923

Mutasarrıfs in Hasa

Nafiz Pasha   1871–1872
Mehmet Pasha   1872–1873
Faiz Pasha   1873–1874
Bazi` Pasha   1874–1875
Mazyad Pasha   1875–1876
Said Bey (first term)   1876–1877
Hüseyin Bey   1877
Said Pasha (first term)   1877–1879
Said Bey (second term)   1879–1880
Abdülgani Pasha   1880–1881
Said Pasha (second term)   1881–1885
Nazih Pasha   1885–1886
Mehmet Salih Pasha   1886–1887
Rifaat Bey   1887–1890
Akif Bey   1890–1891
Said Pasha (third term)   1891–1894
Ibrahim Pasha   1894–1896
Abdallah Pasha   1896
Said Pasha (fourth term)   1896–1900
Musa Kazım Efendi   1900–1901
Tevfik Bey   1901–1902
Sayyid Talib Pasha   1902–1904

APPENDIX 1

Faik Pasha 1904–1905
Necib Pasha 1905–1907
Reşid Pasha 1907
Mumtaz Efendi 1908
Mahmud Mahir Bey 1908–1909
Arif Bey 1909
Ali Suad Bey 1909
Nedim Bey 1911
Abbas Hilmi Bey 1912
`Abd al-`Aziz al-Sa`ud Pasha 1914

Appendix 2

Register of Officials, Notables, and Tribes

`Abd al-`Aziz al-Rashid (Ibn Rashid). Amir of Jabal Shammar, 1897–1907; most powerful Arab opponent of Mubarak, whom he defeated at Sarif in 1901; allied with Ottomans to combat resurgence of Sa`udi power in Najd.

`Abd al-`Aziz al-Sa`ud. Founder of the third and present realm of Sa`udi Arabia; broke power of Ibn Rashid and in 1913 drove Ottomans from Hasa.

`Abd al-Rahman b. Faisal al-Sa`ud. Brother of Sa`ud and `Abdallah. Sought supremacy in Najd in 1870s; stirred 1874 revolt in Hufuf; briefly held Riyadh after death of Sa`ud in 1875. Retired with son Ibn Sa`ud to Kuwait in 1891.

`Abdallah b. Faisal al-Sa`ud. Wahhabi amir of Riyadh. Named to succeed his father in 1865, but challenged by his brother Sa`ud. Civil war caused turmoil in Najd and Hasa; defeats led him to seek support from Midhat in Baghdad. Lost Ottoman support but was able to rule in Riyadh, 1875–1887, but his power was small. Overthrown by Ibn Rashid, died 1889.

Abdülhamid II. Ottoman sultan, 1876–1909; actively involved in political affairs, trying to maintain Ottoman territorial integrity and to rally Muslim solidarity behind him as caliph.

Ahmad al-Thani. Brother of Shaikh Qâsim and rival for authority in Qatar; courted Ottoman support against Qâsim in 1905 but was killed before Istanbul took action.

Ahmet Feyzi Pasha. Marshal of VI Corps in Baghdad; pushed for military occupation of Kuwait in 1901, eventually leading to crisis resulting in status quo agreement; commander of 1904 military expedition to Qasîm, then transferred to put down revolt in Yemen.

`Ajman. Bedouin tribe of the Hasa interior, ranging north and west of `Uqayr. Strongest tribe of eastern Arabia, fitfully cooperative with the Ottomans.

Akif Pasha. *Mutasarrıf* in Hasa, 1889–1890; author of ambitious reform proposal; fell sick and died before most reforms could be implemented.

APPENDIX 2

Al Murra. Bedouin tribe, ranging south and west of `Uqayr. Bellicose and generally outside Ottoman control.

Arif Pasha. *Vali* of Basra, 1896–1897; first supported making Mubarak *kaymakam* of Kuwait, then advised removing him; recalled due to chaos in his administration.

Bani Hajir. Bedouin tribe of the Gulf coast from `Udayd to Kuwait. Frequently slipped out of Ottoman control in times of government weakness.

Bani Khalid. Bedouin tribe of Hasa. Paramount in Hasa until defeated by the Wahhabis; cooperated with the Ottomans. Many tribesmen settled throughout eastern Arabia.

Bazi` b. `Ara`ir. Shaikh of the Bani Khalid tribe in Hasa, appointed *mutasarrıf* in 1874. Unpopularity among the people caused the revolt of 1874 and his subsequent dismissal.

Crow, F. E. British Consul in Basra, 1903–1914.

Curzon, Lord. Viceroy of India, 1899–1905; firm advocate of expansion of British influence in Arabia.

Faisal al-Sa`ud. Wahhabi amir of Riyadh, father of `Abdallah and Sa`ud, whose rivalry to succeed to the amirate gave the Ottomans the opportunity to take over Hasa. Died in December 1865.

Hafız Mehmet Pasha. *Vali* of Basra 1892–1893. Commanded expedition to Qatar that was defeated by Shaikh Qâsim; relieved of post after the debacle.

Hamdi Pasha. *Vali* of Basra, 1893–1896, 1899; firm opponent of Mubarak but never able to execute plans for his removal due to influence of Mubarak's friends in Ottoman government.

Ibn Rashid. Amir of Ha'il and head of the southern Shammar tribe; see Muhammad al-Rashid (1872–1897), `Abd al-`Aziz al-Rashid (1897–1906).

Ibn Sa`ud. Amir of Riyadh; see `Abd al-`Aziz al-Sa`ud.

`Isa b. `Ali al-Khalifa. Shaikh of Bahrain, 1869–1923. Installed by Britain, signed series of agreements that made his domain a British protectorate.

Jarrah al-Sabah. Brother and lieutenant of Muhammad al-Sabah; killed with Muhammad by Mubarak in 1896.

Kemball, Col. C. A. British Persian Gulf Resident in Bushire, 1900–1904.

Khaz`al, Shaikh. Shaikh of Muhammara from 1897; close ally of Mubarak.

Knox, S. G. British Resident in Kuwait, 1904–1908.

Lansdowne, Marquis of. British Foreign Secretary, 1900–1905.

Lascelles, Sir Frank. British ambassador in Berlin, 1895–1908.

Mahmud Nedim Pasha. Succeeded Ali Pasha as Grand Vezir in 1871, engineered removal of Midhat from Baghdad in 1872.

Manasir. Bedouin tribe ranging between Qatar and Abu Dhabi. Wholly beyond state control, sometimes raided Ottoman territory.

Meade, M. J. British Resident in Bushire, 1897–1900; advocate of forward policy in Gulf, notably in Kuwait.

Mehmet Salih Pasha. *Mutasarrıf* in Hasa, 1886–1887; first in a series of reformist *mutasarrıfs*.

Midhat Pasha. *Vali* of Baghdad province, 1869–1872. Noted reformer of provincial administration. Undertook Ottoman return to eastern Arabia in 1871. One of the leading liberals of the *Tanzimat*, he served twice briefly as Grand Vezir but fell foul of the autocratic Sultan Abdülhamid. He was exiled in 1881 to Ta'if in western Arabia, where he was strangled in 1884.

APPENDIX 2

Mubarak al-Sabah. Took part in Qatar campaign of 1892 as head of Ottoman Arab auxiliaries; killed two of his brothers to take over the shaikhdom of Kuwait in 1896; survived as a thorn in the Ottomans' side through his own political skill and help from Britain.

Muhammad al-Khalifa. Shaikh of Bahrain, 1843–1868. Deposed by Britain for violation of maritime peace, imprisoned in India after taking part in 1868 invasion of Bahrain, which Britain reversed by installing Shaikh `Isa. Released in 1888, lived until his death (1890) in Mecca on an Ottoman pension.

Muhammad al-Rashid. Shaikh of the southern Shammar tribal confederation, based in Jabal Shammar around Ha'il. Took advantage of Wahhabi weakness to overthrow Sa`udi rule in Riyadh, 1887. Treated alternately with respect and suspicion by the Ottomans, who for a time considered using him as their viceregent among Arabia's nomads.

Muhammad al-Sabah. Shaikh of Kuwait, 1892–1896; killed by brother Mubarak.

Muhlis Pasha. *Vali* of Basra, 1904–1906; conducted negotiations with `Abd al-Rahman al-Sa`ud and Mubarak in 1905 that led to peaceful Ottoman entry in Qasîm.

Muhsin Pasha. Military commandant, later also *vali*, of Basra (1897–1901); a key ally of Mubarak who blunted Ottoman efforts to take Kuwait.

Muntafiq. Powerful tribal alliance in southern Iraq; Ottoman manipulation of leaders caused repeated unrest, notably under Sa`dun Pasha.

Mustafa Nuri Pasha. *Vali* of Basra, 1901–1904; involved initially in efforts to pressure Shaikh Mubarak (affair of the *naqib*, embargo on food shipped from Basra to Kuwait); later established amicable relations with Mubarak.

Mutayr. Bedouin tribe ranging between Kuwait and the Najd interior. Allies of Ibn Sa`ud and Mubarak al-Sabah, enemies of Ibn Rashid. Limited Ottoman control.

Nafiz Pasha. Military commander of the expedition to Hasa in 1871, named the first *mutasarrıf* of the new Necd *sancak*.

Naqib al-Ashraf. Dean of Basra's community of the Prophet Muhammad. See Rajab Efendi.

Nasir b. Mubarak. A leader of the 1868 invasion that overthrew the pro-British shaikh of Bahrain. After Britain intervened to install `Isa in the shaikhdom, Nasir returned to the mainland, where he continued to scheme against the British-backed ruler while receiving an Ottoman stipend.

Nasir al-Sa`dun. Paramount chief of the Muntafiq tribal confederation in southern Iraq, *vali* of Basra province at its creation in 1875. Restored peace in Hasa after 1874 revolt.

O'Conor, Sir Nicholas. British ambassador in Istanbul, 1898–1908.

Pelly, Col. Lewis. British Resident (agent) in the Gulf, 1862–1873. Aggressive proponent of strong, forward British policy in the area.

Qâsim al-Thani. Shaikh of Qatar, named *kaymakam* by Midhat in 1871. Retained more independence than officials in Hufuf and Qatif, leading to tensions with Ottomans. Tried to resign office and encouraged bedouin lawlessness in 1890s, in 1893 led open revolt. Unwillingly retained title of *kaymakam* thereafter but generally ignored duties of office. Died 1913.

Rajab Efendi. *Naqib al-Ashraf* of Basra, used by the sultan as an intermediary in disputes between the government and Arab leaders, including Mubarak al-Sabah and Qâsim al-Thani.

APPENDIX 2

Receb Pasha. Marshal of the VI Army Corps in Baghdad and ally of Mubarak.

Rıza Ali. Basra naval commandant; submitted proposal for security measures in the Gulf and Arabia in 1884; made *vali* of reconstituted Basra *Vilayet* in 1884.

Ross, Col. E. C. British Resident in the Gulf, 1873–1890. Concluded agreements with shaikhs that brought Bahrain and Trucial Oman under British protection.

Sa`dun Pasha. One of the leading shaikhs of the Muntafiq tribal confederation; frequently in rebellion against Ottomans in 1890s and 1900s; ally of Mubarak at battle of Sarif in 1901, later enemy at battle of Hadiyya in 1910; killed by Ottomans in Syria in 1911.

Said Pasha. *Mutasarrıf* in Hufuf, 1877–1879, 1881–1885, 1891–1894, 1896–1900. Native of Baghdad, a capable governor who established a good rapport with the bedouins and other inhabitants of Hasa.

Said Pasha, Küçük. Ottoman Grand Vezir, 1879–1880, 1880–1882, 1882, 1882–1885, 1895, 1901–1903, 1908, 1911–12; urged restraint in handling Kuwait and Britain after the 1901 status quo agreement.

Salisbury, Marquis of. Prime Minister, 1895–1902, Foreign Secretary, 1895–1900; accelerated British abandonment of commitment to integrity of Ottoman empire.

Sa`ud b. Faisal al-Sa`ud. Brother of `Abdallah, claimant to the Wahhabi leadership. During war with his brother gained the upper hand, held Riyadh from 1873 to his death in 1875. After 1875 his sons continued his struggle against `Abdallah, the Ottomans, and Ibn Rashid.

Shammar. Great tribal confederation, half in Iraq north of Baghdad, half in northen Arabia in Jabal Shammar, the area around Ha'il; southern Shammar led by Al Rashid amirs.

Talib Pasha. Son of the *naqib al-ashraf* of Basra; ally of Mubarak al-Sabah; *mutasarrıf* of Necd, 1902–1904.

Tevfik Pasha. Ottoman foreign minister, 1895–1908.

Wratislaw, A. C. British Consul in Basra, 1898–1903.

Yusuf al-Ibrahim. Head of the anti-Mubarak party in the struggle for Kuwaiti leadership; attempted several assaults on Kuwait by sea; joined forces with Ibn Rashid; died in Ha'il in 1906.

Notes

Abbreviations Used in the Notes and Bibliography

BEO	Bab-i Ali Evrak Odası
DH.ID	Dahiliye.Idare
DH.KMS	Dahiliye.Kalem-i Mahsus
DH.MUI	Dahiliye.Muhâberât-i Umûmiye Idaresi
DH.SN.THR	Dahiliye.Sicill-i Nüfûs, Tahrirât
KMNB	SS. Kyril and Methodius National Library, Sofia
ML.VRD	Maliye.Vâridât
MMV	Meclis-i Mahsus-i Vükelâ
MV	Meclis-i Vâlâ/Meclis-i Vükelâ
ŞD	Şûrâ-yı Devlet
Y.MTV	Yıldız.Mütenevvî Mâruzât Evrakı
YEE	Yıldız Esas Evrakı
Y-A HUSUSÎ	Yıldız-Sadaret-Hususî Mâruzât Evrakı
Y-A KÂMIL	Yıldız-Kâmil Pasha Evrakı
Y-A RESMÎ	Yıldız-Sadaret-Resmî Mâruzât Evrakı

Preface

1. *American Historical Review* 92, no. 4 (October 1987), 1013.

Preliminaries

1. Issawi, *Fertile Crescent*, pp. 408–10, 468–69.
2. Pelly, *Reports*, p. 84. The figures represent currency values in Riyadh in the decade before the Ottomans returned to eastern Arabia.
3. Twenty-five years after Pelly visited Riyadh, 1 kran apparently was worth about 5 kuruş, meaning that 20 krans = T£1. YEE 31/76–118/76/139, 15 Teşrin-i evvel 1306/27 October 1890.

INTRODUCTION

Introduction

1. A few of these documents have been published, including Halaçoğlu, "Midhat Paşa," for Hasa; Bostan, "Zor Sancağı," for Dair al-Zor; Bostan, "Muhammad Hilâl Efendi," for Yemen; Göyünç, "Trablusgarb," for Tripoli (Libya).

2. In addition to narrower articles, these most useful broader studies include: Ochsenwald, *Religion*, for the Hijaz; Rogan, "Bringing the State Back," for Transjordan; Le Gall, "Pashas," for Tripoli and Binghazi; Gerber, *Ottoman Rule*, and Kushner, "Ottoman Governors," for Jerusalem; and Akarlı, *Long Peace*, for Mount Lebanon.

3. For a very good elaboration of this reform process, see Findley, "Evolution," pp. 3–29.

4. For the classic description of the early Ottoman pattern of absorbing territories, see Inalcık, "Methods."

5. A sharpening interest in this and related matters of administrative practice is shown by the recent publication of a collection of essays on the subject: Farah, *Decision Making*. The theme of the book is loosely interpreted, however, and the essays unfortunately lack focus as a group. See also Findley, "Decision-Making."

1. The Setting

1. The area between Kuwait and Qatar—the Eastern Province of today's Saudi Arabia—was known by a number of variant names when it was under Ottoman control, including Lahsa, al-Ahsa, and Hasa. These names could refer also to Hufuf, the main settlement in the region. In this study "Hasa" will be used and will refer exclusively to the region.

2. *Basra Salname*, 1308, p. 141; Raunkiaer, *Wahhabiland*, p. 137. The Ottoman figure includes the numerous springs at Hufuf and Qatif. Unlike those sources, the water found by digging on the coastal plain was often brackish. Although water was plentiful, a number of Ottoman officials and soldiers complained about its quality.

3. Further geographical information on Hasa will be given later. That information, provided by Midhat Pasha after his inspection of the newly conquered territory in 1871, is of interest because it was the fullest description of the region available to the government in Istanbul throughout the period under study and thus helped to shape administrative policy over four decades.

4. Al-Rasheed and al-Rasheed, "Politics of Encapsulation," pp. 96–97; Salibi, *Arabia*, pp. 11–12.

5. Pelly, *Report*, p. 27.

6. Salibi, *Arabia*, p. 163.

7. Lorimer, *Gazetteer*, 1:1000.

8. Şûrâ-yı Devlet (ŞD) 2184/6, petition of ʿAbdallah b. ʿIsa to Council of State, 12 Kânun-i evvel 1315/24 December 1899; Pelly, *Report*, p. 10.

9. Irade Dahiliye 44930, enclosure II, p. 2, 22 Kânun-i evvel 1287/3 January 1872.

10. *Basra Salname*, 1308, pp. 132–33.

11. William Palgrave, *Narrative*, pp. 352–53, 356–57, 362–64, 367–69; *Basra Salname*, 1308, p. 135.

12. Palgrave, *Narrative*, pp. 351, 363. Kornrumpf ("Beschreibungen," p. 81) gives the size of the largest town, Hufuf, as perhaps 30–40,000 in the Ottoman period.

2. THE RESURRECTION OF OTTOMAN ROLE IN THE GULF

13. See map of tribal areas (map 2). *Dira* boundaries were rather fluid, but the map gives a general idea of tribal ranges.

14. Bidwell, ed., *Arabian Personalities*, pp. 139, 140, 142.

15. The Qaramita, an Ismaili Shi`ite sect, broke away from the Abbasid caliphate in Baghdad at the beginning of the tenth century. They established an independent state centered in Hasa, from which they controlled much of Arabia and frequently attacked Syria and Iraq into the eleventh century.

16. Ilhan, "Katif," pp. 783–84. The most complete account of the first Ottoman era in Hasa is Mandaville, "Province of Al-Hasa," pp. 486–513.

17. Saldana, *Nejd*, pp. 16, 31–32.

18. The British tie to Basra shifted to Kuwait on several occasions. When the Safavis held Basra from 1775 to 1779, trade and the British desert post to Aleppo circumvented their old terminus by using Kuwait. Later, in 1793, a dispute with the government of Süleyman Pasha of Baghdad caused the Company Factor and British Resident and his staff to move to Kuwait, where they remained for two years. Lorimer, *Gazetteer*, pp. 1002–4, 1289–90.

19. Trade between Bombay and the Persian Gulf in 1801–2 had a value of £290,000; in 1821/22, £678,000; 1841/42, £796,000; 1857/58, £1,440,000. Only a small part of that trade passed through Basra, but commerce in that port (most of which was carried in ships bearing the British flag, although usually owned by Indian and Gulf natives) expanded mightily in the last third of the century, from £348,000 in 1864 to £2,826,000 in 1900. See Issawi, *Fertile Crescent*, pp. 174, 176–78, 197, 261.

20. Examples of these constraints can be found in Lienhart, "Authority," pp. 61–75. Lienhart's essay offers a very informative explication of the general characteristics of traditional shaikhly leadership in eastern Arabia.

21. Kelly, *Britain*, p. 526.

22. For example, British protests to Amir Faisal checked his plans for attacks on Bahrain and Oman in disputes over the payment of tribute (*zekât*) to Riyadh in 1859 and 1865–66. See Kelly, *Britain*, pp. 512, 646–54.

23. The Sa`udi Shaikh `Abdallah (amir of Riyadh, 1866–1870, 1875–1889) tried to claim treaty relations with Britain in his contest with the sultan of Oman in 1866, based upon the receipt of "'friendly letters from the British Authorities, and ... the Wahhabee government consider a friendly letter to be synonymous with a Treaty Agreement.'" India Office: India Foreign Proceedings (Political), Range 437, vol. 67, June 1866. Cited in Kelly, *Britain*, pp. 654–55.

2. The Resurrection of the Ottoman Role in the Gulf

1. These included the Hatt-i Hümayun of 1856, which promised legal, financial, and administrative reforms corresponding to European practice, and the land law of 1858, which improved rights of ownership. See Davison, *Reform*, chs. 2–3; Lewis, *Emergence*, pp. 115–19.

2. This was the office of the Grand Vezir and the administrative center of the empire; under Sultan Abdülhamid II (1876–1909) it lost some of its practical power and independence as the sultan became more closely involved in directing political affairs.

3. Two of the leading lights of the *Tanzimat*, they alternated as Grand Vezir throughout the decade until their deaths in 1869 and 1871, respectively.

2. THE RESURRECTION OF OTTOMAN ROLE IN THE GULF

4. Gharaybiya, *Muqaddimat*, pp. 397–98. The support was probably more verbal than substantive, and in any case less than reliable. The Qahtan abandoned ʿAbdallah for Saʿud, only then to desert Saʿud out of resentment for a perceived slight.

5. Kelly, *Britain*, p. 718; Lorimer, *Gazetteer*, p. 1128. The Saʿudi amirs had paid tribute to the Ottoman state periodically after their defeat by Mehmet Ali of Egypt. Faisal eventually stopped paying the tribute, but ʿAbdallah offered to resume it in return for assistance.

6. Saldana, *Expansion*, p. 12.

7. "We cannot make our policy at sea depend on Arab politics ashore; we cannot attempt to make our interference to prevent an expedition by sea depend on the justice or injustice of the claims which the expedition is intended to assert. To do so would involve us in the intricate domestic relations of the Arab tribes, which we neither know nor are capable of understanding." Foreign Secretary (Government of India) Aitchison's note on the possibility of preventing the Ottoman expedition by sea, 3 May 1871. In Saldana, *Expansion*, p. 15.

8. Kelly, *Britain*, p. 718; Goldberg, *Foreign Policy*, p. 25; Kumar, *India*, p. 113; Winder, *Saudi Arabia*, p. 252. Winder cites Longrigg (*Four Centuries*) in dismissal of Ottoman strategy. "In all probability there was no particular consideration motivating the Ottoman government to undertake this expedition. 'The deepest reason was the persistent, unceasing land-hunger of the Turks, ever grasping at useless and embarassing possessions, ever willing to annex fresh hostile subjects and barren sands.' "

9. Kelly, *Britain*, p. 718; Davison, *Reform*, p. 267.

10. Ahmida, *Modern Libya*, pp. 30–31.

11. Lorimer, *Gazetteer*, p. 1448–49.

12. Issawi, *Middle East*, pp. 146.

13. Lorimer, *Gazetteer*, pp. 1407, 1453.

14. Caravans had abandoned the desert route for the northern one after several brutal attacks by bedouins in the 1850s. Issawi, *Fertile Crescent*, pp. 247–49.

15. Lewis, *Nomads*, p. 30; Irade Meclis-i Mahsus 1553, 18 Cemazi el-evvel 1286/ 26 August 1869.

16. Kelly, *Britain*, pp. 399, 502, 515; Lorimer, *Gazetteer*, p. 888.

17. Since his accession in 1843, Shaikh Muhammad had been troubled by rivals from another branch of the Al Khalifa. The rebels found support from Amir Faisal al-Saʿud and several tribes in Hasa and Qatar. Muhammad and the shaikh of Abu Dhabi attacked the Qatar coast in 1867, causing great damage. His unwillingness to make reparation for this breach of the maritime truce led to Britain's deposition of Muhammad and appointment of his brother ʿAli as shaikh. At this point the shah's government lodged a protest, the sultan's did not. Coming under the protection of the Saʿudi amir, Muhammad crafted an alliance of ʿAli's enemies. This band attacked and killed ʿAli, but another member of the victorious rebel coalition promptly realized his own claim to the shaikhdom by imprisoning Muhammad. This again brought the British Resident of Bushire and four naval vessels to Manama. They shelled several forts, dispersed the rebels, sent Muhammad and four other ringleaders to prison in India and proclaimed ʿIsa b. ʿAli the new shaikh of Bahrain. Lorimer, *Gazetteer*, pp. 892–89.

18. Farah, *Protection*, p. 35.

2. THE RESURRECTION OF OTTOMAN ROLE IN THE GULF

19. Irade Dahiliye 42435, 25 Zilhicce 1286/28 March 1870; Usul-i Irade Dosya 77, Midhat to Grand Vezir, 8 Zilkade 1286/9 February 1870. These documents refer to the naval force only in discussing the advantages of Kuwait as a support station.

20. Irade Meclis-i Mahsus 1624, Gurre-i Receb, 1287/27 September 1870. At the urging of a Hadhramawti shaikh, two of the five ships were again assigned to Arabia. They were to patrol the Hadhramawt coast in support of Amir Ghalib of the Al Kathir tribe, who claimed a long-standing desire to serve the sultan. Ghalib had lost control of the ports of Shihr and Mukalla to the Al Yafi` tribe and asked for help to return them to the just administration of the sultan. If necessary the Ottoman commander was to land some troops with cannon, although the government was unprepared to commit full support in a poorly understood situation. Nevertheless, this is an early example of Istanbul's interest in extending its sphere of influence to the south Arabian coast.

21. Ayniyat 851/20, 23 Muharrem 1284/27 May 1867; Ayniyat 851/27, 22 Cemazi el-âhir 1324/21 October 1867.

22. The widely known 1867 Henri Kiepert map of "L'Empire Ottoman en Europe et en Asie," for instance, shows the "République de Koueit ou Kourein."

23. Usul-i Irade, Dosya 77, Midhat to Grand Vezir, 28 Kânun-i sani 1285/9 February 1870.

24. Irade Dahiliye 42435; Ayniyat 851/74, 7 Muharrem 1287/9 April 1870. The *zaptiyes* never were assigned to Kuwait. Such a police force would have been unwelcome to the inhabitants, who clearly preferred not to assume the burdens of absorption into the empire. Just as the Ottomans had not wanted to arouse conflict by opening a customs post in Kuwait, they preferred not to send any gendarmes. Since the Kuwaitis paid no taxes, it also would have been more efficient for the authorities to deploy the police in other, revenue-producing areas. In addition to that fiscal constraint, the *kaymakam*'s administration made *zaptiyes* unnecessary: as Midhat put it, since the people of Kuwait were like members of a large family, few disputes went beyond the capacity of the family head, the *kaymakam*, to settle. Irade Dahiliye 44930, enclosure II, p. 1.

25. Irade Meclis-i Mahsus 1667, 3 Kânun-i evvel 1286/15 December 1870.

26. The only other evidence of British material support for Sa`ud is the claim of the explorer Charles Doughty that Pelly gave the Wahhabi leader flour during this period of general hunger and misery (Winder, *Saudi Arabia*, p. 258). Winder concludes, however, that "Pelly followed a correct policy as between the Turks and Saud."

27. This powerful tribe's *dira* extended from the Syrian desert to northern Najd. They neighbored, and were enemies of, the Shammar. Settled groups of the `Anaza also lived in central Najd.

28. `Abdallah must have sought an expedition of the type that Midhat eventually organized, instead of direct support of his own campaign.

29. Irade Meclis-i Mahsus 1667, Grand Vezir to sultan, 2 Muharrem 1288/24 March 1871.

30. Irade Meclis-i Mahsus 1667, Midhat to Grand Vezir, 13 Kânun-i sani 1286/25 January 1871.

31. As happened from time to time, this assessment underestimated the capacities of the Arabs. The Bahrainis had already proven their ability to conduct such an operation by blockading Qatif and the Hasa coast in 1854. See Kelly, *Britain*, p. 505.

2. THE RESURRECTION OF OTTOMAN ROLE IN THE GULF

32. Although Midhat combined civil and military authority in Baghdad *Vilayet*, and the VI army corps had its headquarters in the capital, the ever-present potential for unrest in the province prevented use of most of the present security forces. Midhat thus had to petition Istanbul for troops based in Aleppo.

33. Irade Meclis-i Mahsus 1667, 2 Muharrem 1288/24 March 1871.

34. Saldana, *Expansion*, pp. 16, 20; Kelly, *Britain*, p. 728. By such a definition Midhat was not declaring an imminent intention of conquering those areas, but rather he sought to keep formal Ottoman claims in public view. The official gazette of Baghdad province in 1871 similarly declared that Algerian Arabs were Ottoman subjects; it seems unlikely that Midhat seriously considered launching an invasion of Algiers from Basra at that time. See Davison, *Reform*, p. 276.

35. Unlike Midhat's later reports, this document never mentions "Wahhabis," and the words used in referance to Sa`ud's movement (*isyan, tuğyan, fesad, mefasid, hareket-i bagiyâne*) mix secular meanings of rebellion with occasional overtones of moral decay. Use of a term such as *fitne*, which appears later in documents during Sultan Abdülhamid's reign, would have cast the debate more clearly in religious terms.

36. This statement came in reply to Iranian protests at Britain's actions in the Muhammad-`Isa struggle. Britain also promised to inform Iran about any necessary future punitive measures against the shaikh of Bahrain. Lorimer, *Gazetteer*, p. 896.

37. Lorimer, *Gazetteer*, pp. 890–91.

38. Lorimer, *Gazetteer*, pp. 893–95.

39. Lorimer, *Gazetteer*, pp. 898–99; Kelly, *Britain*, pp. 682–63.

40. Bahrain was the only trucial signatory to renounce explicitly all marine warfare against signatory and nonsignatory foes, receiving in return British naval protection. That undertaking was included in the 1861 Convention. Saldana, *Expansion*, p. 16; Kelly, *Britain*, pp. 526–27.

41. Pelly's "tenure of the Residency was to be marked, not only by indecorous quarrels with other political officers, but also by ill-judged or inept acts of policy, which were to involve his government more deeply than was wise in the politics of the Arabian shore." Kelly, *Britain*, p. 575. Pelly owed his appointment and protection from punishment to Sir Bartle Frere, a governor of Bombay and later a member of the India Council.

42. Saldana, *Expansion*, p. 16.

43. Saldana, *Expansion*, pp. 17–21.

44. Saldana, *Expansion*, p. 15.

45. Saldana, *Expansion*, p. 21, quoting an Indian Government memorandum. Such an understanding would reflect the Sublime Porte's view of the matter as primarily an attempt to stop decay within the empire, not as an issue of Great Power rivalry.

46. Kelly, *Britain*, p. 719.

47. Saldana, *Expansion*, p. 15.

48. "This expedition is like the little rent in the embankment, insignificant in itself and easily repaired at first, but if not repaird [sic], certain to end in the destruction of the whole work." Note by Foreign Secretary (India), 3 May 1871, on the effects of allowing Ottoman troop movements by sea. Saldana, *Expansion*, p. 16.

49. Pakalın, *Sadrâzamlar*, 1:235.

50. Şimşir, "Midhat Paşa," pp. 237–339 (pp. 267–339 reprint British and Ottoman

2. THE RESURRECTION OF OTTOMAN ROLE IN THE GULF

Foreign Ministry documents on the 1876–77 Constantinople Conference, in which Midhat rejected European proposals on the Balkans). See also Davison, *Reform*, pp. 390–94.

51. Lewis, *Emergence*, p. 178. Abdülhamid was determined, however, to be rid of the troublesome reformer. He banished him to the Hijaz, where he was strangled in 1884.

52. Pelly gave these estimates of the size of the force, some of which marched overland, the rest proceeding by Ottoman and (300) Kuwaiti boats. Saldana, *Expansion*, p. 44. The sultan ordered the use of six or seven battalions (*tabur*s) and several other units (Irade Meclis-i Mahsus 1667). A full *tabur* would nominally number about 800 men, but Saldana (p. 23) and Midhat (Irade Dahiliye 44930, 22 Kânun-i evvel, 1287/3 January 1872) mention in other contexts only about 500 men per unit, making Pelly's estimate reasonable.

53. Midhat, *Tabsıra-i Ibret*, p. 110.

54. Saldana, *Expansion*, p. 45; Kelly, *Britain*, p. 729.

55. Irade Meclis-i Mahsus 1703, 14 Cemazi el-âhir, 1288/31 August 1871. That the consul seemed to be equally or better informed than Midhat must have strengthened the *vali*'s suspicions about British involvement with Sa`ud.

56. Irade Dahiliye 44551, 17 Şaban 1288/1 November 1871; Hijaz *Vali* and Mecca Amir to Grand Vezir, Gurre-i Receb 1288/16 September 1871. Similar conditions had helped to prevent `Abdallah from invading Oman in 1870 (Saldana, *Expansion*, p. 46).

57. Midhat minimized the problems of disease in Arabia when reporting to Istanbul, but he did cite autumn as a dangerous season. Irade Dahiliye 44930, enclosure I, p. 1.

58. Irade Meclis-i Mahsus 1703 and enclosed telegram from Midhat to the Grand Vezir, dated 10 Ağustos 1287/22 August 1871.

59. Irade Dahiliye 44551. It is interesting that `Abdallah chose to appeal to the amir of Mecca and the *vali*, whose role was primarily military, instead of to Midhat and Nafiz Pasha, the military commander in Hasa, to the east. It is tempting to ascribe the choice to the development of mistrust between `Abdallah and the latter two officers, but a more plausible explanation is that the Hijaz was closer to the Wahhabi amir's first haven after fleeing Riyadh, the territory of his kinsmen the Qahtan, than was Hasa. It should also be noted that `Abdallah subsequently sought refuge in Hufuf.

60. Irade Meclis-i Mahsus 1703.

61. Irade Dahiliye 44551, 16 September 1871.

62. Irade Dahiliye 44551, 16 September 1871. Muhammad had been imprisoned by Sa`ud, freed by the Ottomans, and then kept under the watchful eye of his brother's allies. The Ottoman authorities probably instigated the call for `Abdallah to come to Hasa.

63. Kelly, *Britain*, pp. 736–77.

64. Lorimer, *Gazetteer*, p. 970. Concerning `Abdallah's new, uncooperative character, Winder writes that after the battle of Juda (21 December 1870), the defeated amir became "by turns, and increasingly, both an irritating and a pathetic figure." Winder, *Saudi Arabia*, p. 251.

65. Kelly, *Britain*, p. 730; al-Mansur, *Tatawwur*, p. 140. A Kuwaiti boat, with that town's ruler Shaikh `Abdallah al-Sabah aboard, accompanied an Ottoman steamer,

2. THE RESURRECTION OF OTTOMAN ROLE IN THE GULF

according to one British report (see Kelly); other information indicated that Nafiz Pasha entrusted the mission entirely to Shaikh `Abdallah (see Mansur). Midhat did not identify the Ottoman representative sent by Nafiz. Irade Dahiliye 44930, enclosure I, p. 5.

66. Crystal, *Oil*, pp. 27–34.
67. Mansur, *Tatawwur*, p. 140.
68. Irade Dahiliye 44930, enclosure I, p. 5.
69. Mansur, *Tatawwur*, p. 140.
70. Irade Dahiliye 44930, enclosure I, p. 5. Midhat stated that Muhammad was elderly and left administration increasingly to his son, which raises the possibility that Qâsim requested aid in his father's name.
71. Under an agreement brokered by Britain to settle relations between Bahrain and Qatar after the turmoil of 1868, Muhammad al-Thani agreed to pay 4,000 riyals to an Al Khalifa tributary shaikh in Qatar and 5,000 to the Al Khalifa shaikh in Manama, via the British Resident (Kelly, *Britain*, p. 675). On this occasion, however, the British consul in Baghdad repeated to Midhat the Indian government's denial of any interference in Qatar or demand for money. Irade Dahiliye 44930, enclosure I, pp. 5–6.
72. Irade Dahiliye 44930, enclosure I, pp. 5–6.
73. Kelly, *Britain*, p. 730; Mansur, *Tatawwur*, pp. 140–41; Saldana, *Expansion*, p. 49; Lorimer, *Gazetteer*, p. 803.
74. British reports speak of the Ottoman troops in Qatar arriving and staying through January 1872, but Midhat's account of 3 January states that the soldiers had been recalled after a successful 34-day peacekeeping campaign. Irade Dahiliye 44930, enclosure I, p. 6; Lorimer, *Gazetteer*, p. 803. Lorimer wrote that Midhat ordered a permanent occupation of Qatar by 100 soldiers (300 according to Mansur, p. 141), who were replaced by 1873 by a squad of *zaptiyes*. Midhat's reports to Istanbul show, however, that he had no plan to expend many resources on Qatar. Because Britain had no treaty relations with Qatar, its ships presumably called at Doha less frequently than at Bahrain or Abu Dhabi, which made its information sketchier.
75. Mansur, *Tatawwur*, p. 141, specifies a term of two and a half years; Lorimer, *Gazetteer*, p. 804.

3. Midhat Pasha's Inspection of Hasa and His Plan for Its Development

1. Following his return from the inspection tour, Midhat submitted four documents to the Sublime Porte, all dated 22 Kânun-i evvel 1287/3 January 1872. These reports are enclosed in Irade Dahiliye 44930, dated 15 Zilhicce 1288/25 February 1872. The first enclosure describes events relating to the campaign of Nafiz Pasha. Enclosure II gives details of the military, administrative, and economic conditions of the various parts of Hasa. The third report concerns the financial costs and benefits of the assumption of regional administration. Enclosure IV gives the provisional guidelines for administration and development of the newly formed Necd *Sancak*.
2. This situation was not unique; Doha, for instance, also depended on distant wells. Two scarce commodities, water and safe harbors, rarely coincided.
3. Irade Dahiliye 44930, enclosure II, pp. 1–2. The unimportant forts included that of Qatif itself, `Anik (on the road from Qatif to Dammam), and Darin on Tarut island; Midhat proposed Badrani for the new military center.

3. MIDHAT PASHA'S INSPECTION OF HASA

4. A British traveler in Arabia ten years earlier remarked on the numerous signs of accessible ground water and abandoned settlements between Hufuf and Qatif. He stated that hundreds of inhabitants had recently emigrated to Bahrain, the Iranian and Omani coasts, as well as points further north in Arabia. Palgrave, *Narrative*, p. 371.

5. Kelly, *Britain*, pp. 759, 765, 788; Lorimer, *Gazetteer*, pp. 973–74.

6. A ship drawing two or three feet (less than one meter) could enter the harbor; one with twice that draft had to anchor two to three miles (3–5 km) offshore. Irade Dahiliye 44930, enclosure II, p. 2.

7. Guardhouses were established at `Uqayr, Bir Yaman (3½ hours from the port), Jafar (between Bir Yaman and Hufuf), and in numerous locations around the Hufuf oasis. Irade Dahiliye 44930, enclosure II, p. 3.

8. According to Lorimer (*Gazetteer*, pp. 2297, 2299), the average annual date production of Hufuf and Qatif was 75,000 tons at the turn of the century. This compared well with Basra, which produced most of the dates exported from Iraq. Hasa dates were also of very high quality.

9. Pelly, *Report*, pp. 84–85.

10. The only relevant figure provided by Midhat was his statement that revenues from Hasa, extracted with the people's consent (that is, with the approval of a new administrative council), reached T£35,000 for the first year of Ottoman administration. This sum included not only the tithe (nominally a 10% tax on agriculture), as well as a 2½% tax on some livestock, but also income from abandoned lands taken over by the state treasury (Irade Dahiliye 44930, enclosure II, p. 6). Farmers working land technically owned by the state also had to give the treasury more than a tenth of their crops, as will be shown below. The single sum reported by Midhat as revenue thus can give no safe indication of the state of Hasa's economy in 1871–72.

11. Irade Dahiliye 44930, enclosure IV, p. 4.

12. Since these processes differ in difficulty, the degree of optimism in Midhat's prediction is uncertain. The first means of gaining production would be less costly and time-consuming than the second; the third would be the easiest, but because water was not a limiting factor within the oases before Midhat proposed development of irrigation systems, the scope for intensification of agriculture on currently farmed land must have been limited. It is probable, however, that Midhat foresaw increasing productivity also through agricultural extension services, such as the introduction of better seeds.

13. Midhat did not mention the three-year drought then experienced in Arabia as a factor in the economic decline. Because the difficulty of raising ground water increased with elevation and distance from the coast, the Najd interior undoubtedly suffered from the lack of rain more severely than did the oases of Hasa.

14. Irade Dahiliye 44930, enclosure IV, p. 1 (section 3).

15. A *tapu senedi* did not confer an actual right of ownership, but rather usufruct rights to the land. The state retained ultimate ownership of the land, but in practice *tapu* holders gradually assimilated most of the rights of ownership.

16. This method would apply if the farmer of an adjoining plot needed to expand his crop area. The first two means of selling rights applied to lands near towns where springs or wells already existed for irrigation, and the land was measured in tenths of a *cerib* (about 25 square feet). Such small areas suggest that the land was being farmed intensively. Irade Dahiliye 44930, enclosure IV, p. 2 (section 5).

3. MIDHAT PASHA'S INSPECTION OF HASA

17. Under the conditions of the 1858 land law, the holder of mîrî land normally could not plant trees or erect buildings without the permission of the government. Midhat expressly sanctioned the planting of trees on distributed land in Hasa, as he did also in Iraq, because of the importance of the date crop to the region's economy. Irade Dahiliye 44930, enclosure IV, p. 2 (section 5).

18. Irade Dahiliye 44930, enclosure IV, p. 2 (section 5). It was in the state's interest to give bedouins economic incentives to settle. This would largely solve the bedouin problem with one neat stroke. If the Bani Hajir, for example, received free land around Dhahran, they would greatly strengthen and protect the settled community instead of forming its major threat. Economic output would rise with the added security and the increase in cultivated area, while the noted availability of abandoned land ensured that the settlement of tribesmen would not dislocate or disturb present farmers. The key to success, however, lay in persuading the nomads to settle and to invest large amounts of time and labor before gaining much reward.

19. Jwaideh, "Midhat," pp. 119–22.

20. It seems that the last period of economic growth in Arabia was in the mid-1850s, when good weather and relative political tranquillity produced bumper crops. A cholera epidemic soon thereafter spread misery, however, and the tensions arising from the unwelcome Wahhabi government in Hasa checked growth. Palgrave stated that Hufuf's population had fallen over a generation from 30,000 to 23–24,000 (Pelly estimated 20,000 for the entire district around Hufuf, a figure significantly less than those of Palgrave and Midhat; Pelly, *Report*, p. 85). Palgrave also reported that the governor in Hufuf tried to cow resistance by dragooning leading townsmen into military expeditions, thereby disrupting the economy (*Narrative*, pp. 162–63, 351, 357). It is worth noting that Hasawis similarly resented being pressed into emergency service to battle bedouin raiders at the end of the 1880s. The inhabitants of Hufuf successfully petitioned Amir Faisal for replacement of the governor in 1863–64 (Winder, *Saudi Arabia*, p. 178), but Pelly noted continuing Wahhabi-Hasawi mistrust in 1865. He also wrote of Mubarraz as a ruin. Nevertheless, he remarked upon the livelier atmosphere to be found in the oasis area than was present elsewhere in Faisal's realm (Pelly, *Report*, pp. 63–64). Economic conditions undoubtedly worsened during the `Abdallah-Sa`ud civil war.

21. Miles, *Countries*, pp. 395–96. For a cataloguing of the problems besetting agriculture around Hufuf in the past, see Philipp, "Probleme," pp. 43–46.

22. Twitchell, *Saudi Arabia*, p. 46.

23. Palgrave, *Narrative*, p. 356.

24. Lorimer, *Gazetteer*, p. 2297; Palgrave, *Narrative*, pp. 356–57; Twitchell, *Saudi Arabia*, pp. 21, 22–23.

25. Y.MTV 67/84, Supervisor of the Sultan's Privy Purse to Yıldız, 7 Eylûl 1308/19 September 1892; Y.MTV 203/60, 17 Mayıs 1316/30 May 1900.

26. Irade Dahiliye 44930, enclosure IV, pp. 1–2, 3 (sections 3, 7). The division of the crop between state and peasant generally amounted to equal halves, although ratios varied. A peasant given land already containing date palms kept one quarter of the fruit and all ground crops (cereals, vegetables, etc.) for seven years, after which he gained an equal ownership of the grove if he had tended the land properly. If the peasant planted palms on empty state land under a coplantation arrangement with the state (*mugarese*), the treasury received half of the fruit and ground crops. If the peas-

3. MIDHAT PASHA'S INSPECTION OF HASA

ant decided not to plant trees on land capable of supporting them, the ground crop (which could include cotton, indigo, or sugar cane) would be divided in half after the state received the *öşür* and repayment for seeds. Some of this arrangement conformed to regulations in Iraq, where the share taken by the government was to diminish over time. For example, in the *mukataa* of Hindiyya south of Baghdad, the government had taken previously two-thirds of the rice crop, although the peasants had provided their own seeds; Midhat lowered the tax only to 50% in his first year as *vali*, but he promised further reductions of a tenth in each of the next two years, with possible further future relief for those of proven good will (Issawi, *Fertile Crescent*, pp. 466–67). In addition to the prescribed tax reductions after a period of faithful cultivation, Midhat probably anticipated similar gradual reductions for seasonal (nonfruit) farmers, if for no other reason than that the need for government (or holders of land gained at auction) to provide seeds would ease as peasant wealth increased.

27. As *vali* of Baghdad Midhat had become very familiar with this practice, in which tenants were overwhelmed by debts owed to landholders (Issawi, *Fertile Crescent*, pp. 348–49, 466–67). The relatively limited availability of land and the presence of a wealthy and powerful landholding class (including the Wahhabi ruling families) would sustain the system in Hasa as well. Some of the agricultural decline noted by Midhat and Palgrave undoubtedly resulted from the flight of peasants seeking to escape a profitless situation. Midhat therefore instructed that the new restriction of the landholder's share of each crop should apply not only to state land farmed out directly to the peasantry (*fellahan*), but also to land sold at auction to non-peasant bidders. The regulation was to be announced and spread in Arabic, presumably in order that both landholder and tenant should know their rights and obligations (enclosure IV, pp. 1–2, section 3).

28. Irade Dahiliye 44930, enclosure II, pp. 3, 6; enclosure III, p. 1; in enclosure I, p. 4, Midhat argued for the expulsion of "the wicked men who are called Wahhabi ulema and who are the sole reason for the continuous ruined and untended state of a great part of the land and people."

29. Irade Dahiliye 44930, enclosure IV, p. 1 (section 2).

30. Midhat promised the notables of Hasa that nothing would be taken beyond the tithes when the territory was brought under official Ottoman administration—a promise that would prove quite hampering in later years. Meclis-i Mahsus-i Vükela minutes (MV) 23/28, 5 Ağustos 1303/17 August 1887.

31. Lorimer, *Gazetteer*, p. 1440.

32. Jwaideh, "Midhat," p. 116.

33. Lorimer, *Gazetteer*, p. 1442. That project turned out to be a white elephant.

34. Davison, *Reform*, p. 163. In 1910 Basra municipality voted to raise a statue of him in recognition of his efforts.

35. Midhat's belief was not quite accurate. While Britain did not levy any kind of tax in return for extending protection to a community, the shaikhs did have rudimentary means of gathering revenue, including customs and fees on pearling boats. Tribute, such as Qatar paid to Bahrain, should also be considered a tax.

36. Midhat, *Tabsıra-i Ibret*, pp. 114–15; Ottoman Ministry of Foreign Affairs, *Necd*, p. 8.

37. Midhat's four detailed reports on the results of his inspection tour of Hasa

3. MIDHAT PASHA'S INSPECTION OF HASA

show that he was aware of potential problems, although he maintained throughout them an optimistic, reassuring tone. His insistence that the native population welcomed the Ottomans wholeheartedly seems categorical—yet he feared that demolition of a few dilapidated forts around Qatif could cause unrest. He claimed that the Wahhabis posed little threat, especially since control of the coast gave mastery of the interior, but he still felt a need to attack Riyadh.

38. Beersheba in Palestine and numerous towns in Transjordan, for example, were founded or developed for this purpose. Gerber, *Ottoman Rule*, pp. 23–24; Rogan, "State," pp. 45–46.

39. On Indian tribes and British tribal policy, see Bose, "Eastern Himalayan"; Choudhury, "Evolution"; Gilmartin, *Empire*, pp. 11–26; Moon, *Conquest*, pp. 906–14.

40. Lorimer, *Gazetteer*, pp. 1426, 1435, 1441.

41. Jwaideh, "Midhat," pp. 116–17.

42. Jwaideh, "Midhat," p. 118.

43. Irade Dahiliye 44930, enclosure I, pp. 1, 2–3.

44. Irade Dahiliye 45052, 18 Muharrem 1289/28 March 1872. The ʿAjmani shaikh, Mansur b. Manakhir, did not settle down to a quiet farmer's life: British reports associated him with several acts of piracy in 1878 (Lorimer, *Gazetteer*, p. 975). When pacification by armed strength did not succeed, Nafiz's successors gave Mansur a stipend of T£3 per month from 1875 to 1903. DH.MUI 54–1/13, 18 Ağustos 1325/31 August 1909.

45. Irade Dahiliye 45052, Midhat to Grand Vezir, 16 Şubat 1287/28 February 1872. It made a formidable, diversified garrison, including not only regular infantry but also mounted troopers, gendarmes, artillerymen, and a few auxiliaries.

46. Irade Dahiliye 44930, enclosure III, p. 2; Midhat expected the first year's military budget to reach T£9–10,000, but less considerable sums would be needed as Hasa's affairs settled into a routine.

47. Pelly estimated tribal size (presumably in number of tents or fighting men) as follows: Bani Khalid and ʿAjman in Hasa, 2,000; Bani Hajir, 500; Al Murra, 600 (Pelly, *Report*, p. 86). Palgrave listed tribal populations as: ʿAjman, 6,000; Bani Hajir, 4,500; Bani Khalid, 3,000; Al Murra, 4,000. Fighting strengths were about one tenth of each total (Palgrave, *Narrative*, p. 299). Fifty years later British estimates of tribal fighting strength reached roughly three times the above numbers (Bidwell, *Arabian Personalities*, pp. 139–43). In 1909 a member of the Al Rashid estimated the ʿAjman to number 60,000, the Al Murra 25,000 and the Bani Hajir and Dawasir at 70,000 combined (DH.MUI 18–2/32, 17 Muharrem 1327/8 February 1909). The Ottomans estimated 15,000 nomads in Hufuf *Kaza* in 1875 and 285,625 in the entire *sancak* in 1896 (Kornrumpf, "Beschreibungen," p. 80). Saʿud was reported to have a "considerable" force with him at about this time, but most of these probably were from the Najd interior (Saldana, *Expansion*, p. 47). Of these tribes, the Bani Khalid were most likely to cooperate with the Ottoman administration.

48. Irade Dahiliye 44930, enclosure II, pp. 5–6.

49. Pelly, *Report*, p. 85.

50. Ochsenwald, *Religion*, pp. 32–35.

51. Agmon, "Bedouin Tribes," p. 58.

52. KMNB, F 265A, AE 212. This document, dated 9 Mayıs 1288/22 May 1872, is a financial accounting of presents given to Arab shaikhs in Iraq, Kuwait, and Hasa. It

3. MIDHAT PASHA'S INSPECTION OF HASA

has been torn into three pieces, of which the middle strip is now missing, but the remaining parts list gifts given to (among others) `Abdallah al-Sabah, his brother Muhammad, the shaikh of Jafar, and a certain Shaikh `Abdallah and his companions who traveled from Necd to Baghdad.

53. Irade Dahiliye 44930, enclosure III, p. 2.

54. Irade Dahiliye 44930, enclosure I, pp. 3–4. KMNB, F 273A, AE 232 is a statement of expenses incurred by the Necd *Sancak* administration in the month of Kânun-i sani 1287/January 1872. Listed among the salary payments is one of T£9 to "former Qatif Amir `Abd al-`Aziz al-Sudayri." The only other payment to an Arab leader mentioned is one of T£10 to one of the Bahraini shaikhs, Hamad al-Khalifa, to defray expenses of a journey to (Trucial) Oman.

55. Irade Dahiliye 44930, enclosure III, p. 2. British information reported that Qâsim did not become *kaymakam* until 1876 (Lorimer, *Gazetteer*, p. 804). The Ottomans themselves later fell into some confusion about Qâsim's history. Two officers investigating the 1893 uprising in Qatar related that a Shaikh Sayf of the once-influential Musallam tribe had become *kaymakam* after the death of Qâsim's father Muhammad, but that Qâsim somehow tricked him into resigning the post (YEE 14/250/126/8, p. 7). This story seems wholly fanciful. Midhat definitely assigned the office to Qâsim, and there is little evidence to suggest that the Ottomans later stripped it from him.

56. Irade Dahiliye 44930, enclosure I, p. 3.

57. Saldana, *Expansion*, pp. 17, 22, 42. It is worth noting, moreover, that the expedition to Riyadh proposed in August-September 1871 was to be undertaken at the request, and with the cooperation, of `Abdallah. Irade Dahiliye 44551, 4 Eylûl 1287/16 September 1871.

58. Enclosure I of Irade Dahiliye 44930, in particular, concerns Midhat's relations with `Abdallah and is the main source of information used in the next three paragraphs.

59. Irade Dahiliye 44930, enclosure I, p. 3. `Abdallah was mistaken in charging that the Ottomans had publicly revoked all Sa`udi right to rule in Arabia, as Midhat was quick to point out; Nafiz Pasha had dismissed only the claims of Sa`ud to the amirate early in the campaign.

60. Since Hufuf lay some six days' journey from Riyadh, this ultimatum gave `Abdallah only two or three days to consider his reaction.

61. Irade Dahiliye 44930, enclosure I, pp. 3–4.

62. Kelly, *Britain*, pp. 736–38; Lorimer, *Gazetteer*, pp. 969–70. Both sources claim that suspicions, or informed warnings, about Ottoman intentions caused `Abdallah's flight; machinations of the Riyadh ulema receive no mention.

63. Irade Dahiliye 44930, enclosure I, p. 3.

64. Mubarraz was later amalgamated into the Hufuf *Kaza*. The eventual structure of the *kazas* is unclear. By the end of the century there were *kazas* at Qatif and Qatar, but Hufuf *Kaza* may have been amalgamated into the *sancak* structure.

65. Irade Dahiliye 44930, enclosure IV, p. 1 (section 1).

66. Davison, *Reform*, pp. 146–50, 163.

67. Irade Dahiliye 44930, enclosure III, p. 2.

68. It is interesting to note, however, that the Ottomans were paying a salary to the former "Amir of Qatif," `Abd al-`Aziz al-Sudayri, in 1872 (see note 54 above). It

3. MIDHAT PASHA'S INSPECTION OF HASA

is possible that he was an appointee of the Sa`udi amir of Riyadh, trusted, because of his (Wahhabi?) roots in Sudayr in Najd, to act as the Sa`udis' viceregent in the more cosmopolitan (non-Wahhabi) port of Qatif. If this were the case, then he seems to have switched allegiance without great difficulty to the Ottomans, who came to Qatif, after all, in support of Amir `Abdallah. The Ottomans in turn probably did not trust any ex-Sa`udi official enough to leave in control of such an important area, but they may well have kept him "on retainer" to advise during the transition to full Ottoman administration. It is interesting to note that St. John Philby found that Ibn Sa`ud similarly had kept on some ex-Ottoman officials to help his administration in Hasa after World War I.

69. Irade Dahiliye 44930, enclosure I, p. 5.
70. Lorimer, *Gazetteer*, pp. 1443–44; Yücel, "Midhat," pp. 175–83.
71. Irade Dahiliye 44930, enclosure III, p. 3; Ayniyat 851/133, 28 Şevval 1288/10 January 1872.
72. The government tried to gain closer oversight (if not full administrative control) of pious endowments at various times in the nineteenth century, including this period. In 1870 Istanbul passed a law giving the government either full administrative or close supervisory rights over such endowments. For more information on *vakıf* reform and a case study of how the process worked in the *sancak* of Jerusalem, see Gerber, *Ottoman Rule*, ch. 8.
73. Irade Dahiliye 44930, enclosure IV, p. 3 (section 6).
74. Ayniyat 851/148, 15 Rebi el-evvel 1289/23 May 1872.

4. The Chance for Adjustment and Stability, 1872–1893

1. MV 23/28, 5 Ağustos 1303/17 August 1887.
2. Philipp, "Probleme," p. 50; Kornrumpf, "Beschreibungen," p. 81.
3. Yıldız-Bab-i Asafi (Sadaret)-Resmî Evrak (Y-A Resmî) 60/12, 26 Teşrin-i evvel 1307/7 November 1891.
4. Sinan, *Ta'rikh*, p. 91. The data, taken from a government *Salname*, purportedly cover the entire *kaza*, but the population estimate (7,900, compared to 8,000 for Doha in Y-A Resmî 60/12) shows a limitation to the *kaza* capital. It is possible that this account confuses the Doha secondary school with that of Hufuf. In 1895–96 there were reported to be only three such schools in all of Basra province, and to have two of them in Arabia seems unlikely. McCarthy, *Statistics*, p. 119. Yet, at least in later years, the government did see education as an important tool in pacifying the Arabian peninsula and making it "Ottoman."
5. Provincial *Salname*s listed twenty elementary schools in the entire *sancak* in 1882–83 and no other public or private schools except religious *medreses*; by 1900 there were twenty elementary schools in Hufuf alone, as well as the state-run institutions. In all, roughly one-third of Basra province's elementary schools were in Arabia. Kornrumpf, "Beschreibungen," p. 81; McCarthy, *Statistics*, 117.
6. Midhat, *Tabsıra-i Ibret*, p. 118.
7. Saldana, *Expansion*, p. 46.
8. *Basra Salname*, 1308, p. 169.
9. Midhat, *Tabsıra-i Ibret*, pp. 126–88; Irade Dahiliye 44794, Midhat to Grand Vezir, 22 Kânun-i evvel 1287/3 January 1872.
10. Kelly, *Britain*, p. 738.

4. CHANCE FOR ADJUSTMENT AND STABILITY

11. Irade Dahiliye 44794, Midhat to Grand Vezir, 8 Kânun-i evvel 1287/20 December 1871.
12. Lorimer, *Gazetteer*, p. 1450.
13. Lewis, *Emergence*, p. 453; Issawi, *Turkey*, pp. 361–63, 367. The Council, answerable to foreign creditors, assumed direct control of 12% to 15% (e.g., T£3,300,000 in 1908) of imperial revenues in order to assure service of the debt. Loan repayment continued to burden the Ottoman, and later Turkish, government into the 1920s.
14. British political officers in the Gulf noted frequent complaints about official extortion in Hasa. Saldana, *Expansion*, pp. 55–56.
15. Saldana, *Expansion*, p. 56; ŞD 2184/6, Former Treasurer Necd to Commander Necd, 9 Mayıs 1317/21 May 1901.
16. Midhat, *Tabsıra-i Ibret*, pp. 123–24.
17. *Basra Salname*, 1308, p. 152. The question of how to define revenues collected—and how to collect needed revenue without breaking the agreed tax limits of 1871—could be a problem for Istanbul. As noted earlier, the government asked the populace for services instead of monetary payments in 1887. Earlier the same year the Basra government had been asked to take part in raising a domestic loan. Basra assigned a share of T£1,800 to Hasa, which could only produce T£370 in riyals. The Hasawis sent the money as a contribution (*iane*) instead of as part of the loan. Accepting it as such would break the rules governing the loan, however—so the government kept the money, credited the sum to Hasa's tax account (which was always in arrears), and had the decision published in the Baghdad and Basra newspapers. KMNB 273A/236, Basra *Vali* to Finance Minister, 14 Kânun-i evvel 1302/26 December 1886; MV 15/59, 28 Kânun-i evvel 1302/9 January 1887.
18. ŞD 2184/6, Necd Mutasarrıf's report, 19 Haziran 1305/1 July 1889; ŞD 2184/6, Necd Commander's report, 4 Kânun-i evvel 1315/16 December 1899; ŞD 2184/6, Necd Commander's report, 12 Kânun-i evvel 1315/24 December 1899.
19. ŞD 2184/6, 19 Haziran 1305/1 July 1889; Y-MTV 239/20, Basra *Vali* to Yıldız Palace, 4 Kânun-i sani 1318/17 January 1903.
20. Saldana, *Expansion*, p. 56.
21. Y-Kâmil Pasha 80–38/3790; *Basra Salname*, 1308, p. 152. Even if the former figure refers to the number of trees (as seems likely), not groves, the revenue report is still very low.
22. *Bağdad Salname*, p. 215. The decline of returns in 1880/81 may have been a result of the troubles with the `Ajman. In general the figures given in *Salnames* sometimes seem reasonable, at other times patently fabricated. It is at least dubious that Hasa's revenue in 1881/82 matched that of the previous year to the last *kuruş*. The figure may well have been given because the real one was unavailable due to lateness in submitting accounts by the Hasa and/or Baghdad Treasuries.
23. Yıldız-Mehmet Kâmil Pasha (Y-Kâmil) 86–38/3790. The probable author of the report was Mehmet Salih Pasha (1886–87).
24. KMNB, F 273A, AE 236, Basra *Vali* to Finance Minister, 14 Kânun-i evvel 1302/26 December 1886; MV 15/59, 28 Kânun-i evvel 1302/9 January 1887; Irade Meclis-i Mahsus 4699, petition of thirty-two Hasawi notables, 1 Haziran 1305/13 June 1889.
25. ŞD 2157/22, Necd Treasurer's report, 13 Kânun-i evvel 1298/25 December 1882.

4. CHANCE FOR ADJUSTMENT AND STABILITY

26. MV 19/67, 22 Nisan 1303/4 May 1887; ŞD 2184/6, prisoners' petition, 13 Kânun-i evvel 1315/25 December 1899. The traders received three-year jail terms.
27. MV 78/55, 16 Kânun-i sani 1309/28 January 1894. The kuşlu riyal or dollar had sunk in value from T£0.20 to T£0.12.
28. *Basra Salname*, 1308, pp. 152–53.
29. Irade Dahiliye 45621, 24 Cemazi el-âhir 1289/29 August 1872.
30. Irade Dahiliye 45592, Baghdad *Vali* to Grand Vezir, 6 Rebi el-âhir 1289/13 June 1872; Irade Dahiliye 45621, Baghdad *Vali* to Grand Vezir, 12 Ağustos 1288/24 August 1872.
31. Lorimer, *Gazetteer*, p. 1131; Winder, *Saudi Arabia*, p. 257. At the end of 1883 a German traveler met this `Ajmani shaikh in Ha'il. The shaikh had spent seven years imprisoned in Niş (now in Serbia) after being seized when he came to Hasa, he claimed, on a safe-conduct to talk with the Ottomans. He blamed Midhat for this, but the full details of the case are certainly open to question. Other shaikhs (including at least one `Ajmani) were still coming to Hasa on safe-conduct to treat with the Ottomans—and were being treated well—not long before Midhat's departure from Baghdad. No shaikh would have trusted a safe-conduct so soon after an incident such as that alleged by the man in Ha'il. Euting, *Tagbuch*, p. 81; Irade Dahiliye 45052, 9 Kânun-i sani 1287/21 January 1872.
32. Ayniyat 851/172, 19 Cemazi el-evvel 1289/25 July 1872.
33. Kelly, *Britain*, p. 741; Lorimer, *Gazetteer*, p. 971; Winder, *Saudi Arabia*, pp. 256–58. The sons of Faisal were not the only aspirants to the amirate. A son of another former amir tried to win Ottoman appointment to office in Riyadh in 1879, but he picked the wrong method. Traveling from Basra around Arabia, he called on every British official near his route to try to win London's backing in Istanbul. Given Ottoman suspicions of British interference in Arabia, any such recommendation would kill his hopes. The pretender reached Istanbul, but nothing further was ever heard from him. His nephew similarly tried to interest the Khedive of Egypt in supporting his appointment in 1895, but also without success. Winder, p. 266; Lorimer, p. 1135.
34. Lorimer, *Gazetteer*, pp. 971–2; Winder, *Saudi Arabia*, p. 257.
35. Irade Meclis-i Mahsus 2052, 8 Muharrem 1291/25 February 1874, and Baghdad *Vali* to Grand Vezir, 6 Şubat 1289/18 February 1874; Midhat, *Tabsıra-i Ibret*, pp. 122–3; Lorimer, *Gazetteer*, p. 1132; Kelly, *Britain*, p. 741. Both Kurdish and Arab irregulars (*başıbozuk*) were included in this force.
36. Irade Meclis-i Mahsus 2052, 8 Muharrem 1291 and 6 Şubat 1289. The gendarmes may not have been much less expensive to keep than the regular troops, because the Ottomans had to offer high pay to raise a sufficient force. ŞD 2149/23, 20 Şubat 1288/4 March 1873; ŞD 2149/27, 18 Nisan 1289/30 April 1873.
37. Ayniyat 851/195–196, 4 Şevval 1290/25 November 1873.
38. Irade Meclis-i Mahsus 2052, 8 Muharrem 1291 and 6 Şubat 1289; Ayniyat 851/206, 11 Muharrem 1291/28 February 1874.
39. The Ottomans could have expected the appointment of Bazi` (sometimes referred to as Barrak) to have met with `Ajmani approval, because relations between the neighboring tribes were normally peaceful. The restoration of a Bani Khalid shaikh to a dominant position, however, quickly stirred latent tensions.
40. ŞD 2149/40, former Necd *Muhasebeci* to Council of State, 5 Kanun-i evvel 1290/17 December 1874 and 15 Ağustos 1291/27 August 1875.

4. CHANCE FOR ADJUSTMENT AND STABILITY

41. Ayniyat 849/159, 2 Cemazi el-âhir 1291/17 July 1874.
42. Kelly, *Britain*, p. 762.
43. *Basra Salname*, 1308, p. 175. This explanation was published some fifteen years after the revolt, and the original Ottoman conclusions may have been colored by the development of Sultan Abdülhamid's Pan-Islamic policy, which would sharpen attacks on such potential religious rivals as the Wahhabis.
44. ŞD 4159/40, 15 Ağustos 1291.
45. Ayniyat 851/258–259, 29 Rebi el-âhir 1294/13 May 1877.
46. Ayniyat 849/195, 7 Şaban 1292/8 September 1875.
47. Irade Dahiliye 49335, 25 Cemazi el-âhir 1292/29 July 1875. The new administrative unit was first constituted as an independent *sancak* but then later made a full-fledged *vilayet*.
48. Irade Meclis-i Mahsus 2216, 2 Muharrem 1292/8 February 1875; Baghdad *Vali* to Grand Vezir, 23 Kânun-i sani 1290/4 February 1875 (two telegrams). Mazyad's appointment, and the honors bestowed upon him, dismayed those in Hasa who had suffered reprisals at the hands of the Muntafiq relief force, but he did manage to keep the peace. ŞD 2149/40, 15 Ağustos 1291.
49. Irade Meclis-i Mahsus 2398, Basra *Vali* to Grand Vezir, 20 Kânun-i sani 1291/1 February 1876.
50. The British government received reports that ʿAbdallah sporadically negotiated with the Ottoman authorities for appointment as *mutasarrıf*. The negotiations all failed, because ʿAbdallah found the Ottoman conditions too severe and the Ottomans never regained faith in his trustworthiness. Saldana, *Nejd*, pp. 41–42, 44.
51. The Ottoman position at that time was precarious, because war with Serbia (1876) and, disastrously, Russia (1877–78), plus uprisings in Bosnia and Bulgaria, diverted the government's attention and military resources to the Balkans.
52. Kushner, "Governors," p. 276.
53. DH.MUI 27–1/15, Necd *Mutasarrıf* to Basra *Vali*, 15 Eylûl 1324/28 September 1908. The *mutasarrıf* argued that it would be impossible to elect a Hasawi representative to the Ottoman parliament because no census had ever been taken and because no Hasawis were fluent in Ottoman Turkish; their Arabic could be no substitute, because their dialect was unique. An example of an Arabic speaker who failed in Hasa was Mahmud Mahir Bey, an Albanian who had last served as *kaymakam* of Sidon (Lebanon) prior to coming to Arabia. Within months Hasawi complaints of his ignorance of local conditions led to his recall. DH.MUI 50–1/21, personnel report (*tercüme-i hal*) of Mahmud Mahir Bey; DH.MUI 50–1/21, petition of 92 people to Grand Vezir, 2 Mart 1325/15 March 1909.
54. Saldana, *Expansion*, pp. 53–61; Lorimer, *Gazetteer*, pp. 979–81; Irade Meclis-i Mahsus 2398, 20 Safer 1293/17 March 1876, and Basra *Vali* to Grand Vezir, 23 Şubat 1291/6 March 1876; Irade Meclis-i Mahsus 2525, 5 Safer 1294/19 February 1877; Irade Dahiliye 1318-L-23, Şevval 1318/February 1901. Their terms in office, of course, were not always calm, as Sayyid Talib's brief and unglorious career in Hasa attests (see chapter 7).
55. DH.MUI 4–2/26, Baghdad Deputy *Vali* to Interior Minister, 22 Haziran 1325/5 July 1909.
56. The unhealthy coastal climate speeded the substitution of irregulars for the more valuable regular troops and the reduction of garrison strengths. Some posts

4. CHANCE FOR ADJUSTMENT AND STABILITY

were so small that they clearly served little purpose beyond showing the Ottoman flag. A British naval officer in 1878 found, for example, that the garrison at Ra's Tanura consisted of a corporal and four soldiers. The troops were an eclectic group, hardly well-trained regulars. Another British officer visited Doha in 1876. He found a garrison of 30–40 *zaptiyes*, one of whom, a sergeant, was a native of Peshawar and had fought in India before drifting into Ottoman service in Basra at the start of Midhat's Hasa campaign. Since then he had served in Hufuf, Qatif, and now Doha. Kelly, *Britain*, pp. 768, 789. The *Basra Salname* of 1308/1890–91 reported (pp. 130–31) a security force in Hasa/Najd of 290 men, 102 of whom were mounted.

57. The most serious outbreaks of violence occurred in 1878, when Sa`ud's sons stirred a revolt in which Dammam was captured and Qatif besieged; 1880, when the `Ajman attacked Hufuf, only to be defeated by a forewarned *mutasarrıf*; and after 1889, when attacks on caravans became common. Lorimer, *Gazetteer*, pp. 983–84.

58. A petition from some Hasawi traders to the Grand Vezir in 1892 claimed that they were responsible for paying subsidies, merely using the Ottoman officials as intermediaries (Y-A Resmî 60/12, 22 Mayıs 1308/3 June 1892). Subsidies were by no means unique to Hasa; the Ottomans commonly paid tribes in other provinces (Ochsenwald, *Religion*, pp. 32–34; Bidwell, *Arabian Personalities*, p. 100). The subsidies in Hasa were insignificant in comparison to those paid in the Hijaz; in 1893–94, for example, the Ottomans sent T£40,751 to Hijazi tribes, who could disrupt the Hajj. It is noteworthy that outside the empire's borders, but in a similar situation and time, Sultan Turki of Oman also relied on subsidies to tribes for their submission. Disappointed with this policy's results, after 1874 he preferred to rely on alliances with select tribes, although he continued to pay token subsidies to tribes in the Omani interior (Landen, *Oman*, p. 360).

59. DH.MUI 54–1/13, Necd Commander to VI Corps Marshal, 22 Nisan 1325/5 May 1909; Necd Treasurer to War Ministry (memorandum and table), 18 Ağustos 1325/31 August 1909. The Ottomans phased out the payments over the period from 1901 to 1903.

60. Nafiz Pasha, on his own initiative before following Midhat out of the region, apparently began the stipend of dates to the Al Thani shaikhs of Qatar, first Muhammad, then Qâsim. The state also gave the Al Sabah shaikhs of Kuwait a stipend from 1872. Irade Meclis-i Mahsus 5117, Council of State memorandum, 16 Şubat 1306/28 February 1891; Usul-i Irade Dosya 77, Basra *Vali* to Interior Minister, 31 Kânun-i sani 1315/12 February 1900.

61. There was an element of willingness in the arrangement that made it more than a straightforward, compulsory payment of tax to the government. The shaikh of `Udayd, for example, in whose territory Ottoman authority was always dubious, sent about T£10 per year to Hasa via Qâsim al-Thani. He also had the Ottoman flag sent by Midhat in 1871, which he flew when Ottoman officials visited `Udayd. By these actions he built a reserve of good will that he could call on if threatened by the shaikh of Abu Dhabi. Kelly, *Britain*, p. 769.

62. An instance of this occurred in 1895. The *mutasarrıf* raised the level of tribute demanded from the Hasa tribes. The `Ajman declared that they could not pay until they had recovered property looted by the Mutayr, whereupon the Ottomans joined forces with the `Ajman to attack the rival tribe. Lorimer, *Gazetteer*, p. 985.

4. CHANCE FOR ADJUSTMENT AND STABILITY

63. Y-Kâmil 86–38/3790, for example, suggested that messengers between Basra and Hasa frequently encountered bedouin raiders.

64. Gerber, *Ottoman Rule*, pp. 20–27; Le Gall, "Pashas," pp. 91–93; Rogan, "Limits of Ottoman Rule," pp. 45–50; Bailey, "Bedouin Tribes," pp. 321–32.

65. Kelly, *Britain*, p. 768; Mansur, *Tatawwur*, p. 146. This figure was reported in 1876 and a roughly similar one in 1878. A decade later the Ottomans were dissatisfied with Qâsim, deeming him obligated to pay them more from his various mercantile and tax monopolies.

66. Zahlan, *Creation*, pp. 52–53; Yıldız Esas Evrakı (YEE), 14/250/126/8, a report on the Qatari uprising of 1893, accused Qâsim of working with Britain to destabilize the country, smuggling guns and supplies to various tribes, and causing Hasa to be harried. (An earlier petition from some leading Hasawis also placed blame on Abu Dhabi. Y-A Resmî 60/12, 22 Mayıs 1308/3 June 1892.) It is probable that the shaikh did allow contraband to pass through his territory, at the least, and his ties to such troublesome tribes as the Bani Hajir and Manasir were apparently close in 1893: members of these tribes fought for him against the Ottomans. The British Resident by 1892 also thought that Qâsim was in league with the raiders, although he had no involvement in the matter (Kumar, *India*, p. 126).

67. Gavin, *Aden*, pp. 203–4; Landen, *Oman*, pp. 124, 139–40; Lorimer, *Gazetteer*, p. 1136; YEE 31/76–118/76/139.

68. Lorimer, *Gazetteer*, pp. 2557–70. Britain's most immediate concern was the passage of arms through Iran to Afghanistan, however, and thus was slower to attack directly the trade along the Ottoman Arabian coast.

69. Y.MTV 37/93, VI Corps commander to Yıldız, 6 Şubat 1304/18 February 1889; YEE 31/76–118/76/139; YEE 14/250/126/8, p. 1; Bab-i Ali Evrak Odası (BEO) 59642, undated (probably 1896) p. 1. Guns may also have been smuggled into the main Ottoman ports under the noses of officials who were bribed to be blind.

70. The VI (Baghdad) Corps in the period 1870–1900 was the worst-equipped unit in the army but had improved markedly by 1914 (Longrigg, *Four Centuries*, p. 314). The local gendarmerie in Hasa would have had even shoddier equipment. The VI Corps probably was denied the best equipment in part because of its high percentage of Shi'i soldiers (90% by one estimate) whose loyalty was uncertain. A proposal was made in 1889 to replace some of these troops with men from the (Sunni) IV (Erzincan) and V (Damascus) Corps (YEE 14/366/126/9, 8 Kânun-i sani 1304/20 January 1889, pp. 3–5). On Ottoman concerns about Shi'ism in Iraq in 1891–1907, see Deringil, "Struggle," pp. 45–62.

71. Y-A Resmî 60/12, 19 Kânun-i sani 1307/31 January 1892; Saldana, *Expansion*, pp. 57, 60. *Mutasarrıf* Akif Pasha in 1889 revived Midhat's sensible suggestion that a regular camel corps could best control mobile marauders, but due to the state's lack of money the army continued to rely heavily on infantry. At the end of his fourth and final term as *mutasarrıf* in 1901, Said Pasha was still trying to convince his superiors that it would be more cost-effective to use a camel corps drawn from local tribesmen than to keep a large garrison of regular infantry to police Hasa (see chapter 3). The Ottomans tried with some success a similar scheme in other remote, tribal areas exempt from conscription, notably among the Kurds of northern Iraq and Muslim tribesmen of Albania (Landau, *Politics*, p. 57; Yapp, "Modernization," p. 351). Although some locals joined the gendarmerie who were often given the main responsibility for

4. CHANCE FOR ADJUSTMENT AND STABILITY

defending Hasa, the government failed to maintain a permanent effective tribal fighting force in Arabia, in spite of Said Pasha's efforts. Presumably doubts about the wisdom of arming local Arabs, as well as initial equipage costs, hobbled the idea.

72. Ochsenwald, *Religion*, p. 162; Saldana, *Nejd*, p. 49. The Ottoman capture from Ibn Rashid of Jawf, a town due east of Aqaba on the northern limit of the Great Nafud desert, reportedly impressed him, predisposing him to cooperate with the Ottomans.

73. Lorimer, *Gazetteer*, p. 1137.

74. YEE 13/112–48/112/6.

75. YEE G/119-I et al./119/138 contain correspondence from Ibn Rashid, including a letter of thanks and good wishes dated 7 Rebi el-evvel 1306/11 November 1888, and several notes about Arabian horses sent to the sultan.

76. YEE 14/366/126/9, p. 1 of a memorandum on political conditions in Basra *Vilayet*, dated 8 Kânun-i sani 1304/20 January 1889.

77. The government showed great concern about the security threat posed by independent south Arabia in the 1870s and 1880s: 1876–79 and 1884–86 were periods of active planning for an extension of authority, direct or indirect, into Oman and Dhufar. By 1888, however, the Ottomans apparently recognized that Sultan Turki held power more securely than they did in Arabia. Sensing an Omani ability to cause unrest in the Hijaz, the government tried to establish good relations with Masqat, for example by trying to establish a regular Ottoman postal steamer service between Bab al-Mandab and Basra (Y-A Hususî, 214/46).

78. A simplified history of Oman over the last two centuries could be reduced to the recurrent struggle between the conservative interior, which looked to the Ibadi imamate for leadership, and the more moderate coast, which supported the sultan in Masqat. The last great imamate-sultanate conflict before 1888 ended in 1871 with the death of the Imam `Azzan b. Qays.

79. British officials did discuss proclamation of a formal protectorate over Oman during the estrangement from Sultan Faisal, but the matter apparently was kept secret from Omani representatives (Landen, *Oman*, p. 369).

80. YEE 14/366/126/9, pp. 1–2, 4–5. This affair is rich in irony. Since the Ottomans in effect adopted Midhat's view that there were no independent shaikhs in Arabia, that earlier ties to Najd and present bonds of religion held all of the peninsula to the empire, it is amusing that any Ottoman official would equate Ibn Rashid's lack of official title with an absence of relationship to the government. It is also amusing that the British eventually absolved the Ottomans of complicity in this plot, accusing Qâsim al-Thani of urging Ibn Rashid to invade Trucial Oman as part of his feud with Abu Dhabi (Lorimer, *Gazetteer*, p. 821).

81. Kumar (*India*, pp. 128–29) states that the plan collapsed when Ibn Rashid was distracted by the unruliness of `Abdallah b. Faisal's brother and successor as head of the Wahhabis, `Abd al-Rahman. `Abd al-Rahman's sudden revolt against Rashidi control in Riyadh, however, did not occur until 28 July 1890, long after the invasion scheme was hatched.

82. YEE 14/366/126/9, p. 1.

83. MV 37/1, 19 Teşrin-i evvel 1304/31 October 1888; YEE 31/76–118/76/139, 15 Teşrin-i evvel 1306/27 October 1890. A German visitor to Ha'il in 1892 found that Ibn Rashid's relations with Istanbul were troubled, in part because of his numerous opponents in Istanbul. Nolde, *Reise*, pp. 55–56.

4. CHANCE FOR ADJUSTMENT AND STABILITY

84. YEE 31/76–118/76/139, pp. 2–3; Y-A Resmî 60/12; and Irade Askeriye 1310-M-16, VI Army *Müşir* to Minister of War, 25 Temmuz 1308/6 August 1892; Lorimer, *Gazetteer*, p. 1137. By 1892 suspicion had hardened to conviction that Ibn Rashid was collaborating with Britain, and that the two allies were preparing to squeeze the Ottomans out of Arabia, Ibn Rashid advancing from the interior and the British from the sea. This alliance existed only in the minds of Ottoman officials; there was some discussion within Indian government ranks of the advisability of making overtures to Ibn Rashid in 1889, but the suggestion was never adopted (Kumar, *India*, p. 129).

85. The Ottomans continued to suspect Ibn Rashid's motives, although they did not challenge him directly. When the amir of Ha'il assumed control over the town of al-ʿUla, formerly attached to the *vilayet* of the Hijaz, and levied *zekât* on the inhabitants, the government sought an amicable solution that would not cause Ibn Rashid undue embarrassment (Y-A Resmî, 60/17, 9 Ağustos 1308/21 August 1892). This may well have been the result of Sultan Abdülhamid II's leniency toward Arab leaders potentially useful to his Islamist policy.

86. Irade Meclis-i Mahsus 4301, memorandum (of the Necd Administrative Council?), 12 Temmuz 1304/24 July 1888; Irade Meclis-i Mahsus 4699, Necd *Mutasarrıf* to Basra *Vali*, 9 Haziran 1305/21 June 1889. It also helped to revive the desire to establish full, direct authority over Riyadh, which could have solidified Hasa's western and southern defenses. Despite doubts about Ibn Rashid's reliability, it is likely that an 1888 attempted attack on a caravan coming from Riyadh to Hufuf resulted from the lack of his control over the area and tribes involved (Manasir and Dawasir) rather than his active encouragement of unrest. The raids probably were also a spillover into Hasa of the turmoil that Ibn Rashid's conquest of Riyadh had brought to central Arabia. A large Ottoman garrison in Riyadh might prove a better check on these bedouin raiders than was the distant amir of Ha'il.

87. The Ottoman propensity for tactical, rather than strategic, planning in Hasa (i.e., do what is necessary to avert crises but do not form a cohesive plan of improvements) is illustrated by the state's treatment of the Saʿudis. Having attempted to cripple Wahhabi power for almost two decades and having had the satisfaction of seeing Ibn Rashid capture Riyadh, the government gave pensions to ʿAbd al-Rahman and his son, ʿAbd al-ʿAziz (who later resurrected the Saʿudi amirate as today's Saudi Arabia), no doubt in part for possible future use should Ibn Rashid become too troublesome (Lorimer, *Gazetteer*, p. 1140). Other former leaders given Ottoman pensions included Muhammad al-Khalifa, former shaikh of Bahrain, and Fadhl b. ʿAlawi, who held the south Arabian port of Salala and its Dhufari hinterland from 1876 to 1879 (Y-A Resmî, 44/34, 29 Zilhicce 1305/7 September 1888; Kelly, *Britain*, pp. 773–75). The government supported Muhammad al-Khalifa and his family despite difficulties caused by an empty Treasury. Abdülhamid supported Fadhl after the shaikh had to flee Dhufar, and Fadhl became one of the sultan's close coterie of Pan-Islamic strategists, responsible for southern Arabia and India (Landau, *Politics*, pp. 67, 71, 322–23).

88. The Omani imamate, and to some degree the sultanate of Masqat, also had such authority, but its scope was limited largely to Ibadi south Arabia. The severe orthodoxy of Wahhabism might have limited the legitimacy of the Saʿudi amir in the eyes of Hasawi town dwellers, but the many bedouin tribes following the Hanbali *madhhab* would have had more respect for his stature.

89. By the early 1880s Istanbul had not lost all its former appreciation of London

4. CHANCE FOR ADJUSTMENT AND STABILITY

but rather considered Britain the best of a bad lot among the Great Powers. In one sense the government could almost accept the British takeover of Cyprus and even Egypt, because it helped ensure against a Russian conquest of India. Britain was still the most effective Ottoman ally in European diplomacy, and loss of India would reduce it to a useless, third-rate power. In another sense, however, the Ottomans greatly feared these marks of growing British interest and influence in the Muslim world. Some in Istanbul favored a policy of preventing any rapprochement between Britain and Russia, which would ease a restraint on St. Petersburg, or between Britain and France, which would allow both countries more freedom to expand in the Middle East (Y-Kâmil 86–37/3623, thought to be dated 1881).

90. Saldana, *Expansion*, pp. 83–85. Zubara had been a stronghold of Bahraini influence in Qatar before the British intervened in Bahraini affairs in 1868. Shaikh `Isa of Manama maintained a claim to sovereignty over the port in the 1870s, at least in part to prevent his enemy Nasir b. Mubarak from launching an invasion from it. Qâsim al-Thani sided with Nasir against Bahrain and Zubara, thus presumably prompting the attacks on Qatari ships. Qâsim and Nasir led an attack on Zubara that destroyed the town in 1878. Zahlan, *Creation*, p. 48.

91. Saldana, *Expansion*, p. 92. By 23 June 1879 the value of stolen property reached 67,008.25 krans (£2,680), of which the government was officially interested in the recovery of 8,834.25 krans (£353). The government was most concerned with compensation due British subjects who had lost goods or money, but a deepening protective instinct for Bahrain stirred a more unofficial interest in the numerous reported attacks on property belonging to the islands' subjects.

92. Lorimer, *Gazetteer*, pp. 975–96; Saldana, *Expansion*, pp. 93–94; Kelly, *Britain*, p. 793. The town near Dhahran was apparently a transshipment point for the pirates, who neither resided nor stored their plunder there. The two Ottoman naval ships did not maintain station off Hasa because their engines broke down.

93. The Viceroy of India was most instrumental in opening the question of Ottoman sovereignty over Qatar. The Consul in Baghdad opined that the peninsula was Ottoman territory, while the Gulf Resident had a shifting stance, admitting rule by Basra over Qatar in October 1878 but denying it outside Doha in January 1879 (Kelly, *Britain*, pp. 788, 796–98).

94. Kelly, *Britain*, 799ff., 830; Saldana, *Expansion*, pp. 100–13; Lorimer, *Gazetteer*, pp. 977–99. The decision to pursue pirates in Ottoman waters was taken despite a finding by the Crown Law Officers that such acts were illegal according to international law.

95. Saldana, *Expansion*, p. 97. In March 1881 the *vali* of Baghdad relayed to the British Consul a report from the *mutasarrıf* in Hufuf that stated that the man most suspected of piracy was innocent of such crimes.

96. Saldana, *Expansion*, p. 93. The author's reference to the accountant as "presumably a Turkish subject" seems to indicate that the British never investigated the details of his case, although the raider was finally delivered to Bahrain for execution. The governments of Bahrain and Hasa made numerous demands of each other for the extradition of criminals and debtors, rarely successfully (Lorimer, *Gazetteer*, pp. 909, 915–17).

97. Viceroy (Lytton) to Secretary of State (India), 22 May 1879, in Kelly, *Britain*, pp. 769, 771–72. The sultan's government would have appreciated the viceroy's rea-

4. CHANCE FOR ADJUSTMENT AND STABILITY

soning, similar to the Ottoman view of Bahrain, that no independent shaikhdom existed at 'Udayd simply because none had been recognized by Britain. "If such a plea [of Ottoman jurisdiction] were admitted, it would be set up by every petty chief along the coast, who might have good reasons for desiring to evade control or chastisement." The Ottoman government naturally considered that Britain had used this very process to establish a position in Arabia that contributed to local unrest. In the later case of Kuwait, British officials would argue that Shaikh Mubarak was independent, because he had approached their government directly.

98. Ottoman alarm and indignation over this event increased with receipt of a report that a British warship took part in the attack (Kelly, *Britain*, pp. 770–71). A British double standard must have been apparent to some who had greater familiarity with Arabian affairs. Colonel Nixon, the British consul in Baghdad, for example, argued in 1876 and 1879 for establishment of a tributary relationship with the Trucial shaikhs and the sultan of Masqat; Britain otherwise had no legal grounds for opposing extension of Ottoman sovereignty over their territories (Kelly, *Britain*, p. 797).

99. Although local officials may have taken the lead in struggling against the rise of British influence, Istanbul was certainly not consistently uninvolved. A case in which the British vice consul in Basra pushed the case of a brother of the shaikh of Bahrain in a dispute with a Qatifi merchant in 1887–88, for example, was discussed twice by the Council of Ministers. The council directed the *vali* of Basra to deliver to the vice consul a written rejection of Britain's right to interfere in a dispute between Ottoman subjects. The Council also established a commission to recommend measures to secure the Ottoman Gulf coast against foreign threats. The commission's investigations helped to spur the spate of reform proposals for the Necd *sancak* in the late 1880s. MV 25/48, 14 Teşrin-i evvel 1303/26 October 1887; MV 28/69, 7 Şubat 1303/19 February 1888.

100. Had Istanbul reinforced the Basra squadron, Britain would have been made uncomfortable by the perceived challenge to its naval supremacy. In the late 1880s Britain muted some complaints about piracy out of fears of an increased Ottoman naval presence in Gulf waters and tried to encourage Ottoman security efforts restricted to the mainland (Lorimer, *Gazetteer*, p. 988).

101. The confused affair of the Bahrain raider and the Qatif accountant-embezzler may well have arisen because the *mutasarrıf* had not yet received the order from Basra to deliver the raider to the shaikh of Bahrain, as the *vali* of Basra later claimed (Saldana, *Expansion*, p. 93). In such cases, when local affairs had relevance to Great Power diplomacy, the governor of Hasa could not act without orders (Y-Kâmil 86–1/38, 12 Nisan 1295/24 April 1879), and the troops normally had to await orders from the War Ministry (Y-A Resmî 60/12, 19 Kânun-i sani 1307/31 January 1892). The Hasa authorities may similarly have remained unconvinced about the guilt of accused men because so much time elapsed between the commission and the report of crimes, which made the collection of evidence difficult.

102. Kelly, *Britain*, pp. 807–9. The new consul in Baghdad (Nixon was replaced because the viceroy thought him too "pro-Turkish") thought that the Ottoman government would prefer continuance of the unrest. "They are seeking . . . [a] quarrel and a pretext to interfere and conquer [Bahrain]." The vice consul in Basra agreed with him, asserting that the only reason why the Ottomans continued to hold Hasa was in hopes of seizing Bahrain's pearl banks. These judgments seem rather harsh,

4. CHANCE FOR ADJUSTMENT AND STABILITY

since conditions in Iraq and Hasa made internal security, not expansion, the prime Ottoman concern at this time. While the Ottoman government in all likelihood did not instigate the attacks, its concerns about security did not preclude attempts to use the turbulent conditions to extend the sultan's sway by stealth (cf. the later plan to use Ibn Rashid to absorb Oman), however, and the Ottomans never fully gave up hope of one day bringing Bahrain under their control. The *vali* of Basra in 1879 did try to win the shaikh of Bahrain's agreement to establishment of a coaling station on his territory "for the purpose of strengthening friendly ties." He sent a trusted representative to talk with Shaikh `Isa and persuade him to shun Iranian and British intermediaries in trying to resolve problems. As inducement the *vali* promised to take effective action to ensure peace and punish pirates. Y-Kâmil Pasha 86–1/38; Y-Kâmil 86–38/3790.

103. Kelly, *Britain*, p. 808.

104. Lorimer, *Gazetteer*, pp. 994–95. By 1897 Indian trade had fallen to one third or one half of previous levels. Local lawlessness also contributed much to the decline. It is possible that some local Ottoman officials felt tempted at times to view piracy as a means to drive British-protected traders away from the Arabian coast. Indian traders were regarded as the thin edge of a British wedge entering the peninsula.

105. This was naturally not the case when the benefits of disclosure of treaty details outweighed the drawbacks. Copies of the Maritime Truce agreements were provided to the Sublime Porte in 1871 after the Grand Vezir intimated that Midhat's expedition could not be sure of not disturbing the truce if the Ottomans had no knowledge of the agreements' contents (Kelly, *Britain*, p. 727).

106. The most striking case of this involved Oman, where previous Anglo-French competition culminated in a jointly declared guaranty of Omani independence in 1862. The agreement was negotiated between London and Paris, and the relevant authorities in India remained ignorant of it for almost two decades. A Protectorate thus became impossible. When a formal supremacy in Oman became desirable in 1892, this hurdle was cleared by conclusion of an Anglo-Omani commercial treaty that contained a secret bond by the Masqat sultan not to cede in any form any territory to a foreign power other than Britain. Because the sultan depended upon British money and military power to survive, this gave Britain a virtually unchallengeable position in Oman without a formal protectorate (Landen, *Oman*, pp. 200, 222–23). In regard to Bahrain, any move to assume a protectorate would inevitably draw strong protests from Istanbul and Tehran (Kelly, *Britain*, p. 805).

107. The activities of several French agents in Masqat and Trucial Oman in 1891 disturbed the British more than did the coincidental Ottoman designs for expansion, while it was feared that Russia instigated the renewed Iranian claims to Bahrain, Qatar, and Trucial Oman in 1886–87. The appearance of French, American, and even Japanese ships in the Gulf in 1880 also helped to convince Britain of the need for firmer ties to Bahrain. External threats could be met by posting more ships and men in the area, thus indicating readiness for immediate, forceful reaction, or by concluding exclusive agreements with local rulers, thereby establishing a preemptive, lasting position in the land and substituting the threat of future retaliation for the expensive reality of a large permanent military presence. There is a nice touch of irony in this. The growth of Europe's (especially Britain's) ability to project power beyond Suez prompted the Ottoman grab at Arabia in 1870–71; the growing European (especially

4. CHANCE FOR ADJUSTMENT AND STABILITY

French) presence in the Red Sea and the Gulf twenty years later spurred Britain to a similar "grab" consolidating its hold on the region (Lorimer, *Gazetteer*, pp. 919–20, 922; Kelly, *Britain*, p. 835; Gavin, *Aden*, pp. 197–98).

108. Kelly, *Britain*, p. 825. Ross and Shaikh `Isa concluded that the ruler could more easily resist Ottoman and Iranian advances if he could refer to a general undertaking, backed by a Great Power, not to allow foreign posts in Bahrain. The Resident undoubtedly also wished to curb the shaikh's propensity to correspond directly with the Ottomans in matters, such as piracy, where he felt that British efforts were not producing results (Kelly, *Britain*, p. 794; Farah, *Protection*, pp. 63–65, 67–68).

109. Kelly, *Britain*, pp. 825–26; Lorimer, *Gazetteer*, p. 922; Farah, *Protection*, pp. 66–67.

110. Kelly, *Britain*, p. 826.

111. Landen, *Oman*, pp. 220–21.

112. Kelly, *Britain*, pp. 834–36.

113. YEE 18/94–25/94/44, Mart 1298/March 1882. Some of these reports have been transcribed and published. For instance, see Bostan, "Zor Sancağı," pp. 163–220; Bostan, "Muhammad Hilâl Efendi," pp. 301–26; Göyünç, "Trablusgarb," pp. 235–46. For an unpublished description of the Najdi interior, submitted by a member of the noted Zuhayr family of Basra, see YEE 14/256/126/8, 21 Rebi el-evvel 1308/4 November 1890.

114. Y-A Resmî 5/21, 2 Safer 1297.

115. The boat was in the Shatt al-Arab, fifteen miles (24 km) south of the city, when it was attacked. The British foreign secretary, Lord Salisbury, did not approve of Ambassador Layard's protest to the Ottoman foreign minister in this case. Layard had acted on his own initiative, and his note to the minister included a vague threat of consequences that the Sublime Porte would wish to avoid. At the time (late 1879) the London and India governments were debating the limits of permissible intervention in the piracy problem, and the Foreign Office preferred not to raise the matter with Istanbul before reaching a decision, especially since it considered such protests to have little effect. The Porte's embarrassment and frustration at this recurrence of piracy presumably were more intense because it recently had taken a series of steps to combat the problem, including the dispatch of several ships, the replacement of the Basra *vali*, and forceful orders to the Basra naval commander to redouble his policing efforts. Kelly, *Britain*, p. 810; Saldana, *Expansion*, p. 95; Y-A Resmî 5/21.

116. Midhat had alerted the Porte to the need for shallow draft vessels for transport along the Hasa coast, but the Ottoman ships were still usually suited for use in deeper water. The continuing disrepair of the Basra naval yard apparently precluded construction of ships designed for local conditions. Because the slope of the seabed is quite gentle in the western Gulf (35cm/km), deep draft steamers had to stand well off the shore, making close scrutiny difficult. This raises the question of how the British navy, also using relatively large ships, could attempt to police the coast and even pursue pirates onto land. The British scheme was more limited than the Ottoman, however: it proposed chasing robbers found outside the three-mile limit, following them into Ottoman territorial waters and on land to the limit of ship's gun range. The last part of the pursuit could be carried out by men loaded into the ship's small boats. Such oared craft would suit for a ship-to-shore chase, less well for the routine coastal inspection involved in preventive policing.

4. CHANCE FOR ADJUSTMENT AND STABILITY

117. A coal depot on Bahrain would have solved this problem admirably. The depot at Qatif or Ra's Tanura proposed by Midhat must not have been maintained, or even built, perhaps because of the difficulty of transferring coal in bulk between deep draft ships and shore.

118. The severity of the shallows problem was indicated earlier by Midhat's statement that the water depth near Qatif can be as little as one or two feet at low tide.

119. The specified level of consumption (5 kantars/600 lbs/275 kg to cover 10 miles/16 km in one hour) still restricted their range if no convenient depot were established. At that rate, travel between Basra and Hasa would take almost ten tons of coal each way.

120. Y-A Resmî 27/19, Meclis-i Vükela memorandum, 17 Kânun-i sani 1297/29 January 1882.

121. YEE 14/88–10/88/12, proposal of steps necessary to improve Basra *Sancak*'s security and economy, Gurre-i Eylûl 1296/13 September 1880; Lorimer, *Gazetteer*, pp. 1505–7.

122. The *mutasarrıf* in Hasa early in 1881 apparently denied the truth of British claims of recent attacks (Saldana, *Expansion*, p. 97). 123. Y-A Resmî 27/19, 17 Kânun-i sani 1297/29 January 1882; 27 Şubat 1299/10 March 1884 for report summaries.

124. The document actually refers to a Shammar-Mukalla conflict, which was unlikely because of the great distance between the two. A local struggle over Mukalla had ended in 1881 with expulsion by Britain of its *naqib*, who claimed to be an Ottoman subject; "Shammar" likely was a misprint for nearby "Shihr." Since Ottoman knowledge of Arabia was generally rudimentary at best, such a mistake is understandable. As to the other incidents, the Italians settled in Assab in 1880. The French purchased Obokh island in 1862 and extended their claim to Djibouti in 1884; they also landed at Shaikh Sa`id, on the Yemen side of the Bab al-Mandab, in 1884, much to the south of the area cited in the Ottoman report (Gavin, *Aden*, pp. 171–72, 197–98). Another (non-European) foreign influence feared by the Ottomans was the Mahdist movement that appeared in the Sudan in 1882. Mahdism's threat to the sultan's religious legitimacy produced a forceful reaction in the Hijaz and a desire to patrol Arabia's coasts in order to prevent Wahhabi-Sudanese cooperation (Y-Kâmil 86–36/3578; Ochsenwald, *Religion*, pp. 202–3).

125. Saldana, *Expansion*, pp. 70, 114; Issawi, *Economic History*, pp. 149–50. Two gunboats, apparently part of the earlier planned coastal squadron, were launched in Istanbul for service in the Gulf in May 1883. They presumably helped suppress the piracy outbreak of that year, in which the Ottomans had some success in retrieving stolen goods. The administration in addition tried to reduce British dominance of Tigris-Euphrates shipping, a market that the Ottoman-Oman Company was supposed to serve. It also is likely that a new commander arrived at the Basra naval yard; the officer's report (Y-A Resmî 27/19) has the tone of a new commander's assessment of a post's problems.

126. Y-A Resmî 27/19, 25 Kânun-i evvel 1299/6 January 1884, *Necd ve Zufar Kıtalarınca Görülen ve Edilen Tahkikat Iktizası Derece-i Vücubda Olan Bazı Icraat ve Teşkilat ile Basra Tersanesinin Islah ve Imarı Hakkında Nezaret-i Celilelerine Takdimine Ictisar Ettiğim Layihadır*. Rıza Ali repeated many points in a second report, drawn up by the Basra *Meclis-i Idare* under his direction (ŞD 2158/10, 22 Temmuz 1301/3 August 1885).

4. CHANCE FOR ADJUSTMENT AND STABILITY

127. Sultan Abdülhamid and his advisers had the most benevolent view of the Arab shaikhs, seeing them as likely supporters of the sultan's policy of Islamism. While other Ottoman observers in the Porte and provinces doubted Arab trustworthiness, they usually allowed their suspicions narrower scope than did Rıza. Midhat and the commanding general in Hasa thought the bedouins unreliable but judged the settled population content under Ottoman rule. Suspicion of Ibn Rashid did not preclude the expectation that he could be replaced by a more pliable rival. The government also was too ready to accept statements of loyalty from shaikhs who were interested primarily in military aid at times of crisis, as happened in Oman. It is worth noting that the British detected a similar growing Ottoman disgust with the shaikhs and a preference for direct appeals to the people in Yemen at about this time (Gavin, *Aden*, p. 207).

128. This document reflected the growth of Islamism under Abdülhamid II, of which the resurrection of the sultan's claim to be caliph was one aspect. In contrast to the generally secular tone of Midhat's and the Porte's documents in 1870/71, this report emphasized the religious threat posed by Britain. The troublesome Indian traders were Zoroastrians (*mecusiyülmazhab*); missionaries and other British representatives cloaked their plots to subvert the faithful in Islamic guise; and many on the coast who had lived without proper guidance converted to Christianity.

129. These ships would make regular three-month patrols, inspecting conditions, solving problems that might draw in outsiders, and doubtless keeping the local leaders in check. The chiefs' loyalty was to be further secured by the award of honors and other reassurances, a tactic on which Abdülhamid came to rely heavily.

130. The Sultan of Masqat, for example, received from India a large subsidy (£8,500) in lieu of tribute formerly paid by Zanzibar; the Ottomans, who had a bare Treasury and no influence in Zanzibar to compel payment of the tribute, could not be expected to continue the subsidy if they displaced the British (Landen, *Oman*, pp. 200–201, 209).

131. The suggestion that sail, not steam, ships be used was very practical. Sail ships could stay on station longer than steamers, were often of shallower draft, and were cheaper to build and maintain. Even so, the Basra naval yard would need heavy equipment, workshops, dry dock and slipway, 200-man barracks, hospital, bath house, mosque, offices, and a 40-pupil naval preparatory school. These improvements would have been very useful for Ottoman control in Iraq and Hasa, but they probably would not have helped progress toward the stated goal as much as was hoped. Even if the Omanis and Dhufaris welcomed extension of Ottoman rule, including patrols of ships and tax collectors among the pearl fisheries, this costly force increase still stood little chance of driving the famously stubborn British from the area.

132. The government's attempts to hinder British commerce on the rivers had caused demand far to outweigh supply of shipping. The Oman company's riverain trade had disappeared as its ships were allowed to decay, leaving it with only paper revenues. A reformed and enlarged company could make those revenues real and increasing. Extension of service to all of Arabia and the Persian coast would help to spread Ottoman influence, reduce the people's dependence on foreigners, transport pilgrims on the Hajj, and save the Treasury at least T£10,000–15,000 per annum for carrying grain from Basra to the Hijaz.

133. The only current channel markers were four buoys placed by the British

4. CHANCE FOR ADJUSTMENT AND STABILITY

India Steam Company. The commander wanted to remove all foreign control of navigation by placing Ottoman buoys and marking lights from the entrance of the Shatt al-Arab to Basra and by putting all ships under pilots from Basra and Kuwait in order to prevent foreigners from becoming familiar with the channel's peculiarities. In case of war this could be an important element of Basra's defense. Tolls charged on shipping would repay the expense of these moves. The commander also included a general statement of the need to secure and fortify Kuwait, whose port would be very valuable to an enemy invading Iraq.

134. The confirmation was included in a report on a broad range of conditions in Baghdad province. The inspector was not a naval man, but rather a former judge (*naib*) of Baghdad city.

135. Y-A Resmî 27/19, 29 Kânun-i evvel 1300. The marker placement was a long-standing goal of the Navy Department, which had signed an agreement on 18 April 1881 with two Frenchmen for the erection of such lighthouses (Y-A Resmî 27/19, 27 Şubat 1299/10 March 1884).

136. Lorimer, *Gazetteer*, pp. 1534–40; Issawi, *Economic History*, pp. 146–50. The government tried to launch a new shipping line in 1888 but continued to have trouble providing ships and keeping them from breaking down or sinking. The most lasting Ottoman actions in this sphere were the continuing disputes with the British government and Euphrates and Tigris Steam Navigation Co. (Lynch Bros.) over shipping rights.

137. Saldana, *Expansion*, pp. 70–71. A few more gunboats trickled in later, as the government continued to feel the need for ships to aid communication and security from Basra to Qatar. By September 1893 the squadron consisted of four steamers, a gunboat, three coastal cutters, and several derelict hulks. Most of these were of little use for patrolling the Arabian coast, however: they drew too much water to come within three or four miles of the coast (except at a handful of ports), were in poor condition and could well sink in rough weather. An immediate reinforcement of four ships, including two of quite shallow draft, was recommended (YEE 14/250/126/8, 10 Eylûl 1309/22 September 1893, pp. 13, 16–17).

138. The yard still lacked a dry dock and other facilities necessary to repair large ships in 1893, as a result of which the navy continued to have to send ships to Istanbul or foreign dockyards (YEE 14/250/126/8, p. 16). It was able to assemble the prefabricated parts of two advanced-design steamers and four barges for river transport in 1904, but naval ships for river and Gulf service generally continued to come from Istanbul instead of being built locally (Issawi, *Fertile Crescent*, p. 249). In 1910–11, Basra received more money in the naval budget than any department except the central administration (McCarthy, *Statistics*, p. 201).

139. Lorimer, *Gazetteer*, p. 1517; YEE 14/250/126/8, 10 Eylûl 1309/22 September 1893, p. 12. The problems besetting the drawn-out construction of the Faw fortifications illustrate the unforeseeable snags that often hampered execution of reform plans. Work continued steadily for almost three years, but an outbreak of cholera in 1889 caused a five-month suspension. Then a succession of changes in the project leadership, arguments between a project head and the War Ministry, and the death of another supervisor made progress sporadic at best.

140. Lorimer, *Gazetteer*, pp. 806–7. In 1888 the *vali* of Basra visited Shaikh Qâsim. In order to persuade the shaikh to cooperate with the Ottoman intrusion into his

4. CHANCE FOR ADJUSTMENT AND STABILITY

domain, the *vali* promised him a title and decoration. As a result, a coal depot was established, and a 250-man garrison and a steam launch were assigned to the town. Qâsim remained recalcitrant, however, and the Ottoman means of control grew slowly.

141. YEE 14/366/126/9, 8 Kânun-i sani 1304/20 January 1889. This report on the security of Basra *Vilayet* stressed the continuing need to make its best harbor defensible. Even were the Shatt closed to the British by the placement of a few guns and the scuttling of several hulks in the channel, if they could capture Kuwait they could besiege Basra within hours.

142. The hope of controlling the pearl trade did not die, however: in 1896 Qatari pearl boats reportedly were offered Ottoman flags (which they refused) and an Ottoman warship was stationed off the peninsula for the boats' "protection" (Saldana, *Expansion*, pp. 71–72).

143. Y-A Resmî 27/19, 15 Teşrin-i sani 1300/27 November 1884. As was mentioned above, the Naval Council budgeted T£31,600 for four vessels in 1880, while Midhat purchased a ship (albeit a large steamer) for T£39,877 while *vali* of Baghdad (Yücel, "Midhat," p. 178).

144. Presumably in recognition of Rıza's services, including his role in resurrecting Basra province, he became acting *vali* later in 1884, replacing the first appointee, and then full governor the following spring (Y-A Resmî 29/14; Lorimer, *Gazetteer*, p. 1502).

145. Y-Kâmil 86-38/3790.

146. The revenues were estimated to be not less than T£60–70,000 to Hasa's T£40,000. The Najd-Hasa ratio in Pelly's estimate of revenues in 1865 was closer to 1:2 than 3:2 (Pelly, *Report*, p. 85).

147. Zahlan, *Creation*, pp. 51–52; Farah, *Protection*, pp. 78–79. The *mutasarrıf* hoped to collect revenues of at least T£5,000 in Qatar and to gain access to an estimated annual revenue in Bahrain of T£50,000, much of it from the pearl trade currently dominated by Indian merchants.

148. Lorimer, *Gazetteer*, p. 983. A survey of Qatif *Kaza*'s date palms was made in 1903 and a population census attempted two years later there and in Hufuf. There may also have been an attempt to reintroduce the *tapu* system to Hasa in or around 1891; the imposition of new laws on land tenure, succession and probate duties reportedly were among the causes of unrest among the people of Qatif at that time (Lorimer, *Gazetteer*, p. 982).

149. The customs rate on exports depended upon destination, from 1% for India to 8% for Iran (Lorimer, *Gazetteer*, p. 995). It is unclear what, if any, taxes might be levied on goods bound for Ottoman territory such as Yemen.

150. The *mutasarrıf* gave a cost of only T£1,000–1,500 for either project, which either the Treasury or the local government could bear. He expected the `Uqayr customs to produce annually up to T£2,000 at the present level of trade. Although he did not mention it, either improvement could also have permitted a naval vessel to use `Uqayr as its base port.

151. Although a *sancak* was usually only a subordinate part of a *vilayet*, in a few cases a region too small to be a province but for some reason (such as remoteness) not suitably governable from a regional capital, it could be administered by a *mutasarrıf* answering directly to Istanbul. One such area was the *sancak* of Zor in the Syrian desert, to which the governor in Hasa referred in his proposal.

4. CHANCE FOR ADJUSTMENT AND STABILITY

152. Le Gall, "Pashas," pp. 1–2, 182–87; Gerber, *Ottoman Rule*, p. 7; Akarlı, *Long Peace*, pp. 31–33; Karal, *Osmanlı Tarihi*, p. 341. Binghazi had the added delicacy of position brought about by the need for the Ottomans to coexist with a reasonably influential Arab religious figure, Muhammad b. Ali al-Sanusi, much as they had to coexist with the Al Sa`ud much of the time in Arabia.

153. Even Binghazi's position was not as extreme as Hasa's. Binghazi had an intermittent telegraph connection to Tripoli in the early twentieth century, but shipping was always the main means of communication. It made sense to have Binghazi look northeast directly to the Porte for instructions rather than to Tripoli, about 600 miles (1000 km) overland to the west and itself often only tenuously connected to Istanbul. Le Gall, "Pashas," pp. 103–6.

154. Irade Meclis-i Mahsus 4699, Necd *Mutasarrıf* to Basra *Vali*, 9 Haziran 1305/21 June 1889; Interior Minister to Grand Vezir, 26 Eylûl 1305/8 October 1889; MV 49/20, 20 Rebi el-evvel 1307/14 November 1889. Sultan Abdülhamid, at least, was reluctant to exempt the local military from the regulations barring troop movements without orders from the high command. He did not act on an earlier Council of Ministers recommendation to grant an exemption, wanting to hurry the extension of the telegraph to Hasa instead. MV 37/17, 23 Teşrin-i evvel 1304/4 November 1888; Irade Meclis-i Mahsus 4301, 8 Rebi el-evvel 1306/12 November 1888.

155. Irade Meclis-i Mahsus 4699, Necd *Mutasarrıf* to Basra *Vali*, 9 Haziran 1305/21 June 1889; Interior Minister to Grand Vezir, 26 Eylûl 1305/8 October 1889; MV 49/20, 20 Rebi el-evvel 1307/14 November 1889; ŞD 2184/6, Necd Commander to Basra *Vali*, 4 Kânun-i evvel 1315/16 December 1899; Ochsenwald, *Religion*, pp. 84–90.

156. Lorimer, *Gazetteer*, p. 982.

157. Irade Meclis-i Mahsus 4699, petition of thirty two Hasawi notables, approved by Hasa administrative council, 1 Haziran 1305/13 June 1889; Lorimer, *Gazetteer*, p. 807. The notables, who included a number of traders, wanted two ships to operate between Basra and `Uqayr to improve commerce as well as communications.

158. Irade Meclis-i Mahsus 4699, 11 Cemazi el-âhir 1307/2 February 1890; Necd *Mutasarrıf* to Basra *Vali*, 9 Haziran and 14 Eylûl 1305/21 June and 26 September 1889 ; Interior Minister to Grand Vezir, 26 Eylûl 1305/8 October 1889; MV 49/20, 20 Rebi el-evvel 1307/14 November 1889. Akif's report was adopted first by the commission formed in 1887 to investigate security along the Gulf coast following British intervention in the case between a Qatifi merchant and a brother of the shaikh of Bahrain.

159. In 1887 the garrison had been reduced by a third to a mere four companies of gendarmes, who may have totaled no more than 100 men. They were to be reinforced by two more companies of donkey-mounted troops, plus 500 camel-mounted gendarmes who could pursue bedouin raiders into the desert. Irade Meclis-i Mahsus 4699, 11 Cemazi el-âhir 1307/2 February 1890; Necd *Mutasarrıf* to Basra *Vali*, 9 Haziran and 14 Eylûl 1305/21 June and 26 September 1889.

160. Saldana, *Expansion*, p. 57.

161. Irade Meclis-i Mahsus 4699, 11 Cemazi el-âhir 1307/2 February 1890; Necd *Mutasarrıf* to Basra *Vali*, 9 Haziran 1305/21 June 1889; Interior Minister to Grand Vezir, 26 Eylûl 1305/8 October 1889; Lorimer, *Gazetteer*, pp. 806–7; Sinan, *Ta'rikh*, p. 91; Y-A Resmî 60/12, 19 Kânun-i sani 1307/31 January 1892. The harbor master was reassigned to Qatif.

4. CHANCE FOR ADJUSTMENT AND STABILITY

162. An example of the rivalries that could complicate reform was the enmity of the Hasa military authorities for *Mutasarrıf* Rifaat Bey, which reportedly distracted him and may have caused his dismissal before he could institute real reforms. One root of the disagreement was supposedly the military and civilian leaders' rival claims to a dead man's estate. It was rumored that the military commander had Rifaat assaulted and abused, although the British doubted the truth of this. Saldana, *Expansion*, p. 57; Lorimer, *Gazetteer*, p. 980. This was just a partial explanation, however. There developed a deep-seated and long-running competition for dominance in Hasa between the military and civil services that went far beyond this incident and was to cause more problems in the future. ŞD 2184/6, Akif Pasha's report, 19 Haziran 1305/1 July 1889.

163. Y-A Resmî 60/12. The dates are uncertain. A petition from 36 Hasawi traders to the Grand Vezir, dated 22 Mayıs 1308/3 June 1892, states that the attacks occurred three years earlier. Lorimer (*Gazetteer*, p. 984) merely notes the outbeak of disturbances about 1890. The savagery of the first two attacks, which occurred in quick succession, clearly shocked the traders, who told of men, women, and children killed or left to die in the desert, of children taken as slaves, and of the theft of money and goods beyond reckoning. It should also be noted that the Bani Hajir apparently made a vigorous return to piracy in 1891–93.

164. Saldana, *Expansion*, p. 58. The government had also reappointed Said in 1881 after the ʿAjman attacked Hufuf, and he had brought about a similar reconciliation after lengthy negotiation. Said sometimes seemed to have more trouble operating in the Ottoman political milieu than in the Arab, being relieved of his position on (at least) one occasion because of irritating his superiors. Irade Dahiliye 1311-Ş-48, Interior Minister to Grand Vezir, 9 Şubat 1309/21 February 1894.

165. Lorimer, *Gazetteer*, pp. 984–85. A *rafiq*, or escort, was a kind of safe-conduct, because his presence and role as protector of the travelers would have to be respected by other members of his tribe. Although generally effective, the practice carried no guaranty: in 1894 some Dawasir tribesmen raided a caravan under the protection of a Dawsiri *rafiq*. Upon discovery of this, however, the Dawasir made restitution.

166. Y-A Resmî 60/12, 22 Mayıs 1308. This was not an empty threat. Continuing tax disputes caused over 130 merchants and other Hasawis to flee to Bahrain in 1894–95, where they remained until they reached a compromise on future assessments with the government (Saldana, *Expansion*, p. 59).

167. Y-A Resmî 60/12, 19 Kânun-i sani 1307/31 January 1892; 30 Haziran 1308/12 July 1892. The Ottomans' inability to maintain an effective garrison in Hasa during much of the time of their rule there is amazing. Time after time troop levels were stripped down to woeful inadequacy for reasons of economy, disease, or need elsewhere. Security often devolved upon small gendarmerie units. Bedouin attacks usually resulted. In 1888 the Hasa command was so weak that it had to call upon the citizens of Hufuf to help drive off a band of bedouin raiders. Istanbul tried to make the most of the meager resources devoted to Hasa by giving the local commander the authority to act against threats without having to await clearance by Basra and Istanbul, but this could not resolve every problem. Irade Meclis-i Mahsus 4301, 12 Temmuz 1304, and Council of Ministers memorandum, 30 Teşrin-i evvel 1304/11 November 1888; Irade Meclis-i Mahsus 4531, 11 Zilhicce 1306/8 August 1889; Y-A Resmî 60/12, 25 Temmuz 1308.

4. CHANCE FOR ADJUSTMENT AND STABILITY

168. Y-A Resmî 60/12, 25 Temmuz 1308, 5 Ağustos 1308/17 August 1892; Saldana, *Expansion*, p. 58. These forces followed the emergency dispatch of a rifle battalion. Half of the later troops went to Hufuf and the others were divided between Qatif and Qatar. These troops had some success in punishing raiders and in preventing attacks.

169. Y-A Resmî 60/12, 19 Kânun-i sani 1307, Basra *Vali* to Grand Vezir. The reported unrest in Qatif in 1891, the merchants' petition in 1892 and the emigration of Hasawis to Bahrain in 1894–5 all indicate continuing deep dissatisfaction with the government. Some complaints were apparently gradually resolved, however. The *vali* of Basra made an inspection tour of Hasa in October 1892, which resulted in the arrest of the *kaymakam* of Qatif on unspecified charges (Saldana, *Expansion*, p. 58).

170. Zahlan, *Creation*, pp. 52–53; Lorimer, *Gazetteer*, pp. 811, 813, 822.

171. ŞD 2158/10 is full of these complaints, many of which were written by a member of the Qatar *Kaza* Administrative Council, Shaikh Muhammad b. `Abd al-Wahhab al-Qubhan.

172. YEE 14/250/126/8, p. 2. Qâsim had flirted with the British ten years earlier, seeking some means of breaking their habit of forcing him into actions he disliked. Perhaps aware of this, and always suspicious of British subversion, the Ottomans read too much into the repeated contacts between Qâsim and the Resident in 1887–89, in which Qâsim was warned about his actions against Bahrain and Abu Dhabi and about his policies toward Indian traders and piracy off Qatar. The shaikh resented outside interference, be it British or Ottoman, and it was largely the increase of the latter in Doha that eventually tilted Qâsim toward Britain. Farah, *Protection*, p. 74; Lorimer, *Gazetteer*, pp. 812–14.

173. ŞD 2158/10, document 75, draft of Council of State's response to proposal for action (no date).

174. Irade Meclis-i Mahsus 5117, 27 Şaban 1308/8 April 1891; Council of State memorandum, 16 Şubat 1306/28 February 1891; MV 63/77, 10 Mart 1307/22 March 1891.

175. Mansur, *Tatawwur*, pp. 146–49, Zahlan, *Creation*, pp. 51–53.

176. YEE 14/250/126/8, p. 2.

177. YEE 14/250/126/8, p. 2; Sinan, *Ta'rikh*, p. 94; Mansur, *Tatawwur*, p. 150.

178. YEE 14/250/126/8, p. 2. According to Sinan (*Ta'rikh*, p. 94), Qâsim claimed that the money was a payment by the poor people of Qatar to meet the demands of the Ottomans, who held the country in their hands. He also offered to surrender 400 rifles.

179. YEE 14/250/126/8, p. 3. Three hours' travel time from Doha, Waqba was Qâsim's headquarters. The *vali* either did not realize this or greatly underestimated the strength of Qâsim's bedouin supporters, because the Ottoman force was too small for a full attack on a heavily defended fort. The column included 230 infantry, 100 horse-mounted gendarmes, 40 camel-mounted Arab auxiliaries, some marines, and a 3-pound gun.

180. YEE 14/250/126/8, p. 3. In this, as in many other details of the affair, the Ottoman, Arab, and British accounts differ widely. Non-Ottoman histories state that the battle began at Waqba, then shifted to Thaqab (Sinan, pp. 94–95), Sha'b (Mansur, p. 152), or Misaymir (Lorimer, p. 823); Misaymir lies south of Doha, far from Waqba, and is clearly wrong. The large number of bedouins cited may well have included

5. THE CASE OF KUWAIT

inhabitants of Waqba town, who were the first to attack the column, according to these sources. Qâsim later told the Ottoman investigating officers that this band comprised bedouins who, having been dispersed as the *vali* wished, were attracted by the gunshots of the sudden Ottoman attack on the shaikh's position. There is little solid evidence gainsaying his account of the attackers' identity, although the investigators did not credit much of his tale of events. For example, he also claimed not to have taken part in the fighting, which contradicted the evidence of eyewitnesses interviewed by the officers. YEE 14/250/126/8, p. 5.

181. Lorimer, *Gazetteer*, p. 824; Mansur, *Tatawwur*, 153–54; Kumar, *India*, pp. 126–27. Qâsim also asked permission of the shaikh of Bahrain to settle in northern Qatar, where the Bahraini claimed jurisdiction, and of the shaikh of Abu Dhabi to be allowed to remove to 'Udayd. Either move would also have brought British protection, albeit more indirectly.

182. YEE 14/250/126/8, p. 6.

183. YEE 14/250/126/8, p. 5.

184. This was an early instance of the use of unofficial local intermediaries to solve problems with Arab leaders, a tactic that Sultan Abdülhamid II came to favor in Arabia. Abdülhamid was often reluctant to use brute force against Muslims, and it was probably the shelling of Doha's residents that actually caused Hafız Mehmet's dismissal.

185. YEE 14/250/126/8, pp. 5–6; Mansur, *Tatawwur*, p. 154. According to Mansur, the shaikh of Qatar was to pay one quarter of his domain's income.

186. YEE 14/250/126/8, p. 6. The Ottomans in this period seem to have contemplated more seriously than usual a military solution to the problems of sovereignty over Bahrain and its role in the arms trade. Such was the fear of an imminent attack from Qatar in August 1892 that Indian traders in Manama loaded their possessions on boats in preparation for flight. The *kaymakam* of Qatif in 1893 pressed the claim to Bahrain to the point of requiring Bahraini boats in Qatif to fly the Ottoman flag. Qâsim and the *naqib* also discussed a quick strike on Bahrain, but the Ottomans did not pursue the scheme (Farah, *Protection*, pp. 84–85; YEE 14/250/126/8, p. 6).

187. YEE 14/250/126/8, p. 6; Bostan, "Uprising," p. 87.

188. MV 78/13, 22 Kânun-i evvel 1309/3 January 1894.

189. Zahlan, *Creation*, p. 54; Lorimer, *Gazetteer*, p. 824. Its patience almost exhausted by Qâsim's willfulness, intrigues, and breaches of the peace, the government was tempted to break its tie to him in 1899 but thought twice before allowing him to become a free agent again. Y-A Resmî 94/10, 15 Temmuz 1314/27 July 1898; BEO 97352, 4 Ağustos 1315/16 August 1899.

190. Nolde noted (*Reise*, p. 69) during his travels in the Arabian interior that 1893 proved that the Ottomans could neither rule the desert directly nor understand the Arabs well enough to govern it indirectly.

5. *The Case of Kuwait*

1. Abu Hakima, *Kuwait*, pp. 104–6, 123. In sheer size, Kuwait was a fairly substantial town. Pelly reckoned that the population numbered 20,000 in the early 1860s (Crystal, *Kuwait*, p. 8); Midhat estimated that the town had 5,000–6,000 buildings in 1871. Irade Dahiliye 44930, enclosure II, p. 1.

5. THE CASE OF KUWAIT

2. The vague notion of the Indian government after the turn of the century that Midhat installed a customs post for a short time seems baseless (Saldana, *Koweit*, p. 6). It is also clear that no effective action had resulted from earlier suggestions for improving Kuwait's defenses.

3. Irade Dahiliye 1310-M-31, 23 Muharrem 1310/16 August 1892; *Basra Salname*, 1308, pp. 76–77.

4. YEE 14/250/126/8, p. 17. The officers investigating the Qatar incident termed Kuwait the most important entry point for arms, while the British considered that the trade there began only after Mubarak seized power. Lorimer, *Gazetteer*, p. 2569.

5. "Basra Vilayeti'nden Gelen" registry lists a message to Istanbul on 25 Mayıs 1309/6 June 1893: "Kuveyt Kazasının taht idareye alınması hakkında ittihazı lazımgelen tedabir hakkında." The file relating to this message, BEO 13640, could not be found in the archives.

6. Muhammad's predecessor, Shaikh `Abdallah, had also received a stipend of dates for at least part of his time as *kaymakam* of Kuwait. Ayniyat 851/164, 27 Receb 1289/30 September 1872.

7. Khaz`al, *Ta'rikh*, pp. 146–47, 149, 151–52. Although Kuwait clearly suffered less disturbance than other parts of Arabia, Khaz`al may overstate its pacificity. The 1894 Bani Hajir attack on several Kuwaiti boats was apparently a retaliation for a raid by a relative of Shaikh Muhammad (Mubarak?), in which the victims lost livestock and four men (Lorimer, *Gazetteer*, p. 1016).

8. Saldana, *Koweit*, p. 7.

9. Busch, *Britain*, p. 97; Bidwell, *Kuwait*, i/2/1 (section 1/document 2/enclosure 1), Government of India to Lord Hamilton (Secretary of State for India), 24 February 1897.

10. Khaz`al, *Ta'rikh*, I, pp. 136–38, 145—46, 149–52. Mubarak also took part in a peacemaking operation at the end of the Muntafiq uprising in 1881, although he apparently was not acting under direct Ottoman orders.

11. BEO 27268, 20 Mart 1310/1 April 1894. Mubarak had won the *Nişan-i Mecidi* and the rank of *Kapıcı Başı* in 1871 for his service in the campaign in Hasa (Ayniyat 851/119, 28 Cemazi el-evvel 1288/15 July 1871; Ayniyat 851/128, 15 Şaban 1288/30 October 1871; Ayniyat 851/140, 3 Muharrem 1289/13 March 1872).

12. BEO 27268. One proposal was a promotion of two grades. The Basra *vali* disapproved of this for a number of reasons. Any previous service of Mubarak had been forgotten, and although he had gone to Hasa at the bidding of the VI Corps commander, he had been of no use in Qatar. He had squeezed money out of the Kuwaitis for so-called defense costs, and by joining with the `Ajman to raid the Bani Hajir he had caused turmoil among the tribes. Since the *vali* arrived in Basra, he had seen no service of Mubarak or his brother the *kaymakam* that deserved a reward. He further protested that with the proposed promotion (*mir-i miran*, roughly the civil equivalent of brigadier general) Mubarak would outrank the *kaymakam*, who held the grade of *mirülümera* (equivalent to a colonel). The *vali* raised some valid points—Mubarak certainly had not hastened to help Hafız Mehmet Pasha in Qatar—and the two-grade promotion was not awarded.

13. Lorimer, *Gazetteer*, pp. 1015–16.

14. Crystal, *Kuwait*, p. 11.

15. Irade Dahiliye 44930, enclosure II, p. 1.

5. THE CASE OF KUWAIT

16. Khaz`al, *Ta'rikh*, I, p. 153. This interpretation began to win wide circulation in the 1950s. H. R. P. Dickson (*Kuwait*), formerly a British official and a devoted admirer of his country's small protégé, was instrumental in spreading this story. He seems to have been eager to prove Mubarak's independence and Arabness to the followers of Nasser and the Iraqi regime, which looked to history to justify its threat to seize Kuwait. Expanding the story several years later in a time of feverish Arab nationalism, Khaz`al spared no effort to make Mubarak into an exemplar of the perfect Arab hero. He even purports to quote Mubarak as saying "We are Arabs; we must remain Arabs and do what is in our power to preserve our Arabness [`*urubatuna*] and combat all that would subvert it" (*Ta'rikh*, II, p. 13). There is absolutely no evidence that Mubarak felt any "Arabian" motivation in 1896 or thereafter, yet this explanation has been adopted by later historians, such as Futuh al-Khatrash (*Ta'rikh*, p. 16). If "Arab" consciousness underlay the crime, would not Mubarak have also killed the "Ottoman" leader, Yusuf, instead of striking while he was away from Kuwait? He had already killed the Ottoman-appointed *kaymakam*; killing an unofficial agent could hardly have made Istanbul's reaction much worse.

17. Kumar, *India*, pp. 137–38; Khaz`al, *Ta'rikh*, I, pp. 153–54; Dickson, *Kuwait*, p. 137; Harraz, *Dawla*, p. 171.

18. Although the *vali* of Basra, Hamdi Pasha, clearly seems to have disliked the independent Sabah family and Mubarak in particular, he never roused Istanbul's interest in a change of Kuwait's administration before May 1896. His suggestion subsequent to the assassination of Muhammad and Jarrah that the town should be occupied took the Porte by surprise and caused much annoyance, since it had already determined that there was no need to strip the Al Sabah of power. While he (and Yusuf al-Ibrahim, of whom the Porte knew nothing before mid-1896) went farther than Istanbul wished in opposing Mubarak after the coup, it is unclear how actively he may have pursued an anti-Sabah policy on his own initiative before that event. Among the charges leveled against him by the Interior Minister in advocating his dismissal was his unnecessary hounding of some of the province's Arabs; he was certainly on bad terms with some notables, but their innocence of wrongdoing was often debatable (on the *naqib* of Basra and a shaikh of the Bani Asad, see Lorimer, *Gazetteer*, pp. 1504, 1508; see also note 28 below). This accusation appeared, however, only after Mubarak had petitioned the Porte. His initial telegram probably resembled several sent shortly thereafter, which contained strong denunciations of Hamdi as a terrible persecutor. BEO 66196, Interior Minister to Grand Vezir, 25 Haziran 1312/7 July 1896; petition from 119 Arabs supporting Mubarak, 10 Temmuz 1312/22 July 1896; Mubarak to Grand Vezir, 18 Ağustos 1312/30 August 1896. It is noteworthy that the 22 July message charged Hamdi with improper threats only over the previous three months.

19. Bidwell, *Kuwait*, i/3/1 (see note 9), Memorandum of Capt. Whyte (Basra Consul), 22 March 1897.

20. Rashid, *Ta'rikh*, pp. 39–44. Rashid clearly had mixed feelings about Mubarak. While noting some admirable qualities (bravery, determination) in the shaikh, he could only deplore his despotism and devotion to money (*Ta'rikh*, pp. 132, 135).

21. Qana`i, *Safahat*, pp. 25–77. This fraternal argument was of long standing. A close friend of the Sabah family in Basra temporarily created peace in 1892 by settling a yearly stipend of 10,000 rupees on Mubarak. The death of the friend in

5. THE CASE OF KUWAIT

1894/95 revived the dispute. Even more than Rashid's, Qana`i's account of the 1896 events contradicts the version of the "Arabists" (Dickson et al.): the losers, especially Shaikh Muhammad, receive sympathetic treatment, while Mubarak is sharply criticized for his method of seizing power and for his misuse of it later in his reign. Qana`i judged Mubarak a good governor in his first decade of rule, however, when he still followed the precepts of his predecessors.

22. Khaz`al, *Ta'rikh*, I, p. 154. Perhaps the best short analysis of the question in English is in Rush, *Al-Sabah*, pp. 119–20. Unfortunately, Rush does not include the sources of much of his information.

23. Lorimer, *Gazetteer*, p. 1018.

24. Bidwell, *Kuwait*, i/3/1, Memorandum of Capt. Whyte, 22 March 1897.

25. Akarlı ("Economic Policy," p. 459) cites an Ottoman report of 1891 on the spread of corruption, based on need for most officials, on greed for top appointees. In Iraq, Deringil ("Struggle," pp. 55–56) for example refers to the arrears of the small salaries due to religious teachers. Much of the bureaucracy in border regions far from Istanbul, such as Iraq, suffered severely from being paid neither promptly nor well. Distance from the center made difficult the discipline of the better-paid top echelon (e.g., the *vali*, *defterdar*, and commanders of the military services). Responsible only for limited sections of the Ottoman provincial presence, these authorities could always blame each other for problems with little fear that anyone in Istanbul had independent knowledge of local conditions. A graphic example of this was the turmoil in Basra in 1897.

26. Bidwell, *Kuwait*, i/3/1; Rashid, *Ta'rikh*, II, p. 53. Although often referred to as Abdülhamid's astrologer, Ebülhuda (Abu al-Huda al-Sayyadi) was really one of the sultan's key aides in efforts to rally Muslim support to the Ottomans. See Abu Manneh, "Sultan Abdulhamid," pp. 131–53.

27. BEO 66196, Basra *Vali* to Interior Ministry, 28 Nisan 1312/10 May 1896.

28. Bidwell, *Kuwait*, i/3/1. Hamdi "was an honest man and on the whole a satisfactory administrator, but neither brilliant nor popular." Hot-tempered, arbitrary, and aggressive against corruption, he made many enemies. Lorimer, *Gazetteer*, p. 1502; Longrigg, *Four Centuries*, p. 300, also noted that Hamdi "passed the average in honesty and capacity." Some accounts suggest that Yusuf al-Ibrahim instigated the resistance to Mubarak (Rashid, *Ta'rikh*, II, p. 53; Khaz`al, *Ta'rikh*, II, p. 16; Mansur, *Kuwayt*, p. 53; Harraz, *Dawla*, pp. 171–72; Khatrash, *Ta'rikh*, II, pp. 26–27), but Hamdi was an independent point of opposition.

29. BEO 66196, Basra *Vali* to Interior Ministry, 28 Nisan 1312/10 May 1896; 29 Nisan 1312/11 May 1896.

30. BEO 66196, Minister of Interior Affairs to Grand Vezir, 30 Nisan 1312/12 May 1896.

31. BEO 60415, Grand Vezir to Basra, 25 Haziran 1312/7 July 1896; Irade Hususiye 17 Safer 1315, War Department memorandum, 2 Temmuz 1313/14 July 1897; Bidwell, *Kuwait*, i/1/1, Memorandum of Mr. Stavrides (legal adviser, British Embassy, Istanbul), 30 June 1896; Busch, *Britain*, pp. 95–97.

32. Bidwell, *Kuwait*, i/1/1.

33. Rashid, *Ta'rikh*, II, p. 53.

34. A useful piece of disinformation, which erased the relatives who would presumably be most interested in vengeance for the death of Muhammad and Jarrah.

5. THE CASE OF KUWAIT

35. BEO 66196, report of War Minister, 3 Haziran 1312/15 June 1896.
36. Bidwell, *Kuwait*, i/1/1; Rashid (*Ta'rikh*, II, p. 53) also noted the order to desist but gave no date.
37. BEO 66196, Interior Minister to Grand Vezir, 25 Haziran 1312/7 July 1896.
38. BEO 66196, Basra *Vali* to Interior Minister, 26 Haziran 1312/8 July 1896, and 3 Temmuz/15 July.
39. BEO 64548, Grand Vezir to Basra *Vali*, 22 Teşrin-i evvel 1312/3 November 1896 referring to telegram of 170 Kuwaitis to Council of State (Şura-yi Devlet). Yusuf had ties to India but was not British-protected. The epistolary campaign also tried to convince the Ottomans that Yusuf had killed the two shaikhs (Rashid, *Ta'rikh*, II, p. 54).
40. Arif Pasha was formerly *Mutasarrıf* of Karasi in Hüdavendigâr (Bursa) province. BEO 63228, 15 Eylûl 1312/27 September 1896.
41. BEO 70267, memorandum by Interior Minister, 25 Mart 1313/6 April 1897, based on reports from the *vali* dated 12 Kânun-i sani 1312/24 January 1897 and 19 Mart 1313/31 March 1897. It is an indication of how totally at sea the government felt itself to be in handling the Kuwait crisis that much of the *vali*'s last message addressed the Porte's queries about Kuwait's location, population, and past and present modes of government.
42. The British consul in Basra reported that Arif had accepted a present of T£7,000 from Mubarak (Bidwell, *Kuwait*, i/3/1). Arif's later shift away from accommodation with Mubarak may have resulted from bribery by Yusuf al-Ibrahim; a falling out following the assignment of a quarantine officer to Kuwait in February; or merely a short memory concerning Mubarak's largess. Ironically the posting of the quarantine officer was not primarily a political move but rather part of a program to prevent the spread of a plague (*veba; taun*) epidemic from Iran and India. From late 1896 to July/August 1897 all ships and goods from Iran, Bahrain, Masqat, and Muhammara had to pass through quarantine, and restrictions lasted even longer for arrivals from Bombay. A program of protective measures was ordered for all ports from Basra to Qatar (including Bahrain). Given many Arabs' preference for trade through Kuwait because of its lack of a customs post, the state needed to extend sanitary controls there in order to contain the spread of the disease. Mühimme 11575, 5 Kânun-i evvel 1312/17 December 1896; 11737, 25 Kânun-i evvel 1312/6 January 1897; 11804, 1 Kânun-i sani 1312/13 January 1897; 11852, 8 Kânun-i sani 1312/20 January 1897; 12825, 17 Temmuz 1313/29 July 1897.
43. BEO 70267, 25 Mart 1313/6 April 1897; BEO 71844, Council of Ministers memorandum, 23 Zilhicce 1314/25 May 1897. The eventual plan of operation proposed shipping at least 1,200 men by sea, with half a battery of artillery, who would rendezvous at Kuwait with a further 500 mounted Arabs from the area of Muntafıq and the Syrian desert. The government clearly took Mubarak's ability to rally support among townspeople and bedouins more seriously than had Hamdi a year earlier. Y-A Resmî 87/88, Meclis-i Mahsus-i Vükela memorandum, 13 Temmuz 1313/25 July 1897.
44. Shaw, *History*, pp. 206–7.
45. The sultan issued several irades (Hususiye) seeking information about Mubarak and Kuwait in 1896; these became much more common several years later, when a number of documents on this and related problems also began to appear in the Yıldız Palace records.

5. THE CASE OF KUWAIT

46. Rashid, *Ta'rikh*, II, pp. 46–47; Lorimer, *Gazetteer*, p. 1017. Mubarak later told a British official that "his nephews had lived on good terms with him after their father's [sic] death, and that it was in consequence of the intrigues of Sheikh Yusuf that they had turned against him." (Bidwell, *Kuwait*, i/23/4, Maj. Meade [British Resident, Persian Gulf] to Government of India, 25 September 1897.) According to Qana`i (*Safahat*, p. 29), Sa`ud b. Muhammad, and some days later the others, fled to Yusuf in Qasr Sabiya, whence they all later escaped to Basra. The young men may have remained in Kuwait for as long as a month, although their stay was probably shorter. The *vali* confirmed the presence of five sons of the murdered men in Basra on 9 July 1896. Hamdi took an interest in the boys' fates after their arrival in Basra. Shortly before he was dismissed, he inquired about the possibility of sending the three youngest (Khalid, Hamud, and `Adhbi) to the tribal school (*Aşiret Mektebi*) in Istanbul, which Abdülhamid had founded to Ottomanize children of important tribal leaders. BEO 61784, 25 Ağustos 1312/6 September 1896 (this document could not be found in the archives); for more information on the tribal school, see Rogan, "Aşiret Mektebi."

47. That his nephews were so young undoubtedly inclined Mubarak to shift his attention to the more experienced Yusuf. Jarrah's son Hamud was only aged 13 in 1896; Muhammad's sons Sabah, Sa`ud, and Khalid were respectively 21, 19, and 13 years old. Muhammad's two other sons, `Ali (36) and `Adhbi (11), played lesser roles in this family struggle. Bidwell, *Kuwait*, Al Sabah genealogical table.

48. Rashid, *Ta'rikh*, II, pp. 52–53; Qana`i, *Safahat*, p. 29.

49. An example of one of Mubarak's telegrams—in which he charged Yusuf with the murders, purchasing influence in Istanbul, and generally being a troublemaker from India looking to cause tribal unrest and to destroy the Sabahs (who, including the author, were well known for their devotion and service to the Ottomans)—is found in BEO 76587, sent to the head of the Council of State on 28 Nisan 1313/10 May 1897. One specific charge, about Yusuf buying influence in Istanbul, was later proven false (BEO 76587, Post and Telegraph Minister to Council of State head, 24 Haziran 1313/6 July 1897), but changed circumstances kept Mubarak safe from any bad consequences.

50. Rashid, *Ta'rikh*, II, pp. 54–55.

51. Busch, *Britain*, p. 101; Bidwell, *Kuwait*, i/3/1 and i/23/4.

52. Bidwell, *Kuwait*, i/23/4.

53. Bidwell, *Kuwait*, i/5, India Office to Bidwell, 7 April 1897; Busch, *Britain*, p. 98.

54. See note 9 above.

55. Bidwell, *Kuwait*, i/1/1, Stavrides memorandum, 30 June 1896; Busch, *Britain*, pp. 95–97.

56. Bidwell, *Kuwait*, i/19/3, Commander Baker to Rear-Admiral Drummond, 4 August 1896; Busch, *Britain*, p. 101.

57. Anderson, *Eastern Question*, pp. 251, 254–58, 262–63.

58. Busch, *Britain*, pp. 98–99; Kumar, *India*, pp. 138–41; Bidwell, *Kuwait*, i/5–18, i/23/4.

59. Bidwell, *Kuwait*, i/10, Salisbury to Currie (Ambassador Istanbul), 17 July 1897.

60. Busch, *Britain*, p. 99.

61. Most strongly in the Resident, Maj. Meade.

5. THE CASE OF KUWAIT

62. Bidwell, *Kuwait*, i/12, Currie to Salisbury, 21 July 1897.
63. Busch, *Britain*, p. 99.
64. Y-A Resmî 104/30, Basra *Vali* to Interior Minister, 25 Haziran 1313/7 July 1897.
65. Rashid, *Ta'rikh*, pp. 57–60; Qana`i, *Safahat*, pp. 29–30 (wrote that Jabir al-Sabah also sent Mubarak warning from Faw); Busch, *Britain*, p. 100; Bidwell, *Kuwait*, i/8, Currie to Salisbury, 16 July 1897.
66. BEO 75045, Grand Vezir to Interior Minister, 21 Ağustos 1313/2 September 1897, referring to memorandum from Minister of War, 28 Safer 1315/29 July 1897. Inhabitants of Zubayr, between Basra and Kuwait, had sent a string of anti-Mubarak messages to the Porte and might now also take action on their own. See for example a telegram with 112 signatures to the head of the Council of State, BEO 76587, 9 Haziran 1313/21 June 1897.
67. Y-A Resmî 104/30, Basra *Vali* to Minister of Interior, 22, 25 and 30 Haziran 1313/4, 7 and 12 July 1897; Irade Hususiye, 14 Safer 1315/15 July 1897.
68. Y-A Resmî 104/30, 30 Haziran 1313/12 July 1897. This story, so similar to that told by Qâsim al-Thani in 1893 to deflect Ottoman retribution, seems to have been misinformation fed to the Ottoman officer by Mubarak or his men, who may have been the source of a similar story about a British offer of protection the year before. Y-A Resmî 104/30, 22 Haziran 1313/4 July 1897.
69. Y-A Resmî 104/30, 25 Haziran 1313/7 July 1897; Irade Hususiye, 14 Safer 1315, enclosure dated 10 Temmuz 1313/22 July 1897. Yusuf's nephews assured the sultan that Mubarak's brother Jabir had planted in the boats the rifles that were discovered there, but to no visible effect.
70. Saldana, *Koweit*, pp. 12–13.
71. Y-A Resmî 104/30, 22 Haziran 1313; Irade Hususiye 17 Safer 1315/17 July 1897, enclosure dated 2 Temmuz 1313/14 July 1897.
72. Y-A Resmî 87/88, Council of Ministers memorandum, 13 Temmuz 1313/25 July 1897; Y-A Resmî 88/3, Council of Ministers memorandum, 20 Temmuz 1313/1 August 1897.
73. BEO 76587, Salim (?) b. Jarrah to head of the Council of State, 27 Eylûl 1313/9 October 1897.
74. BEO 76587, Grand Vezir to Receb Pasha, 24 Eylûl 1313/6 October 1897. This was but a new part of a sporadic campaign to force a resolution of the inheritance dispute by legal means. At some time before March 1897, for example, the Basra court (*mahkeme-i bidayet*) ruled that the revenues of disputed groves at Faw should be held in trust by Hajji Mahmud Efendi of the Basra administrative council until final judgment of the case. Mubarak ignored the ruling (BEO 79027, Interior Minister to Grand Vezir, 19 Teşrin-i sani 1313/ 1 November 1897). The land involved in the September 1897 dispute was a small parcel that had been registered in Shaikh Muhammad's name and thus clearly could be claimed by his sons. Mubarak later tried to get his nephews to accept it in settlement of all their inheritance claims, although its value was small.
75. BEO 75613, Grand Vezir to Interior and Naval Ministers, 7 Eylûl 1313/19 September 1897; BEO 75931, Grand Vezir to Finance Minister, 15 Eylûl 1313/27 September 1897; BEO 76522, Basra *Vali* to Interior Minister, 28 Eylûl 1313/10 October 1897; Grand Vezir to Naval Minister, 30 Eylûl 1313/12 October 1897; BEO

5. THE CASE OF KUWAIT

76587, Basra *Alay Beyi* to Grand Vezir, 12 Eylûl 1313/24 September 1897; Basra *Defterdar* to Finance Minister, 12 and 13 Eylûl 1313/24 and 25 September 1897; Interior Minister to Grand Vezir, 21 Eylûl 1313/3 October 1897; Finance Minister to Grand Vezir, 22 Eylûl 1313/4 October 1897; Finance Ministry Council memorandum, 27 Eylûl 1313/9 October 1897; Grand Vezir to VI Army Corps commander, 24 Eylûl 1313/6 October 1897; BEO 76519, Grand Vezir to Basra *Vali*, 30 Eylûl 1313/12 October 1897; Basra *Vali* to Grand Vezir, 2 Teşrin-i evvel 1313/14 October 1897.

76. Replacement of Arif was already being discussed in Istanbul before the war of words reached full force, primarily because Receb Pasha complained about the *vali*'s inability to check the renegade Muntafiq shaikh, Sa`dun Pasha. BEO 75045, Grand Vezir to Interior Minister, 21 Ağustos 1313/2 September 1897.

77. Irade Dahiliye, 6 Cemazi el-evvel 1315/3 October 1897.

78. BEO 76328, Grand Vezir to War and Interior Ministers, 23 Eylûl 1313/5 October 1897.

79. Opinions of Receb in Istanbul are hard to ascertain. His unswerving support for Mubarak might have stirred suspicion about his impartiality, but his high rank and distance from the Gulf seem to have saved him from the worst of the war of words in Basra. Qâsim al-Thani apparently was the first explicitly to charge Receb with taking bribes and supporting Mubarak purely for personal gain (BEO 79027, Qâsim to Interior Minister, 27 Kânun-i sani 1898/8 February 1898).

80. BEO 78415, Grand Vezir to Interior Minister, 19 Teşrin-i sani 1313/1 December 1897.

81. Bidwell, *Kuwait*, i/27/2, Baghdad Consul Loch to Government of India, 22 December 1897; Busch, *Britain*, p. 103.

82. Rashid, *Ta'rikh*, II, pp. 61–62. Rashid described Said as a close friend of Mubarak. They had many opportunities for contact during Said's previous terms in office, since Mubarak's standing as a leader of the bedouins tied to Kuwait inevitably made him of interest to the *mutasarrıf*s. For instance Said's predecessor, Ibrahim Bey, wrote at least once to Mubarak in May 1895, perhaps in conjunction with the `Ajmani-Mutayr dispute of that year. BEO, Basra Vilayeti'nden Gelen catalogue no. 263, entry for 5 Mayıs 1311/17 May 1895.

83. BEO 78127, Basra *Vali* (Arif) to Grand Vezir, 5 and 14 Teşrin-i sani/17 and 26 November, 4 Kânun-i evvel 1313/16 December 1897; Arif and Basra Commandant (Muhsin) to Grand Vezir, 25 Teşrin-i sani 1313/7 December 1897; BEO 78777, Interior Minister to Grand Vezir, 22 Teşrin-i sani 1313/4 December 1897.

84. Y-A Resmî 92/69, memorandum by the War Minister, 9 Nisan 1314/21 April 1898; Y-A Resmî 90/25 and 90/30, memoranda of Council (*meclis*) and Committee (*encümen*) of Ministers, 23 Teşrin-i sani 1313/5 December 1897; Y-A Resmî 90/56, memoranda of Council and Committee of Ministers, 6 Kânun-i evvel 1313/18 December 1897. The force in Basra was to keep up the pretense of targeting Qatar, but rumor quickly pinpointed the real objective.

85. Y-A Resmî 90/56, Council of Ministers memorandum, 6 Kânun-i evvel 1313/18 December 1897; BEO 79027, Grand Vezir to Interior Minister, 6 Kânun-i evvel 1313. The investigation was briefly delayed at the start when the first person chosen to go asked to be excused. The arduous journey, and the scant pleasures awaiting the traveler in Basra, made this an unattractive task, as it had been also for Receb Pasha.

5. THE CASE OF KUWAIT

86. BEO 78930/79027, Interior Minister to Grand Vezir, 5 Kânun-i sani 1313/17 January 1898.
87. Y-A Resmî 90/56, Committee of Ministers memorandum, 6 Kânun-i evvel 1313/18 December 1897.
88. Y-A Resmî 91/29, Council of Ministers memorandum, 18 Şubat 1313/2 March 1898; Y-A Resmî 92/69, Council of Ministers memorandum, 19 Nisan 1314/1 May 1898.
89. YEE 14/255/126/8, "Basra Körfezi ve Hükümet-i Seniye ile Ingiltere'nin Münasebatı hakkında bir Layiha Bendekâne," by Halil Halid, 21 Şubat 1313/5 March 1898, pp. 2, 5–6.
90. YEE 14/255/126/8, pp. 7–8.
91. Y-A Resmî 92/69, War Minister memorandum, 9 Nisan 1314/21 April 1898; Council of Ministers memorandum, 19 Nisan 1314/1 May 1898.
92. Receb Pasha was still acting in Mubarak's interests. Having requested the return of his reserves, he then wanted in mid-May to send some or all of the gathered units to Qatar after the residents of Doha attacked members of the garrison. Istanbul saw no need for such severe action, however. BEO 84151, Grand Vezir to Basra *Vali*, 2 Mayıs 1314/14 May 1898; Y-A Resmî 93/21, Council of Ministers memorandum, 27 Mayıs 1314/8 June 1898; Y-A Resmî 94/10, Council of Ministers memorandum, 15 Temmuz/27 July 1898.
93. Y-A Resmî 91/29, Council of Ministers memorandum, 18 Şubat 1313/2 March 1898; Y-A Resmî 92/69, Council of Ministers memorandum, 19 Nisan 1314/1 May 1898.
94. Y-A Resmî 93/21, 27 Mayıs/8 June 1898.
95. The government had become very concerned about the signs of decay visible throughout Iraq. Its three rich provinces now absorbed money from the central treasury instead of contributing to it. In May 1898 the government appointed a commission to inspect in succession Mosul, Baghdad, and Basra provinces. Its members would recommend reforms in administration of settled and tribal areas, schools, fiscal affairs, agriculture and river control, and religious affairs. Y-A Resmî 93/8, Committee of Ministers memorandum, 11 Mayıs 1314/23 May 1898.
96. That the Basra government later came to agree about its own weakness is suggested by the previously aggressive Hamdi (reappointed *vali* in March 1899) Pasha's recommendation of use of local notables to whom Mubarak might pay greater heed. Y-A Resmî 104/30, Basra *Vali's* report, 7 Eylûl 1315/19 September 1899.
97. BEO 88003, Grand Vezir to Basra *Vali* and Interior Minister, 8 Ağustos 1314/20 August 1898.
98. Bidwell, *Kuwait*, i/34/1, Acting Baghdad Consul to Istanbul Ambassador, 6 October 1898.
99. Bidwell, *Kuwait*, i/26/2, Commander of warship "Pigeon" to Resident Bushire, 7 November 1897.
100. Y-A Resmî 104/30, Basra *Vali* (Anis Pasha) to Grand Vezir, 10 Ağustos 1314/22 August 1898; Bidwell, *Kuwait*, i/48/2, Basra Consul to Acting Consul-General Baghdad, 20 December 1898.
101. Bidwell, *Kuwait*, i/71/2, Resident to Government of India, 30 January 1899.
102. Most notably Lord Curzon; Busch, *Britain*, p. 106.
103. Landen, *Oman*, pp. 240–44. Regarding the Russian challenge, not only the

5. THE CASE OF KUWAIT

British regarded it seriously. The Ottoman London Vice-Consul's analysis of the Gulf asserted that the area was the object of a major struggle for influence between the two powers that might lead to war. The loser of the contest for influence, he warned, would look for compensation elsewhere in Ottoman lands.

104. Busch, *Britain*, pp. 106–7.

105. Plass, *England*, p. 249.

106. "There can be no doubt that Sheikh Mubarak . . . is quite ready to ask for British or Turkish protection, as appears best for his own interests, and I doubt if we would have heard much of his desire for our help if the Turks had at once acknowledged him." Bidwell, *Kuwait*, i/23/4, Meade to Government of India, 25 September 1897.

107. Bidwell, *Kuwait*, i/23/4, Meade to Government of India, 25 September 1897; i/27/2, Baghdad Consul-General to Government of India, 22 December 1897.

108. Bidwell, *Kuwait*, i/33, Meade to Bidwell, 28 March 1898.

109. One of those who had earlier opposed involvement in Kuwait, Indian Political Secretary Sir William Lee-Warner, for example, now remarked in August 1898, "I wish that we had secured Koweit a year ago." Busch, *Britain*, p. 105.

110. Bidwell, *Kuwait*, i/71/3, translation of Arabic Bond, 23 January 1899; Busch, *Britain*, pp. 110–12.

111. Busch, *Britain*, pp. 105–9; Kumar, *India*, pp. 141–46; Plass, *England*, pp. 250–57; Bidwell, *Kuwait*, i/40 and 41, Foreign Office to India Office, 4 and 18 January 1899.

112. Bidwell, *Kuwait*, i/71/2, Meade to Government of India, 30 January 1899.

113. Bidwell, *Kuwait*, i/71/3; i/71/5, Government of India to Meade, 12 February 1899; i/71/9, Meade to Government of India, 19 February 1899.

114. Bidwell, *Kuwait*, i/71/7, Government of India to Meade, 17 February 1899.

6. Kuwait, 1899–1913

1. When Meade arrived at Kuwait, an Ottoman corvette was anchored there. Bidwell, *Kuwait*, i/71/2; i/74/2, Basra Consul Wratislaw to Baghdad Acting Consul-General Melvill, 2 February 1899 and i/83/1, Wratislaw to Istanbul Ambassador O'Conor, 22 April 1899.

2. It is worth noting that the *naqib* continued to act as intermediary in this period. Bidwell, *Kuwait*, i/78/2, Wratislaw to Melvill, 25 February 1899.

3. BEO 92060, Yusuf b. Ibrahim to Grand Vezir, 9 November 1898 and 11 January 1899; Grand Vezir to Basra *Vali*, 5 Teşrin-i sani 1314/17 November 1898. Y-A Resmî 100/6, Basra *Vali* to Grand Vezir, 22 Kânun-i evvel 1314/3 January 1899; Interior Minister to Grand Vezir, 11 and 27 Şubat 1314, 3 Mart 1315/ 23 February, 11 and 15 March 1899; Council of Ministers memorandum, 2 Mayıs 1315/14 May 1899 (also MV 98–2/25).

4. Raunkiaer, *Wahhabiland*, pp. 39–40, 49; Khaz`al, *Ta'rikh*, II, pp. 296–97. Some of these taxes were quite onerous and undoubtedly aided the later growth of anti-Mubarak feeling in Kuwait. The customs duty started at 5% but later increased to 10%. Owners of buildings also had to pay a tax worth one third of their property's value.

5. Bidwell, *Kuwait*, i/86/2, Wratislaw to O'Conor, 3 May 1899. The end of duty-free trade through Kuwait presumably was of little comfort to the Ottomans.

6. KUWAIT, 1899–1913

6. Ibid.
7. Bidwell, *Kuwait*, i/86, O'Conor to Salisbury, 6 June 1899.
8. Y-A Resmî 104/30, Hamdi to Grand Vezir, 2 Ağustos 1315/14 August 1899. Hamdi was right; he merely did not know how far that fear had already drawn Britain into Kuwaiti affairs. He therefore actively encouraged the British government to raise the issue in Istanbul, thinking that it could be reassured there that the Ottomans had no such intention. Bidwell, *Kuwait*, i/95/1 and i/119/1, Wratislaw to O'Conor, 3 June and 28 July 1899; i/116, O'Conor to Salisbury, 11 September 1899.
9. As noted above, for instance, Hamdi was quite ready to use local notables as intermediaries. He also sent one to persuade Mubarak to make a reasonable settlement with his nephews (Bidwell, *Kuwait*, i/119/1). When Muhsin and members of the *naqib*'s family began a campaign of complaints against him, Hamdi took the additional step of asking for an irade for every action on Kuwait, so that he could not be accused later of exceeding his authority. Y-A Resmî 104/30, 7 Eylûl/19 September 1899.
10. Y-A Resmî 104/30, Hamdi to Grand Vezir, 2 Ağustos 1315/14 August 1899; Muhsin to Sublime Porte, 17 Ağustos 1315/29 August 1899; Council of Ministers memorandum, 14 Teşrin-i sani/26 November 1899.
11. Y-A Resmî 104/30, Doha garrison commander to Najd commander, 26 Haziran 1315/8 July 1899; Najd Commander to Grand Vezir, 7 Ağustos 1315/19 August 1899. This false rumor (perhaps encouraged by Qâsim?) was accepted because it seemed to explain Britain's known attentions to Mubarak.
12. Y-A Resmi 104/30, Hamdi to Grand Vezir, 26 Ağustos 1315/7 September 1899.
13. Busch, *Britain*, pp. 188–89; Bidwell, *Kuwait*, i/120, i/121, i/123, O'Conor to Salisbury, 13, 14, and 15 September 1899; Y-A Resmî 104/30, Imperial Chief Secretary's memorandum, 31 Ağustos 1315/12 September 1899. The two sides' impressions of the talks were quite different. O'Conor thought that the foreign minister was receptive to his suggestions and had not objected to the statement that Britain had "very friendly relations" with Kuwait's ruler. The foreign minister's report noted the existence only of Anglo-Kuwaiti trade ties, which the Ottomans already recognized, and seized upon O'Conor's statement that his government had absolutely no designs on Kuwait. Britain merely wanted to avoid drawing it to the attention of another power.
14. "*Gayet cahil*." Hamdi suggested his secret assault on Kuwait because he was afraid that Mubarak would not be sophisticated enough to withstand the Resident's subversions. Y-A Resmî 104/30, Hamdi to Grand Vezir, 5 Ağustos 1315/17 August 1899.
15. Y-A Resmî 104/30, Hamdi to Grand Vezir, 24 Eylûl 1315/6 October 1899. Hamdi's report was not pursued because he had again fallen out of favor, victim of a campaign of abuse by Mubarak and his supporters, such as the *naqib*'s son Talib, who had come to Istanbul as his father's agent to lobby the palace. The probably true story of the appeal to the shah was assiduously spread by Mubarak, presumably in hopes of pressuring Britain into deepening its support. Lorimer, *Gazetteer*, p. 1025; Bidwell, *Kuwait*, i/129, Wratislaw to O'Conor, 2 October 1899. Mubarak tried to develop friendly relations with many powers at various times, including France, Germany and, most notably, Russia.
16. Y-A Resmî 104/62, Council of Ministers memorandum, 5 Kânun-i evvel 1315/17 December 1899.

6. KUWAIT, 1899–1913

17. Usul-i Irade Dosya 77, Basra *Vali* (Muhsin) to Interior Minister, 31 Kânun-i sani 1315/12 February 1900.

18. The stipend was perhaps given as cash because regular payments, akin to a salary, gave greater leverage than one large gift per year. Given the poverty of Istanbul and especially of Basra, regular payment was probably too much to hope for, however.

19. Bidwell, *Kuwait*, ii/45, Basra Consul (Shipley) to O'Conor, 7 July 1900; ii/45/2, Shipley to Resident (Kemball), 15 June 1900. The consul noted in July that in minor matters "Mubarek has ... shown a certain deference to Mohsin Pasha, such as applying to the latter for advice and assistance."

20. Busch, *Britain*, pp. 195–96. He gave Meade a unilateral declaration prohibiting the arms trade through Kuwait in May, but if he acted on it, it was only to stop the trade of others. Since Mubarak was always very alert to the possibility that he could suffer the same fate that he meted out to his brother Muhammad, he made sure to control the supply of weapons in his territory as much as possible—just as did the Ottomans. Raunkiaer, *Wahhabiland*, p. 43; Plass, *England*, p. 247. He also agreed to permit regular stops by British steamers but then reversed his decision.

21. Usul-i Irade Dosya 77, Imperial Chief Secretary's minute, 18 Eylûl 1316/30 September 1900.

22. Busch, *Britain*, pp. 193–94.

23. Plass, *England*, pp. 266–67; Busch, *Britain*, pp. 190–92; Bidwell, *Kuwait*, ii/25/2, Memorandum of Extra Assistant Resident Gaskin, 5 February 1900. That the railway would be of undoubted economic benefit to the port (as the Germans apparently pointed out to Mubarak) was a strong inducement to the shaikh to accept the plan. Britain's local representatives clearly recognized the risk that Mubarak might be tempted to back the plan, regardless of the 1899 agreement. Just as the Ottomans bid for Mubarak's allegiance with medals and money, Britain's Gulf officials could only recommend giving constant, full political support to Mubarak as a way of reminding him of where his best interests lay. If Mubarak had not given them a misleading account of his meetings with the Germans, their anxiety about his reliability might have pushed London into a diplomatic crisis with Berlin and Istanbul.

24. Y-A Resmî 104/74, Committee of Ministers memorandum, 12 Kânun-i evvel 1315/24 December 1899. The final convention for the project reflected this thinking by naming Basra as the terminus but reserving to the contracting company the right to extend the railway to another point on the Gulf. Busch, *Britain*, pp. 203–4.

25. For more information on the background of Ibn Rashid's relations with the Ottomans and activities in Arabia, see chapter 7.

26. It is impossible to know whether Muhammad would have continued his restraint if he had lived past the last days of that year.

27. BEO 116611, Grand Vezir to Interior Minister, 14 Eylûl 1316/27 September 1900. Yusuf could be forgiven for thinking that, with Muhsin master of Basra and Istanbul apparently semi-reconciled with Mubarak, he must look elsewhere for support.

28. Rashid, *Ta'rikh*, II, pp. 63–64.

29. Musil, *Neğd*, p. 245.

30. Busch, *Britain*, pp. 197–98; Bidwell, *Kuwait*, ii/92, Wratislaw to de Bunsen

6. KUWAIT, 1899–1913

(secretary, Istanbul embassy), 22 November 1900; Lorimer, *Gazetteer*, p. 1027; Musil, *Neğd*, p. 245; Rashid, *Ta'rikh*, II, pp. 64–65.

31. BEO 116746, Grand Vezir to Interior Minister, 17 Eylûl 1316/30 September 1900; Busch, *Britain*, p. 197.

32. BEO 117903, Grand Vezir to Interior Minister, 17 Teşrin-i evvel 1316; BEO 116401, Grand Vezir to Interior Minister, 9 Eylûl 1316/22 September 1900; Bidwell, *Kuwait*, ii/92. The intermediaries were the *naqib*'s brother, Ahmad, and `Abd al-`Aziz's agent in Basra, while Talib was again sent to Kuwait. The amir was so angry because Sa`dun, after several clashes with the Rashidis, had escaped with considerable booty. One of the goals of the advancing troops was to force the return of the Shammar property; knowledge of this may have swayed the amir, in combination with the news that Yusuf was to be pardoned.

33. Bidwell, *Kuwait*, ii/92.

34. Rashid, *Ta'rikh*, II, pp. 66–9; Qana`i, *Safahat*, pp. 30–33; Lorimer, *Gazetteer*, pp. 1028–9; Abu Hakima, *History*, p. 113; Bidwell, *Kuwait*, iii/77/1, Kemball to Government of India, 20 April 1901.

35. Bidwell, *Kuwait*, iii/87, Wratislaw to O'Conor, 15 May 1901; iii/87/1, Abbas Aliof to Mubarak, early May 1901. Aliof (Aliev) was a trader from the Caucasus who visited Kuwait every year to buy lamb skins. He was the contact between Mubarak and the Russian Consulate in Baghdad. He and another merchant first visited Kuwait in 1899 for political as well as trade purposes. The Russian warship *Gilyak* followed up their efforts with a visit to Kuwait in 1900, during which Mubarak had extensive discussions with the Russian Consul from Basra. In the spring of 1901, Mubarak used those contacts to ask Russia to raise its flag over Kuwait. Rezvan, *Ships*, pp. 7–8.

36. Busch, *Britain*, pp. 200–204; Kumar, *India*, pp. 195–98.

37. Muhsin's ignorance was partly a matter of closing his eyes and hoping all would turn out well. He was now regarded with suspicion by Abdülhamid, whose concern for the integrity of his empire was growing ever sharper. The *vali* feared that he might be dismissed at any time; provocative behavior by his friend Mubarak could have precipitated his recall. Bidwell, *Kuwait*, iii/36, Wratislaw to O'Conor, 16 March 1901; iii/73, Wratislaw to O'Conor, 10 April 1901.

38. BEO 121889, War Minister to Grand Vezir, 22 Şubat 1316/7 March 1901; BEO 122116, Interior Minister to Grand Vezir, 7 Şubat 1316/20 February 1901. This was one piece of information passed on by Muhsin. It was based on letters from `Abd al-`Aziz to Qâsim seized by Mubarak's men. A similar incident occurred in 1897, when the shaikh's supporters produced an incriminating letter from Qâsim to Muhammad Ibn Rashid.

39. The sultan sent his brother-in-law, Kazım Pasha, to counsel patience to Ibn Rashid. His presence probably restrained the amir until Kazım returned to Iraq a week before the battle; as a gesture of the sultan's good intentions, Kazım seems to have brought word of Yusuf al-Ibrahim's pardon. Yusuf returned to Baghdad with Kazım. This pacification was undermined, however, by Mubarak's ignoring the sultan's order to return to Kuwait. Bidwell, *Kuwait*, iii/36; iii/41/1, Kemball to Government of India, 11 March 1901; iii/77/1; BEO 122410, Grand Vezir to Interior Minister, 5 Mart 1317/18 March 1901.

40. BEO 123146, *Müfettiş* Celal Bey to Receivership of Customs (*Rüsumat Emaneti*), 21 Mart 1317/3 April 1901; Grand Vezir to Muhsin, 29 Mart/11 April;

6. KUWAIT, 1899–1913

Muhsin to Interior Minister, 19 Mart/1 April; Muhsin to Grand Vezir, 31 Mart/13 April.

41. Receb was appointed commander of the troops in Tripoli on 17 Safer 1316/8 June 1898 (`Azzawi, Ta'rikh, p. 8:130). It was later suggested by the British consul that a Rashidi agent had bribed the new Marshal. Bidwell, *Kuwait*, iii/93, Wratislaw to O'Conor, 3 June 1901.

42. Said Pasha, *Hatıratı*, p. 2/1:336.

43. Bidwell, *Kuwait*, iii/57 and iii/68, O'Conor to Foreign Secretary (Lansdowne), 2 and 20 May 1901.

44. Mühimme 16956, Grand Vezir to Health Minister, 29 Nisan 1317/12 May 1901; Bidwell, *Kuwait*, iii/68.

45. Irade Dahiliye 36/5 Cemazi el-evvel 1319, Muhsin to Grand Vezir, 8 Temmuz 1317/21 July 1901.

46. They were aimed first at demonstrating Ottoman sovereignty to Britain, leaving open the possibility that Mubarak could remain in Kuwait. The loss of independence, money, and prestige following such a development would be enough to make Mubarak reluctant, however.

47. Bidwell, *Kuwait*, iii/92, Wratislaw to O'Conor, 1 June 1901; iii/116 and 135, O'Conor to Lansdowne, 20 August 1901; Rashid, *Ta'rikh*, II, pp. 74–75. Mubarak also sent a letter from Kuwait, restating his loyalty and asking, among other things, that his subsidy be continued. Istanbul discovered only much later, and much to its annoyance, that the Basra administration had stopped paying the subsidy without consulting the Porte, because Mubarak "did not ask for it." DH.MUI 30–2/28, Basra *Vali* to Interior Minister, 18 Mart 1326/31 March 1910; Interior Minister to Grand Vezir, 30 Mart 1326/12 April 1910.

48. Busch, *Britain*, pp. 200–203. The request was denied partly because of some officials' continuing concern about the legality of British moves in territory recognized in even a vague way as Ottoman; more important was the wish to avoid disputes with Berlin and Istanbul that could complicate the war effort against the Boers in South Africa and the Baghdad Railway negotiations.

49. Irade Dahiliye 36/5 Cemazi el-evvel 1319, Muhsin to Grand Vezir, 8 and 12 Temmuz 1317/21 and 25 July 1901; Council of Ministers memorandum, 18 Temmuz 1317/31 July 1901.

50. Busch, *Britain*, p. 203.

51. Usul-i Irade Dosya 77, Imperial Chief Secretary's memorandum, 4 Temmuz 1317/17 July 1901.

52. Irade Dahiliye 36/5 Cemazi el-evvel 1319, Council of Ministers memorandum, 18 Temmuz 1317/31 July 1901.

53. Based at Samawa, a week's march from Kuwait, the troops were intended to overawe the troublesome Muntafiq chief, Sa`dun, who had clashed again with the amir's men in July. Irade Dahiliye 36/5 CA 1319, 18 Temmuz/31 July 1901; Bidwell, *Kuwait*, iii/105 and 128, O'Conor to Lansdowne, 9 and 29 August 1901. Despite Sultan Abdülhamid II's penchant for bypassing the Porte and ignoring its advice (a prime example of which was his use of private emissaries in the Kuwait question), it is unlikely that he intended to order directly an attack on Kuwait. Private governance of necessity relied on individuals or small groups of trusted men; a complicated operation, such as a military campaign, would require the assistance of the central bureaucracy, thus drawing in the Porte.

6. KUWAIT, 1899–1913

54. Muhsin, for example, chose to view the military maneuvers as potentially aimed at Kuwait and thus largely to blame for Mubarak's rapprochement with Britain. Y-A Resmî 114/46, Muhsin to Interior Minister, 13 and 17 Ağustos 1317/26 and 30 August 1901.

55. Usul-i Irade Dosya 77, Council of Ministers memorandum, 15 Ağustos 1317/28 August 1901. The Treaty of Berlin, in particular, cropped up in diplomatic discussions.

56. Bidwell, *Kuwait*, iii/103, Ambassador Berlin (Lascelles) to Lansdowne, 30 July 1901; iii/135, O'Conor to Lansdowne, 20 August 1901; Busch, *Britain*, pp. 202–3; Plass, *England*, pp. 285–86.

57. Bidwell, *Kuwait*, iii/140, Lansdowne to O'Conor, 3 September 1901; iii/141, 157 and enclosures, and 160, Lansdowne to Lascelles, 3, 11 and 12 September; iii/165, Lascelles to Lansdowne, 13 September; Busch, *Britain*, pp. 207–8; Plass, *England*, pp. 290–94.

58. Said Pasha, *Hatıratı*, II/1, pp. 185–87; Karal, *Osmanlı*, pp. 433–34. The French navy's action in this, the Lorenzo and Tobini affair, was repeated by a multinational fleet in 1905 to force Abdülhamid to accept an International Finance Committee for Macedonia.

59. Gavin, *Aden*, p. 217; Bidwell, *Kuwait*, iii/135. Ottoman troops and men of an allied shaikh moved into a fort at al-Darayja, on the disputed border between Aden and San`a. Four hundred men and a battery from Aden attacked the position on 27 July 1901; the Arab auxiliaries decamped, leaving the Ottomans outgunned. These had to withdraw, having suffered about one hundred casualties.

60. The sultan credited Britain's problems in the Boer War with forcing it to heed Ottoman protests and to give up her plan to occupy Kuwait. Abdülhamit, *Hatıratım*, pp. 151–52.

61. Y-A Resmî 114/23, Council of Ministers memorandum, 24 Ağustos 1317/6 September 1901.

62. Indicative of the problems contained in this agreement is the Ottoman Foreign Ministry's history of the dispute (*Kuveyt*, p. 5), which marks 1901 as the real start of the Kuwait problem.

63. The distinction between the concepts seems to have an enduring fascination for the British. Consider Canada or Australia, for example, where the monarch's face may appear on money as the nation's titular head of state, but where any attempt by London to alter the course of domestic events would cause a furor.

64. Y-A Resmî 114/46, Foreign Minister to Grand Vezir, 28 Ağustos 1317/10 September 1901; Busch, *Britain*, pp. 205–9; Ottoman Foreign Ministry, *Kuveyt*, p. 5.

65. Plass, *England*, p. 296; Usul-i Irade Dosya 77, copy of memorandum, apparently from the German Foreign Ministry, recommending an immediate accord with one of the aggrieved powers and then the referral of the second case to The Hague.

66. Y-A Resmî 114/46, Muhsin to Interior Minister, 13 and 17 Ağustos 1317/26 and 30 August 1901. Either immediately or within a short time Mubarak began for a time to sign letters just as "Ruler (Hakim) of Kuwait." BEO 135903, Interior Minister to Grand Vezir, 3 Mart 1318/16 March 1902.

67. Y-A Resmî 114/46, Council of Ministers memorandum, 12 Eylûl 1317/25 September 1901. When queried about his young friend's reported activities in a letter from the *vali*, Mubarak admitted that Ibn Sa`ud had gone to Najd but claimed that the purpose of the journey was to look for a wife. The Ottomans did not give much credence to this explanation.

6. KUWAIT, 1899–1913

68. Said Pasha, *Hatıratı*, p. 2/1:313.
69. Y-A Resmî 114/46, 12 Eylûl 1317; Bidwell, *Kuwait*, iii/179, O'Conor to Lansdowne, 26 September 1901. Istanbul evidently took pains to maximize the gains from the replacement. The new *vali*, Mustafa Nuri Pasha, formerly commander of troops at Üsküp/Skopje, presumably arrived in Basra without the prejudices common to his predecessors who had served before in Iraq. Like Muhsin, he was simultaneously governor and military commander of Basra, which increased the likelihood of stable administration. The sultan seemed to trust him, using him and his brother in his Kuwait initiatives of December 1901.
70. Busch, *Britain*, p. 209; Bidwell, *Kuwait*, iii/179.
71. Busch, *Britain*, p. 209.
72. Bidwell, *Kuwait*, iii/264/3, Imperial Chief Secretary to Basra *Vali*, 16 Teşrin-i evvel 1317/29 October 1901; iii/264/2, Basra *Naqib* to Mubarak, 26 Receb 1319/10 November 1901.
73. Y-A Resmî 114/46, 12 Eylûl 1317/25 September 1901.
74. Busch, *Britain*, p. 211.
75. Plass, *England*, p. 302.
76. Consul Wratislaw in Basra believed that the *naqib* had made some sort of demand for submission "but was unable to obtain any definite reply from Mubarek." The *naqib* asserted that, after consultation with Bushire, the shaikh said that he owed the sultan no allegiance, and that the government should address itself to Britain in future. Bidwell, *Kuwait*, iii/248, de Bunsen to Lansdowne, 12 December 1901.
77. Rezvan, *Ships*, p. 74.
78. Rezvan, *Ships*, pp. 13–14, 80, 85, 90–91, 114–15, 136–37.
79. Said Pasha, *Hatıratı*, p. 2/1:316; Bidwell, *Kuwait*, iii/229, Lansdowne to de Bunsen (Chargé d'Affaires, Istanbul), 4 December; iii/231*, de Bunsen to Lansdowne, 5 December 1901.
80. Said Pasha, *Hatıratı*, pp. 2/1:316–17; Usul-i Irade Dosya 77, Irade, 5 Ramazan 1319/16 December 1901; Busch, *Britain*, p. 212.
81. Said Pasha, *Hatıratı*, pp. 2/1:313–14; Usul-i Irade Dosya 77, Irade, 17 Şaban 1319/28 December 1901.
82. Bidwell, *Kuwait*, iii/221, O'Conor to Lansdowne, 8 November 1901.
83. Usul-i Irade Dosya 77, Chief Imperial Secretary memorandum, 18 Teşrin-i evvel 1317/31 October 1901; Bidwell, *Kuwait*, iii/203, Secretary Cairo Legation to Lansdowne, 9 October 1901.
84. Said Pasha, *Hatıratı*, p. 2/1:314.
85. Usul-i Irade Dosya 77, Imperial Secretary to Grand Vezir, 5 Ramazan 1319/16 December 1901; BEO 132596, Grand Vezir to Mustafa Nuri, 14 Kânun-i evvel 1317/27 December 1901; Said Pasha, *Hatıratı*, pp. 2/1:316–7.
86. Usul-i Irade Dosya 77, Imperial Secretary to Grand Vezir, 25 Ramazan, 2, 8 and 16 Şevval 1319/6, 12, 18 and 26 January 1901. This was not the only occasion on which Britain landed guns, removing any doubt in Istanbul that London had withdrawn them out of some lasting weakness.
87. BEO 132345, Grand Vezir to Finance Minister, Basra *Vali* and Military Commander, 4 Kânun-i evvel 1317/17 December 1901; 132584, Grand Vezir to Basra *Vali*, 14 Kânun-i evvel/27 December; 132733, Grand Vezir to Finance Minister, 18 Kânun-i evvel/31 December. The government at first offered him

6. KUWAIT, 1899–1913

T£2,000, which had to be boosted to T£3,000 and T£1,000 worth of food before he agreed.

88. BEO 133388, Grand Vezir to Mustafa Nuri, 6 Kânun-i sani 1317/19 January 1902; Mustafa Nuri to Grand Vezir, 7 Kânun-i sani/20 January.

89. Usul-i Irade Dosya 77, Chief Imperial Secretary to Grand Vezir, 12 Ramazan 1319/23 December 1901.

90. Usul-i Irade Dosya 77, Chief Imperial Secretary to Grand Vezir, 17 Zilhicce 1319/27 March 1902.

91. Gavin, *Aden*, pp. 217–22; Said Pasha, *Hatıratı*, pp. 2/1:317–28.

92. Said Pasha, *Hatıratı*, pp. 2/1:314–15; BEO 134067, Marshal Feyzi to War Minister, 20 Kânun-i sani 1317/2 February 1902; BEO 134247, Mustafa Nuri to Grand Vezir, 27 Kânun-i sani/9 February; BEO Basra'dan Gelen catalogue, Mustafa Nuri to Grand Vezir, 27 Kânun-i sani, 1, 18, 21 Şubat 1317/9, 14 February, 3, 6 March 1903; BEO 134673, 134868, 135640, Grand Vezir to Mustafa Nuri, 6, 12, 28 Şubat 1317/19, 25 February, 13 March 1903.

93. Said Pasha, *Hatıratı*, p. 2/1:372; Usul-i Irade Dosya 77, Chief Imperial Secretary to Grand Vezir, 12 Ramazan 1319/23 December 1901.

94. BEO 120426, Grand Vezir to Naval Minister, 28 Kânun-i evvel 1316/10 January 1901; BEO 134067, Feyzi to War Minister, 20 Kânun-i sani 1317/2 February 1902.

95. BEO 135903, Interior Minister to Grand Vezir, 3 Mart 1318/16 March 1902.

96. Busch, *Britain*, p. 217; Bidwell, *Kuwait*, iv/88, O'Conor to Lansdowne, 16 March 1902.

97. Plass, *England*, p. 308.

98. In a similar scenario some months later, the *mutasarrıf* of Necd proposed the appointment of several officials and the dispatch of some gendarmes to an island between Qatif and Kuwait to forestall an Anglo-Kuwaiti scheme to wrest it from the Ottomans. BEO 146319, Necd *Mutasarrıf* to Basra *Vali*, 14 Ağustos 1318/27 August 1902. For a strong reaffirmation of Abdülhamid's claim to legitimate grounds to act to protect his rights in his empire, including Najd and Kuwait, in the face of British protests about troop movements, see Usul-i Irade Dosya 77, Chief Imperial Secretary to Grand Vezir, 16 Zilhicce 1319/26 March 1902. Referring also to events in Yemen and Hasa, that document and others suggest that the sultan, chafing under the status quo agreement, still was very active in directing Ottoman affairs in Arabia, trying to get the more reluctant ministers' assistance in a forward policy.

99. BEO 134247, Mustafa Nuri to Grand Vezir, 27 Kânun-i sani 1317/9 February 1902; BEO 136435, Interior Minister to Grand Vezir, 13 Mart 1318/26 March 1902. This mail service lapsed again later, due to insecurity along the route, but was restarted again after Mubarak's relations with the Ottomans thawed in 1905. Qasim, *al-Khalij*, p. 283, states that the Ottomans built way stations for the mail at their new posts at Umm Qasr and Bubiyan, although neither was on the direct route from Hasa to Basra. It is also worth noting that the *vali*'s message makes clear that he and the VI Corps commander also communicated directly with the palace concerning this and other problems in Hasa, again indicating Abdülhamid's close interest in the area.

100. London seems to have received very little solid information about the case. The consul in Basra noted, almost as an afterthought, that the desert routes were unsafe and that Ibn Rashid's main supporter in Zubayr had warned against travel to

6. KUWAIT, 1899–1913

Kuwait on pain of death. Otherwise the government's attention was drawn to it only by Ottoman complaints, which the Foreign Office did not take seriously. Bidwell, *Kuwait*, iv/51, Wratislaw to O'Conor, 10 January 1902; iv/94, Lansdowne to Ottoman ambassador, London, 20 March 1902.

101. Bidwell, *Kuwait*, iv/104, O'Conor to Lansdowne, 29 March 1902.

102. Busch, *Britain*, pp. 213–14; Bidwell, *Kuwait*, iv/59, O'Conor to Lansdowne, 14 February; iv/76 and iv/89, Wratislaw to O'Conor, 8 and 15 February 1902.

103. Bidwell, *Kuwait*, iv/136, Wratislaw to O'Conor, 31 March 1902. The *vali* refused the money, suggesting that Mubarak donate it to the strapped Basra Treasury instead.

104. Bidwell, *Kuwait*, iv/136; BEO 135903, Interior Minister to Grand Vezir, 3 Mart 1318/16 March 1902. It is possible that Mubarak softened his new practice of signing messages as "Ruler of Kuwait." His use of a similar title on a letter much exercised the *vali* in 1905, arguing either a change in the shaikh's practice or the *vali*'s ignorance of the recent history of the Kuwait question. Bidwell, *Arabia*, ii/47, Acting Basra Consul to Istanbul Embassy, 24 February 1905.

105. Usul-i Irade Dosya 77, Imperial Secretary to Grand Vezir, 13 and 17 Mart 1318/26 and 30 March 1902; Bidwell, *Kuwait*, iv/101, iv/119 and iv/1114, O'Conor to Lansdowne, 27 March, 1 and 2 April 1902.

106. Getting Mubarak to agree to proposals also was not a mere formality. He bluntly refused to establish a quarantine post in 1908, for example. Busch, *Britain*, pp. 310–11.

107. Finnie, *Lines*, p. 28. A copy of the 1899 document was finally given to Istanbul in 1912, while the 1907 bond remained unpublicized until its discovery by researchers in 1963.

108. The situation is captured beautifully in the Minutes of a subcommittee of the Committee for Imperial Defence of 2 March 1908: (Mr. Morley:) "Now, Sir Richmond, tell us how we stand jurisprudentially in Koweit." (Sir R. Ritchie:) "Whenever we write to the Foreign Office we always say, 'The Sheikh of Koweit, with whose status the Secretary of State for Foreign Affairs is acquainted;' and similarly when the Foreign Office write to us they adopt a similar form." Quoted in Plass, *England*, p. 243.

109. BEO 146372, Grand Vezir to Mustafa Nuri, 7 Teşrin-i sani 1318/20 November 1902; BEO 147490, Grand Vezir to Mustafa Nuri, 12 Kânun-i evvel 1318/25 December 1902; Usul-i Irade Dosya 77, Chief Imperial Secretary to Grand Vezir, 19 Kânun-i evvel 1318/1 January 1903; BEO 147732, Grand Vezir to Interior and Foreign Ministers, 21 Kânun-i evvel/3 January 1903. The statement by the authors of a later Foreign Ministry historical report (*Necd*, p. 10), who seem to have had only limited access to some official records, that the Porte incited Ibn Rashid to advance on Kuwait does not agree with the available documents.

110. BEO 144592, Mustafa Nuri to Interior Minister, 26, 27 and 30 Ağustos 1318/8, 9 and 12 September 1902; Interior Minister to Grand Vezir, 2 Eylûl/15 September; Foreign Minister to Grand Vezir, 16 Eylûl/29 September; Busch, *Britain*, pp. 219–21. In June 1902 Yusuf had felt so alarmed by events in Najd and by Mubarak's growing alliance with Yusuf's powerful neighbor, Shaikh Khaz`al of Muhammara, that he attempted to reach a settlement with his enemy. Mubarak refused. Out of frustration, Yusuf and several of the nephews prepared a raiding

6. KUWAIT, 1899–1913

party in hopes of catching Kuwait unprepared for a sea attack. News of the plan leaked, however, and a British warship intercepted the party. During the ensuing chase, one British sailor was killed and two others wounded. The British conducted their own investigation of the affair, which led to the demands for action against Yusuf, the nephews, and the *vali*. The Ottomans questioned the conclusions of the inquiry, in which they did not take part. Abdülhamid continued to credit the idea, planted in 1896 by Mubarak, that Yusuf was a British-paid agent provocateur (Abdülhamit, *Hatıratım*, p. 150). No decisive action was taken over the incident. The attack was, however, the last grand scheme by Yusuf, who died in Ha'il in 1906.

111. BEO 241415, Post and Telegraph Minister to Grand Vezir, 18 Kânun-i evvel 1323/31 December 1907; BEO 241590, Grand Vezir to Basra *Vali* and Reform Committee (Baghdad), 20 Kânun-i evvel/2 January 1908; BEO 248993, Basra *Vali* to War Minister, 9 Şubat/22 February; War Minister to Grand Vezir, 10 Mayıs 1324/23 May 1908; Grand Vezir to Basra *Vali*, 13 Mayıs/26 May.

112. Istanbul wanted to know, for example, what connection Mubarak might have to Sa`dun and his land dispute with another tribe. Since Sa`dun had been given by design land far from Mubarak, the *vali* discounted any connection. BEO 199769, Basra *Vali* to Grand Vezir, 28 Ağustos 1321/10 September 1905; Grand Vezir to Basra *Vali*, 31 Ağustos/13 September; Basra *Vali* to Grand Vezir, 1 Eylûl/14 September.

113. BEO 187460, Grand Vezir to Basra *Vali*, 24 Kânun-i sani 1320/6 January 1905. The British Agent assigned to Kuwait in 1904 estimated the annual trade in arms through that port at roughly 12,000 rifles, of which about half reached Iran. Some of the rest went to Najd and elsewhere in Arabia, but most of it was smuggled into Iraq. Bidwell, *Arabia*, iii/75/2, Capt. Knox to Major Cox (Resident Bushire), 21 February 1905.

114. BEO 191285, Grand Vezir to Basra *Vali*, 1 Nisan 1321/14 April 1905; BEO 248520, Muhalhal al-Sa`dun to Grand Vezir, 3 Mayıs 1324/16 May 1908; Rashid, *Ta'rikh*, II, pp. 96–97; Basra'dan Gelen catalogue, 3 Kânun-i evvel 1325/16 December 1909 and 17 Mart 1326/30 March 1910. It is possible that the government wanted to harass Mubarak, not just to prevent extension of his influence in sensitive areas. Khaz`al, *Ta'rikh*, II, p. 79, lumps a second transaction with the Sa`dun purchase dispute as evidence of such harassment. On the other hand, it is worth noting that Muhalhal al-Sa`dun's petition in BEO 248520 complains that the local authorities had taken no action on his charge that Mubarak had seized his property. The problem with Sa`dun Pasha may also have been caused by his lack of a title to the land. After an earlier round of outlawry, Sa`dun had been allocated land rented from the state, as well as a salary—two rewards that could be revoked if he caused fresh trouble. Y-A Resmî 124/56, Council of Ministers memorandum, 4 Şubat 1319/17 February 1904; BEO 199769, Basra *Vali* to Grand Vezir, 1 Eylûl 1321/14 September 1905.

115. BEO, Basra'dan Gelen catalogue, 27 and 28 Mart 1320/9 and 10 April 1904. This followed Mustafa Nuri's earlier warning to the Porte that Mubarak was plotting to return the Sa`udis to power in Najd (BEO, Basra'dan Gelen catalogue, 10 Haziran 1318/23 June 1902). It is also interesting to note that the Ottoman Foreign Ministry's 1917 report on Najd (*Necd*, p. 10) states that "Shaikh Mubarak, together with his allies," continued to press Ibn Rashid, defeating him in battles in August and October 1904.

116. BEO, Basra'dan Gelen catalogue, 10 Ağustos 1321/23 August 1905.

6. KUWAIT, 1899–1913

117. Abdülhamit, *Hatıratım*, p. 151; Busch, *Britain*, p. 228; Bidwell, *Arabia*, iii/55/3, Kuwait Agent Knox's notes of Mubarak's account of February meetings, 28 February 1905. Abdülhamid's memoir specifies no date for Mubarak's saving the amir from Britain's clutches. In February 1905 a certain coldness ruled his relations with the Ottomans, since he refused to renounce his British ties and, as the amir did, swear his loyalty to the sultan. He may have been momentarily miffed by the deportation of several Sa`udi informants from Basra in January, one of whom, he claimed, owed him money. Nevertheless he very likely kept in touch with the Palace, and within several months relations had warmed again.

118. BEO 180244, Grand Vezir to Basra *Vali*, 23 Ağustos 1320/5 September 1904; BEO, Basra'dan Gelen catalogue, 24 Ağustos/6 September. The *vali* did not receive credit for his action from Britain; the Consul later accused him of spreading malicious lies about British activity. Bidwell, *Arabia*, iv/15/1, Basra Consul Crow to O'Conor, 14 June 1905.

119. BEO, Basra'dan Gelen catalogue, 15 and 19 Kânun-i evvel 1320/28 December 1904 and 1 January 1905; Usul-i Irade, Dosya 77, Chief Imperial Secretary to Grand Vezir, 1 Kânun-i sani 1320/14 January 1905; BEO 186211, Grand Vezir to Foreign Minister, 1 Kânun-i sani/14 January; BEO 186671, Grand Vezir to Baghdad *Vali*, 10 Kânun-i sani/23 January; BEO 187439, Grand Vezir to Baghdad and Basra *Valis*, 24 Kânun-i sani/6 February; Basra *Vali* to Grand Vezir, 25 Kânun-i sani/7 February.

120. Just before meeting Mubarak and `Abd al-Rahman, the *vali* asked the Grand Vezir for instructions on the proper steps to be taken, "in view of the fact that on no matter does the Kuwait *kaymakamlık* carry on official dealings with the *vilayet*." Basra'dan Gelen catalogue, 27 Kânun-i sani 1320/9 February 1905.

121. Irade Hususiye, 26 Muharrem 1323/2 April 1905; BEO 190526, Grand Vezir to Basra *Vali*, 21 Mart 1321/3 April 1905; Irade Hususiye, 8 Safer 1323/14 April 1905.

122. BEO, Basra'dan Gelen catalogue, 4 Nisan 1321/17 April 1905.

123. Hüsni, *Necd*, pp. 266–67. Hüsni was an officer who deserted because he feared that Ibn Rashid was plotting to have him murdered. Mubarak talked with him several times while he waited for a ship in which to begin his intended return to Istanbul. According to what Hüsni learned, Mubarak tried to isolate the British Agent from the Kuwaiti people. The shaikh also refused to allow the British to carry out any projects to improve Kuwait, saying that he had accepted British protection only for himself and his personal rights; the land and other property belonged to the Ottoman state. If the British wanted to carry out any improvements, they would have to approach the Ottoman government first.

124. Bidwell, *Arabia*, iii/30, Crow to O'Conor, 22 April 1905. For an example of another report, submitted to the British Consul in Basra by a confidential informant, that stressed a growing Anglophobia in Mubarak, see Bidwell, *Arabia*, v/58/3, forwarded to O'Conor on 30 September 1905.

125. In response to Ottoman complaints that the Agent violated the status quo, the Foreign Office had informed Istanbul that the appointment was temporary. The *vali* might well have used this information to press Mubarak, if the shaikh appeared to be emboldened by the appointment. Y-Maruzat Defteri 12685, memorandum of a special committee of ministers, 31 Teşrin-i evvel 1320/13 November 1904.

126. Farah, *Protection*, ch. 5; Lorimer, *Gazetteer*, pp. 938–42. `Isa was rivaled in power by his nephew, `Ali. When Britain recognized `Isa's son, Hamad, as the heir

6. KUWAIT, 1899-1913

apparent to the shaikhdom, `Ali started to cause unrest in Manama. His men beat a European employee of the German trading firm Wonckhaus in an argument over corvée labor and then assaulted and robbed some Iranian merchants. Sensitive to the international problems that might arise from the incidents, Britain delivered an ultimatum demanding payment of compensation and deportation of the guilty men, including `Ali. These and other conditions were designed to demonstrate where the real power in Bahrain lay. `Isa balked at some of the demands, which in sum were very humiliating. He finally had to bow to British pressure tactics, which included holding Hamad as a hostage for a time. Driving the lesson home, the British warned `Isa that they would not tolerate further rejection of their advice on important matters, and Hamad was told that ultimate recognition of his claims depended on his future conduct.

127. Bidwell, *Arabia*, vi/17/1, Crow to O'Conor, 4 January 1906; BEO 198922, Grand Vezir to Muhlis, 14 Ağustos 1321/27 August 1905; BEO 199723, Grand Vezir to Muhlis, 30 Ağustos/12 September; Grand Vezir to Naval Minister, 30 Ağustos/12 September; BEO 203562, Muhlis to Imperial Chief Secretary, 21 Teşrin-i sani 1321/4 December 1905. The agent became a convenient means of ingratiation; he apparently received an Ottoman decoration several years later. BEO, Basra'dan Gelen catalogue, 30 Mayıs 1323/12 June 1907; BEO 231219, Grand Vezir to Basra *Vali*, 7 Haziran/20 June.

128. BEO 223227, Basra *Vali* to Grand Vezir, 22 Kânun-i evvel 1322/4 January 1907; Grand Vezir to Basra *Vali*, 25 Kânun-i evvel/7 January; Usul-i Irade Dosya 77, Chief Imperial Secretary to Grand Vezir, 25 Kânun-i evvel /7 January.

129. BEO 230322, Basra *Vali* to Grand Vezir, 14 Mayıs 1323/27 May 1907; Grand Vezir to Basra *Vali*, 24 Mayıs/6 June.

130. Plass, *England*, p. 388.

131. BEO 297912, Grand Vezir to Mubarak, 25 Teşrin-i sani 1327/8 December 1911. The telegram, however, was to acknowledge receipt of Mubarak's message of friendship and loyalty to the sultan on the Greater (*Kurban*) Bayram. The lapse of principle regarding Mubarak's title seems to have been momentary; several months later he was again referred to as "Kuveyt Kaymakamı." BEO 299568, Grand Vezir to Interior Minister, 14 Kânun-i sani 1327/27 January 1912.

132. Khaz`al, *Ta'rikh*, II, p. 81.

133. BEO 299568, Mubarak's letter of thanks, 16 Safer 1330/3 February 1912.

134. Mubarak's relations with Ibn Sa`ud at this time were still much warmer than they were to become by 1915. By then Mubarak felt that the ideal situation was to have the two Najdi leaders bleed each other into insignificance. He wrote to both Ibn Sa`ud and the Rashidi amir, professing his support and urging each to attack the other. Unfortunately for Mubarak, his secretary disapproved of such underhandedness and sent each man the letter meant for his opponent. Rashid, *Ta'rikh*, II, p. 126; Rihani, *Ta'rikh*, p. 152.

135. Raunkiaer, *Wahhabiland*, pp. 24, 30-32.

136. Mubarak pled ill health to avoid going to Basra to receive his medal in 1912 (BEO 299568, Basra *Vali* to Interior Minister, 3 Kânun-i sani 1327/16 January 1912). He did visit his Faw estates and travel up the Shatt when the Ottomans appeared relatively benign, however (BEO, Basra'dan Gelen catalogue, 28 Ağustos 1322/ 10 September 1906).

137. Şevket, *Günlüğü*, p. 45.

6. KUWAIT, 1899–1913

138. It is interesting to note that Mubarak's sons and successors, Jabir and Salim, permitted and even encouraged the passage through Kuwait of supplies for the Ottomans in World War I. Finnie, *Lines*, pp. 42–44.

7. Arabia, 1896–1914

1. Y.MTV 203/60, telegram of 13 Hasawis to War Minister, 17 Mayıs 1316/30 May 1900. The case against the officer was not clear, since 26 Hasawis sent another telegram insisting that he was a just and fair man (Y.MTV 203/60, War Minister's memorandum, 5 Haziran 1316/18 June 1900).

2. BEO 59642, "Memalik-i Iraniye'den Bender Buşir'de Mukim Ingiltere Devlet-i Fahimesi Cenral Konsolosunun Hilaf-i Uhud Tecavüzatına Havi Layıhadır," by Ibrahim Pasha.

3. See the Interior Minister's complaint against Hamdi in chapter 5.

4. BEO 123162, Marshal Feyzi to Ministry of War, 14 Mart 1317/27 March 1901, for example, reports the confiscation of 256 rifles, plus ammunition, from such a Bahraini boat.

5. Lorimer, *Gazetteer*, pp. 831–33.

6. The Ottomans suspected, for instance, that Qâsim gave Ibn Rashid modern Martini rifles. BEO 114077, Major Hüsni (Qatar commander) to Interior Ministry, 31 Mart 1316/13 April 1900.

7. BEO Dahiliyeden Gelen catalogue 65/3–14 (1316), no. 5160, 22 Şubat 1316/7 March 1901.

8. A German visitor to Doha in 1904 found the garrison in a poor state and master of only what its guns could reach. Burchardt, "Ost-Arabien," pp. 312–13.

9. Y-A Resmî 93/21, Council of Ministers memorandum, 27 Mayıs 1314/8 June 1898.

10. BEO 198475, Doha garrison commander to VI Corps Marshal, 20 Haziran 1321/3 July 1905.

11. BEO 198475, Doha garrison commander to VI Corps Marshal, 5 Temmuz 1321/18 July 1905; Burchardt, "Ost-Arabien," p. 313.

12. Y-A Resmî 94/10, Council of Ministers memorandum, 15 Temmuz 1314/27 July 1898.

13. BEO 198475, 20 Haziran 1321; Lorimer, *Gazetteer*, p. 824.

14. Lorimer, *Gazetteer*, pp. 828–30.

15. Rihani, *Ta'rikh*, pp. 154–55; Goldberg, *Policy*, pp. 66–67; Lorimer, *Gazetteer*, p. 835.

16. BEO 198475, Doha garrison commander to VI Corps Marshal, 20 Haziran, 5 and 10 Temmuz 1321/3, 18 and 23 July 1905.

17. BEO 205916, Grand Vezir to Interior Minister, 4 Kânun-i sani 1321/17 January 1906.

18. Telegram from Basra *Vali* to Interior Minister, 14 Teşrin-i evvel 1326/27 October 1910, reproduced in Arabic translation in Mansur, *Tatawwur*, pp. 230–31.

19. Lorimer, *Gazetteer*, p. 831.

20. Some of the tribe, which had been dominant in Doha earlier in the last century, left Wakra for Kuwait in 1910 because of problems with Qâsim, although the details of the dispute are unclear. Sinan, *Ta'rikh*, p. 96; Khatrash and Mansur, *Masadir*, document summary 32, p. 153.

7. ARABIA, 1896–1914

21. MV 84/70, 30 Nisan 1311/12 May 1895; MV 87/42, 15 Mayıs 1312/27 May 1896; Khatrash and Mansur, *Masadir*, document summaries 13, 14, 24, 25a, 27, 36b, 39b, 52.

22. Khatrash and Mansur, *Masadir*, summarizes an undated letter from Qâsim to the *mutasarrıf* in Hufuf, demanding settlements at Zubara and `Udayd to protect the peace against bedouin unrest (no. 52, p. 161).

23. Lorimer, *Gazetteer*, p. 826. Khatrash and Mansur, *Masadir*, summarize a report (no. 22b) of 28 Teşrin-i sani 1327/11 December 1911 that discusses `Abdallah al-Thani's influence over Qatari affairs and his leanings toward the British. `Abdallah had been officially appointed Qâsim's deputy on the understanding of continuing loyalty to the government just four years before (photocopy of *buyruldu*, dated 4 Teşrin-i sani 1323/17 November 1907, in Mansur, *Tatawwur*, p. 217).

24. Lorimer, *Gazetteer*, p. 985.

25. ŞD 2184/6, Former Hufuf Paymaster to Necd Commander, 9 Mayıs 1317/22 May 1901. Hasawis were still too poor to pay an assessed education tax at this time.

26. Irade Maliye 21/L.1318, 19 Şevval 1318/9 February 1901.

27. ŞD 2184/6, deposition (*isticvab*) of Necd *zaptiye* soldier Ahsa'lı `Abdallah b. Hasan, 30 Kânun-i sani 1315/11 February 1900. ŞD 2184/6, petition of `Abdallah b. `Isa, 12 Kânun-i evvel 1315/24 December 1899 mentions *zaptiye* soldiers in the "Hamidiye" guardhouse in Hufuf, referring presumably to the troops rather than to a barracks named after the sultan. Saldana (*Expansion*, p. 60) mentions Said's recruitment of auxiliaries without defining them as Hamidiye gendarmes.

28. Saldana, *Expansion*, p. 60.

29. BEO Dahiliyeye Giden catalogue, no number, 6 Mayıs 1318/19 May 1902; BEO 148399, Grand Vezir to Interior Ministry, 6 Kânun-i sani 1318/19 January 1903. Lorimer (*Gazetteer*, p. 985) reported the dispatch of 200 cavalry to Hasa in 1902, but this force either wasted away or was withdrawn after early 1904, when Burchardt ("Ost-Arabien," p. 310) reported the presence of a half battalion of mule troopers. A new mule-mounted corps had to be organized in 1906. BEO 213421, Grand Vezir to Interior Minister, 28 Mayıs 1322/10 June 1906; BEO 219707, Basra *Vali* to Grand Vezir, 10 Teşrin-i evvel 1322/23 October 1906.

30. Nomads regularly visited towns to buy and sell goods. Since at such times they were most vulnerable not only to the gendarmerie but also other bedouins, they often came only after receiving a safe-conduct from the authorities. BEO 216786, VI Corps Marshal to War Minister, 25 Mayıs 1322/7 June 1906. Similarly when Ottoman officials passed through bedouin-controlled areas, they found it wise to ensure peaceful relations by paying a protection fee (*al-khuwa*). Burchardt, "Ost-Arabien," pp. 311–12.

31. ŞD 2184/6, 16 Şevval 1317/17 February 1900.

32. ŞD 2184/6, Necd Commander's report, 19 Kânun-i evvel 1315/31 December 1899.

33. The date of his final replacement is rather unclear, but he seems to have been unwelcome in Hasa after 1903, when he was allowed to return to Basra because of "illness." Lorimer, *Gazetteer*, p. 981; Kornrumpf, "Beschreibungen," p. 86; BEO 163230, Grand Vezir to Interior Minister, 11 Eylûl 1319/24 September 1903.

34. DH.MUI 54–1/13, 22 Nisan 1325/5 May 1909.

35. Lorimer, *Gazetteer*, pp. 985–86; BEO 138890, Grand Vezir to Interior Ministry, 9 Mayıs 1318/22 May 1902. Government and town dweller alike must have espe-

7. ARABIA, 1896–1914

cially enjoyed the capture of a caravan of supplies intended for the Al Murra accused of partaking in an earlier raid.

36. Lorimer, *Gazetteer*, pp. 981–82; Y-A Resmî 119/58, Petition of Head of the Qatif Imperial Properties Commission, 2 and 4 Şubat 1318/15 and 17 February 1903; VI Corps Marshal to War Ministry, 2 Şubat/15 February; Basra *Vali* to Interior Minister, 4 and 6 Şubat/17 and 19 February; Interior Minister to Grand Vezir, 9 Şubat/22 February; Y-A Resmî 120/92, Petition from Muhtars, 22 Şubat/7 March; Interior Minister to Grand Vezir, 16 Mart/29 March.

37. For a discussion of the difficulties the government faced in finding administrators willing to grapple with the challenges of managing affairs in Arabia (aside from civil-military tensions), see Irade Dahiliye 1322-i-48, civil officials commission memorandum, 6 Teşrin-i sani 1320/19 November 1904.

38. Abu `Alieh, "Dirasa," p. 122.

39. When Said Pasha left Hasa, he put annual revenue at T£60,000. Three years later Burchardt reported annual income of T£35,000, well below Said's estimate of T£54,000 for military expenses alone in 1900. There are very few records in Istanbul about Hasa's finances. Several that do exist from this period suggest that the central Treasury had little information about Necd, except that it was not producing much revenue. Lorimer, *Gazetteer*, p. 983; Burchardt, "Ost-Arabien," p. 310; ML.VRD 4178, accounts of provincial and sub-provincial tax receipts, 1319/1903–04, pp. 80–81; ML.VRD 4247, accounts book, 1321/1905–06.

40. Irade Maliye 5/R.1323, 2 Rebi el-âhir 1323/6 June 1905. The results of the survey indirectly confirm the decline in Hasa's economic health. The survey increased revenue by 120,000 küsur kuruş to a total of 900,000. The küsur kuruş was a debased coin, however, whose value varied from place to place. If a rough value of T£1=120 küsur kuruş is used, the *öşür* on dates (virtually the only taxed produce) realized only about T£7,500 in Qatif in 1903–after the survey. With Hufuf in earlier years producing twice as much as Qatif, it seems likely that the tithe in all of the *sancak* reached only T£20–25,000 at this time.

41. BEO 177123, Grand Vezir to Basra *Vali*, 21 Haziran 1320/4 July 1904; BEO 182427, Basra *Vali* to Grand Vezir, 24 Ağustos/6 September; War Ministry to Grand Vezir, 27 Eylûl/10 October; Ministry of Military Preparedness, undated; Grand Vezir to Basra *Vali*, 7 Teşrin-i evvel/20 October; BEO 186285, War Ministry to Grand Vezir, 23 Kânun-i evvel 1320/5 January 1905.

42. BEO 183343, VI Corps Marshal to War Minister, 18 Teşrin-i evvel 1320/31 October 1904.

43. Abu `Alieh, "Dirasa," pp. 122–23; Lorimer, *Gazetteer*, pp. 983, 995–96; BEO 170941, Grand Vezir to Interior Ministry, 9 Şubat 1319/22 February 1904; BEO 179815, Interior Minister to Grand Vezir, 9 Ağustos 1320/22 August 1904; BEO 212368, Grand Vezir to Interior Minister, 9 Mayıs 1321/22 May 1905.

44. *Ulema* and other notables of Hufuf and the surrounding area, for instance, threatened to desert their homes if the poll tax were imposed, just as they had in 1900 in protesting the tax increases. Irade Maliye 21/L.1318, Finance Minister's report, 9 Kânun-i evvel 1316/22 December 1900; BEO, Basra'dan Gelen catalogue, Mart 1322/March-April 1906.

45. At least eleven men held the *mutasarrıflık* between 1900 and 1909; many also held the military command. When the civil and military duties were split, both

7. ARABIA, 1896–1914

mutasarrıfs and garrison commanders rotated frequently. See appendix for a list of *mutasarrıfs* and their terms in office.

46. BEO 104585, Council of Ministers memorandum, 19 Cemazi el-âhir 1317/25 October 1899; Grand Vezir to Interior Minister, 24 Teşrin-i evvel 1315/5 November 1899.

47. Bidwell, *Kuwait*, iv/107, O'Conor to Lansdowne, 25 March 1902. By 1899 Istanbul was sending both food and money to Ibn Rashid, but more warlike supplies were restricted until 1903. BEO 80094, Grand Vezir to Interior Minister, 1 Kânun-i sani 1314/13 January 1899.

48. Musil, *Neğd*, p. 245; Goldberg, *Policy*, p. 49; BEO 114077, report by Doha garrison commander, 31 Mart 1316/13 April 1900; Interior Minister to Grand Vezir, 20 Eylûl 1316/3 October 1900.

49. For a discussion of Europe's destruction of Arabia's pre-modern commercial economy and domination of its replacement, see al-Naqeeb, *Society and State*, chs. 2–4. Wanting to be provocative, Naqeeb makes some dubious statements, including the assertion that Wahhabism-Sa`udism was an "indigenous national resistance" (pp. 41–42), but his points usually deserve careful consideration.

50. Goldberg, *Policy*, p. 48.

51. `Abd al-Rahman al-Sa`ud had received a stipend during much of his "exile" in Kuwait; he was a potential weapon against the Rashidi amirs, should they prove too wayward. The stipend was cut off for a time, probably as a result of the 1901 campaign that finished at Sarif. It was restored after he made his peace with the government later in 1901 (BEO 126191, Grand Vezir to Interior Minister, 20 Haziran 1317/3 July 1901).

52. BEO 168582, Grand Vezir to Basra and Baghdad *valis*, 27 Kânun-i evvel 1319/9 January 1904; BEO 168823, Grand Vezir to Basra *Vali*, 23 Kânun-i evvel/5 January, and Basra *Vali* to Grand Vezir, 29 Kânun-i evvel/11 January; BEO, Basra'dan Gelen catalogue, Basra *Vali* to Grand Vezir, 31 Kânun-i evvel 1319/13 January.

53. BEO 157622, Grand Vezir to Interior Minister, 16 Haziran 1319/29 June 1903; Irade Dahiliye 1321-N-14, 29 Ramazan 1321/19 December 1903.

54. As in the case of Kuwait at this time, the sultan's interest in taking action in Najd was greater than the Porte's (Hüsni, *Necd*, pp. 3–4).

55. Bidwell, *Arabia*, i/14/2, Extract of (Consular?) Diary to Government of India for week ending 28 November 1904; Lorimer, *Gazetteer*, pp. 1147–48; Goldberg, *Policy*, pp. 58–59. Hüseyin Hüsni, who took part in the Najd operations in 1904–5, described a number of ways in which Ibn Rashid and his men contributed to the defeat at Bukayriya in July 1904. Perhaps most galling was the Rashidi bedouins' treatment of wounded soldiers, stripping them of everything and leaving them to die in the desert (Hüsni, *Necd*, pp. 220–28).

56. A petition from this messenger, which included avowals of Ibn Sa`ud's friendship and loyalty, is among the enclosures of Irade Dahiliye 1322-L-48 (21 Şevval 1322/29 December 1904).

57. Irade Dahiliye 17/19 Cemazi el-evvel 1323/22 July 1905.

58. Shaikhs were to be given the title of *sancakdar* (standard-bearer) and banners showing on one side the phrase "*Innama al-Mu'minuna Ikhwa*" (Truly Believers are brothers) and on the other the Ottoman arms.

59. The government planned to station two battalions in Qasîm during the first

year, and thereafter only one. In comparison Hasa had seven battalions in 1903–4. BEO, Basra'dan Gelen catalogue, 29 Nisan 1319/12 May 1903; Burchardt, "Ost-Arabien," p. 310.

60. Hamzah, *Qalb*, p. 368.

61. BEO 193339, Basra *Vali* to Grand Vezir, 2 Mayıs 1321/15 May 1905.

62. BEO 193339, 2 Mayıs 1321. The merchant was given promissory notes to be redeemed by the Basra Treasury. As ever denuded of funds, the Treasury redeemed them only at a discount. The merchant proved less willing to do business with the Ottomans subsequently. Hüsni, *Necd*, pp. 246–47.

63. BEO 194492, Finance Minister to Grand Vezir, 25 Mayıs 1321/7 June 1905; BEO 195031, War Minister to Grand Vezir, 24 Mayıs 1321/6 June 1905; Grand Vezir to Syria, Baghdad, and Basra *Valis*, 2 Haziran/15 June; Bidwell, *Arabia*, iv/24, O'Conor to Lansdowne, 24 July 1905; v/68, Basra Consul Crow to O'Conor, 18 November 1905.

64. Bidwell, *Arabia*, v/68. These unidentified Arabs may well have included Sa`udi supporters, but the main culprits were presumably followers of Ibn Rashid.

65. Lorimer, *Gazetteer*, pp. 1154–55.

66. Goldberg, *Policy*, p. 73; Bidwell, *Arabia*, viii/7/1, Acting Consul Jidda to O'Conor, 19 June 1906.

67. Hüsni, *Necd*, pp. 250–51, 254, 271–72.

68. Hüsni, *Necd*, pp. 68, 244–46, 251; Irade Hususiye 18 Ramazan 1323/16 November 1905; Irade Dahiliye 17/19 Cemazi el-evvel 1323/22 July 1905.

69. Hamzah, *Qalb*, p. 368. Ibn Rashid was succeeded by his eldest son, Mut`ib. Mut`ib ruled Ha'il less than one year before being murdered by a member of the rival branch of the Al Rashid. Between 1906 and 1908 four different Rashidi amirs of Ha'il were killed in battle or by assassination.

70. Part of the problem was the expense of supply through the Hijaz. In searching to improve delivery of necessities, Hüseyin Hüsni learned from Qasimi traders that grain brought from Kuwait would cost less than half that carried from Madina. Avoiding the area around Ha'il, moreover, might reduce the excessive rate of pilferage. Sultan Abdülhamid's known opinions of both Shaikh Mubarak and Ibn Rashid made any such suggestion to alter the route politically unwise, however. *Necd*, pp. 248–50.

71. Hüsni, *Necd*, pp. 160–61; BEO 141637, Grand Vezir to Basra *Vali* and Finance Minister, 10 Temmuz 1318/23 July 1902.

72. Goldberg, *Policy*, pp. 70–71.

73. BEO 228642 and 230322, Grand Vezir to Basra *Vali*, 24 Nisan/7 May and 24 Mayıs 1323/6 June 1907; Kornrumpf, "Beschreibungen," p. 86.

74. Goldberg, *Policy*, p. 86.

75. On several occasions reports reached Istanbul that officials had sided with Ibn Sa`ud. Given the frequent tensions among the civil and military authorities, it is possible that this was used as a convenient charge to force the dismissal of rivals. BEO 183343, Marshal Feyzi Pasha to War Minister, 18 Teşrin-i evvel 1320/31 October 1904; BEO 216786, VI Corps Marshal to War Minister, 25 Mayıs 1322/7 June 1906; Abu `Alieh, "Dirasa," p. 127.

76. Burchardt, "Ost-Arabien," pp. 308–12; Raunkiaer, *Wahhabiland*, pp. 47–48, 132–36, 142–43.

77. BEO 216786, 25 Mayıs 1322/7 June 1906.

7. ARABIA, 1896–1914

78. DH.MUI 4–2/26, 22 Haziran 1325/5 July 1909; DH.MUI 37–2/20, Necd *Mutasarrıf*'s report, 14 Eylûl 1325/27 September 1909.

79. BEO 221665, Grand Vezir to Basra *Vali*, 22 Teşrin-i sani 1322/5 December 1906; BEO 221902, Grand Vezir to War and Interior Ministers, 28 Teşrin-i sani/11 December; BEO 222350, Basra *Vali* to Grand Vezir, 12 Kânun-i evvel/25 December; BEO 253340, Grand Vezir to Basra *Vali*, 6 Ağustos 1324/19 August 1908; BEO, Basra'dan Gelen catalogue, 13 Ağustos 1324/26 August 1908; BEO, Basra'dan Gelen catalogue, 25 Nisan 1325/8 May 1909; DH.MUI 54–1/13, Grand Vezir to Interior Minister, 21 Kânun-i evvel 1325/3 January 1910; Lorimer, *Gazetteer*, pp. 986–87.

80. Inalcık, "Recession," p. 85; Hamzah, *Qalb*, p. 371; Safran, *Saudi Arabia*, p. 34.

81. Musil, *Neğd*, pp. 246–48.

82. There were several incidents that annoyed Britain in 1910, including the Ottoman occupation of an island near `Uqayr that the shaikh of Bahrain also claimed. The initiative in these schemes apparently lay with local authorities, however, and the British fear that the Young Turks were determined to strengthen their position in Arabia seems to have been exaggerated. Busch, *Britain*, pp. 319–20.

83. Şevket, *Günlüğü*, pp. 45, 152.

84. Busch, *Britain*, pp. 319–40; Şevket, *Günlüğü*, p. 177. For a discussion of the agreement's relevance to Kuwait, and of some reasons for Istanbul's willingness to accept the basic British proposals for determining the borders, see Finnie, *Lines*, pp. 35–38. A further possible explanation for acceptance of Britain's idea of the proper border was simply that the government had no solid information on which to anchor an alternate position. Presumably because of the general disorder in Istanbul, the Porte could find no information on official relations with Kuwait after 1871, or on the present compass of Mubarak's influence. It requested information from Basra, but the equal chaos there made the provincial authorities of little help. BEO 301361, Grand Vezir to Basra and Baghdad *Vali*s, 10 Mart 1328/23 March 1912; BEO 310745, Grand Vezir to Basra Deputy *Vali*, 1 Şubat 1328/14 February 1913; BEO 311041, Basra Deputy *Vali* to Grand Vezir, 10 Şubat/23 February, and Grand Vezir to Basra Deputy *Vali*, 12 Şubat/25 February; BEO 311104, Grand Vezir to Basra Deputy *Vali*, 16 Şubat 1328/1 March 1913.

85. Goldberg, *Policy*, p. 85; Qasim, *Al-Khalij*, p. 310.

86. Goldberg, *Policy*, pp. 90–01, 99–100, 104; Ottoman Foreign Ministry, *Necd*, p. 11; Şevket, *Günlüğü*, p. 34, 143. Ibn Sa`ud apparently raised the question of Qatar and Oman himself, in order to stir Britain into action against an Ottoman return to Hasa.

87. Ottoman Foreign Ministry, *Necd*, pp. 12–14; Goldberg, *Policy*, pp. 106–8, Appendix A.

88. Şevket, *Günlüğü*, pp. 49, 83; BEO, Vilayatdan Gelen catalogue, 12 Ramazan 1331/15 August 1913; Musil, *Neğd*, p. 248.

89. DH.ID 145–1/4, Post and Telegraph Minister to Interior Minister, 31 Mart 1328/12 April 1912; Interior Minister to Post and Telegraph Minister, 7 Nisan 1328/20 April 1912.

Conclusion

1. Zahlan, *Qatar*, pp. 61–68.
2. Finnie, *Lines*, pp. 42–43, 57–61.

Glossary

BEYTÜLMAL MÜDIRI: *sancak* Treasury supervisor.
BUYRULDU: decree (e.g., of appointment to office).
DEVE RÜSUMU: camel tax.
DIRA: range over which a bedouin tribe customarily circulates.
ILTIZAM: tax farm, or contracting out the right to collect taxes.
KAYMAKAM: administrator of a *kaza*.
KAZA: administrative district of a *sancak*.
MECLIS-I DEAVI: claims tribunal (*kaza*).
MECLIS-I IDARE: administrative council at all levels of provincial administration, drawn from local leaders and officials.
MÜDIR: local administrator of the smallest unit (*nahiye*) of the Ottoman provincial hierarchy, serving under a *kaymakam*.
MUTASARRIF: subprovincial governor, administrator of a *sancak*.
MUTASARRIF MUAVINI: deputy governor of a *sancak*.
NAIB: Shari`a court judge.
NAQIB AL-ASHRAF: dean of the local community of descendents of the Prophet Muhammad. The government frequently used members of the family of the Basra *naqib*, including Rajab Efendi and Talib Pasha, for political assignments in Arabia.
ÖŞÜR (AR. `USHR): canonical tithe of agricultural produce levied on settled population.
QANUN/KANUN: secular state law.
RÜSUM-I IHTISABIYE: excise taxes.
SANCAK/MUTASARRIFLIK: district of a *vilayet*, governed by a *mutasarrıf*.
SUBLIME PORTE: office of the Grand Vezir in Istanbul and seat of the central administration of the empire.
TAHRIRAT KÂTIBI: correspondence secretary.
TEMYIZ-I HUKUK: court of appeal (*sancak*).
VALI: governor of a *vilayet*.
VILAYET: province, largest administrative district of the empire.
ZEKÂT (AR. ZAKAT): canonic tax of one-fortieth, levied on bedouin livestock.

Bibliographical Note

There is an excellent reason why this kind of study has not been written before: in comparison to sources of information on many other areas of the Ottoman empire, those concerning eastern Arabia are very limited. Ottoman records in Istanbul are the richest source, yet they are still being catalogued and are not yet fully available for research. Ottoman record collections that were used in preparing this study are described in the following Bibliography section. Important papers produced by Ottoman provincial officials in what are now Iraq and Saudi Arabia, such as court records and tax registers, either have not survived or are at present inaccessible. A few Ottoman official publications that contain valuable information are available, such as the provincial gazettes (*salname*) of Basra and Baghdad. These contain lists of officials, statistics, and accounts of provincial history. The Foreign Ministry also produced a series of pamphlets in 1917 that recounted the development of disputes with Britain in Arabia. Varying in depth of detail, they generally are strongest on recent history and often reproduce important diplomatic notes and agreements.

The other major collections of contemporary records that have survived and are freely open to research are those of the British and Indian governments. They had no representatives stationed in eastern Arabia, except in Kuwait during the last years of the period covered, so the British archives are not as rich concerning mainland affairs as they are for many other Ottoman provinces. These records have been used heavily by scholars of Gulf history, and many of the documents have been published. Robin Bidwell's edited volumes of documents from the Foreign Office Confidential Print make available the most important government correspondence regarding Kuwait and Arabia during the important decade 1896-1906; they are very valuable resources. Bidwell also edited *Arabian Personalities*, a British government guide for political and intelligence officers working in Arabia, originally published in 1917. It gives much useful information about settled and nomadic tribes and other groups. India Office papers have not been published, but the works of J. G. Lorimer and J. A. Saldana are based on Indian records. Composed at a time of tension between the two empires, Lorimer's *Gazetteer* seems to delight in pointing out perceived instances of Ottoman malefaction. Lorimer amassed a wealth of information, however, and his book is an excellent reference tool.

Memoirs and travelogues of a handful of European and Ottoman officials and explorers usefully supplement archival evidence. Pelly and, in particular, Palgrave have left very informative descriptions of central and eastern Arabia just prior to the resurrection of Ottoman rule. Given Ottoman concern about foreign influence, however, very few travelers were permitted in eastern Arabia after 1870. Burchardt and Raunkiaer were rare exceptions. Their unusual access makes their accounts, although sketchy, quite valuable. Useful Ottoman memoirs are similarly uncommon. Ali Haydar Midhat edited *Tabsıra-i Ibret*, part of the autobiography of his father, Midhat Pasha. The book is quite informative concerning Midhat's actions in Iraq and Hasa, as well as his view of events there after his departure from Baghdad in 1872. The other memoirist with personal knowledge of eastern Arabia was Hüseyin Hüsni. His book is partly a description of conditions found in Ottoman Arabia but mostly concerns his experiences as a military officer there, especially in Qasîm in 1904-1906. An outspoken graduate of the elite Harbiye military college, Hüsni found himself serving in remote areas such as Najd, where he thought the Ottoman government was operating in ignorance. Having antagonized Ibn Rashid, out of fear for his life he finally joined the stream of deserters from the Qasîm army. His book explains why he did so. It is both fascinating and informative. The diaries or memoirs of Sultan Abdülhamid II and two grand vezirs, Küçük Said Pasha and Mahmut Şevket Pasha, give views of Gulf affairs from Istanbul after 1900.

Contemporary accounts of affairs written by Arabs are rare. Chroniclers, such as Ibn `Isa, were much more concerned with events in Najd and practically ignored the Ottomans. For Kuwait we have the *Ta'rikh Kuwayt* of `Abd al-`Aziz al-Rashid. Published in 1926, it is a useful account of Mubarak's machinations in search of independence but is of sometimes uncertain accuracy, as it relies heavily on local historical traditions. Yusuf al-Qana`i witnessed many of the events of this period that he described much later in *Safahat min Ta'rikh al-Kuwayt*, which is a condensed history of Kuwait to the death of Shaikh Mubarak.

Western and Arab scholars have written a number of regional histories using the British records and sometimes Arabic sources. Two very thorough works in English are the books by J. B. Kelly and Briton Busch. Based upon records in London, they concentrate on British policies and views. Kelly is too ready to adopt the rather scornful attitude toward the Ottomans and at least in part the Arabs that some British officials had, but both books have become the standards for Gulf history of this period. Ravinder Kumar's book is not as useful, since it is based overwhelmingly on records in India, thus missing much that was decided in London. It does provide some information for the period 1880–1894 that is not covered by Kelly or Busch. Arab historians have also published works based on these sources. The best of these are Jamal Qasim's *Al-Khalij al-`Arabi* and Fuad Hamza's *Qalb Jazirat al-`Arab*. Jens Plass's *England zwischen Russland und Deutschland* is an excellent work that uses otherwise-ignored German and French records. Its main drawback is the short time period of its coverage. Even less well known than German and French papers are the Russian records; Efim Rezvan has fortunately published translations of some very interesting reports of Russian officials who visited the Gulf in his *Russian Ships in the Gulf, 1899–1903*.

Several accounts of individual countries are certainly worth reading. Mahmud Sinan and `Abd al-`Aziz al-Mansur have written solid histories of Qatar. Mansur and Futuh al-Khatrash have also published the very useful *Masadir Ta'rikh Qatar*, which includes summaries of about sixty Ottoman documents in Doha. Jill Crystal's books should be consulted for their comments on the nature of society and the role of shaikhs in Kuwait and Qatar, although they concentrate on the post-1914 period. Anyone interested in the subject of traditional leadership in Arabia before the intrusion of outside powers must read Peter Lienhardt's illuminating article on the domestic political limits under which Gulf Arab shaikhs operated. Bayly Winder's *Saudi Arabia in the Nineteenth Century* is the standard history of Najd in this period and makes good use of Arabic chronicles as well as Western accounts. Winder concentrates on political history; for a provocative look at socioeconomic change induced by European penetration into the region, see Naqeeb's *Society and State in the Gulf*. Jacob Goldberg's book gives an interesting account of Ibn Saud's practical Great Power diplomacy, by which he sought to minimize the threat from his would-be Ottoman overlords, a policy earlier followed by Mubarak al-Sabah and Qâsim al-Thani.

It is never wise to study an area in isolation, so it is fortunate that solid studies of neighboring countries in the Gulf and Arabia are available.

Using British records, Talal Farah has written a very good study of Bahrain from the accession of Shaikh ʿIsa to World War I. Robert Landen's book is authoritative on developments in Oman in this period. As Busch did for the Gulf, R. J. Gavin has produced a very sound study of Aden under British rule. He gives some information on Ottoman views of tribal problems that were also present in eastern Arabia. Iraq is surprisingly understudied. Because so little has been published in English on Iraq before 1900, Longrigg's old study remains the main guide to the period. ʿAzzawi's multivolume chronicle of Iraq contains useful facts gleaned from Ottoman and Arabic sources but is not an integrative history. Some good articles on narrower aspects of Iraq in the last century, such as those by Jwaideh and Deringil, have filled a few of the historiographical gaps.

In recent years a number of works have been published that also allow comparison of eastern Arabia's experiences with those of other Ottoman provinces in the Middle East. William Ochsenwald has written an excellent account of the Hijaz under Ottoman rule during the Tanzimat and Hamidian periods. His book details the structure of, and change in, society in western Arabia. It also discusses a number of problems that confronted the Ottomans on the eastern side of the peninsula as well. Palestine has been well studied, and the works of Gerber and Kushner about Jerusalem are very illuminating about Ottoman methods of administration. Engin Akarlı's *The Long Peace* is a welcome addition to the historiography on Lebanon, which previously slighted the Ottoman role in that territory's post-1860 development. Michel Le Gall similarly brings to light for the first time much information about Ottoman rule in Libya before the Italian conquest. Eugene Rogan presents an excellent sketch of social and political trends in Transjordan, another of the understudied desert, tribal territories of the Ottoman empire, with which useful comparisons to Ottoman Arabia can be traced. Rogan's forthcoming book, *Ottomans, Merchants, and Missionaries*, should plug a large hole in current knowledge of the nineteenth-century Middle East.

Finally, a few works that help to give a broader perspective on the Ottoman empire in this era should be mentioned. Two classic studies of reform and change in the empire are Bernard Lewis' *The Emergence of Modern Turkey* and Roderic Davison's *Reform in the Ottoman Empire*. They are still highly regarded and are recommended reading. Carter Findley has done admirable work on the bureaucratic history of the empire. Charles Issawi's series of nineteenth-century Middle Eastern economic history books are excellent introductions to a field that is still less clearly understood than is its political history. Jacob Landau's book is recommended for those interested in the role of Pan-Islam in Sultan

Abdülhamid II's state. For the general diplomatic history of the age, M. S. Anderson's *The Eastern Question* remains the standard. It is based on Western European sources and pays remarkably little attention to the Ottoman perspective, despite the empire's inevitably central role in the piece. The course of relations with Europe after 1798 is but one of many topics in Ottoman history that still awaits proper treatment.

Bibliography

Unpublished Archival Sources

Almost all of the Ottoman government documents that form the base of this study were found in the Başbakanlık Arşivi in Istanbul. They were drawn from five broad collections and one uncatalogued dossier.

Bab-i Ali Evrak Odası Ayniyat (Ayniyat): Correspondence issuing from the Grand Vezir's office to other ministries and to the provinces was copied in the defters (registers) of this collection. Five defters (848–852) contain copies of messages to Baghdad and Basra in the period from 1866 to 1879; some correspondence from 1879 to 1892 is also to be found in the Arabian Provinces (Arabistan Vilâyetleri) defters (1516–1525). This system was discontinued in 1892 and replaced by the BEO Gelen-Giden system.

Bab-i Ali Evrak Odası Gelen-Giden (BEO): This voluminous collection (over 300,000 files) contains the rough drafts of correspondence from the Grand Vezir's office to the various ministries and provincial authorities beginning in 1892. Files often include copies of relevant correspondence, and the numbers of previous related files are usually noted on the front cover of individual drafts. Although the correspondence coming to the Grand Vezir was not systematically saved, the contents of messages were summarized in catalogues covering each province or ministry (e.g., Basra'dan Gelen) with the numbers of related draft files noted.

Dahiliye Nezareti (DH): Correspondence and memoranda of the Interior Ministry have recently been catalogued and opened up for research. Almost all of the documents date from the twentieth century and, divided into thirteen subclassifications, concern a broad array of administrative issues. Subclassifications used in this study include Idare (DH.ID), Kalem-i Mahsûs (DH.KMS), and Muhâberât-ı Umûmiye Idaresi (DH.MUI). As in the BEO collection, each dossier contains the draft of a message and copies of documents concerning the issue addressed.

Irade: An irade was a decree issued by the sultan. An irade often resembled a file rather than a simple order: it might contain not only a proposal from the Grand

Vezir, at the bottom of which the sultan's chief secretary wrote an authorization for action, but also the papers which led the Grand Vezir to make his recommendations. These documents could include messages and memoranda from provincial authorities and ministers in Istanbul. Irades were classified by the governmental department concerned in the immediate problem; most of the decrees mentioned in this work were addressed to the Interior Ministry (Dahiliye), but others involved the Council of Ministers (Meclis-i Mahsus-i Vükela) or were more broadly phrased demands for information or action generated from the Palace instead of the Porte (Hususiye). Irades were numbered in sequence by department (e.g., Dahiliye 44930) until 1892, when they began to be numbered in recurring sequences every month (e.g., 1312-N-33=33d Irade of Ramazan 1312).

Meclis-i Vükela Mazbataları (MV): These papers, collated as defters, summarize discussions about issues brought to the attention of the Council of Ministers (the "cabinet" of the Ottoman government in Istanbul). Each entry includes a brief summary of the problem under consideration and of the Council's recommendation for action.

Şûrâ-yı Devlet Evrakları (ŞD): The Council of State (Şûrâ-yı Devlet) dealt with issues involving state administrative affairs, including judicial matters and complaints about officials. Dossiers of documents involved in discussion of some issues were kept and have recently been opened for research. Given the absence or unavailability of court records and foreign consular reports from eastern Arabia, the documents in this collection are especially valuable for gaining a clearer picture of common life and practices in the area under the Ottomans.

Usul-i Irade Dosya 77: This is an uncatalogued package of papers concerning three long-running problems with Britain: Kuwait, Yemen, and `Aqaba. The messages and reports in these files were key documents underlying important decrees issued by the sultan over the years addressing these disputes.

Yıldız-Bab-i Asafi: Correspondence from the Grand Vezir to Sultan Abdülhamid II has been divided into several document classifications, all of which are identified by the initial abbreviation Y-A (e.g., Y-A Kâmil). The most broadly based collection is that marked Y-A Resmî, which contains files on matters of particular interest to Abdülhamid from throughout his reign. Other collections (e.g. Kâmil, Mâruzat, Hususî) contain documents related to more specific matters or officials. Much like the Irades, these files contain background documents, such as petitions or dispatches from the provinces.

Yıldız Esas Evrakları (YEE): Sultan Abdülhamid II collected documents that particularly interested him in a private library in the Yıldız Palace. He kept a wide variety of papers, but typical of this classification are reports on thorny problems and provincial issues, proposals for reform, and messages from important Muslim Arab leaders, such as Ibn Rashid.

Yıldız-Mütenevvî Mâruzât (Y.MTV): As the name of this classification suggests, its contents include reports to Abdülhamid II on the entire spectrum of domestic and foreign issues in which the sultan was interested. This collection is the correspondence coming from departments and people outside of the Grand Vezir's office. Its files are generally much briefer than those in the other Yıldız classifications noted above.

BIBLIOGRAPHY

Another collection of Ottoman documents that includes papers related to Arabian affairs is in the Sts. Cyril and Methodius National Library (KMNB) in Sofia, Bulgaria. These documents, in which correspondence about financial matters predominates, were sold to Bulgaria as scrap paper in 1931. The purchasers fortunately recognized the value of the documents and preserved them, although many of the papers had been torn apart. These documents concern all periods and parts of the Ottoman empire.

Published Sources

Abdülhamit, Sultan. *Siyasi Hatıratım.* Istanbul: ARBA, 1987.
Abu `Alieh, `Abd al-Fattah. "Dirasa Ta'rikhiya liMawqif al-Ahsa min al-Istratijiya al-`Uthmaniya." *Al-Dara* 1, no. 4 (December 1975): 116–31.
———. "Al-`Uthmaniyun wa Banu Khalid fil-Ahsa." *Revue d'Histoire Maghrebine* 10, no. 29–30 (July 1983).
Abu Hakima, Ahmad Mustafa. *History of Eastern Arabia, 1750–1800: The Rise and Development of Bahrain and Kuwait.* Beirut: Khayats, 1965.
———. *The Modern History of Kuwait, 1750–1965.* London: Luzac, 1983.
Abu Manneh, B. "Sultan Abdulhamid II and Shaikh Abulhuda al-Sayyadi." *Middle Eastern Studies* 15, no. 2 (May 1979): 131–53.
Agmon, Iris. "The Bedouin Tribes of the Hûla and Baysân Valleys at the End of the Ottoman Rule According to *Wilâyat Bayrût*." *International Journal of Turkish Studies* 5, no. 1 (1990–91): 47–69.
Ahmida, Ali Abdullatif. *The Making of Modern Libya: State Formation, Colonization, and Resistance, 1830–1932.* Albany: State University of New York Press, 1994.
Akarlı, Engin. "Economic Policy and Budgets in Ottoman Turkey, 1876–1909." *Middle Eastern Studies* 28, no. 3 (July 1992).
———. *The Long Peace: Ottoman Lebanon, 1861–1920.* Berkeley: University of California Press, 1993.
Amr, Saleh Muhammad. *The Hijaz Under Ottoman Rule 1869–1914: Ottoman Vali, the Sharif of Mecca, and the Growth of British Influence.* Riyadh: Riyad University Publications, 1978.
Anderson, M. S. *The Eastern Question, 1774–1923: A Study in International Relations.* New York: St. Martin's Press, 1966.
`Azzawi, `Abbas. *Ta'rikh al-`Iraq bayna Ihtilalayna*, vols. 7–8. Baghdad: Sharika al-Tijara wal-Tiba`a al-Mahduda, 1955–56.
Bailey, Clinton. "The Ottomans and the Bedouin Tribes of the Negev." In Gad G. Gilbar, ed., *Ottoman Palestine, 1800–1914: Studies in Economic and Social History*, pp. 321–32. Leiden: E. J. Brill, 1990.
Bağdad Vilayeti Salnamesi. Baghdad Matbaası, 1301/1883–84.
Basra Vilayeti Salnamesi. Basra Matbaası, 1308/1890–91.
Basra Vilayeti Salnamesi. Basra Matbaası, 1318/1900–1901.
Bidwell, Robin, ed. *The Affairs of Arabia, 1905–1906*, 2 vols. London: Frank Cass, 1971.

BIBLIOGRAPHY

———. *The Affairs of Kuwait, 1896–1905*, 2 vols. London: Frank Cass, 1971.
———. *Arabian Personalities of the Early Twentieth Century*. New York: Oleander Press, 1986.
Bose, M. L. "Eastern Himalayan Frontier and Development of Government Therein During the British Period." In N. R. Ray, ed., *Himalaya Frontier in Historical Perspective*, pp. 127–43. Calcutta: Institute of Historical Studies, 1986.
Bostan, Idris. "Basra Körfezinin Güney Kesimi ve Osmanlılar (1876–1908)." *Osmanlı Araştırmaları* 9 (1989): 311–22.
———. "The 1893 Uprising in Qatar and Sheikh Al Sâni's Letter to Abdülhamid II." *Studies on Turkish-Arab Relations* 2 (1987): 81–89.
———. "Muhammad Hilâl Efendi'nin Yemen'e Dair Iki Lâyihası." *Osmanlı Araştırmaları* 3 (1982): 301–26.
———. "Zor Sancağı'nın Imâr ve Islâhı Ile Alâkalı Üç Lâyiha." *Osmanlı Araştırmaları* 6, (1986): 163–220.
Burchardt, Hermann. "Ost-Arabien von Basra bis Maskat auf Grund eigener Reisen." *Zeitschrift der Gesellschaft für Erdkunde zu Berlin* (1906): 305–22.
Busch, Briton C. *Britain and the Persian Gulf, 1894–1914*. Berkeley: University of California Press, 1967.
———. "Britain and the Status of Kuwait, 1896–1899." *Middle East Journal* (Spring 1967): 187–98.
Buzpınar, Ş. Tufan. "Abdülhamid II and Sayyid Fadl Pasha of Hadramawt: An Arab Dignitary's Ambitions (1876–1900)." *Osmanlı Araştırmaları* 13 (1993): 227–39.
———. "The Hijaz, Abdulhamid II, and Amir Hussein's Secret Dealings with the British, 1877–1880." *Middle Eastern Studies* 31, no. 1 (January 1995): 99–123.
Cheesman, R. E. *In Unknown Arabia*. London: Macmillan, 1926.
Choudhury, D. P. "Evolution of British Tribal Policy in the North-East Frontier of India (1865–1814)." In N. R. Ray, ed., *Himalaya Frontier in Historical Perspective*, pp. 113–26. Calcutta: Institute of Historical Studies, 1986.
Cottrell, Alvin J. et al., eds. *The Persian Gulf States: A General Survey*. Baltimore: Johns Hopkins University Press, 1980.
Crystal, Jill. *Kuwait: The Transformation of an Oil State*. Boulder: Westview Press, 1992.
———. *Oil and Politics in the Gulf: Rulers and Merchants in Kuwait and Qatar*. New York: Cambridge University Press, 1990.
Davison, Roderic H. *Reform in the Ottoman Empire, 1856–1876*. Princeton, N.J.: Princeton University Press, 1963.
Deringil, Selim. "The Struggle Against Shiism in Hamidian Iraq: A Study in Ottoman Counter-Propaganda." *Die Welt des Islams* 30 (1990): 45–62.
Dickson, Harold R. P. *Kuwait and Her Neighbors*. London: George Allen and Unwin, 1956.
Euting, Julius. *Tagbuch einer Reise in Inner-Arabien*. Leiden: E. J. Brill, 1896 and 1914.
Farah, Caesar. "The Anglo-Ottoman Confrontation in Yemen, 1840–1849." *International Journal of Turkish Studies* 3, no. 2 (1985–86): 69–93.
Farah, Caesar, ed. *Decision Making and Change in the Ottoman Empire*. Kirksville, Mo.: Thomas Jefferson University Press at North East Missouri State University, 1993.

BIBLIOGRAPHY

Farah, Talal Toufic. *Protection and Politics in Bahrain, 1869–1915*. Beirut: American University of Beirut, 1985.
Findley, Carter V. *Bureaucratic Reform in the Ottoman Empire: The Sublime Porte, 1789–1922*. Princeton, N.J.: Princeton University Press, 1980.
———. "Decision-Making in the Ottoman Empire." In *V. Milletlerarası Türkiye Sosyal ve Iktisat Tarihi Kongresi*, pp. 867–77. Ankara: Türk Tarih Kurumu, 1990.
———. "The Evolution of the System of Provincial Administration as Viewed from the Center." In David Kushner, ed., *Palestine in the Late Ottoman Period: Political, Economic, and Social Transformation*, pp. 3–29. Leiden: E. J. Brill, 1986.
Finnie, David. *Shifting Lines in the Sand: Kuwait's Elusive Frontier with Iraq*. Cambridge: Harvard University Press, 1992.
Gavin, R. J. *Aden Under British Rule, 1839–1967*. New York: Barnes and Noble Books, 1975.
Gerber, Haim. *Ottoman Rule in Jerusalem, 1890–1914*. Berlin: Klaus Schwarz Verlag, 1985.
Gharayiba, `Abd al-Karim M. *Muqaddima Ta'rikh al-`Arab al-Hadith, 1500–1918, al-Juz' al-Awwal: al-`Iraq wal-Jazira al-`Arabiya*. Damascus: Matba`a Jami`a Dimashq, 1960.
Gillard, David, ed. *British Documents on Foreign Affairs: Reports and Papers from the Foreign Office Confidential Print*. Part I, Series B, vols. 17 and 18. N.p.: University Publications of America, 1985.
Gilmartin, David. *Empire and Islam: Punjab and the Making of Pakistan*. Berkeley: University of California Press, 1988.
Goldberg, Jacob. *The Foreign Policy of Saudi Arabia: The Formative Years, 1902–1918*. Cambridge: Harvard University Press, 1986.
———. "The 1913 Saudi Occupation of Hasa Reconsidered." *Middle Eastern Studies* 18, no. 1 (January 1982): 21–29.
Göyünç, Nejat. "Trablusgarb'a Ait Bir Lâyiha." *Osmanlı Araştırmaları* 1 (1980): 233–46.
Hagopian, V. H. *Ottoman-Turkish Conversation-Grammar*. London: Groos, 1907.
Halaçoğlu, Yusuf. "Midhat Paşa'nın Necid ve Havalisi ile Ilgili bir Kaç Lâyihası." *IÜEF Tarih Enstitüsü Dergisi* 3 (1972): 149–76.
Harraz, Muhammad Rajab. *Al-Dawla al-`Uthmaniya wa Shibh Jazira al-`Arab, 1840–1909*. Cairo: al-Matba`a al-`Alamiya, 1970.
Hüsni, Hüseyin. *Necd Kıtası'nın Ahval-i Umumiyesi*. Istanbul: Matbaa-yi Ebüzziya, 1328/1910.
Ibn `Isa, Ibrahim b. Salih. *Ta'rikh Ba`d al-Hawadith al-Waqi`a fi Najd*. Riyadh: Dar al-Yamama lil-Bahth wal-Tarjama wal-Nashr, 1966.
Ilhan, Mehmet M. "The Katif District (Liva) During the First Few Years of Ottoman Rule: A Study of the 1551 Ottoman Cadastral Survey." *Belleten* 51, no. 200 (1987): 781–98.
Inalcık, Halil. "Ottoman Methods of Conquest." *Studia Islamica* 2 (1954): 103–29.
———. "Recession of the Ottoman Empire and the Rise of the Saudi State." *Studies on Turkish-Arab Relations* 3 (1988): 67–85.
Issawi, Charles. *The Economic History of Turkey, 1800–1914*. Chicago: University of Chicago Press, 1980.

BIBLIOGRAPHY

———. *The Fertile Crescent, 1800–1914: A Documentary Economic History*. New York: Oxford University Press, 1988.
Issawi, Charles, ed. *The Economic History of the Middle East, 1800–1914: A Book of Readings*. Chicago: University of Chicago Press, 1975.
Jwaideh, Albertine. "Midhat Pasha and the Land System of Lower Iraq." In Albert Hourani, ed., *St. Antony's Papers 16: Middle Eastern Affairs 3*. Carbondale: Southern Illinois University Press, 1963.
Karal, Enver Ziya. *Osmanlı Tarihi*, vol. 8: *Birinci Meşrutiyet ve Istibdat Devirleri (1876–1907)*. Ankara: Türk Tarih Kurumu Basımevi, 1988.
Kelly, John B. *Britain and the Persian Gulf, 1795–1880*. Oxford: Clarendon Press, 1968.
———. "Salisbury, Curzon, and the Kuwait Agreement of 1899." In K. Bourne and D. C. Watt, eds., *Studies in International History*. Hamden, Conn.: Archon Books, 1967.
Khatrash, Futuh A. and `Abd al-`Aziz M. al-Mansur. *Masadir Ta'rikh Qatar, 1868–1916*. Kuwait: Dar Dhat al-Salasil, 1984.
Khatrash, Futuh A. *Ta'rikh al-`Alaqat al-Siyasiya al-Baritaniya al-Kuwaytiya, 1890–1921*. Kuwait: Dar Dhat al-Salasil, 1974.
Khaz`al, Husayn Khalaf Shaikh. *Ta'rikh al-Kuwayt al-Siyasi*. Beirut: Matba`a Dar al-Kutub, 1962.
Khususi, Badr al-Din A. *Dirasat fi Ta'rikh al-Khalij al-`Arabi al-Hadith wal-Mu`asir, al-Juz' al-Thani*. Kuwait: Dar Dhat al-Salasil, 1988.
Kornrumpf, Hans-Jürgen. "Zur Osmanischen Herrschaft in Innerarabien im 19. und 20. Jahrhundert." In *VIII. Türk Tarih Kongresi, III. Cilt*, pp. 1581–1591. Ankara: Türk Tarih Kurumu Basımevi, 1983.
———. "Die Osmanische Herrschaft auf der Arabischen Halbinsel im 19. Jahrhundert." *Saeculum* 31, no. 4 (1980): 399–408.
———. "Neuere Beschreibungen von al-Hasa in Amtlichen Osmanischen Veröffentlichungen." *Der Islam* 55 (1987): 74–92.
Kumar, Ravinder. *India and the Persian Gulf Region, 1858–1907: A Study in British Imperial Policy*. New York: Asia, 1965.
Kushner, David. "Ali Ekrem Bey, Governor of Jerusalem, 1906–1908." *International Journal of Middle East Studies* 28, no. 3 (August 1996): 349–62.
———. "The Ottoman Governors of Palestine, 1864–1914." *Middle Eastern Studies* 23, no. 3 (July 1987): 274–90.
Landau, Jacob. *The Politics of Pan-Islam: Ideology and Organization*. New York: Oxford University Press, 1990.
Landen, Robert G. *Oman since 1856: Disruptive Modernization in a Traditional Arab Society*. Princeton, N.J.: Princeton University Press, 1967.
Le Gall, Michel. "Pashas, Bedouins and Notables: Ottoman Administration in Tripolitania and Benghazi, 1881–1902." Ph.D. dissertation (Near Eastern Studies), Princeton University, 1986.
Lewis, Bernard. *The Emergence of Modern Turkey*. New York: Oxford University Press, 1979.
Lewis, Norman. *Nomads and Settlers in Syria and Jordan, 1800–1980*. New York: Cambridge University Press, 1987.
Lienhardt, Peter. "The Authority of Shaikhs in the Gulf: An Essay in Nineteenth-

BIBLIOGRAPHY

Century History." In R. B. Serjeant and R. L. Bidwell, eds., *Arabian Studies*, vol. II, pp. 61–75. London: C. Hurst, 1975.
Longrigg, Stephen H. *Four Centuries of Modern Iraq*. Oxford: Clarendon Press, 1925.
Lorimer, J. G. *Gazetteer of the Persian Gulf, Oman, and Central Arabia*, vol. I: *Historical*. Calcutta: Superintendent Government Printing, 1915.
Mandaville, Jon E. "The Ottoman Province of al-Hasa in the Sixteenth and Seventeenth Centuries." *Journal of the American Oriental Society* 90 (1970): 486–513.
Mansur, `Abd al-`Aziz M. *Al-Kuwayt wa `Alaqatuha bi`Arabistan wal-Basra, 1896–1915*. Kuwait: Dar Dhat al-Salasil, 1980.
——. *Al-Tatawwur al-Siyasi liQatar fi al-Fatra ma bayna 1868–1916*. Kuwait: Dar Dhat al-Salasil, 1980.
Midhat, Ali Haydar. *Tabsıra-i Ibret*. Istanbul, 1325/1907.
Miles, S. B. *The Countries and Tribes of the Persian Gulf*. London: Harrison, 1919.
Moon, Sir Penderel. *The British Conquest and Dominion of India*. London: Gerald Duckworth, 1989.
Musil, Alois. *Northern Neğd: A Topographical Itinerary*. New York: American Geographical Society, 1928.
Naqeeb, Khaldoun Hasan. *Society and State in the Gulf and Arab Peninsula: A Different Perspective*. New York: Routledge, 1990.
Nolde, Baron Eduard. *Reise nach Innerarabien, Kurdistan, und Armenien, 1892*. Braunschweig: Friedrich Vieweg, 1895.
Ochsenwald, William. *The Hijaz Railroad*. Charlottesville: University of Virginia Press, 1980.
——. *Religion, Society, and the State in Arabia: The Hijaz Under Ottoman Control, 1840–1908*. Columbus: Ohio State University Press, 1984.
——. "The Impact of Ottoman Rule on Yemen, 1849–1914." In *V. Milletlerarası Türkiye Sosyal ve Iktisat Tarihi Kongresi*, pp. 255–65. Ankara: Türk Tarih Kurumu, 1990.
Ottoman Foreign Ministry. *Bagdad Hattı ve Basra Körfezine Müteallık Ingiltere Mutalabatı Hakkındaki Lâyiha ve Marbutatı*. Istanbul: Matbaa-yi Amire, 1327.
——. *Bahreyn Adaları Meselesi*. Istanbul: Matbaa-yi Amire, 1334.
——. *Kuveyt Meselesi*. Istanbul: Matbaa-yi Amire, 1334.
——. *Maskat Meselesi*. Istanbul: Matbaa-yi Amire, 1334.
——. *Muhammara Meselesi*. Istanbul: Matbaa-yi Amire, 1334.
——. *Necd Kıt'ası Meselesi*. Istanbul: Matbaa-yi Amire, 1334.
——. *Şattülarab Meselesi*. Istanbul: Matbaa-yi Amire, 1334.
Özbaran, Salih. "A Note on the Ottoman Administration in Arabia in the Sixteenth Century." *International Journal of Turkish Studies* 3, no. 1 (1984–85): 93–99.
Pakalın, Mehmed Z. *Son Sadrâzamlar ve Başvekiller*, I. Cild. Istanbul: Ahmet Sait Matbaası, 1940.
Palgrave, William G. *Personal Narrative of a Year's Journey Through Central and Eastern Arabia, 1862–63*. London: Macmillan, 1883.
Pelly, Lewis. *Report on a Journey to Riyadh*. New York: Oleander Press, 1978.
Pfullmann, Uwe. "Şammar-Emirat, Sa`udischer Staat, und Kuweit im Spannungsfeld der politischen Interessen der europäischen Mächte und des Osmanischen Reiches 1821–1914." *Asien, Afrika, Lateinamerika* 18 (1990): 643–53.

BIBLIOGRAPHY

Philby, H. St. John B. *The Heart of Arabia: A Record of Travel and Exploration.* London: Constable, 1922.

Philipp, H. J. "Alte und Neue Probleme in Agrarwirtschaft und Agrargesellschaft der Oase al-Hasa (Saudi-Arabien)." *Orient* 28, no. 1 (1987): 38–65.

Plass, Jens B. *England zwischen Russland und Deutschland: Der Persische Golf in der Britischen Vorkriegspolitik, 1899–1907.* Hamburg: Institut für Auswärtige Politik, 1966.

Qana`i, Yusuf b. `Isa. *Safahat min Ta'rikh al-Kuwayt.* Kuwait: Dar Dhat al-Salasil, 1988.

Qasim, Jamal Zakariya. *Al-Khalij al-`Arabi: Dirasa liTa'rikh al-Imarat al-`Arabiya (1840–1914).* Cairo: Matba`a Jami`a `Ayn Shams, 1966.

Rasheed, Madawi. *Politics in an Arabian Oasis: The Rashidi Tribal Dynasty.* New York: I. B. Tauris, 1991.

Rasheed, Madawi and Loulouwa al-Rasheed. "The Politics of Encapsulation: Saudi Policy Towards Tribal and Religious Opposition." *Middle Eastern Studies* 32, no. 1 (January 1996): 96–119.

Rashid, `Abd al-`Aziz. *Ta'rikh Kuwayt, al-Juz' al-Thani min al-Qism al-Awwal.* Baghdad, 1926.

Rashid, Ibrahim, ed. *Documents on the History of Saudi Arabia,* vol. 1: *The Unification of Central Arabia Under Ibn Saud, 1909–1925.* Salisbury, N.C.: Documentary Publications, 1976.

Raunkiaer, Barclay. *Through Wahhabiland on Camelback.* Gerald de Gaury, trans. London: Routledge & Kegan Paul, 1969.

Rezvan, Efim. *Russian Ships in the Gulf, 1899–1903.* Reading, U.K.: Ithaca Press, 1993.

Rihani, Amin. *Ta'rikh Najd wa Mulhaqatihi.* Beirut: Mu'assasa Dar al-Rayhani, 1970.

Rogan, Eugene. "Aşiret Mektebi: Abdülhamid II's School for Tribes." *International Journal of Middle East Studies* 28, no. 1 (February 1996): 83–107.

———. "Bringing the State Back: The Limits of Ottoman Rule in Transjordan, 1840–1910." In Eugene Rogan and Tariq Tell, eds., *Village, Steppe, and State: The Social Origins of Modern Jordan,* pp. 32–57. New York: British Academic Press, 1994.

Rush, Alan. *Al-Sabah: History and Genealogy of Kuwait's Ruling Family, 1752–1987.* Atlantic Highlands, N.J.: Ithaca Press, 1987.

Safran, Nadav. *Saudi Arabia: The Ceaseless Quest for Security.* Ithaca: Cornell University Press, 1985.

Said Pasha, Küçük. *Said Paşa'nın Hatıratı.* Istanbul: Sabah Matbaası, 1328/1910.

Saldana, J. A. *Persian Gulf Gazetteer, part 1: Historical and Political Materials. Precis of Nejd Affairs, 1804–1904.* Calcutta, 1906.

———. *Precis of Koweit Affairs, 1896–1904.* Calcutta, 1906.

———. *Precis of Turkish Expansion on the Arab Littoral of the Persian Gulf and Hasa and Qatif Affairs.* Calcutta, 1906.

Salibi, Kamal. *A History of Arabia.* Delmar, N.Y.: Caravan Books, 1980.

Salih, Nuriya Muhammad Nasir. *`Alaqat al-Kuwayt al-Siyasiya biSharqi al-Jazira al-`Arabiya wal-`Iraq al-`Uthmani, 1866–1902.* Kuwait: Dar Dhat al-Salasil, 1977.

BIBLIOGRAPHY

Şevket Pasha, Mahmut. *Mahmut Şevket Paşa'nın Günlüğü*. Istanbul: ARBA, 1988.
Shaw, Stanford and Ezel K. Shaw. *History of the Ottoman Empire and Modern Turkey*, vol. 2. New York: Cambridge University Press, 1977.
Sinan, Mahmud B. *Ta'rikh Qatar al-`Amm*. Baghdad: Matba`a al-Ma`arif, 1966.
Şimşir, Bilal N. "Midhat Paşa'nın Ikinci Sadrazamlığı ve Ingiltere." In *Uluslararası Midhat Paşa Semineri: Bildiriler ve Tartışmalar*. Ankara: Türk Tarih Kurumu Basımevi, 1986.
Tauber, Eliezer. "Sayyid Talib and the Young Turks in Basra." *Middle Eastern Studies* 25 (January 1989).
Twitchell, K. S. *Saudi Arabia, with an Account of the Development of Its Natural Resources*. Princeton, N.J.: Princeton University Press, 1953.
Wilkinson, John C. *Arabia's Frontiers: The Story of Britain's Boundary Drawing in the Desert*. New York: I. B. Tauris, 1991.
Winder, R. Bayly. *Saudi Arabia in the Nineteenth Century*. New York: St. Martin's Press, 1965.
Wratislaw, A. C. *A Consul in the East*. London: Blackwood, 1924.
Yapp, M. E. "The Modernization of Middle Eastern Armies in the Nineteenth Century." In V. J. Parry and M. E. Yapp, eds., *War, Technology, and Science in the Middle East*, pp. 330–66. New York: Oxford University Press, 1975.
Yasamee, F. A. K. "Abdülhamid II and the Ottoman Defence Problem." *Diplomacy and Statecraft* 4, no. 1 (March 1993): 20–36.
Yücel, Yaşar. "Midhat Paşa'nın Bağdat Vilayetindeki Alt Yapı Yatırımları." In *Uluslararası Midhat Paşa Semineri: Bildiriler ve Tartışmalar*. Ankara: Türk Tarih Kurumu Basımevi, 1986.
Zahlan, Rosemarie Said. *The Creation of Qatar*. New York: Barnes and Noble Books, 1979.

Index

`Abd al-`Aziz al-Rashid, see Ibn Rashid
`Abd al-`Aziz al-Sa`ud, see Ibn Sa`ud
`Abdallah al-Sabah, 22, 92
`Abdallah al-Thani, 173, 237n23
`Abdallah b. Faisal al-Sa`ud, 13, 17, 20, 22–25, 30, 31, 64, 185n23; deposition of, 48–49; Hasa, taxation of, 37, 40; Midhat Pasha and, 46–49, 168; murder of, 69; Ottoman policy toward, 61, 62
`Abd al-Rahman b. Faisal al-Sa`ud, 61, 63, 64, 93, 117, 136, 155, 156
Abdülaziz, 17, 57
Abdülhamid II, 6, 18, 29, 68, 70, 75, 78, 79, 82; Basra food embargo, 126, 127; British-Kuwait status quo agreement (1901), 123, 124, 126, 127, 128, 132; deposition of, 139, 159, 162; Ibn Rashid and, 154, 156–59; Ibn Sa`ud and, 160; Islamism, 108, 209nn127, 128; Kuwait problem, 99, 104, 116, 120, 121, 134; and Mubarak al-Sabah, 125, 139; Mubarak-Ibn Rashid conflict, 119
Abu Dhabi, 26, 66, 72, 147
Aden, 19, 29
Agriculture: governmental interference with, 144; in Hasa, 36–40, 59; in Hufuf, 81; tribal problems and, 43, 44, 46; see also Date farming

Ahmad al-Thani, 88, 89, 145–48
Ahmad Pasha, 109
`Ajman, 12, 31, 35, 65, 66, 161, 163; Midhat's policy toward, 43–44; Mubarak al-Sabah's relations with, 109; Ottoman defeat of, 43, 48; Ottoman policy toward, 61, 63; Qâsim al-Thani, support of, 147; Said Pasha's policy toward, 151; size, 194n47
Akif Pasha, 64, 83–84
Al Bu`Aynayn, 149
Algeria, 19
`Ali al-Khalifa (nephew of `Isa b. `Ali al-Khalifa), 234n126
Ali Pasha, 17, 18, 57
Al Khalifa, 14, 31; shaikhs of Bahrain, 176
al-Khawr, shaikh of, 32
Al Murra, 12, 31, 35, 65, 85, 161; Ahmad al-Thani, support of, 147; Midhat's policy toward, 43–44; Ottoman defeat of, 43, 48; Ottoman policy toward, 61, 63; Said Pasha's policy toward, 151; size, 194n47
Al Rashid, 17, 68, 90; amirs of Ha'il, 175; Najd, Rashidi-Sa`udi conflict in, 134, 136, 137, 140, 153–59, 161
Al Sabah, 14, 31, 55, 92, date groves, 93, 104, 130; *Haripasa* piracy case, 101;

INDEX

Al Sabah, . . . (Continued)
  shaikhs of Kuwait, 176
Al Sa`ud, 13, 14, 62, 64, 69; amirs of
  Riyadh, 175; in Hasa, 45, 48, 49;
  intrafamily feuds, 67; Mubarak and,
  117–18; Najd, Rashidi-Sa`udi conflict
  in, 134, 136, 137, 140, 153–59, 161;
  tribal problems, 66
Al Thani, 14, 31, 32, 33, 55; shaikhs of
  Qatar, 176
`Ammara, 86
`Anayza, 156, 157
`Anaza, 23
Anglo-Arab agreements, 73–74, 77
Anglo-Ottoman accord (1913), 3, 162,
  163
Anglo-Ottoman commercial convention
  (1838), 14
Anglo-Qatari agreement (1868), 88
Arab Gulf, see Persian Gulf
Arabia, 1–5; geography, 9; history,
  12–15; Ottoman empire's return of
  interest in, in nineteenth century,
  16–20; society, 9–12; see also Persian
  Gulf; and specific political divisions,
  e.g., Najd; Yemen
Arab tribal groups, 4, 11, 12; Ibn Rashid
  and, 154; Ibn Sa`ud and, 154;
  Midhat's approach to, 42–49, 52;
  Ottoman policy toward, 42, 65–69,
  72, 142, 156, 168–69, 172; Riza Ali's
  concern with, 77–78; Said Pasha's
  policy toward, 151; Talib Pasha's policy toward, 151; weaponry, 67; see
  also Bedouins; names of specific
  tribal groups, e.g., `Ajman; Bani
  Hajir
Arif Pasha, 98, 100–3, 106
Armenian pogroms, 101
Arms, trade and smuggling of, 3, 18, 67,
  92, 171; Khawr Zubayr, 129;
  Mubarak al-Sabah and, 135, 136,
  226n20; Qatar, 144–45; Said Pasha
  and, 151
Asia, Ottoman interests in, 18, 19, 20
`Asir, 19
`Asiri tribes, 154
Assab, 77

Asur (steamer), 22, 24, 26, 27
`Azzan b. Qays, sons of, 68

Baghdad, province of, 76, 80
Baghdad Railway, 116–17, 121, 129, 133
Bahrain, 3, 20, 23, 25, 29, 32, 172, 173;
  `Abd al-Rahman in, 63; Al Khalifa
  shaikhs of, 176; arms trade, 67;
  British interests and influence in, 1,
  18, 22, 73–74; Hasa, blockade of, 27;
  history, 14, 15; Muhammad al-
  Khalifa's invasion of, 26; Ottoman-
  British agreement (1913), 162;
  Ottoman presence in, 84; piracy, 71,
  73; Qatar, rivalry with, 70; Qatif and
  Dammam, blockade of, 22, 24;
  Shari`a, 83; society, 10; tribes, 66
Balkans, Ottoman position in, 18
Balkan wars, 70, 139, 140, 159, 162
Bani Hajir, 12, 35, 43, 65; Qâsim, sup-
  port of, 87, 109; Said Pasha's policy
  toward, 151; size, 194n47; Talib
  Pasha's policy toward, 151; unrest,
  85
Bani Khalid, 12, 14, 62, 64, 65, 67; size,
  194n47
Basra, 20, 21, 67, 119; administration,
  76, 80, 104, 105, 106, 108; British
  involvement in, 71; history, 13, 14;
  Kuwait, trade dispute with, 114–15;
  Kuwait's attachment to, 92; naval
  yard, 23, 25, 75–80, 171; Necd
  Sancak, 63, 82–83; piracy, 71; quarantine charges (1879), 73; society, 12;
  trade, 11, 185n.19
Basra Gulf, see Persian Gulf
Bazi` b. `Ara`ir, 62, 63, 64, 67, 168
Bedouins, 4, 10, 11, 20, 107, 143, 144;
  arms trade, 67; Ibn Sa`ud's authority
  among, 160; Midhat's approach to,
  42–46, 52; Mubarak's influence
  among, 113, 117, 118, 126; Ottoman
  policies toward, 65–66, 169; Qatar
  revolt (1893), 87, 88, 89; Rashidi-
  Sa`udi conflict, 158; Said Pasha's pol-
  icy toward, 151; settlement of, 42,
  43, 44, 66, 168; unrest and depredations, 69, 82, 84, 85, 86, 129, 149,

INDEX

161, 163, 173; see also names of specific tribes
Berlin Conference (1878), 70
Binghazi, 82, 212n153
Blood feud, 10
Bribery and stipends, 65, 92, 95; Mubarak's date stipend, 116
Bubiyan, 132, 134
Bulgaria, 2, 70
Burayda, 156
Burchardt, Hermann, 160–61
Bushire, 13, 110

Camel corps, 12, 67, 84
Camel post, 81
Caravans, bedouin attacks on, 69, 85, 86, 161, 163
Cemeteries, 56
Coal depots, 77, 84, 208n117
Communications, 6, 7, 16, 20, 51, 91; Basra-Hasa mail service, 130; difficulties of, 72, 81–82, 85; in Hasa, 142, 153, 165, 166, 170; and Ottoman-Ibn Rashid alliance, 159
Corruption, 168, 170; in Kuwait, 91, 95
Crete, 98, 101
Curzon, Lord, 110, 111, 133, 170
Cyprus, 70, 101, 122

Dammam, 22, 34, 35, 37; fall of, to Ottomans (1871), 29
Darin, 83, 84
Date farming: Al Sabah groves, 93, 104, 130; Bani Khalid's seizure of groves, 62; date prices, 144, 168; foreign demand for dates, 56; in Hasa, 35, 36, 38, 39, 40, 45, 51, 59; Mubarak's date stipend, 116; at Qatif, 152; tithe on dates, 58
Dawasir, 12; size, 194n47
Dhafir, 12
Dhahran, 35, 38; piracy, 71; reform proposals for, 80
Dhufar, 78
Dira, 11
Doha, 9, 31, 32, 33, 79; Akif's proposals for, 84; British involvement in, 71; Ottoman presence in, 145–49; port,

83; Qâsim, dissatisfaction with, 87; Qatar revolt (1893), 88, 89; reform proposals for, 81; schools, 56; society, 10, 11
Donkey-mounted troops, 84

Eastern Question, 2
East India Company, 13
Ebülhuda, 95, 99
Education, in Hasa, 51, 52, 55–56
Egypt, 13, 19, 70; British occupation of, 101
Eritrea, 77
Euphrates, see Tigris and Euphrates
Europe: Age of Imperialism, 109–10; Kuwait affair, interest in, 107, 120–21; see also names of specific countries, e.g., France

Fahd b. Sunaytan, 61, 63
Faisal, Sultan (son of Turki b. Sa`id), 68
Faisal al-Sa`ud, 13, 17, 45
Farming, see Agriculture
Faw, 79, 101, 103, 112, 135
Feyzi Pasha, Ahmet, 119, 120, 156, 157
Financial issues: modernization, cost of, 17; money shortages, 6, 7, 84, 153, 166, 167, 169; naval forces, expenditures for, 76; Ottoman coinage, 60; revenue and expenditures, 57; see also Taxation
France, 18, 19, 74, 77, 110; Britain, competition with, 121; Ottoman dispute with, 122
Frere, Bartle, 170, 188n41
Fuad Pasha, 17, 18

General Treaty of Peace (1820), 14
Germany, 110, 164, 165; Britain, competition with, 121; and British-Kuwait agreement (1901), 121–22, 123, 127; railway project, 116–17, 121, 133
Great Britain, 171–73; and `Abdallah-Sa`ud rivalry, 23, 48–49, 61; Aden, control of, 19; Al Thani shaikhs, tribute from, 32; Anglo-Arab agreements, 73–74; and Baghdad Railway, 133; in Bahrain, 22, 23, 27, 73, 74; in

INDEX

Egypt, 19, 101; Ibn Sa`ud and, 160, 163, 164, 173; and `Isa b. `Ali al-Khalifa, 138; and Kuwait, 92, 97, 99–102, 103, 107, 134, 185n18; Kuwait railway terminus sites, 134; Kuwait status quo agreement (1901), 121-32; in Masqat, 23, 74; Mubarak al-Sabah and, 109–12, 113–16, 118–20, 132–42, 172; Muhammad al-Khalifa, deposition of, 21; in Oman, 23, 68; Ottoman agreement with (1913), 3, 162, 163; Ottoman fear and distrust of, 22–26, 28, 52, 70, 72, 77, 79, 80, 82, 83, 96, 132, 133, 134, 136, 144, 153, 171–72; Ottoman territory, British perception of, 93; Persian Gulf, aspirations and influence in, 1–4, 6, 7, 14, 15, 18–21, 26–29, 107, 141; Persian Gulf policy (1871–1892), 69–74; and piracy problem, 14, 26, 70, 71, 73, 75, 102; protectorates, tax policy in, 41–42; Qâsim al-Thani, confrontations with, 87; in Qatar, 144, 147, 148, 149; and Qatar revolt (1893), 88–89; shipping, growth of, 56; trade, 11, 13, 14; tribal problems, approach to, 42; in Yemen, 122
Greece, 98, 101
Gun smuggling, see Arms, trade and smuggling of

Hadhramawt, 20, 77
Hadiyya, battle of, 140
Hafiz Mehmet Pasha, 87, 88, 90
Ha'il, 67, 68, 69, 90, 117, 158; Al Rashid amirs of, 175
Hamad (son of `Isa b. `Ali al-Khalifa), 234n126
Hamdi Pasha, 95, 96, 97, 99, 100, 113–16, 217n18
Hamud al-Sabah, 100
Hanbali, 11, 12
Haripasa (ship), 93, 101
Hasa, 4, 8, 9, 19; Anglo-Ottoman agreement (1913), 162, 163; Bahraini blockade of, 27; Bazi` b. `Ara`ir's administration, 62, 63, 64; British involvement in, 23, 24, 25, 27, 28, 71; communication, difficulties of, 72, 81, 82, 142, 153, 165, 166, 170; economic conditions, 36–42, 57, 173; exports, 81; geography, 69, 184n1; governmental structure, 49–51; history, 12, 13, 14; Midhat's inspection of and plans for, 34–36, 52–53; *mutasarrifs* in, 176–77; Ottoman administration: (1872–1893), 54–69; (1896–1905), 149–53; (last years of), 143–44, 159–66, 169, 173; Ottoman-Ibn Sa`ud agreement (1914), 164; Ottoman reconquest project and campaign in (1871), 17, 18, 20–25, 27–33; Ottoman reform proposals, 74–85; piracy, 70, 71, 72; revenue, 59–60; revolt (1874), 61-62, 90; Sa`udis in, 17, 48, 49, 159–66; shipping connections, 83; social and infrastructural development in, 51–52, 55, 56, 57; society, 10, 11; taxation, 55, 56, 58, 59, 60, 62, 86, 143, 144, 149, 150, 152, 167–68; tribal issues in, 42–49, 66, 85, 143, 144, 154
Herbert, British Consul, 25
Hijaz, 10, 13, 19, 20, 30; government of, 67; Ottoman tribal policy in, 45; Shari`a, 83
Hijaz Railway, 139
Hufuf, 9, 56, 72, 184n1; agriculture, 81; Bazi` b. `Ara`ir's administration, 62, 63; date groves, 59; decline of, 85; economic potential, 36, 37, 38, 40; fall of, to Ottomans (1871), 30; governmental structure, 49, 50, 62; Ibn Sa`ud's capture of, 163; Midhat's evaluation of, 35, 36; mosques and schools, 51, 56; population, 192n20; Qâsim, dissatisfaction with, 87; Qatar revolt (1893), 88; reform proposals, 80; riots and strike (1905), 152; society, 10, 11; tribal problems, 45, 66
Hüsni, Hüseyin, 234n123, 239n55

Ibadis, 10
Ibn Rashid (`Abd al-`Aziz al-Rashid), 8,

INDEX

140, 142, 160, 168; Ahmad al-Thani and, 147; communications, control of, 159; death of, 158; Mubarak al-Sabah, conflict with, 117–20, 124, 126–30, 134, 135, 235n134; Najd, Rashidi-Sa`udi struggle for, 136, 137, 154–59; Ottoman relations with, 68, 154–59

Ibn Sa`ud (`Abd al-`Aziz al-Sa`ud), 4, 8, 90, 93, 117, 132; Abdülhamid II and, 160; British relations with, 160, 163, 164, 173; foreign influence over, 153; Hasa, transfer of power to (1906–1914), 159–66; international recognition, 172; Mubarak al-Sabah and, 124, 140, 142, 160, 235n134; Najd, Rashidi-Sa`udi struggle for, 136, 137, 154–59; Ottoman agreement with (1914), 164; Ottoman relations with, 156, 157, 163, 164; and Qâsim al-Thani, 147; Riyadh, capture of, 129, 130, 155, 160

Ibrahim Pasha, 64, 144–45

India, 3, 11, 15, 26, 27, 28; Anglo-Masqat agreement, 74; Ibn Sa`ud and, 164; Kuwait invasion plot, 103; Kuwait railway terminus sites, 134; maritime policy, 71; Ottoman-British agreement (1913), 162, 163; piracy issue, 70; sultan of Masqat, subsidy to, 209n130; tribal issues, 42, 169

Indian traders, 10, 11, 26, 73, 77

Iran, 11, 103, 107; Russian influence over, 110

Iranian traders, 10, 60

Iraq, 5, 19, 23, 30, 76, 91, 171, 173; British designs on, 82; government, 67; history, 12, 13; Kuwait, claim to, 3; Midhat's financial legacy in, 56, 57; Midhat's reforms and improvements in, 41, 51, 52, 54; Mubarak's claims in, 111–12, 113; Rashidi-Sa`udi conflict and, 155; religious practices, 10; revenue, 59; Sa`ud's wish to dominate, 25; Shammar *dira*, 68; society, 12; taxation, 58; tribal policy, 45–46; waterways, 79; World War I, 3

Irrigation, 40

`Isa b. `Ali al-Khalifa, 26, 27, 73, 74, 138, 173, 186n17, 234n126

Islam, 78, 90, 108, 209n127

Italy, 76, 139, 159

Jabal Shammar, 17, 23, 31, 68

Jabir b. Mubarak, 236n138

Jarrah al-Sabah, 93–94, 96

Jerusalem, 64

Jews, 10

Jubayl, 71

Kapnist, Count, 111

Kazim Pasha, 227n39

Kelly, J. B., 18

Kemball, C. A., 118

Khalifa, Al, *see* Al Khalifa

Khawr Zubayr, 129

Khaza`il, 43

Khaz`al, Husayn Khalaf Shaikh (historian), 94, 216n7, 217n16

Khaz`al (shaikh of Muhammara), 109, 139

Knox, S. G., 134, 136

Kurdish tribal groups, 4

Kuwait, 3, 7, 8, 14, 33, 166; Al Sabah shaikhs of, 176; arms trade, 67; bribery of tribes, 65; British tie to, 92, 97, 113, 114, 134, 173, 185n18; customs regulations, 114; economy, 92; flag, 134; food embargo, 126, 127; geography, 9; history to 1896, 92–94; Mubarak-British relationship, 99–102, 109–12; Mubarak-Ottoman relationship: (1896–1897), 94–102; (1897–1898), 102–9; (1899–1901), 113–21; Ottoman administration, 21–22, 55, 91–93, 172; Ottoman-British agreement (1913), 162; Ottoman policy toward (1902–1914), 132–42; population, 215n1; railway project, 116–17; railway terminus sites, 134; society, 10, 11, 12; status quo agreement (1901), 121–32, 133, 134, 162; sultan's suzerainty and sovereignty, 123

INDEX

Land tenure, 57; in Hasa, Midhat's proposal for, 36, 37–40, 43; in Iraq, 46
Layard, Ambassador, 207*n*115
Legal system, 83, 86
Livestock taxes, 152
Lorenzo and Tobini affair, 229*n*58
Lorimer, J. G., 94, 136, 150
Lynch Company, 19, 21

Macedonia, 99
Mahdist movement, 208*n*124
Mahmud Nedim Pasha, 57
Mahmut Şevket Pasha, 162
Mail service, 81, 130, 134, 138, 170
Manama, 24, 81
Manasir, 65, 85; Qâsim, support of, 87, 109; Talib Pasha's policy toward, 151
Mansur Bey, 24
Maritime issues, 70; Ottoman territorial waters, 71; warfare ban, 72; *see also* Naval forces; Piracy; Shipping
Maritime Peace in Perpetuity, Treaty of (1853), 14
Masqat, 23, 68, 74, 110; Indian subsidy to sultan of, 209*n*130
Mazyad, 63, 64, 67
Meade, M. J., 110, 111, 112, 114
Mecca, amir of, 45–46
Mecca, sharif of, 17, 67, 161
Mehmet Ali, 13
Mehmet Cemalüddin Efendi, 95
Mehmet Salih Pasha, 80–83
Midhat Pasha, 2, 6, 7, 16, 17, 18, 21–25, 27, 28, 29, 54, 167; `Abdallah al-Sa`ud and, 46–49; administrative system, 49-51; financial legacy, 56, 57; flexibility, 171; Hasa, inspection of and reports on, 34–36, 52; Hasa, plans for development of, 36–42, 53; Hasa, social and infrastructural development in, 51–52; Kuwait, 92; and Ottoman Hasa and Qatar campaign, 30, 32, 33; resignation of, 56–57; tribal policies, 42–49, 52, 168
Military forces, British India, 169
Military forces, Ottoman: communication, slowness of, 83; at Doha,

145–49; V Corps, 30; at Hasa, 57–60, 62, 65, 85, 86, 90, 150–53, 162–63, 168; Hasa and Qatar campaign, 29–30; at Hufuf, Midhat's proposals for, 36; and Ibn Saud-Ottoman agreement (1914), 164; Kuwait affair, 102, 103, 105, 106, 107; manpower shortages, 6, 7; modernization, 17; Najd expedition, 153–58; at Qasîm, 136; VI Corps, 30, 107, 119, 201*n*70; and tribal policy, 43, 44, 45, 66–67, 84
Miz`al, 100
Modernization, 6, 17
Mosques, 51, 52, 56
Mosul, 107
Mounted police force, 150
Mubarak al-Sabah, 2, 6, 8, 88, 90, 91–93, 170, 172; German railway project, 117; and Great Britain, 99–102, 109–12, 113-16, 118–20, 132–42; Ibn Rashid, conflict with, 117–20, 124, 126–30, 134, 135; Ibn Sa`ud and, 160; income sources, 114; *kaymakam*, appointment as, 105, 107; land dealings, 135, 140; murder of brothers, 93–94, 96–99, 106, 140; nephews, 97, 99, 102–4, 106–8, 114, 130, 131, 134–36, 220*n*47; Ottoman relations with: (1896–1897), 94–99; (1897–1898), 102–7; (1899–1901), 113–21; (1902–1914), 132–42; and Rashidi-Sa`udi conflict, 136, 156; Russia and, 125–26, 142; Said Pasha and, 151; status quo agreement (1901), 123–32; sultan's ultimatum to (1901), 125
Mubarraz, 11; economic potential, 36, 38; governmental structure, 49, 50; mosques and schools, support of, 51; society, 10
Muhammad al-Khalifa, 20, 21, 26, 186*n*17
Muhammad al-Rashid, 67, 68, 69, 117, 155, 168
Muhammad al-Sabah, 92, 93–94, 96
Muhammad b. `Abd al-Wahhab, 13
Muhammad b. Sa`ud, 13

INDEX

Muhammad b. Thani, 31, 32, 33
Muhammad (brother of `Abdallah b. Faisal al-Sa`ud), 31, 46, 48
Muhammara, 67, 101
Muhlis Pasha, 136–40
Muhsin Pasha, 105, 108, 113, 115, 116, 121, 123, 124, 130, 170; and Mukalla, 77
Mule corps, 67
Muntafiq, 12, 24, 43, 46, 63, 64, 67, 103; Kuwait, conflict with (1910), 140; and Mubarak-Ibn Rashid conflict, 118
Musa Kazim Efendi, 64
Mustafa Nuri Pasha, 131, 230n69
Mutayr, 12, 17
Mut`ib b. `Abd al-`Aziz, 240n69

Nafiz Pasha, 30–33, 47–50, 56, 60
Na`im, 89
Najd, 4, 8, 9, 19, 24, 25, 28–32, 61, 173; and `Abdallah-Sa`ud conflict, 17; administration of, 50–51; British designs on, sultan's fear of, 126; governmental structure, 49; history, 12, 13; Ibn Rashid's control of, 69; Mubarak-Ibn Rashid conflict in, 117–19; new province of (1914), 164; Rashidi-Sa`udi conflict in, 134, 136, 137, 140, 153–59, 161; reform proposals for, 80; society, 10, 11, 12; trade restrictions, 152, 168; tribal issues, 11, 45, 66, 85
Nasir al-Sa`dun, 43, 46, 63, 67, 168
Nasir b. Mubarak, 73, 74
Naval Council, Ottoman, 76, 77
Naval forces, British, 77, 78, 85, 141, 207n116
Naval forces, Ottoman, 21, 24, 27, 85, 171; Basra flotilla, 77; Basra naval yard, 23, 25, 75–80; Kuwait expedition, 102, 103; piracy, control of, 75–76; at Qatar, 145; Riza Ali's proposals for, 78, 79
Necd *Sancak*, 5, 49, 50, 51, 54, 63, 84; Basra's administration of, 82–83; government budget, 60; Hamdi Pasha and, 96

Netherlands, 13
Newspapers, 135
Nomads, *see* Bedouins

Obokh, 77
Oil, 173
Oman, 20, 23, 29, 68–69; history, 12, 14, 15; religious practices in, 10; Riza Ali's proposals for, 78
Oman-Ottoman administration (state shipping line), 79
Ottoman empire: Arabian peninsula, claim to, 13; Asian territories, 18, 19, 20; centralization, 5, 6; coinage, 60; expansionist policies, 6, 12; France, dispute with, 122; geopolitics, 65, 72, 83; German railway project, 117; Great Britain, agreement with (1913), 3, 162, 163; Great Britain, fear and distrust of, 22–26, 28, 52, 70, 72, 132, 133, 134, 136, 144, 153, 171–72; Ibn Rashid, alliance with, 68, 154, 155, 156; and Ibn Rashid-Mubarak conflict, 118–20; Ibn Sa`ud, agreement with (1914), 164; Ibn Sa`ud and, 156, 157, 163, 164, 172; Mubarak al-Sabah and: (1896–1897), 94–102; (1897–1898), 102–9; (1899–1901), 113–21; (1902–1914), 132–42; Persian Gulf, resurrection of interest in, in nineteenth century, 16–20; Persian Gulf presence, in mid-sixteenth century, 16; Persian Gulf states, administration in, 1–8; provincial and local administration, 5, 7, 8, 54, 55, 57, 64, 65, 83, 86, 150, 170–71; Qasîm, occupation of, 136, 137, 138; Qatar, position in, 144–49; Rashidi-Sa`udi conflict, 153–59; reactionary political phase, 6; reform process, 6; religious practices, 10; territorial waters, 71, 78; tribal policies, 42, 65–69, 72, 142, 156, 168–69, 172

Palgrave, William, 40
Paris, Treaty of (1856), 18
Pearl fisheries, 78, 79; taxation of pearl trade, 59, 84

INDEX

Pelly, Lewis, 26, 27, 32, 45, 170; Hasa, economic potential of, 37
Persia and the Persian Question (Curzon), 110
Persian Gulf, 1; British aspirations and influence in, 1–4, 6, 7, 14, 15, 21, 26–29, 107, 141; British policy in (1871–1892), 69–74; international politics of, 2, 110; Ottoman holdings in, in mid-sixteenth century, 16; resurrection of Ottoman interest in, in nineteenth century, 16–20; *see also* Arabia
Petroleum, 173
Piracy, 11, 14, 18, 26, 70–76, 80, 102; Bani Hajir, 35; *Haripasa* case, 101; proposals for dealing with, 83; Qatar, 145
Portugal, 12, 13
Prostitutes, 56
Public safety, *see* Security issues

Qahtan, 12, 17
Qana`i, al-, Yusuf (historian), 94
Qaramanlis, 19
Qaramita movement, 12
Qasîm, 31, 32, 172; Ottoman occupation of, 136, 137, 138, 153–60
Qâsim b. Muhammad al-Thani, 31, 32, 33, 46, 50, 66, 81, 84, 144–49, 160, 169, 172; Ibn Rashid and, 154; Ibn Sa`ud and, 155; Qatar revolt (1893), 87–90; Said Pasha and, 151; tribal allies, 109; Yusuf al-Ibrahim and, 105, 106
Qatar, 3, 9, 25, 26, 108, 164, 172; Al Thani shaikhs of, 176; arms trade, 67; British oversight, 173; governmental structure, 49, 50; history, 14, 15; mosques and schools, 56; Ottoman administration, 55; Ottoman-British agreement (1913), 162; Ottoman campaign in (1871), 29–33; Ottoman position in (1896–1914), 144–49, 166; piracy, 70, 71; revolt (1893), 7, 8, 85–90, 93, 143, 144; society, 10, 12; taxation, 84; tribal issues, 45, 46, 65, 66
Qatif, 9, 11, 22, 24, 56; agriculture, 59, 152; economic potential, 37, 38; fall of, to Ottomans (1871), 29; government of, 49, 50, 62; Ibn Sa`ud's capture of, 163; Midhat's evaluation of, 34, 35; mosques and schools, support of, 51; piracy, 70; society, 10; tribal issues, 45, 66
Qurna, 92

Railroads, 19; German project, 116–17, 121, 129, 133; Hijaz Railway, 139; Kuwait terminus sites, 134; Russian plan for, 110–11
Rajab Efendi, 108, 109, 116, 124–25, 126
al-Rashid (family), *see* Al Rashid
al-Rashid (historian), 94
Ra's Tanura, 29, 34
Raunkiaer, Barclay, 160–61
Receb Pasha, 95, 96, 98, 99, 102, 103, 105, 107, 108, 170; and Qâsim al-Thani, 145
Red Sea, 19, 76, 77
Religion, 10, 12; and Arabs' bond to sultan, 78, 90, 108, 209*n*127
Rifaat Bey, 83, 213*n*162
Riyadh, 64, 68, 69; Al Sa`ud amirs of, 175; Ibn Sa`ud's capture of, 129, 130, 155, 160
Riza Ali, 77–80, 82, 83, 92
Road, Basra-`Ashar, 139
Ross, E. C., 73–74
Russia, 18, 29, 107; Iran, influence over, 110; and Mubarak al-Sabah, 125–26, 142; rail plan, 110–11

Sabah, Al, *see* Al Sabah
Sa`dun Pasha, 118, 135–36, 139, 140
Safavi empire, 12, 14
Said Bey, 64
Said Pasha (*Mutasarrif* in Hufuf), 64, 85–86, 106, 150, 151, 152, 168, 171
Said Pasha, Küçük (Grand Vezir), 124
Sail ships, 209*n*131
Salim b. Mubarak, 236*n*138
Salisbury, Marquis of, 101, 207*n*115
Sancak, 211*n*151
Sarif, battle of (1901), 118
Sa`ud, Al, *see* Al Sa`ud

INDEX

Sa'ud b. Faisal al-Sa'ud, 17, 22–25, 30, 31, 32, 64; 'Abdallah al-Sa'ud, defeat of, 47; grandsons' challenge of Ibn Sa'ud, 163; Hasa, taxation of, 37, 40; Ottoman defeat of, 43, 48; Ottoman policy toward, 61
Saudi Arabia, 3, 91
Sea mail, 81
Security issues, 86, 161; Hasa, Ottoman forces in, 162; independent *sancaks*, 82; local personnel, 57; Midhat's reform proposals, 36; Said Pasha, policy of, 150–51; *see also* Piracy
Shaikhs, 14; Riza Ali's concern with, 77–78
Shakba, 88
Shammar, 12, 68
Shari'a, 83
Shatt al-Arab, 79, 93
Shi'a, 10, 35
Shihr, 77
Shipping, 56, 79, 81, 82, 83
Slave trade, 3, 10, 14, 18, 26
Social services, in Hasa, 51–52, 55, 56
Stavrides, British embassy councilor, 96
Steamer traffic, 19, 21
Sublime Porte, 17, 134; British-Kuwait status quo agreement (1901), 123, 124, 127, 132; Ottoman-British agreement (1913), 162, 163
Sudan, 19
Suez Canal, 18, 19, 70
Süleyman the Magnificent, 12
Sunni tribes, 10, 11
Suq al-Shuyukh, 67
Syria, 10, 13, 19, 20, 173

Talib Pasha, Sayyid, 64, 105, 118, 151, 152, 154, 170
Tanzimat reform era, 6, 17, 18
Tapu system, 38–41, 43, 46, 59, 168, 191n15
Tarut island, 35
Taxation, 86, 171; Akif's suggestions for, 84; Hasa, 55, 56, 58, 59–60, 62, 143, 144, 149, 150, 152, 167–68; Kuwait, 114; Midhat's plan for, 36, 37, 40–42, 51; Qâsim al-Thani, 87; Qatar, 146; Riza Ali's proposals for, 78
Tax farming, 58
Telegraph, 19, 82, 83, 85, 141, 142, 153, 170
Tevfik Pasha, 122, 123, 124
Thani, Al, *see* Al Thani
Tigris and Euphrates, 19, 20, 79
Tobacco and snuff, 56
Trade, 11, 14, 26, 77, 168; bedouin attacks and, 86; Bombay-Persian Gulf, 185n19; Ibn Rashid's disruption of, 155; Indian traders, 10, 11, 26, 73, 77; Iranian traders, 10, 60; Kuwaiti regulations, 114, 115; Mehmet Salih's proposals, 81; nomads, in Najd, 10; port improvements, 83, 84, 85; taxation, in Hasa, 152
Travel, 170; Basra-'Ashar road, 139; *see also* Caravans, bedouin attacks on; Railroads
Tripolitania, 19
Trucial Oman, 14, 164; British interests in, 18, 74; history, 15; Ottoman presence in, 84; piracy, 72, 73; Shari'a, 83
Turki b. Sa'id, 68

'Udayd, 32, 66, 72, 84, 148, 149
Umm Qasr, 129
'Uqayr, 35, 37, 45, 81; 'Abd al-Rahman in, 63; Ibn Sa'ud's capture of, 163
'Utayba, 12
'Utub, 10
'Uyun, 150

Vakif system, 51, 52

Wahhabi movement, 12, 13, 15, 17, 19; authority of, 69; Hasa, misrule in, 35, 36; Muhammad al-Khalifa's disputes with, 20; in Najd, 155; Ottomans, conflict with, 25; restrictions imposed by, 56
Wakra, 32, 148, 149
Waqba, 88
Warba, 132
Washm, 154
Water rights, 144

INDEX

Weapons, *see* Arms, trade and smuggling of
Wine sellers, 56
World War I, 3, 164, 165, 173
Wratislaw, A. C., 131

Yemen, 10, 12, 19, 31, 77, 122, 128
Young Turk movement, 139, 140, 159
Yusuf al-Ibrahim, 94, 97, 99, 100, 102–6, 108, 114, 129, 172, 217n18; Ibn Rashid and, 117; Kuwait, seaborne attack on, 135, 232n110

Zanzibar, 209n130
Zor, 82
Zubara, 31, 70, 71, 84, 96, 148
Zubayr, 129, 130
Zuhaf (corvette), 121, 123